ASIAN AMERICAN SHORT STORY WRITERS

ASIAN AMERICAN SHORT STORY WRITERS

An A-to-Z Guide

Edited by Guiyou Huang

Emmanuel S. Nelson, Advisory Editor

Greenwood Press
Westport, Connecticut • London

Library of Congress Cataloging-in-Publication Data

Asian American short story writers : an A-to-Z guide / edited by Guiyou Huang.
    p. cm.
    Includes bibliographical references and index.
    ISBN 0–313–32229–5 (alk. paper)
    1. Short stories, American—Asian American authors—Bio-bibliography—Dictionaries. 2. Short stories, American—Asian American authors—Dictionaries. 3. American fiction—20th century—Bio-bibliography—Dictionaries. 4. Authors, American—20th century—Biography—Dictionaries. 5. Asian Americans—Intellectual life—Dictionaries. 6. Asian American authors—Biography—Dictionaries. 7. American fiction—20th century—Dictionaries. 8. Asian Americans in literature—Dictionaries. 9. Immigrants in literature—Dictionaries. I. Huang, Guiyou, 1961–

PS153.A84A828 2003
818'.0109895'03—dc21   2002192772
[B]

British Library Cataloguing in Publication Data is available.

Library of Congress Catalog Card Number: 2002192772
ISBN: 0–313–32229–5

First published in 2003

Greenwood Press, 88 Post Road West, Westport, CT 06881
An imprint of Greenwood Publishing Group, Inc.
www.greenwood.com

Printed in the United States of America

The paper used in this book complies with the Permanent Paper Standard issued by the National Information Standards Organization (Z39.48–1984).

10 9 8 7 6 5 4 3 2 1

Copyright Acknowledgment

The author and publisher gratefully acknowledge permission for the use of the following material:

From an e-mail interview conducted between Susan Nunes and Alice D'Amore. Used by permission of Susan Nunes.

CONTENTS

PREFACE

With this volume, Greenwood Press has published five reference works on five major genres in Asian American literature: Emmanuel Nelson's *Asian American Novelists: A Bio-Bibliographical Critical Sourcebook* (2000), Guiyou Huang's *Asian American Autobiographers: A Bio-Bibliographical Critical Sourcebook* (2001) and *Asian American Poets: A Bio-Bibliographical Critical Sourcebook* (2002), and Miles X. Liu's *Asian American Playwrights: A Bio-Bibliographical Critical Sourcebook* (2002). Along with this volume, readers and researchers of Asian American literary writing will be, I hope, well equipped in their study, research, and teaching of the Asian American novel, autobiography, poetry, drama, and short fiction. Of course, this is not to set aside the importance and significance of other genres, such as the essay, written by Asian American authors. Asian American literature has journeyed tortuously since its inception at the end of the nineteenth century; however, it had not been considered an autonomous branch of American literature until the last quarter of the twentieth century. In a matter of two decades—since the 1980s—both creative writing and critical literature by Asian Americans have blossomed, and major developments in both fields have been truly remarkable; as a result, literature by Asian American writers has been studied and taught on a great many campuses across the country. In view of such literary achievements, reference books on Asian American literature are a timely aid to teaching and research.

Asian American Short Story Writers represents forty-nine Asian American authors of short fiction; and like its four predecessors, each chapter consists of four sections: (1) Biography, (2) Major Works and Themes, (3) Critical Reception, and (4) Bibliography, which consists of two parts, Works by the Author (subdivided by genre) and Studies of the Author. Such an organization will lend convenience to the reader whether s/he looks for details about an author's life, or is interested in analysis of major stories, or wants to do further research by following the comprehensive bibliography. While short story writers who are considered major or important by some may not be represented here for space and other reasons, a large number of those included have won major literary awards or other kinds of national and international recognition and have been anthologized in various venues. These stories are worthy of many more studies like this volume. As Amy Ling writes, "For Asian American readers, these stories preserve memory, provide models to emulate, give spiritual sustenance, and embody communal identity" ("Asian American Short Story" 40). And this book will help readers gain insight into Asian American writing as well as the people who create it.

Guiyou Huang

ACKNOWLEDGMENTS

I would like to thank all the contributors, without whose participation this book would not exist. I also want to express my gratitude to Dr. George Butler, Senior Editor at Greenwood Press, and Professor Emmanuel S. Nelson at SUNY-Cortland, for their support. John Donohue, production editor, and Peter Braver, copyeditor, both deserve a special thank-you for their excellent work on the book. Finally, I owe a great debt to my wife, Jennifer Yufeng Qian, and my son, George Ian, for their understanding and support in the year-long process of preparing this book for publication.

INTRODUCTION: THE ASIAN AMERICAN SHORT STORY—THE CASES OF SUI SIN FAR, YAMAMOTO, AND PEÑARANDA

Guiyou Huang

The Asian American short story has not achieved the level of notoriety that the Asian American novel or autobiography has garnered so far. Yet, since Sui Sin Far's publication of her first story, "The Gambler," in 1896 (Ling, "Creating One's Self" 306), and notably since World War II, there has emerged a group of devoted Asian American short-fiction writers. In this introduction I will consider six short stories by three authors from three different time periods of the twentieth century—Sui Sin Far at the turn of the century, Hisaye Yamamoto in the middle of the century, and Oscar Peñaranda toward the end of the century—to survey the thematic scope and historical breadth of the evolution of the Asian American short story over the span of roughly a century. These writers, diverse as they are in gender, ethnicity, cultural backgrounds, and the eras they lived in, all explore the fate and destiny of individuals in relation to issues of race, gender, and identity politics. In their characters' struggles to make sense of their ethnic life and identities, the role of the family often figures prominently, both as a metaphorical and literal anchor of the individual's body and soul, and as a site of contest about the racialization of relationships.

The Asian American writer attempts to create a voice that articulates Asian American experience. The protean expressions of their writing incorporate self-perceptions of Asian Americans. These self-perceptions, inscribed in language, are often put forward as a self-defining strategy to challenge, and ultimately to change, the stigmatized views imposed on them by outside perceivers, often from the dominant culture. A higher level of freedom "to experiment with taboo subjects" in a short story than in a novel "partially accounts for the frequency with which short stories are used to introduce oftentimes stigmatized 'submerged population groups' to a wider reading public," in this case the taboos being race and racism encountered by Asian Americans (Lee 253). It is obvious then that the Asian American writer, by writing what has been experienced, attempts to expose the falsity of stereotypes in order to dismantle them. Stereotypical views of the Asian American, whether as the model minority or as the unassimilable alien, are racially biased and politically motivated and are in urgent need of correction. The ad hominem foreignizing tendency about American Asians constitutes the core of racist efforts in legal, political, and economic terms. In significant ways, then, the Asian American writer writes to expose the ridiculousness of racial stereotyping. To parody John Milton, who wrote *Paradise Lost* to justify the ways of God to man, Asian American authors write at once to *dejustify* the ways of American racism to Asian America and to *delegitimize* the many stigmatizing labels that Asian Americans have been forced to wear since they first landed on the North American continent.

In the short stories I choose to examine in this introduction, racial and gender issues occupy the center of the authors' concerns. Whether the protagonists are male or female, they are almost invariably placed in the context of racialized and politicized discourse—husband pitted against wife, self against other, Oriental against Occidental, child against parent, male against female, employer against employee, and individual against society in the form of groups, institutions, and the government. Since Sui Sin Far is commonly viewed as the first Asian American short fictionist, my examination of the Asian American short story will start with her work.

As many of her short narratives—autobiographical and fictional—demonstrate, Sui Sin Far[1] (1865–1914) is keenly interested in the Asian American experience. As her autobiographical piece "Leaves from the Mental Portfolio of an Eurasian" indicates, she was hardly recognized as having traces of Chinese extraction, and as a result she was usually regarded as a member of the white race. When she was working for a San Francisco newspaper, for example, at the proprietor's suggestion that she obtain subscriptions from Chinatown residents, she found that "the Chinese merchants and people generally are inclined to regard me with suspicion. They have been imposed upon so many times by unscrupulous white people" (120). Although it may be risky to attempt a comparison of a historical writer with a fictional character, one cannot be blind to the similar agonizing frustration and misunderstanding caused by mixed blood, experienced by Sui Sin Far and Faulkner's Joe Christmas in *Light in August*.

Joe Christmas encountered suspicions from people of both the white and black race; even the way he dressed betrays his mixed and displaced identity.[2] Sui Sin Far, likewise, intimately felt the tension between being a perceived white and having indiscernible Chinese blood. Another comparable example is the African American fiction writer Charles Chesnutt (1858–1932), who walked the race borderline all of his life, wrote during roughly the same time period as Sui Sin Far, and explored the disastrous consequences for light-skinned blacks who attempted to pass as white. Joe Christmas, Sui Sin Far, and Charles Chesnutt all have to deal with identity crises on a deep, psychological level, complicated by their mixed racial heritage. Joe's inability to fit into a racially divided society spells his downfall; Chesnutt, taking advantage of his literacy and passing as white, wrote about racial disparities and his own inner turmoil from a biracial perspective, as is apparent in his masterful movement from ostensibly "white" English to the black dialect, in such stories as "The Goophered Grapevine"; Sui Sin Far found herself trapped in a similar bind, but by embracing her Chinese heritage in both her life and writing she created a fictional world of romanticized images of interracial families and relationships.

The famous anthology *The Big Aiiieeeee!* includes Sui Sin Far's "Leaves from the Mental Portfolio" and two other stories, "The Story of One White Woman Who Married a Chinese" and "Her Chinese Husband." In the anthology's eye-catching position between a six-page introduction and the texts of selected writings stands a fiery, passionate ninety-two-page overview of Chinese and Japanese American literature, authored by Frank Chin, sarcastically and provocatively entitled "Come All Ye Asian American Writers of the Real and the Fake." Chin apparently feels appreciated, as a Chinaman, in reading works by Sui Sin Far, who refuses to put down the Chinese man but elevates him instead: "[T]he only Chinese men who are not emasculated and sexually repellent in Chinese American writing are found in the books and essays of Sui Sin Far, Diana Chang, and Dr. Han Suyin" (12). Chin obviously oversimplifies the generic and thematic issues of these Eurasian and Asian American authors, and understates the role that gender plays in these matters; nevertheless, he finds fair representation, and therefore affirmation, of the Asian male's manhood in their writing, to which Sui Sin Far's stories lend expedient textual evidence.

"Leaves from the Mental Portfolio" poses probing questions about racial and national identity. According to Amy Ling, Sui Sin Far's mission in this autobiographical piece is "to right the wrongs by writing them, and the wrong she focused on here was one with which she was personally most familiar: bigotry, which, as a Eurasian, she had experienced from Asians as well as Caucasians" (*Between Worlds* 32). Sui Sin Far's travels from England to Canada and then to the United States, coupled with her biracial heritage, provide her with global outlooks on the self, race relations, and nationalities, issues that would frequently resurface in subsequent Asian American writing. Writing at the turn of the twentieth century when the East and the West were more

sharply divided, and when racial ignorance severely impeded mutual cogni-
zance, Sui Sin Far self-consciously sought a path of life and identity that had
rarely been trodden before. She frequented the library to read books about
China and the Chinese, through which she learned about China's civilization
and about herself. "At eighteen years of age what troubles me is not that I
am what I am, but that others are ignorant of my superiority" ("Leaves" 116).
This statement, implying her inferior treatment by Caucasians, sets in motion
an understanding that Sui Sin Far's short autobiography mandates a mission
of self-discovery as well as an obligation to inform about her ethnic and cultural heritages.

Unlike Joe Christmas who feels deep shame and inferiority in having black
blood in him, Sui Sin Far finds strength in her Chinese heritage and intends
to retain it not for her Chinese mother's sake but for her own. Her realization
that China was a civilized culture enables her to see the Chinese differently
from people around her, such as her employer, Mr. K., who believed that the
Chinese were "more repulsive than a nigger" (117). Sui Sin Far's audacity to
speak up on behalf of herself and the Chinese race is rooted in her belief in
racial equality.[3] Although her "Leaves from the Mental Portfolio" projects a
utopian vision of the blending of races and the browning of the world's population, the optimism it expresses was rare in early Asian American writing.
She was more interested in the individual person's human qualities than characteristics attributable to a particular race or nation. At the end of her portfolio, she claims:

> After all I have no nationality and am not anxious to claim any. In-
> dividuality is more than nationality. "You are you and I am I," says
> Confucius. I give my right hand to the Occidentals and my left to the
> Orientals, hoping that between them they will not utterly destroy the
> insignificant "connecting link." (123)

Joy Leighton considers the Confucian aphorism as "tautological" that "discloses nothing about individuality" (23); however, since the statement does
emphasize difference and separation, it asserts the importance of autonomy:
there should not be racial inequality and anyone, "you" or "I," is equally
inviolable as an independent human being. Unlike many other writers, Sui
Sin Far downplays the significance of a fixed identity determined by nation-
ality; she dismisses narrowly defined nationalism, which is traditionally characterized by patriotic pride in the race that peoples the nation. Sui Sin Far
refuses to accept, in Lisa Lowe's words, "a nationalism that affirms the separate purity of its ethnic culture" (33). Loyalty and devotion to the state have
historically been core components of patriotism and nationalism, but when
one's sense of national consciousness rises to the level of fanatical supremacy,
nationalism merges with racism to create a deadly force against people of
other nations and races. *Light in August* again presents a credible example of

extreme nationalism in the truculent character of Percy Grimm, who maintains "[A] sublime faith in physical courage and blind obedience, and a belief that the white race is superior to any and all other races and that the American is superior to all other white races" (451). In the grand name of nationalism Grimm riddles Joe Christmas with bullets and castrates him while he is still conscious, just to ensure the purity of his race and the sanctity of his white American nation.

Sui Sin Far's nonchalance to nationalism, paradoxically coupled with a keen awareness of racial differences, exhibits a democratized and deracialized view of racial politics, which prompts her to consider interracial marriages like that of her parents. Handicapped and sickly all her life, Sui Sin Far was never married, yet she wrote about married life in "One White Woman," and its sequel, "Her Chinese Husband," because, argues Joy Leighton, writing allows Sui Sin Far, essentially an exile alienated from both her family and society, to "create a fictional family, who can provide each other with sympathy and support at a time when public and familial disapproval leave her isolated from everyone" (11). These stories, though strictly not autobiographical, certainly are personal. "The personal story of what life was like for the Chinese and Eurasians in America at the turn of the century is Sui Sin Far's special contribution to American letters, for she was the first person of any Chinese ancestry to take up this subject" (Ling, *Between Worlds* 40). The pioneering nature of her attention to Chinese American experience aside, Sui Sin Far presents the Chinese American man as a hero, instead of a coward or wife batterer, images of Chinese men one may find in, say, Amy Tan's *The Joy Luck Club* and *The Kitchen God's Wife*.

In "One White Woman," Minnie's first husband, James Carson, is an advocate of women's suffrage. But Carson pays mere lip service to women's rights and entertains no thought, let alone actions, of making his wife his equal. He would read magazine columns of advice to women "who were ambitious to become comrades to men and walk shoulder to shoulder with their brothers" (124). Minnie, on the other hand, shows not even lukewarm admiration for career women, but to please her husband she not only shoulders all household responsibilities but willingly spends time catching up on current politics. The reform-minded husband exhibits inconsistency between talking about women's issues and actually denigrating the role of his own wife, betraying male chauvinistic ideas. His inferior comparison of his wife with clever businesswomen only emphasizes his selfishness and adulterous thoughts about other women. Very much like Winnie's Chinese husband in *The Kitchen God's Wife*, Minnie's white husband, while emotionally abusing her, does not respect the woman he claims he loves, Miss Moran, either, with whom he is writing a book on social reform. The irony cannot be more biting: he intends to reform only society at large while lagging behind the general trend of social progress himself.

Divorce from her white husband and ensuing despair drive Minnie to an almost successful suicide when she is rescued by Liu Kanghi, a Chinese man who kindly places her in the care of his relative's family. Minnie, admittedly, was raised and educated with racial prejudices, but now through the day-to-day contact with her Chinese host family she becomes enlightened about the Chinese race, and an epiphany occurs: "My life's experiences had taught me that the virtues do not all belong to the whites. I . . . lost altogether the prejudice against the foreigner in which I had been reared" (130). This perhaps is the most subversive moment of the story as the narrator discovers virtues in the Chinese that had been either ignored or simply dismissed. What separates the races and hinders communication is rightly identified in this realization of a white woman who is positioned, both by choice and by chance, to know the Other, and whose acquisition of firsthand knowledge of another race supersedes her ignorance and dispels her prejudice. Minnie, however, remains concerned about her daughter who would grow up with a Chinese father and a white mother in a society where white Americans look down upon her for merely becoming the wife of a humble Chinaman. This concern continues in the sequel, "Her Chinese Husband," in which Minnie narrates memories of her Chinese husband after he was shot to death, presumably by some Chinese racists.

"Her Chinese Husband" explores both the fascination and frustration of an interracial marriage. Minnie's American husband is a prospective author of a book on social reform, a fact that suggests the bookish, impracticable facets of his reform goals: the gap between his theory-based (book) reform ideals and his actual conduct toward Minnie, like the widening chasm in their relationship, is never bridged in "One White Woman." In the sequel Minnie's Chinese husband, also reform-minded, is a member of the Reform Club where Chinamen discuss business and politics. A club, as opposed to a book, is geared more toward action, and by implication, Liu is more a man of deeds than of words. But cultural differences in values still surface between the interracial couple. For example, Minnie notes, "[I]f my ideas opposed or did not tally with his, he would very vigorously denounce what he called 'the foolishness of women'" (136). Clearly, Minnie is not conversant with Chinese women's etiquette and her actions (in this case, what she said) may be construed to be disrespectful, even subversive of gender roles, and therefore threaten the Confucian pro-male social order. Trinh Minh-ha, writing about "The Civilization of the Woman in African Tradition" hosted by a group of women in 1972, offers this comment on etiquette: "Observance of the rules of etiquette . . . is a necessity for the survival of the community, not just an empty form with which individuals comply from mere habit" (108). Minnie did not observe the Chinese rule of etiquette, sexist in itself; manners are culture-specific and they fulfill or break culture-specific expectations: Liu needs Minnie to observe Chinese etiquette for *his* survival (saving face) in *his* Chinese community. The demeaning phrase "the foolishness of women" inadvertently paints Liu as a

Confucian sexist who believes in the superiority of the male sex that, when expressing opinions, does not reveal "foolishness."

While Minnie's memories of her Chinese husband are largely sweet and dear, she remains bothered by the racial as well as cultural differences. The narrator indicates that Liu sometimes feels insecure about his marriage with a white woman. The trials and tribulations ignited by this uncertainty are the source of uneasiness in their union; Minnie, too, is baffled by what she calls "the barrier of race" (136). Either in want of a better term or in surrender to popular and stereotypical views, Minnie resorts to the familiar and the stereotypical—race, for an explanation, overlooking a vital factor in the workability of a marriage, culture. As Mark Nathan Cohen argues, "culture structures our behavior, thoughts, perceptions, values, goals, morals, and cognitive processes," and "one's culture tends to blind one to alternatives" (B4). When Liu denounces Minnie's "foolishness of women," he measures her articulateness against his cultural conventions.[4] When she talks in front of *his* people he feels his opinion, and then himself, slighted, and therefore he loses face for being outshined by a woman, though that woman is his own wife. When problems arise, race becomes an easy target in Minnie's search for explanation; race thus becomes scapegoated in the less than perfect intermarriage, and Minnie, the willy-nilly victim of rampant racial stereotyping.

In "Leaves from the Mental Portfolio," "One White Woman," and "Her Chinese Husband," Sui Sin Far raises unresolved questions about race relations, cultural conventions, and ethnic identity. Even though she shows the reader the possibility of interracial marriage, she encounters difficulties in negotiating race and culture, two factors that largely dominate popular perceptions and imaginations of society and people, and that continue to cause people to ask hard-to-answer questions such as "Can we really get along?"[5] On the other hand, while Sui Sin Far denounces racial prejudice and condemns racial violence, she recognizes and respects racial differences. Racial differences are undeniably inherent human attributes, culturally constructed and socially reinforced. While these differences exist and cannot be denied, racial discriminations constitute barriers in human communication, as Sui Sin Far demonstrates in her work. Her stories thus seem to portray its author as a racial differentialist.

Racial differentialism, I propose, may be used as a theory frame for critical discourse on racial politics; such a notion acknowledges racial differences but does not necessarily promote them while affirming racial equality. While it may appear politically unwise to emphasize physical, ethnographical differences complicated by cultural codes, denial of them only begets more ignorance that fertilizes greater prejudice based on racial stereotypes. And in addition to racial and cultural differences, class and gender differences, as Lisa Lowe suggests, should also be acknowledged among Asian Americans, so as to create "greater political opportunity to affiliate with other groups whose cohesion may be based on other valences of oppression" (32). Ultimately, racial differentialism frees the ethnic American—author, critic, and citizen—from the yoke of denial and creates greater space in the critical discourse on racial and identity politics.

As history has repeatedly taught its learners, race is a negligible issue, certainly a tolerable one, in times of peace and prosperity. Sui Sin Far, the first of first-generation Asian American writers, wrote about times prior to World War I, a historical period marked by racial ignorance of varying degrees in all peoples, but not yet plagued by wars involving multiple nations which gave rise to various kinds of nationalisms. By the time Hisaye Yamamoto started to write and publish her short fiction, World War I was well behind and World War II was over also, but memories of them lingered on and haunted the imagination of writers across the world. The ending of World War II witnessed drastic economic and political shifts in virtually all aspects of world affairs and international relations. The United States emerged from the war not only as a big winner, but as one of two world superpowers whose military, political, and economic positions in the postwar world of nations were strengthened, as it supervised the surrender of Germany and Japan while establishing military bases in these and other countries. On the other hand, Japan, defeated by China and its allies, had its expansionist dream crushed, and Japanese descendants abroad, particularly those living in the United States and Canada, suffered humiliation and persecution because of Pearl Harbor and their ancestral/ethnic connections to Japan. It is these Japanese and their experience living and suffering in wartime America that caught the attention of Yamamoto in her stories.

Called "master of indirection and understatement" (Ling, "Asian American Short Story" 40), Yamamoto's (1921–   ) is "among the most highly developed of Asian American writing" (Chan et al. 339). Her "Seventeen Syllables" has been widely critiqued. Two other pieces, "The Legend of Miss Sasagawara" and "Yoneko's Earthquake," often anthologized and well studied too, are my concerns here. Like Sui Sin Far—and many other women writers—Yamamoto concerns herself with women's domestic and public plight under trying circumstances. In Elaine Kim's words, "Yamamoto's stories are consummately women's stories" (160). In "The Legend" Yamamoto examines the alleged insanity of one woman, Miss Sasagawara, whose mother had died in an evacuation camp, after which her father, a Buddhist minister, relocated with her to an internment camp in an Arizona desert. The camp experience of Japanese Americans is Yamamoto's focus in this narrative. The buildings of the camp are numbered, and the numbers seem to subsume the collective identity of the residents. The recurrent mention of building numbers seems to accentuate the government's treatment of Japanese Americans as suspect enemies that would really threaten national security. Camp life was confining and dull to the point of suffocation, where any stir, human or otherwise, would create some degree of excitement among the inmates. Miss Sasagawara's appearance, for example, immediately seized the attention of little girls as well as older women at the camp. The celebrity-like attention Miss Sasagawara received partly resulted from her "abnormal" behavior. The narrator Kiku thus describes her first glance of the new arrival:

> [H]er shining hair was so long it wound twice about her head to form a coronet; her face was delicate and pale, with a fine nose, pouting bright mouth, and glittering eyes; and her measured walk said, "Look, I'm walking!" as though walking were not a common but a rather special thing to be doing. (340)

This depiction presents a woman who did not seem to be experiencing melancholia or suffering from depression; the way she dressed and walked suggests a human being who enjoyed what up to that point life had to offer to her. Kiku uses expressions of envy to describe her first impression of Miss Sasagawara, innocent enough to attribute her temperamental disposition and arrogance to her once being a ballet dancer. But Elsie, the narrator's friend, has more complicated views of her and supplies Kiku with different accounts of Miss Sasagawara, mostly based on hearsay. One major incident Elsie recounts occurred at the barracks where, the Sasagawaras' neighbor, Mr. Sasaki's intention to do a favor was misconstrued by Miss Sasagawara to be spying on her; this incident prompted Mr. Sasaki to think her crazy and started to call her madwoman, which soon picked up currency.

Miss Sasagawara's misinterpretation of Mr. Sasaki's intention of doing a neighborly favor suggests possible paranoia on her part; however, her harsh use of the verb "spy" insinuates the hostile tension going on between the government and the Japanese internees. The government attempted, by isolating its Japanese American citizens, to protect national security and presumed interests of the majority of the American population during the Pacific war in which Japan was a member of the Axis, as President Franklin D. Roosevelt's Executive Order 9066 conveyed it in no equivocal terms.[6] The America of this time period was a body politic that willfully and arbitrarily determined its citizens' degree of patriotism by their ethnicity and national origins.[7] During the three-and-a-half-year internment, writes Frank Chin, the Japanese American Citizens League (JACL), led by Mike Masaru Masaoka, in a gesture to please the government, collaborated with it in its efforts to isolate and intern Americans of Japanese ancestry (52). As Stan Yogi also indicates, "At the time of the war, the JACL advocated cooperation with the government as a sign of loyalty. Because of this, the JACL was targeted as an opportunistic organization suspected of betraying fellow Japanese Americans, particularly issei. In some camps, JACL spokespeople were beaten and threatened" ("Japanese American Literature" 133).

The internees, then, were reasonably concerned about their own safety and well-being and were on alert against covert JACL representatives.[8] This hostile environment divided Japanese Americans into two categories: government supporters (JACL) and government suppressed (internees). The loss of trust among Japanese Americans therefore becomes explicable: some were spying and some were spied on. Amid such intense political hostility, Miss Sasagawara's accusation of Mr. Sasaki spying on her is not totally irrational, nor is the latter's calling her madwoman utterly justifiable. As King-Kok Cheung puts it, "Her hypersensitivity to being spied upon not only mirrors the wartime hysteria and paranoia of the white majority but also reflects back on the plight of her whole ethnic group" (67). The name-calling no doubt shows the psychological pressure accruing from the internment experience where privacy was watchfully guarded but was rudely encroached upon nonetheless.

The plot of "The Legend" unfolds from the perspective of one young girl and her friend, which, as Morrison does in *The Bluest Eye*, reduces the subjectiveness of the narrative as young children look at their world with untainted innocence. On the other hand, because of their innocence and young age, the girls do not comprehend what they see and hear as well as adults do (as is also the case in the next Yamamoto story, "Yoneko's Earthquake"). As Elaine Kim has pointed out, Yamamoto's stories are generally told from the viewpoint of a nisei narrator "who sees the issei as through a glass darkly, without ever fully comprehending the feelings and actions of the older persons. The understanding is incomplete partly because of communication difficulties, but also because of the self-absorption of the *nisei*, who are intent upon conquering other worlds" (158). Their weak comprehension ability and credulous tendency as listeners also raise the issue of reliability about the truthfulness of the narrative. To what extent is the reader willing to believe as true what is told to Kiku, who then retells it secondhand to the reader? Yamamoto, I think, very adeptly uses "legend" to characterize her story to intentionally reduce the reliability of hearsay peppered throughout the story and problematize the discrepancy between truth and perception. Such a tactic makes the reader wonder whether Miss Sasagawara is really insane; or, if she is, who or what is responsible for such a disastrous consequence occurring to a former ballet dancer?

There is little doubt that Miss Sasagawara has undergone traumatic experiences, as suggested by her obsessive behaviors toward young boys. But again, these behaviors are indirectly reported to Kiku by Elsie who heard them from Mrs. Sasaki, the wife of Mr. Sasaki who, according to Miss Sasagawara, had earlier spied on her. Mrs. Sasaki found deviant and therefore unacceptable the behavior of a thirty-nine-year-old woman absorbedly watching young boys play. Another major event is also reported by Elsie, who heard it from Joe Yoshinaga, one of the boys that Miss Sasagawara had earlier watched play with others. Joe reported that he found Miss Sasagawara sitting on his bed, at night, watching him concentratedly. According to these "eyewitness" accounts, twice removed, Miss Sasagawara was mad after all—she certainly did not act by the standards of people who judged her, such as the Sasakis.

The incriminating power of "The Legend" lies in its subversive strategy, and in its intent to expose the detrimental effects that internment caused upon the internee's nervous system and behavioral pattern. Kiku, having recorded the various accounts of Miss Sasagawara's reportedly aberrant actions, finally offers an account from her own knowledge, however limited, of the legendary ballet dancer, as she comments after hearing Elsie's narrative:

> I was impressed, although Elsie's sources were not what I would ordinarily pay much attention to—Mrs. Sasaki, that plump and giggling young woman who always felt called upon to explain that she was childless by choice, and Joe Yoshinaga, who had a knack of blowing up, in his drawling voice, any incident in which he personally played even a small part. (351)

This observation effectively casts both storytellers as untrustworthy sources of information and compromises the reliability of stories about Miss Sasagawara told by Mrs. Sasaki and Joe Yoshinaga. Elsie, as an agency that helped spread these stories, puzzled over the cause of Miss Sasagawara's derangement, and Kiku, the narrator, "sagely explained that Miss Sasagawara had no doubt looked upon Joe Yoshinaga as the image of either the lost lover or the lost son. But my words made me uneasy by their glibness, and I began to wonder seriously about Miss Sasagawara for the first time" (351). Here, loss suffered by Japanese Americans in World War II is thematized by Yamamoto, and later, by many other Japanese American authors.

Yamamoto's structural design for the story is such that toward its close, she makes sure that the reader hears the last word directly from the narrator, who received her last word directly from the subject of her narration, in the form of a long poem written by Miss Sasagawara, "about a man whose life-long aim had been to achieve Nirvana, that saintly state of moral purity and universal wisdom" (352). This poem, a *tour de force*, signed Mari Sasagawara, apparently is autobiographical. Kiku's deliberate use of her personal name, Mari, often ignored by her fellow internees, restores her real identity. The poem explores the resigned life of a Buddhist man after the death of his wife, and oxymoronically praises the father as noble and flawless, while insinuating that the suffering party was the one who had to companion him, namely the daughter. Yamamoto writes, "The poet could not speak for others, . . . she could only speak for herself. But she would describe *this man's devotion as a sort of madness*, the monstrous sort which, pure of itself and so with immunity, might possibly bring troublous, scented scenes to recur in others' sleep" (352; emphasis added).

The narrator's interpretation of the poem casts into question all that has been said and believed about Miss Sasagawara's lunacy. The incrimination of the father as a religious fanatic emphasizes the sensitivity of the daughter as an artist—first a ballet dancer, then a poet—who was vulnerable to harm.

King-Kok Cheung, juxtaposing her reading of the story with Charlotte Perkins Gilman's "The Yellow Wallpaper," asks, "The saintly father with his devotional fanaticism . . . stifles the human yearning of 'someone else'—his daughter. Who then is mad?" (56). The fact that Miss Sasagawara was able to write poetry to explain the troubled relationship with her father seems to bespeak her sanity rather than insanity. If, indeed, she was insane as alleged, the liable ones would be the father and the government, both patriarchal and oppressive. As Stan Yogi puts it, "Miss Sasagawara becomes a symbol of all Japanese Americans who, especially during the war, were thought to be disloyal and consequently interned" ("Japanese American Literature" 136). Hence the story's condemnation of America's state-sponsored practice of racial hate under a legal cover. As W.E.B. Du Bois argues in his column in the *Amsterdam News*: "Most people do not realize that outbreaks of so-called 'racial hate' are practically always organized and not spontaneous. The driving out of people of Japanese descent on the West Coast was not only an attempt to confiscate their savings without return, but to foment and prolong racial antagonism" (284).

Mr. Sasagawara, on the other hand, was not merely practicing Buddhism to achieve Nirvana; it seems that the war, his wife's death, and the government's internment of Japanese forced him to beat an escapist route to avoid worldly troubles. Buddhism is notorious for its renunciatory philosophy, characterized by an unconditional resignation from mundane affairs and intentional indifference to personal losses and gains. Such an analysis of the father's character does not preclude sympathy for the victimized daughter, but it allows us to see the father and the daughter both as victims of war and government discrimination, in addition to viewing the daughter as a double victim of institutional prosecution and paternal negligence due to her mother's death and her father's religious passion. The father is incriminated in the daughter's insanity, so one is left with little room in which to think that he is above blame. The story presents a disturbing portrayal of a displaced family whose members are at odds with each other, pitted against a formidable government and a monstrous war.

In the second Yamamoto piece, "Yoneko's Earthquake," the reader is shown another Japanese American family, which again is dysfunctional and incomplete, for the family's sovereignty was first violated and then it suffered a loss from the abortion of an unwanted pregnancy. The elusive narrative style is perhaps the story's greatest attraction. In a nutshell, the Hosoumes hired a young Filipino, Marpo, to help them on the farm. An earthquake struck, incapacitating Mr. Hosoume and rendering him sexually impotent, necessitating Mrs. Hosoume to tend the farm with Marpo, during which time the two developed an affair. Marpo conquered not just the heart of Mrs. Hosoume but also her daughter Yoneko's, influencing both with his religious zeal and versatile talents. The earthquake marks an important turning point in the lives of all people involved. On Yoneko's part, she narrated what she witnessed, heard, and felt. Realizing that her three hours of prayers to God were not answered, Yoneko concluded that God was nonexistent and therefore she gave up the Christian beliefs that Marpo had inculcated in her. To the contrary, Mrs. Hosoume, originally a non-believer, started to believe in God after the disappearance of Marpo, the abortion of her pregnancy, and the unexpected death of her son Seigo.

Stan Yogi reads "Yoneko's Earthquake" as a chronicling of "the infatuation of a young nisei girl with a Filipino hired hand, while also revealing the disturbing ramifications of her mother's relationship with the same man" ("Japanese American Literature" 135). In a more sophisticated discussion, Yogi views Mrs. Hosoume's adultery with Marpo and Yoneko's hiding of the ring as defiant acts against patriarchy, represented by Mr. Hosoume and the Christian religion ("Rebels and Heroines" 140).[9] The story, like Morrison's *The Bluest Eye* and Yamamoto's own "The Legend," unfolds from the perspective of a child, the ten-year-old Yoneko, a nisei, the hidden focus being on the issei mother, who used to subjugate herself to her husband against whom she now silently rebelled by committing adultery with a man of a different ethnicity and class. The earthquake serves a causal function as the real shake-up occurred between Mr. and Mrs. Hosoume, a quake on the allegorical level that severely tested Yoneko's faith in God, which proved, like the quake itself, only a passing whim.

King-Kok Cheung similarly reads the story as a veiled attack on patriarchy and male dominance. Mr. Hosoume had to cope with the loss of his physical ability, as well as his sexual manhood. Cheung writes, "If Mr. Hosoume thinks his family is turning against him out of scorn, his wife's love affair and ensuing pregnancy must be the ultimate affront to his manhood. . . . [T]he fetus is a terrible reminder at once of cuckoldry and Mr. Hosoume's impotence" (51–52). Elaine Kim, on the other hand, locates an aesthetic slant in the story; that is, she finds creative power in the women of Yamamoto's stories. Kim observes,

> In "Yoneko's Earthquake" and "Seventeen Syllables," the husbands are hard-working and serious but unable to tolerate their wives' efforts to create beauty and poetry. . . . Yamamoto's women . . . possess strength that arises from a combination of madness and a thirst for beauty and meaning in their lives. (162)

Mrs. Hosoume apparently found intellectual beauty in Marpo's versatility and eloquence, qualities that also attracted Yoneko and that she found missing in her own father.

The earthquake, the ring, the crushed dog, and the departure of Marpo all baffle the uncomprehending Yoneko. Marpo, on the other hand, had hankered for the opposite sex but a Japanese woman did not exactly satisfy his sexual fantasies. "As an artist," Yoneko muses, "Marpo painted larger-than-life water colors of his favorite movie stars, all of whom were women and all of whom were blonde, like Ann Harding and Jean Harlow, and tacked them up on his walls" (271). Nonetheless, the focus of Marpo's sexual fantasies finally shifted to Mrs. Hosoume when she accepted his ring—in the married Japanese woman Marpo discovered romance and beauty to which Mr. Hosoume had become oblivious, just as he failed to notice the ring that Yoneko wore on her finger.

But Mr. Hosoume's traditional moral and aesthetic values surfaced when he saw the flamingo nail polish Yoneko was wearing, and ironically, he told his daughter, "You look like a Filipino" (276). This stern remark not only shows Mr. Hosoume's racial bias against Filipinos as a whole,[10] it also links Yoneko to Marpo, and when Mrs. Hosoume came to her daughter's defense, it links her to Marpo, too. In fact her defense represents her awakened consciousness of her own beauty, which had been missed by her husband and now recognized and appreciated by Marpo. Yoneko remembered once hearing someone comparing her mother to "a dewy, half-opened rosebud" (278), further indication that her mother's feminine beauty had not been fully appreciated by her insensitive, unromantic husband. Her presumed consummation with Marpo now fully opened the rosebud. So in defending Yoneko, she also defended, and attempeted to conceal, her own secret liaison with Marpo. But to her husband her defense mounted a contradiction that defied his authority.

Mr. Hosoume's physical handicap increased his sense of vulnerability and the potent threat to his manhood. When he felt contradicted, as he believed he was, his authority as head of the house was defied. Worse still, his authoritative role as master to Marpo was also shaken as the latter stood up to intervene in Mrs. Hosoume's behalf, using the children's presence as an excuse. Mr. Hosoume's observation that "Marpo was beginning to forget his place" (279) represents the master's forced admission of his loss of control over what used to be his domain: the house, the family, his wife and children, and his farm. To correct the imbalance caused by his handicap, Mr. Hosoume threatened Marpo about his job. This segment of the story proves to be most elusive and yet constitutes perhaps its most crucial moment: soon after Mr. Hosoume made his threatening remark, Marpo disappeared, without even saying goodbye to Yoneko and Seigo. Coincidentally, the day of Marpo's mysterious disappearance was also the day of the Hosoumes' visit to the hospital, en route to which Mr. Hosoume recklessly crushed a beautiful collie.

The subterranean connection between Marpo's departure and Mrs. Hosoume's hospital operation is never explicitly stated. Critics such as Cheung, Yogi, and Kim all agree that Marpo impregnated Mrs. Hosoume and that he was fired by Mr. Hosoume for his insolence and disrespect, and more important but unstated, for his adulterous affair with his wife. However, though there might be a danger of "overreading" the text, the temptation to think that Mr. Hosoume killed Marpo is hard to resist. After all, Mr. Hosoume had acted violently toward his own wife, and he did threaten Marpo about his job; and most revealing of all, driving his wife to the hospital he ran over a dog without displaying any show of upset emotions, in contrast to his daughter's wanting to vomit vis-à-vis the same bloody scene.

To a considerable extent, the dog symbolizes Marpo: they were both beautiful; both fell victim to Mr. Hosoume's irascible actions; and both disappeared mysteriously, or certainly so it seemed to Yoneko. The story becomes even more tragic toward its close when Yoneko's five-year-old brother Seigo suddenly dies of an unnamed disease. The death of the boy alters the mother's course of life and belief system and it persuades her, who at first was a nonbeliever, that God's will cannot be violated, as she told her daughter by way of a lesson. "Never kill a person, Yoneko, because if you do, God will take from you someone you love" (282). The critics cited earlier all seem to think that Mrs. Hosoume was referring to her aborted child with Marpo when she said "Never kill a person," working from the assumption that the aborted fetus was a person killed, and to punish the killing, God took away the Hosoumes' unborn child. Again, since the reader is never clearly informed of what exactly happened to Marpo, there is room left in which to speculate about his fate: if the aborted fetus is not regarded as a person, as contemporary pro-choice advocates have generally argued, no one was killed, except possibly Marpo, by Mr. Hosoume. The firing (or perhaps killing) of Marpo and the crushing of the dog thus become Mr. Hosoume's desperate efforts to regain his control, and the violence involved being a means of reasserting his male authority, and ultimately, a futile effort at restoring peace and harmony to his formerly male-dominated home turf, as well as at repairing his damaged, and devalued, manhood.

"Yoneko's Earthquake" explores loss, sexual and gender tensions vis-à-vis patriarchal rule and interethnic relations, and to a lesser extent, the impact of religion on an individual's life.[11] Gender and sexual relations, complicated by racial tensions and attractions, have been given prominent treatment by Asian American novelists and short story writers. Among these authors is Oscar Peñaranda (1944–), a Filipino American[12] writer and poet who has worked at different jobs, including working as a bus boy in Las Vegas in the early 1960s. Peñaranda's story, "Dark Fiesta," like Yamamoto's "Yoneko's Earthquake," is set in a family with an observant child, a schoolboy named Amador. Like Yamamoto, Peñaranda explores an adulterous affair and presents the narrative from a child's perspective. The story, with a simple plot, records a young boy's disconcerting discovery of his father's liaison with his schoolteacher, for whom he maintained respect until his discovery of the affair. In more than one way, "Dark Fiesta" reminds readers of Richard Wright's "The Man Who Was Almost a Man," Faulkner's "Barn Burning," and Arthur Miller's *Death of a Salesman*, for all four works examine, among other things, father/son relationships and the child's gradual, upsetting discovery of the father as something different from what he had previously known. Put differently, the child's discovery of the father's dark, secret side marks a turning point in his life, which causes alienation from the father and eventual departure from home.

In Faulkner's "Barn Burning," Colonel Sartoris Snopes, the son, has always thought of his father Abner as a Civil War hero, but when he finds out that his father is nothing but a coward and arsonist, the disappointment is so overwhelming that he reports his father's arson intent to Major De Spain, whose barn his father plans to burn. As a result De Spain has time to prepare and in the end shoots and kills Abner. Colonel Snopes, on the other hand, runs away from home. The theme of "Dark Fiesta" resembles even more closely Miller's *Death of a Salesman* in respect to the son's discovery of the father's dark secrets. Biff accidentally finds his father Willy Loman making out with a strange woman in a Boston hotel room. Unable and unwilling to tell his mother about the liaison, Biff, who has lost respect for his father, rebels by leaving home. Though he later returns, he is never able to restore his respect nor does he really reconcile with his father.

"Dark Fiesta," dealing with a Filipino family, nicely parallels Faulkner's and Miller's works. Amador, the son of Mr. and Mrs. Ante and the central character, has no interest in going to school, but his parents want him to receive an education. His father seems the more curious of the two parents about his school attendance, as he goes there to fetch him home every day. This enables the father to see Amador's teacher, with whom he conducts regular rendezvous. Amador's parents forbid him to play with a boy named Totoy, who, by contrast, does not attend school because his parents do not believe in education; hence his curiosity about the institution. The two boys seem to look across an unsurmountable wall into each other's yard with curious interest but are unable to cross over and experience what the other has. Totoy, however, persuades Amador to skip school and play with him; he even suggests that Amador secure his teacher's forgiveness by giving her a green apple.

Totoy appears very street-smart and quite worldly for an illiterate person. When Amador asks him about the color and shape of the world—either to show off his own knowledge or to test the range of Totoy's—he does not expect him to know, and yet Totoy answers, "It is crooked" (232), which demonstrates his empirical knowledge of the world and cynical but sophisticated understanding of human nature. Totoy's answer foreshadows the dark fiesta of Amador's discovery of his father's secret rendezvous with his teacher in the hut, and as if the sight of their illicit meeting was not shocking enough, he finds out that his father has killed their family dog who had bitten a boy whose family demanded the dog's liver for wound-healing purposes. The twin discoveries of the dog's killing and of his father's sexual misconduct stun Amador and force him to revise his perceptions of the man: he did not expect him to kill their family dog, nor did he dream of him acting unfaithful to his mother who generously, and innocently, thought his teacher pretty. Amador had revered his teacher and respected his father. The disillusionment induced by his discoveries came so suddenly and violently that when his father emerged from the hut with the teacher and saw him, Amador threw the already rotten apple "far and hard into the dust where the shadows were growing long" (236).

The green apple is an emblematic image of high significance in the story. Its initial green color symbolizes Amador's innocence and inexperience. By the end of the second day, after a chain of events, the apple had rotted just as the world suddenly turned crooked. Throwing it away not only reflects Amador's disillusionment about his father and his teacher, both role models, but also marks his maturity. This disillusionment amounts to nothing less than that experienced by Goodman Brown upon discovering his wife, Faith, and his respected church leaders participating in dark ceremonies in the woods in Hawthorne's "Young Goodman Brown." Amador's apple also invokes the biblical fruit, the eating of which marks the moral and physical fall of man. Ultimately, the flinging away of the rotten fruit represents Amador's rejection of his teacher's and his father's (im)moral values. In the end, like Dave in "The Man Who Was Almost a Man," Colonel Snopes in "Barn Burning," and Biff in *Death of a Salesman*, Amador takes the classic action of rebellion and defiance—running away.

Running away is, for the moment at least, the only way of distancing himself from the people he wants to disassociate from, as well as a mode of defining his own morality and identity; from a narrative point of view, it's a convenient way of bringing the story to a denouement. The rotten apple is inevitably linked to his teacher as it was meant for her in the first place, and the decaying stench to his father, as he killed the dog and lugged its remains to the site of the fiesta. Running away from these rotten things and people signifies a drastic departure from the moral standards of his authoritative superiors. But he also runs away from Totoy and Carding, his friends, toward "the taboo bridge." The only character in the story who mentions the old bridge is Amador's mother, who forbade him to go there because there were ghosts and it was dark on the other side. His mother also believed that the old bridge was ready to fall apart and meant trouble for children. Thus, not only does the bridge symbolize discipline imposed by the mother, but it represents a crossover to the unknown, as suggested by ghosts and darkness on the other side. Yet that is the direction Amador chose to run in, hence the will to break the taboo and to free himself of disciplinarian bounds, and in the end, to defy authority and seek autonomy. Peñaranda's story thus affirms the value of the American spirit of independence by means of rebellion, and "Dark Fiesta," apparently a narrative about a Filipino family, is a real American story of independence with a traceable thematic origin in the American Revolution that established America's nationhood.

Sui Sin Far, Yamamoto, and Peñaranda did not merely concentrate on their own ethnic experiences in America. What they wrote in the stories examined above no doubt transcends ethnic, personal, and cultural boundaries. Their works deal with issues—gender, love, loss, death, and family—that writers of all ethnicities are concerned with. I emphasize the particularities of some Asian American issues to demonstrate the universalities of the human experience in any culture, under any circumstances. As the works of these writers have proved, ethnic differences are always there when one looks for them, but behind and beside(s) the differences always lie the sameness manifest in all humans.

◆ NOTES

1. "Sui sin far," Edith Eaton's own spelling of the modern *shui xian hua*, as has been frequently noted, literally means "water lily" in Chinese.

2. A white shirt and black pants suggest his half white/half black racial identity.

3. Sui Sin Far's vision of racial equality is naively utopian, as she writes in these lines: "Fundamentally, I muse, all people are the same. My mother's race is as prejudiced as my father's. Only when the whole world becomes as one family will human beings be able to see clearly and hear distinctly. I believe that someday a great part of the world will be Eurasian. I cheer myself with the thought that I am but a pioneer. A pioneer should glory in suffering" (117). Rachel Lee comments on this political naivete: "Her fiction and memoir thus operated on the premise that ideal turn-of-the-century readers of "The Inferior Woman" and "Leaves" would grow sympathetic with working-class women and with the Chinese through their vicarious association with them across these pages" (256).

4. According to Cohen, culture, like language, is "made up of its own arbitrary conventions." See "Culture, Not Race," B4.

5. Rodney King's question of this very wording, following the scandalous police brutality perpetrated against him in Los Angeles several years ago, provides good illustration.

6. In this order President Roosevelt cites "the successful prosecution of the war" as justification for his authorization to evacuate Japanese Americans, as "protection against espionage and against sabotage to national-defense material, national-defense premises and national-defense utilities," and this presidential order, observe Philip Foner and Daniel Rosenberg, "helped set a legal precedent in discrimination against Asian Americans" (248). For various accounts on Japanese American relocation, see Foner and Rosenberg, eds., *Racism, Dissent, and Asian Americans from 1850 to the Present*.

7. As readers familiar with the history of World War II well know, while ethnic Japanese on the west coast were interned in concentration camps, ethnic Italians and Germans, whose ancestral countries were Japan's allies, received far better treatment from the government, in fact little different from most other European descendants.

8. The same JACL, however, later spearheaded the Japanese American redress effort.

9. Yogi points out, "Mrs. Hosoume's adultery is a direct violation of patriarchal dominance, and Yoneko's unknowing compliance and silence about the ring's origin suggests generational rebellion against the patriarchy" ("Rebels and Heroines" 140).

10. Mr. Hosoume blatantly states, "for it was another irrefutable fact among Japanese in general that Filipinos in general were a gaudy lot" (277).

11. Grace Kyungwon Hong, analyzing Yamamoto's story, "A Fire in Fontana,"

briefly considers "Yoneko's Earthquake," which she believes shows Yamamoto's long-recognized "fragility of Japanese Americans' claim to property in the United States" (292).

12. Although critics such as N.V.M. Gonzalez and Oscar V. Campomanes have pointed out that many Filipino migrants and their second-generation offspring usually resist usage of the term Filipino American because it occludes the historical and power differentials engendered by the Philippine American colonial experience (62), for its distinguishing function in my discussions of various ethic writers, I rely on the term to differentiate this group from other Asian American groups.

◆ WORKS CITED

Chan, Jeffery Paul, Frank Chin, Lawson Fusao Inada, and Shawn Wong, eds. *The Big Aiiieeeee! An Anthology of Chinese American and Japanese American Literature*. New York: Meridian Books, 1991.

———. "Introduction." In *The Big Aiiieeeee!* Chan et al., eds., xi–xvi.

Cheung, King-Kok. *Articulate Silences: Hisaye Yamamoto, Maxine Hong Kingston, Joy Kogawa*. Ithaca, NY: Cornell University Press, 1993.

Chin, Frank. "Come All Ye Asian American Writers of the Real and the Fake." In *The Big Aiiieeeee!* Chan et al., eds., 1–92.

Chin, Frank, Jeffery Paul Chan, Lawson Fusao Inada, and Shawn Hsu Wong, eds. *Aiiieeeee! An Anthology of Asian American Writers*. New York: Meridian Books, 1997.

Cohen, Mark Nathan. "Culture, Not Race, Explains Human Diversity." *The Chronicle of Higher Education* (April 17, 1998): B4–B5.

Du Bois, W.E.B. "W.E.B. Du Bois on the Internment," In *Racism, Dissent, and Asian Americans from 1850 to the Present*. Philip Foner and Daniel Rosenberg, eds. Westport, CT: Greenwood Press, 1993, 284.

Faulkner, William. *Light in August*. New York: Vintage International, 1990.

———. "Barn Burning." In *Norton Anthology of American Literature*, vol. 2, 5th ed. Nina Baym, gen. ed. New York: Norton, 1998, 1630–42.

Foner and Rosenberg, eds. *Racism, Dissent, and Asian Americans*.

Gonzalez, N.V.M., and Oscar V. Campomanes. "Filipino American Literature." In *An Interethnic Companion to Asian American Literature*. King-Kok Cheung, ed. New York: Cambridge University Press, 1997, 62–124.

Hawthorne, Nathaniel. "Young Goodman Brown." In *Norton Anthology of American Literature*, vol. 1, 4th ed. Baym, gen. ed., 1236–45.

Hong, Grace Kyungwon. " 'Something Forgotten Which Should Have Been Remembered': Private Property and Cross-Racial Solidarity in the Work of Hisaye Yamamoto." *American Literature* 71.2 (June 1999): 291–310.

Kim, Elaine H. *Asian American Literature: An Introduction to the Writings and Their Social Context*. Philadelphia: Temple University Press, 1982.

Lee, Rachel. "Asian American Short Fiction: An Introduction and Critical Survey." In *A Resource Guide to Asian American Literature*. Sau-ling Cynthia Wong and Stephen H. Sumida, eds. New York: MLA, 2001, 252–84.

Leighton, Joy M. " 'A Chinese Ishmael': Sui Sin Far, Writing, and Exile." *MELUS* 26.3 (Fall 2001): 3–29.

Ling, Amy. *Between Worlds: Women Writers of Chinese Ancestry*. New York: Pergamon Press, 1990.

————. "Creating One's Self: The Eaton Sisters." In *Reading the Literatures of Asian America*. Shirley Geok-lin Lim and Amy Ling, eds. Philadelphia: Temple University Press, 1992, 305–18.

————. "The Asian American Short Story." In *Columbia Companion to the Twentieth-Century American Short Story*. Blanche H. Gelfant and Lawrence Graver, eds. New York: Columbia University Press, 2001, 34–41.

Lowe, Lisa. "Heterogeneity, Hybridity, Multiplicity: Marking Asian American Differences." *Diaspora* 1.1 (Spring 1991): 24–44.

Miller, Arthur. *Death of a Salesman*. In *Norton Anthology of American Literature*, vol. 2, 5th ed. Baym, gen. ed., 1919–85.

Morrison, Toni. *The Bluest Eye*. New York: Washington Square Press, 1972.

Peñaranda, Oscar. "Dark Fiesta." In *Aiiieeeee!* Chin et al., eds., 227–36.

Sui Sin Far. "Her Chinese Husband." In *The Big Aiiieeeee!* Chan et al., eds., 133–38.

————. "Leaves from the Mental Portfolio of an Eurasian." In *The Big Aiiieeeee!* Chan et al., eds., 111–23.

————. "The Story of One White Woman Who Married a Chinese." In *The Big Aiiieeeee!* Chan et al., eds., 123–33.

Trinh, Minh-ha. *Woman, Native, Other*. Bloomington: Indiana University Press, 1989.

Wright, Richard. "The Man Who Was Almost a Man." In *Norton Anthology of American Literature*, vol. 2, 5th ed. Baym, gen. ed., 1758–66.

Yamamoto, Hisaye. "The Legend of Miss Sasagawara." In *The Big Aiiieeeee!* Chan et al., eds., 340–52.

————. "Yoneko's Earthquake." In *Aiiieeeee!* Chin et al., eds., 267–82.

Yogi, Stan. "Rebels and Heroines: Subversive Narratives in the Stories of Wakako Yamauchi and Hisaye Yamamoto." In *Reading the Literatures of Asian America*, Lim and Ling, eds., 131–50.

————. "Japanese American Literature." In *An Interethnic Companion to Asian American Literature*. Cheung, ed., 125–55.

PETER BACHO

(1950–)

Rocío G. Davis

◆ BIOGRAPHY

Peter Bacho was born in Seattle in 1950. His father had immigrated to the United States in 1923, and returned to the Philippines to marry his mother in 1949. The family was migratory until 1954, after which his father divided his time between summers working in Alaskan canneries and a job in the city. Bacho grew up in the Central District in Seattle, mainly an African American and Filipino neighborhood at the time. He graduated summa cum laude from Seattle University in 1971, earned a law degree from the University of Washington in 1974, became a City of Seattle Prosecutor in 1985, and a Staff Attorney, U.S. Ninth Circuit Court of Appeals from 1989 to 1990. In 1988, Bacho was Assistant Professor in the Ethnic Studies Department of the University of Washington and Visiting Professor in English and History at the University of California at Irvine in 1994-1995. He lives in Tacoma where he teaches at the University of Washington and is on the editorial board of the *Tacoma News Tribune*.

Bacho has trained in martial arts and American boxing for over thirty years, and works out in his free time. He says that he fights and writes to keep a connection with his forefathers. An important aspect of his creative imagination lies in his understanding of the generation of immigrants that had come before him, and he feels fortunate to have known many of the heroic protagonists of early Filipino American history, notably Chris Mensalvas, the "Jose" in Carlos Bulosan's *America Is in the Heart*.

Bacho's first novel, *Cebu* (1992), won the American Book Award of the Before Columbus Foundation. His second book, *Dark Blue Suit and Other Stories*, won a Washington State Governor's Writers Award and the Murray Morgan

Award in 1998. Bacho's essay collection for young adults, *Boxing in Black and White*, a discussion of major figures in the world of boxing, from Filipino boxer Sammy Santos to Muhammad Ali, made the Best Books List 1999, Children's Center for Books at the University of Illinois. He has just published his second novel, *Nelson's Run*.

◆ MAJOR WORKS AND THEMES

Dark Blue Suit is a collection of twelve semi-autobiographical linked stories about the first-generation Filipino immigrants—the *Manongs* (a respectful term for older men) who came to the United States in the 1920s and 1930s—and their children. Bacho describes the ways the Filipino community in Seattle dealt with one another and the social and political structures of the city, with the loss of a country and racism in a new one, as well as with the manner in which the second generation comes to terms with their past and the demands of the present. The stories, narrated by Buddy, a second-generation Filipino American, set from the 1950s to the present, are largely character portraits. Buddy stresses kinship with the Manongs, appropriating their stories from a consciously American point of view, and engages those of his generation—his friends Rico and Stephie, his half-sister, Sonia—in their attempts to establish themselves in America. In the first story, "Dark Blue Suit," seen through the eyes of himself as a child, Buddy describes an afternoon with the men in Chinatown who await dispatch to the Alaskan canneries. Vince, Buddy's father, is the foreman in charge of selecting the men: "That day, like most days, Dad was also wearing a suit. This one, though, was especially sharp—a somber, dark blue suit, pressed and perfect, fit for a mayor, a movie star, or an Alaskero" (5). The narrator highlights the Filipinos' quiet elegance, the pride that required them to dress impeccably and to look good, particularly in the face of poverty. The boy meets characters that continue to influence his life: his father's cousin Leo, the protagonist of "The Wedding"; Stephie, the daughter of an American prostitute and an unknown Filipino father—possibly either Leo or Vince—who will reappear dramatically in Buddy's life in an eponymous story; and Chris Mensalvas, the protagonist of "A Life Well Lived" and the communist leader whom Buddy first meets dressed as Santa Claus at the Union Christmas party. "A Manong's Heart" centers on Uncle Kikoy, who "loved boxing because it was like life, or at least the life he knew" (103). That sport becomes at once a form of entertainment and a strategy for signifying for the Manongs, as it will later be for Buddy and Rico. Boxing symbolizes the Filipinos' struggle for the right to be treated as equals, and putting on gloves is a way for the Manongs to assert themselves and fight back, "and above all to protect a manhood perpetually threatened by an emasculating society" (Francia 76), a trope for self-making, because "[i]n the ring, a Filipino could beat a white man with his fists and not be arrested" (110).

Accounts of the second generation manifest the liminal position and ambivalence of American-born children. In "Rico" and "Home," Buddy describes a working-class friend trapped between a world he rejected and one that rejected him, who fights a real war—Vietnam—and never recovers. Another half-Filipina woman lost in the gap between the community and mainstream America is Sonia, the protagonist of "Dancer," whose story makes Buddy perceive the choices his parents had made. "The Second Room" outlines Buddy's pursuit of self-defense, and his appreciation for the art of boxing. "August 1968" foregrounds the necessary cultural reassessment that characterized Buddy's adolescent years and his vision of his changing neighborhood. The dialogue between Buddy and Aaron, his African American boyhood friend, in this story illustrates the dramatic tensions that divide many American cities. "But what about us," Buddy asks, "neither black nor white, who lived on the same block and shared the poverty? Did the revolution spare observers?" (54–55).

In the last story, "A Family Gathering," Buddy laments the lack of historical grounding and interest of the new groups of immigrants who "didn't know what the old men had done and, quite frankly, couldn't care less. They wouldn't see the connection between their own comfort and what others had struggled to build. They couldn't see that the old men had heart and did the most with the least, and with a style they can never have and that I'll never see again" (143). His chronicle, then, becomes an exercise in remembrance, his strategy for connection and survival. In different stories, as Buddy records his own efforts at belonging—changing professions, marrying and divorcing twice—he continually looks back at those stories of dignity and resistance, and achieves his own catharsis when he is finally able to stand before his father's tomb and pray. Through these stories, Bacho transforms the Manong into a heroic figure in the United States historical context, using him as an example and model for his narrator.

◆ CRITICAL RECEPTION

The stories in *Dark Blue Suit* have received consistent praise, from both mainstream and Asian American critics. Thomas Keneally calls the book a "superb performance" (back cover); Shawn Wong, situating the collection in the tradition of earlier Filipino American writers like Bulosan, Santos, and Gonzales, points out that it takes the story of immigration further, as it engages the stories of the second generation (back cover). George Leonard affirms Bacho's position as one of "the finest writers of the Filipino experience and one of the finest American realists ... [presenting] an unforgettable picture of Seattle's rainy Chinatown as it really was" (493–94). He suggests that the book itself is "a deeply Filipino act, a debt paid" to the generation of Manongs (495). Anderson Tepper highlights Bacho's "rough-hewn and wistful style," a narrative counterpart to the valedictory the writer pays to a generation of fighters (24). Emily Baillargeon praises Bacho's perception of the con-traditions and possibilities of immigrant life, for he presents the world of Chinatown as at once "an extended family and a dead end for many immigrants," and he portrays fighting not so much as "a mode of self-defence for Buddy as a dance, a choreographed journey towards identity" (12). Bacho's honest, albeit sentimental, chronicle of the immigrant generation recovers and preserves the buried history of unsung heroes.

◆ BIBLIOGRAPHY

Works by Peter Bacho

Short Story Collection

Dark Blue Suit and Other Stories. Seattle: University of Washington Press, 1997.

Novels

Cebu. Seattle: University of Washington Press, 1991.
Nelson's Run. Holliston, MA: Willowgate Press, 2002.

Essays

Boxing in Black and White. New York: Henry Holt and Co., 1999.

Studies of Peter Bacho

Baillargeon, Emily. "Pinoy Stories." *Seattle Weekly Books Quarterly* (Winter 1997): 12.
Davis, Rocío G. *Transcultural Reinventions: Asian American and Asian Canadian Short Story Cycles.* Toronto: TSAR, 2001.
Francia, Luis H. "America Is in the Dark." *A. Magazine* (October 1997): 76.
Leonard, George J., and Diane Rosenblum, eds. "A Reader's Guide to *Cebu* and *Dark Blue Suit* Based on Interviews with Its Author, Peter Bacho." In *The Asian Pacific American Heritage: A Companion to Literature and Arts.* George J. Leonard, ed. New York: Garland Press, 1999, 481–95.
Tepper, Anderson. "Dark Blue Suit and Other Stories." *The New York Times Book Review* (October 26, 1997): 24.
Tizon, Alex. "The Filipino Fight, beyond the Boxing Ring." *The Seattle Times*, Arts Alive Section (November 16, 1997): 17.

HIMANI BANNERJI
(1942–   )

Chandrima Chakraborty

◆ BIOGRAPHY

Himani Bannerji was born in 1942 in what is now Bangladesh. She came to Canada in 1969 and began her teaching career in Canada working as a part-time instructor at Atkinson College (York University), Toronto. She is currently an Associate Professor in the Department of Sociology at York University. She has published books on poetry, fiction, and theory, and numerous essays on racism, feminism, politics, and culture. Her short stories have been published in various books and journals.

◆ MAJOR WORKS AND THEMES

Bannerji's short stories voice the oppression of the female sex irrespective of their age, class, or geographical location. They deal with the condition of female immigrants in Canada and the religious and societal structures of gendered discrimination in India. The narrative voice in all the stories is that of a female South Asian immigrant.

The immigrant conflict between home as a physical site in Canada and home as an emotional tie to the country of birth is evident in a number of stories. The physical geography of Canada in "On a Cold Day" is emphasized through the "white cold light" and the "cold whiteness of the city" (33). In "The Colour of Freedom," "the whiteness" and "stifling monotony and purity of snow" are contrasted with the "yellow sun" of the narrator's childhood "in a far away country" (177). The mother in "The Other Family" sees her daughter "walking alone through an alien street in a country named Canada" and remembers "the sun, the trees and the peopled streets of her own country!"

(141). In "The Day It Rained," rain reminds the omniscient narrator of "that day of rain—in another country, in another time" (27).

"On a Cold Day" confronts directly the forces of cultural domination and racial intolerance in Canada. Devika, a female immigrant of South Asian origin, on her way to work, sees a brown woman's body sprawled on the sidewalk. It takes her a moment to recognize the difference between the dead woman and herself. She concludes: "A woman from either India or Pakistan or Bangladesh or Sri Lanka, or for that matter from Trinidad or Guyana, or Africa or Fiji" (29). Bannerji's enumeration of the various nation spaces that the victim could belong to critiques the Western homogenization of individuals (immigrants/foreigners) based on skin color. Her list of countries reminds the reader of the colonial past with its history of slavery, indentured labor, forced and voluntary migrations, and the transcultural nature of today's globalized world.

Devika changes her name to Debbie after a counselor convinces her that employers want "to be able to pronounce their employees' names without going to heritage classes" (30). She wears high heels to work, although her feet hurt, and her clothes are "a set of costumes or disguises" (32)—all desperate efforts to somehow survive in the West (and not die like Asima). It is significant that Bannerji presents Asima's restless movements before she jumps from her seventh-floor balcony but does not provide a reason for her decision. The momentary identification of Devika with Asima at the beginning of the story and the narration of Devika's racist experiences reveals the existential condition of non-white woman immigrants in Canada and provides possible reason(s) for Asima's suicide. This is made explicit at the end of the story when the shopkeeper articulates his inability to offer a prayer for the dead woman for the lack of her name, and Devika tells him that the dead woman's name was Devika Bardhan. According to Mukherjee, Devika Bardhan's transformation into Debbie Barton "marks a loss as final as death, even though Devika does not die a physical death" (xii). The coerced transformation of Devika into Debbie raises questions of discrimination, loss of self with (re)naming, and the denial of the immigrant woman's right to be different.

This theme of identity gets played out at the intergenerational level in "The Other Family" where a young girl's drawing of her family with blue eyes, blond hair, red beard, and white skin makes her shocked mother respond in anger and pain. The daughter's defense—"all our books have this same picture of the family. . . . And everyone else drew it too" (143)—represents second-generation immigrants' interpellation into the discourse of the majority culture. The mother's reaction makes the girl conscious of her difference from the model textbook Canadian family. The next day she goes back to school and adds the "other" family—a dark-skinned, dark-haired family—next to the blond family, without erasing the white family. This reveals that in the child's consciousness there have emerged complex and contested forms of belonging and identity formation, which interrogate self/other dichotomies, held by the mother's generation. She redraws the contours of the cultural landscape by including her marginalized/invisible family within the cultural parameters of the dominant discourse.

While "The Other Family" depicts the confusion of South Asian children socialized in the North American context, "The Day It Rained" presents a young South Asian girl's uncertainty and feelings of trepidation on her entry into "womanhood." Her first menstrual cycle dislodges her from her childhood "of joy and boundless activities" (27) and places her forever into "the suffocating atmosphere of the female world" (29). In a moment her "outer world" is transformed to the "other world," the world of men. The patriarchal societal structures that function around the separation of spheres into home/inner (= female) and the world/outer (= male) restrict her freedom and imprison her in traditional notions of womanhood.

The prison metaphor common in Bannerji's poetry is used in "The Day It Rained" and in "The Colour of Freedom" to represent a South Asian woman's life. In "The Colour of Freedom" the child character considers her family "in a prison that my father guarded" (181). Presented from a child's point of view, her fears of her father's violent outbursts and incomprehension of the Hindu-Muslim riots in her hometown poignantly express the need for domestic reform and the dismal events of the freedom struggle. The faith of the Indian masses in Gandhi's power to heal the pain and anger caused by interreligious clashes is evocatively portrayed when the mother and daughter go to see Gandhi who was passing through their town. Neither of them, nor the people standing near them, are able to get a glimpse of the Mahatma, but their rickshaw puller comments with certainty: "Whatever his words may be, we won't have riots here again" (189).

Faith in political redemption is replaced by faith in religion as capable of liberating man from the cycles of births and re-births in "The Moon and My Mother." The narrator's elderly mother is excited about the American expedition to the moon. A widow, who has believed in the Hindu scriptures' views on rebirth and transmigration of souls, is shocked to hear that the men on the moon "only found darkness" and not "pitrilok—the world of our fathers," that is, her dead ancestors (191). The disillusionment that results from this Western scientific discovery leads her to debunk old, traditional belief systems, but without any other system to replace the old structures, she is left with no solace on her deathbed. She is now afraid to die, as she knows that "there is nothing on the other side of death" (195).

Bannerji uses the female immigrant narrative voice to foreground the oppression of women and children across geographical boundaries through the narrators' reminiscences of their country of birth. Her stories voice the female characters' frustration at the entrenched societal structures of discrimination, gendered upbringing, and racism. Her fiction forcefully discloses racism as a lived reality in the lives of non-white communities. They are politically necessary for an immigrant community striving to find its voice and claim a space in the cultural and literary landscape of the Canadian nation. However, Bannerji's didacticism impinges into the omniscient narrative mode in such an obvious manner that it blunts the power of her critique.

◆ CRITICAL RECEPTION

No critical essays on Bannerji's short stories are available. Most critics find fault with Bannerji's poetry and fiction for an inclination for "discussion" in her works. Mukherjee, in an interview with Bannerji, says, "The Other Family" "could generate a discussion of what is happening at school . . . how our children are unobtrusively being assimilated into this so-called Canadian culture" (152). Verghese regards the images of the country of birth, which are found in South Asian works like Bannerji's, as "nostalgia specific to the immigrant," and "These images, this nostalgia, is the brick and mortar of the South Asia we immigrants carry with us in North America" (xv).

◆ BIBLIOGRAPHY

Works by Himani Bannerji

Short Stories

"The Day It Rained." *Fireweed* 21 (Summer/Fall 1985): 27–31.
"The Other Family." In *Other Solitudes: Canadian Multicultural Fictions*. Linda Hutcheon and Marion Richmond, eds. Toronto: Oxford University Press, 1990, 141–45. Rpt. in *Immigrant Experiences: Exploring Fiction, Poetry and Non-fiction*. Dom Saliani, ed. Toronto: Harcourt Brace, 1995, and in *The Language We Share: A Canadian Cross-cultural Reader for Learning English*. Eva C. Karpinski and Marlene Lecompte, eds. Toronto: Harcourt Brace, 1995.
"On a Cold Day." In *Her Mother's Ashes, and Other Stories by South Asian Women in Canada and the United States*. Nurjehan Aziz, ed. Toronto: TSAR, 1994, 26–34.
"The Moon and My Mother." In *Contours of the Heart: South Asians Map North America*. Sunaina Maira and Rajini Srikanth, eds. New York: Asian American Writers' Workshop, 1996, 188–96.
"The Colour of Freedom." *West Coast Line* 26–27 (September 1998–February 1999): 177–91.

Poetry

A Separate Sky. Toronto: Domestic Bliss, 1982.
Doing Time: Poems. Toronto: Sister Vision Press, 1986.

Novels

The Two Sisters. Toronto: Kids Can Press, 1978.
Coloured Pictures. Toronto: Sister Vision Press, 1991.

Non-fiction

With Linda Carty, Kari Dehli, Susan Heald, and Kate McKenna. *Unsettling Relations: The University as a Site of Feminist Struggles*. Toronto: Women's Press, 1991.

The Writing on the Wall: Essays on Culture and Politics. Toronto: TSAR, 1993.

Thinking Through: Essays on Feminism, Marxism and Anti-racism. Toronto: Women's Press, 1995.

The Mirror of Class: Essays on Bengali Theatre. Calcutta: Papyrus Publishers, 1998.

The Dark Side of the Nation: Essays on Multiculturalism, Nationalism and Gender. Toronto: Canadian Scholars' Press, 2000.

Jibanananda, Sudhindranath Ebang (Essays on Modern Bengali Poetry). Calcutta: Dey's Publishing, 2000.

Edited Books

Returning the Gaze: Essays on Racism, Feminism and Politics. Toronto: Sister Vision Press, 1993.

With S. Mojab and J. Whitehead. *Of Property and Propriety: The Role of Gender and Class in Imperialism and Nationalism*. Toronto: University of Toronto Press, 2001.

Essays

"Introducing Racism: Notes Towards an Anti-Racist Feminism." *Resources for Feminist Research* 16.1 (1987): 10–12. Rpt. in *Women, Law and Social Change: Core Readings and Current Issues*. 2nd ed. T. Brettel Dawson, ed. North York, ON: Captus Press, 1994.

"The Sound Barrier: Translating Ourselves in Language and Experience." *Fireweed* 30 (Summer 1990): 121–34. Rpt. in *Language in Her Eye: Views on Writing and Gender by Canadian Women Writing in English*. Libby Scheier et al., eds. Toronto: Coach House Press, 1990, and in *By, For and About: Cultural Politics*. Wendy Waring, ed. Toronto: Women's Press, 1995.

"Re: Turning the Gaze: Racism, Sexism, Knowledge and the Academy." *Resources for Feminist Research* 20.3 (1992): 5–11. Rpt. in *Beyond Political Correctness: Toward the Inclusive University*. Stephen Richer and Lorna Weir, eds. Toronto: University of Toronto Press, 1995.

"Writing 'India,' Doing Ideology: William Jones' Construction of India as an Ideological Category." *Left History* 2.2 (Fall 1994): 5–36.

"Beyond the Ruling Category to What Actually Happens: Notes on James Mill's Historiography in *The History of British India*." In *Knowledge, Experience, and Ruling Relations: Studies in the Social Organization of Knowledge*. Marie Campbell and Ann Manicom, eds. Toronto: University of Toronto Press, 1995, 49–64.

"On the Dark Side of the Nation: Politics of Multiculturalism and the State of 'Canada.'" *Journal of Canadian Studies* 31.3 (Fall 1996): 103–28. Rpt. in *Literary Pluralities*. Christl Verduyn, ed. Peterborough, ON: Broadview Press, 1998.

"Geography Lessons: On Being an Insider/Outsider to the Canadian Nation." In *Dangerous Territories: Struggles for Difference and Equality in Education*. Leslie G. Roman and Linda Eyre, eds. London: Routledge, 1997, 23–42.

"Politics and the Writing of History." In *Nation, Empire, Colony: Historicizing Gender and Race*. Ruth Roach Pierson and Nupur Chaudhuri, eds. Bloomington: Indiana University Press, 1998, 287–301.

"A Question of Silence: Reflections on Violence against Women in Communities of Colour." In *Scratching the Surface: Canadian Anti-Racist Feminist Thought*. Enakshi Dua and Angela Robertson, eds. Toronto: Women's Press, 1999, 261–77.

"The Paradox of Diversity: The Construction of a Multicultural Canada and 'Women of Colour.'" *Women's Studies International Forum* 23.5 (September–October 2000): 537–60.

"Projects of Hegemony: Towards a Critique of Subaltern Studies' 'Resolution of the Women's Question.'" *Economic and Political Weekly* 35.11 (2000): 902–20.

Studies of Himani Bannerji

Chakraborty, Chandrima. "Himani Bannerji." In *Asian American Poets: A Bio-Bibliographical Critical Sourcebook*. Guiyou Huang, ed. Westport, CT: Greenwood Press, 2002, 37–44.

Interview with Arun P. Mukherjee. In *Other Solitudes*, Hutcheon and Richmond, eds., 146–52.

Jacob, Susan. "Breaking the Circle: Recreating the Immigrant Self in Selected Works of Himani Bannerji." In *Intersexions: Issues of Race and Gender in Canadian Women's Writing*. Coomi S. Vevaina and Barbara Godard, eds. New Delhi: Creative, 1996, 189–96.

Mukherjee, Arun P. "Introduction." In *Her Mother's Ashes*, Aziz, ed., ix–xvii.

Verghese, Abraham. "Foreword." In *Contours of the Heart*, Maira and Srikanth eds., xiii–xv.

SUSHAM BEDI
(1945–   )

Alice D'Amore

♦ **BIOGRAPHY**

Susham Bedi was born on July 1, 1945 in Ferozpur, Punjab. She wrote during her undergraduate years at Delhi University in India, participating in literary competitions and publishing in various magazines, and has since proven herself an influential Indian American novelist and short story writer. As she writes of Anisha abandoning the warm days of India for the chilled evenings of Belgium in the short story "Ice-Armor," Bedi herself left India for Brussels in 1974, serving as a correspondent for the *Times of India* until 1979, when she traveled with her family to the United States. That same year she earned her doctorate from Punjab University, completing her dissertation, "Innovation and Experimentation in Contemporary Hindi Drama," and publishing the text five years later. She joined Columbia University as a professor of Hindi language and literature in 1985. Throughout her professorship, she has also served as coordinator of Columbia's Hindi-Urdu Language Program because of her multilingual proficiency in English, French, Hindi, Urdu, Punjabi, and Sanskrit. In addition to her academic endeavors, Bedi also acted as a New York correspondent for "Letters from Abroad," a BBC program produced in the early 1990s. Like Dhira in her short story "The Search," Bedi has embraced America as a diverse and enriching atmosphere where she can explore the boundaries of her talents, which are many, and allow her children to do the same. An acclaimed actress since her early days on Indian television in the late 1960s and 1970s, she has appeared on *Law & Order: Special Victims Unit* and in Krutin Patel's award-winning film *ABCD*, as well as various televised commercial advertisements.

Currently, Bedi is developing two novels, a second short story collection, and poetry as well as producing Hindi reading and listening comprehension materials for the language classroom. Her literary work has been translated into English and Urdu.

◆ MAJOR WORKS AND THEMES

Throughout her short stories, Bedi's major themes describe the cultural and geographical displacement experienced by her characters, male and female. "In the Park" details the cultural fall of a displaced Indian male and his inability to influence his "Americanized" daughter following the cataclysmic events induced by a single day's excursion into Central Park. She also explores the effects of cultural displacement on two transplanted Indians in a story of cultural and religious conflict, "Avsaan" ("A Death in America"). The story recounts the funeral of an Americanized Indian, Divakar, and the impact the occasion has on his less-pliant Indian counterpart, Shankar. In a comic description of the suddenly dead Divakar, a middle-aged, twice-divorced, atheistic medical doctor and recent father, Bedi portrays the loss of cultural values experienced by the Americanized Indian. The story concludes with Shankar's pathetic and futile attempt to resurrect his sole connection with his homeland by interrupting the Christian ceremony, as arranged by Divakar's American widow, to intone sacred Hindu verses from the *Bhagavad Gita* to his lost friend.

The wonder of Bedi's artistry is her ability to convey her own experiences to the reader through her stories and novels; Bedi's personal relocation and subsequent emotional and spiritual transition appear in each of her characters, regardless of gender. The theme of the displaced Indian woman pervades Bedi's collection of short stories entitled *Chiriya aur Cheel* (*The Sparrow and the Kite*), published in 1995. In "The Search," Dhira, an Indian woman on a quest for identity, finds herself dissatisfied with the sacrifices she has made for her family. She is torn between her nurturing Indian family values and the liberating American ideals of individuality and gender equality she desires to pursue. Though living in an individualistic America, she finds herself intellectually unchallenged and in constant domestic service to her husband and children. She looks wistfully back upon the years she spent teaching at Daulatram College in India. Torn between the selfless enjoyment she takes from serving her family and the inspiration of her feminist American acquaintance Ellen, she feels apathetically "comfortable with her slow and predictable, challengeless domestic life" while realizing that she lacks personal fulfillment (25). She listens silently as her husband, Sameer, clarifies a woman's "duties," noting, "A woman gives love and in return receives it. When the American woman emphasizes individuality, she is doing something just for herself. She does not enjoy the central place that a woman in traditional cultures does as a mother or a wife" (26). However, Dhira also realizes the paradox of the male position in society, reflecting, "Men also get married, but they don't give up their individuality, their autonomy, the realization of their potential" (26). It is her communion with a native American at the zoo, a wizened explorer of India who resembles her father, that draws Dhira to the rediscovery of her native identity. He speaks of the Indian people and their "inner freedom." "They taught me to truly respect my inner self and follow its lead," he tells Dhira, offering an outlet for her inner strength through a reunion with the supportive nature of her culture as it is perceived by a fellow displaced "outsider." Through her epiphany, she is able to confront her husband, negotiate her individual needs, and achieve self-actualization while remaining the supportive core of her family.

In a paper she presented at the Illinois Humanities Festival in Chicago in 1995, "Conflict and Transformation: An Indian Experience of Love and Marriage," Bedi further explores the role of the female in an Indian relationship. Reflecting on the contrasting love affairs between Indian deities, the monogamous Sita and Ram and the promiscuous Krishna and Radha, she notes, "Although their true love is certainly tested after marriage . . . in both cases it is the woman who, through her suffering, tolerance and perseverance, saves the marriage," as Dhira proves in "The Search." Regarding the imbalance of power between the sexes, Bedi contemplates the traditional role of the female in Indian society: "[W]omen in India are brought up to understand themselves primarily in relation to others. A woman's role in the society is defined as daughter, daughter-in-law, wife and a mother. She is not supposed to have the demands of an individual." Bedi embodies this lack of individuality in Anisha, the central character of the story "Ice-Armor."

In "Ice-Armor" Bedi again explores the role of the Indian woman in marriage; however, the cultural complications in this story grow more complex because the story portrays an interracial relationship, not the simple traditional clash faced by Dhira in "The Search." "Ice-Armor" involves the psychological transition of Anisha, an Indian woman displaced among the "faces with cold, frozen, false smiles" of Brussels (23). Her marriage to the Belgian Jean has become a monotonous round of drinking, silence, irritation, and "lifeless, emotionless, dry kisses. Kisses that taste like frozen pieces of meat in their mouths" (25). As her father had warned, the initial "romantic haze" of the relationship soon succumbs to what he defined as the "huge gulf between the two of you, your values, culture, way of life" (24). Too late she realizes that "somewhere in the man she sat with in the balmy, colorful Delhi evenings, lived the cold, foggy, grey evenings of Brussels" (24). Considering her place in Jean's life, Anisha reduces her role to that of an automaton: "Using the machines in the house over and over—the dishwasher and the washing machine—she felt that she too had turned into a machine. She was a machine that ran all the others" (24). Unable to adapt to the city's harsh noises, cold air, and frigid inhabitants, her depression becomes overwhelming. Severe headaches plague her daily, and she finds herself growing dependent upon prescription medication that only succeeds in "leaving her sicker than before when it wears off, numbing her body and mind" (25). Where Dhira overcomes her struggle in "The Search," finding the strength to draw supportive elements of her culture into her new environment, Anisha experiences a spiritual and cultural death, a descent into emptiness and despair resulting from her geographical displacement. Where Dhira earns the respect of her husband with "the look of firm resolve on her face," Anisha succumbs to the oppression of her surroundings: "She has begun to feel that her life is simultaneously tugged in two directions—between noise and emptiness. The open, lively, effervescent world outside has turned into a corpse inside her and has begun to smell. . . . She is dressed in a frigid, frozen armor of ice. She only feels secure if she has it on" (26–27).

◆ CRITICAL RECEPTION

Though Bedi writes only in Hindi, a growing tide of scholars has risen to translate her works into English; David Rubin, Geeta Patel, and Tahira Naqvi, recognizing the importance of Bedi's message to America's assimilation of all cultures, have translated several of her stories and novels. However, since she has published all her work in India, most criticism of Bedi's writing is available only in her native Hindi, her work as displaced as many of her characters. Nonetheless, Indian American websites and news publications have recently begun to promote her novels and poetry. The website *India in New York* has described Bedi's works as those that "explore the immigrant experience—immigrants' struggle[s] and their cultural as well as psychological conflicts" (http://www.indiainnewyork.com). For example, in "Broadway," she personifies the famous strip of New York City as a silent observer of the fall of the traditional immigrant's American Dream. The seams of the dream, as envisioned by a displaced Indian family whose breadwinner struggles to support his brood by opening a "casket business," fray and unravel when he is murdered and ironically buried in his own creation. Though the story ends tragically, Bedi seems to suggest that there is hope in a return to culture—not merely a physical return to the homeland, but an internal spiritual return to strength and self-respect also seen in Dhira's actions in "The Search" and Kamani's self-discovery in "Colors of Fall."

While conveying Bedi's recurring theme of dislocation to the reader is of greatest importance in her work, Brunda Moka-Dias's study of Bedi's novels warns that "one needs to be aware that the politics of translation is complex—issues of language, style, and culture have to be carefully negotiated, often with no satisfactory or alternative solutions" (16). Of course, the possibility exists that the author's intended message and style may be lost in translation, but addressing this issue in her interview with Eileen Tabios, Bedi states, "Always, the meaning of the story gets conveyed. But in some parts, my style does not get translated. This is unfortunate because literature is not just about meaning—it's style, how you say things. It's what Art is about" (Tabios 84). Despite the possible loss of what Bedi calls her "circular style," it is still apparent that her American audience will continue to grow, due to her ability to engage the reader's empathy for her characters despite the cultural chasms of race, religion, and gender, which separate them from English-speaking readers.

◆ ACKNOWLEDGMENT

I wish to thank Dr. Jim Nechas for his unwavering guidance in his review of my work.

◆ BIBLIOGRAPHY

Works by Susham Bedi

Short Stories

"Homecoming." *Pratibha* 13.3 (1994): 13–20.
"Vibhakt." *Hans* (February 1994): 37–42.
"Ice-Armor." Trans. Geeta Patel. *Journal of South Asian Literature* 30.3–4 (1995): 23–27.
"Avsaan." *Samkaleen Bhartiya Sahitya* 66 (1996): 151–56.
"In the Park." In *Odyssey: Stories by Indian Women Writers Settled Abroad*. Divya Mathur, ed. New Dehli: Star, 1998, 103–11.
"Sarak ki Laya." *Abhivyakti* (Online web magazine), 2001. http://www.abhivyakti-hindi.org. Accessed October 31, 2001.

Short Story Collection

Chiriya aur Cheel. Dehli: Parag, 1995.

Novels

The Fire Sacrifice. Trans. David Rubin. London: Heinemann, 1993.
Lautna. Delhi: Parag Prakashan, 1993.
Katra-dar-Katra. Chandigarh: Abhishek, 1994.
Itar. Delhi: National Publishing House, 1997.
Gatha Amerbel ki. Delhi: National Publishing House, 1999.
Nava Bhum Ki Ras-katha. Delhi: National Publishing House, 2001.

Academic Publications

Innovation and Experimentation in Contemporary Hindi Drama. New Dehli: Paraga Prakasana, 1984.
"Growing Up with India These Fifty Years." *The Asian Pacific American Journal* 6.2 (1997): 45–49.

Conference Papers

"Quest for Identity: Grappling with the Literary Self in the Diaspora." Meeting of
    United States Association for Commonwealth Literature and Language Stud-
    ies, May 6, 2001, Providence, Rhode Island.
"Conflict and Transformation: An Indian Experience of Love and Marriage." Illinois
    Humanities Festival, November 10–12, 1995, Chicago, Illinois.

Studies of Susham Bedi

Embree, Ainslie. Rev. of *The Fire Sacrifice. Journal of South Asian Literature* 28.1–2 (1993):
    357–58.
"The Flames and Ashes of Diaspora." Rev. of *The Fire Sacrifice. Asian Times* (February
    15, 1994): 13.
India in New York: "For and about People from the Subcontinent." http://www.indiain
    newyork.com/iny01212000/Women/HindiNovelist.html. Accessed Septem-
    ber 30, 2001.
"Looking for New Horizons." Rev. of *Havan. The Frontier Post* (March 12, 1993): 4.
Moka-Dias, Brunda. "Susham Bedi." In *Asian American Novelists: A Bio-Bibliographical
    Critical Sourcebook.* Emmanuel S. Nelson, ed. Westport, CT: Greenwood Press,
    2000, 13–17.
Madhu, Sandhu, ed. *Women Novelists at the Eve of the 21st Century.* Delhi: Nirmal
    Publications, 2000, 53–63 and 127–35.
Rao, Sucheela. Rev. of *The Fire Sacrifice. World Literature Today* 69.2 (1994): 429.
Sharma, Bulbul. "In Alien Land." Rev. of *The Fire Sacrifice. Indian Express* (April 24,
    1994): 7.
Tabios, Eileen. "Susham Bedi: A Reconciliation with Translation." *The Asian Pacific
    American Journal* 5.2 (1996): 81–93.
"Writers at Home in the West." Rev. of *The Fire Sacrifice. India Mail* (December 14,
    1993): 4.

CECILIA MANGUERRA BRAINARD

(1947–   )

Alicia Otano

◆ BIOGRAPHY

Cecilia Manguerra Brainard was born in Cebu, Philippines, the youngest of Mariano F. Manguerra and Concepcion Cuenco Manguerra's four children. She began keeping a diary at the age of nine, after her father's death. The need to write about her experiences growing up in Cebu ("Ubec" in her works of fiction) presaged a vocation in this field: she graduated from Maryknoll College in Quezon City with a B.A. in Communication Arts in 1968.

In 1969, Brainard immigrated to the United States to study filmmaking at UCLA graduate school. There, she married Lauren Brainard, with whom she has three children. From 1969 to 1981 she worked as a documentary scriptwriter and as a fundraiser for a non-profit organization. In 1981, she decided to take writing classes and began her career in writing. From 1982 to 1988 she wrote a bimonthly column, "Filipina American Perspective," for the *Philippine American News*. Writing for this now defunct newspaper offered the possibility of exploring the experience of living in the United States as a Filipina and the impetus to explore memories of her childhood in the Philippines. Her contributions to the column were published as a collection of essays entitled *Philippine Women in America*. During this time she started publishing short stories and essays in various magazines and journals both in the Philippines and in America. These short stories first appeared in the periodicals *Focus Philippines*, *Philippine Graphic*, *Mr. and Ms. Magazine*, *Katipunan*, *Amerasia Journal*, *Bamboo Ridge Journal*, *The California Examiner*, and others. Short story anthologies like *Making Waves* (1989), *Forbidden Fruit* (1992), *Songs of Ourselves* (1994), and *On a Bed of Rice* (1995) have also included her work.

Brainard is the author and editor of nine books, has published over 250

essays, and written three dozen stories. The best-known and most widely received of her works are her two short story collections: *Woman with Horns*
(1987) and *Acapulco at Sunset* (1995), and a novel, *Song of Yvonne* (1991), published in the United States as *When the Rainbow Goddess Wept* (1994). She collected and edited *Fiction by Filipinos in America* (1993) and *Contemporary Fiction
by Filipinos in America* (1997). In 1985 her short stories were awarded the Fort-
ner Prize and in 1989 she was awarded both the California Arts Council Artists' Fellowship in Fiction and the Honorable Mention Award of the Philippine
Arts, Letters and Media Council. Her commitment to education was reflected
in the Los Angeles Board of Education's Special Recognition award in 1991.
She is a founding member of PAWWA (Philippine American Women Writers
and Artists) and was awarded the Outstanding Individual award from the
city of Cebu in 1995. She currently lives in Santa Monica, California, where
she teaches creative writing part-time and is the Director of the Philippine
American Literary House.

♦ MAJOR WORKS AND THEMES

A common theme links Brainard's fiction: she engages the Filipino legends
and history, superstitions, folktales, native traditions, and the Catholicism she
learned as a child into fiction set in the past or in contemporary times. Many
of her short stories reflect her interest in historiography: in her collections,
stories set during the Spanish colonization coexist with those set during the
American occupation, problematizing versions of the Philippine's complex
cultural history. In "The Magic Spring," in *Women with Horns*, a young girl
visits a spring believed to make women beautiful and meets a young man
avenging his mother's death. Their conversation reflects a mixture of Catholic
and native beliefs and strategies of coping with pain. In her second collection,
Acapulco at Sunset, a Catholic priest struggles to convert the natives but ends
up drawn into their system of beliefs. "There is a rawness here, a wildness
that I find invigorating. . . . Who am I to say that the way they dress, their
songs and stories are not right for them?" the title character asks in "Temp-
tations of Padre Joaquim" (32).

Brainard also explores the psychological impact of diverse foreign occupations on the Filipino people during different time periods. Historical facts
take on life when they are narrated by those anonymous people living then,
their stories illustrating universal experiences. On a formal level, she deftly
handles narrative strategies like point of view as part of her nuanced representation of story and history. In "Woman with Horns," Dr. Gerald McAllister,
an American doctor trying to clear the islands of cholera, has performed his
job brilliantly: "Thanks to his vaccination program, the epidemic was now
under control. This success was another feather in his cap, one of the many
he had accumulated during his stay in the Philippine Islands" (9). His life

crammed with many activities is, in reality, empty. One of his colleagues voices what he has long suspected about himself: " 'You bastard!' He said, 'All you think about is work. You have no soul' " (17). His attraction to an island girl, also a widow, will finally awaken his soul to the human component behind his inoculation programs. Similarly, in "The Black Man in the Forest" an aging general battles with an influx of feelings which will lead him to perform an act of mercy. After killing the young African American soldier who has wounded him, he is moved by his final cry: "Sara" (21), which leads him to see, for the first time, the dead enemy soldier as a human being who must be spared the cannibalism practiced by one of his own men, "Liver-eater." This progression of characters toward the moment of revelation or discovery about their own lives is documented through Brainard's manipulation of point of view. It is a conscious manipulation that renders multilayered versions of reality: though externally things seem quite normal, the reader soon discovers a latent tension in the manner in which the focalizer perceives his or her circumstances. The focalization process becomes a window to their souls, giving a humane angle to historical facts and revealing timeless truths.

Self-imposed physical exile for the sake of a better life or self-imposed psychological exile where characters do not have to leave the Philippines to feel the mental anguish associated with such an experience is a recurring theme in many of the short stories. Brainard also deals with the theme of marriage, which embodies the "cultural, social, and biological reproduction, that is, the executor of group interests to which individual desires are subjugated" (Adler 45), creating impressive psychological depth. Marriage, too, becomes a form of exile. In *Acapulco at Sunset*, exile can be seen in the different time periods featured. In "Chino's Dream," the protagonist, who joins the Spanish expedition heading for Alta California to start up a settlement in 1780, wants a better life. His only mistake is believing all the empty promises that fuel his imagination: "For weeks, Jose, who had signed up in September, talked of nothing else but what the settlers would get. He spoke about the monthly salary and regular rations for three years. He had a way with words so all these came to life in my head" (4). "Leaving" is a way of ending an unhappy life. Mental escape or physical escape, however, does not guarantee happiness; instead it often leads to deception and anguish. In "Acapulco at Sunset" the protagonist narrates: "Papa had told me that with Santiago as my husband, I and my children will not lack anything; he was right" (14). As she desperately waits for the yearly letters from home brought by the galleon *Nao de Manila*, she takes refuge in memories of her former life. This woman's nostalgia is no different from that felt by the protagonist of "Lucy and Ben," set in the 1990s. Lucy has also found a better life in America, but visits home always set off a wave of nostalgia and a sea of doubts whenever she sees her former boyfriend Ben. A successful middle-aged businessman, he finally confesses that "this life

I have isn't a life" (100). The protagonist, however, rises above her memories: self-awareness brings a final freedom from the past—and the exile into memories, when she sees his "limitations; understood that he did not have and never had the gumption to choose for himself the woman he really loved, that (like a business deal) he surrendered Lucy for money" (101). The multilayeredness of Brainard's narratives, which negotiate history, exile, and identity, clearly establish her place in Asian American literature.

◆ CRITICAL RECEPTION

The critical acclaim for Brainard's short stories has been positive both in the Philippines and in the United States. The psychological wealth of her writing, manifest in her handling of point of view, is an important contribution to Asian American fiction. Leonard Casper alludes to this manipulation of perspective when he notes how the effects of war are negotiated in the stories "Miracle at Santo Niño Church" and "The Blue-Green Chiffon Dress" in *Women With Horns* (72). In the first, Tecla, a deranged woman who practically lives in a church, suffers nightmares about the Japanese who bayoneted her family. In the second, a teenage girl wears "the perfect dress" to a party where she meets a very young American soldier with only six months left in Vietnam. In both stories, war is focalized as it is experienced, the protagonists touched by different degrees of loss.

Isagani R. Cruz writing for the *Philippine Star* notes: "Brainard's short stories are refreshingly new, therefore comfortably old-fashioned; they are delightfully conventional, therefore startlingly innovative. . . . Or perhaps more precisely put, they are new fiction, written as though they are old, or old fiction, written as though they are new" (20). This critic highlights Brainard's interweaving of the elements of fiction in *Acapulco at Sunset*: "In Brainard's stories, Acapulco and Intramuros are the same, and at the same time, completely different places. Dead characters and live characters talk to each other nonchalantly. A young poor boy falls in love with an older rich woman, and by loving her, kills her. Filipinos find their identity in, of course, San Francisco but not so ordinarily in Alaska. The green card—actually blue—spells the difference between authenticity and an authentic life, between dreaming and the American dream" (20). Les Adler praises Brainard's original use of the theme of exile in *Acapulco at Sunset*: "Brainard enriches the conventional understanding of exile by applying the concept to Filipino experience in the Philippines. She is thereby able to show that the cultural and social issues that a Filipino/a faces while in exile are universal Filipino experiences"(45). Her chronicles of Filipino history and myth, as well as of contemporary living, become narratives of survival and adaptation to a constantly changing world.

◆ BIBLIOGRAPHY

Works by Cecilia Manguerra Brainard

Short Story Collections

Women With Horns and Other Stories. Quezon City: New Day, 1987.
Acapulco at Sunset and Other Stories. Manila: Anvil, 1995.

Novels

Song of Yvonne. Quezon City: New Day, 1991.
When the Rainbow Goddess Wept. New York: Dutton, 1994. Rpt. New York: Plume, 1995.

Edited Works

Coed., *Seven Stories from Seven Sisters: A Collection of Philippine Folktales.* Los Angeles: PAWWA, 1992.
Fiction by Filipinos in America. Quezon City: New Day, 1993.
Coed., *The Beginning and Other Asian Folktales.* Los Angeles: PAWWA, 1995.
Contemporary Fiction by Filipinos in America. Manila: Anvil, 1997.

Studies of Cecilia Manguerra Brainard

Adler, Les. "Acapulco at Sunset." *Filipinas* 26 (Spring 1996): 45.
Beltran, Marie G. "Woman with Stories and Other Concerns." *Filipinas* (May 1995): 29, 56.
Casper, Leonard. "Cecilia Manguerra Brainard." In *American Ethnic Writers,* vol. 1. David Peck, ed. Pasadena, CA: Salem Press, 2000, 71–73.
Cruz, Isagani R. "The Pleasures of Ubec, Otherwise Known as Cebu." *Starweek: The Sunday Magazine of the Philippine Star* (October 29, 1995): 20.
Hidalgo, Cristina Pantoja. *Filipino Woman Writing: Home and Exile in the Autobiographical Narratives of Ten Writers.* Manila: Ateneo de Manila University Press, 1994.
Huebler, Dana. "An Interview with Cecilia Manguerra Brainard." *Poets and Writers Magazine* (March–April 1997): 96–105.
Ty, Eleanor. "Cecilia Manguerra Brainard." In *Asian American Novelists: A Bio-Bibliographical Critical Sourcebook.* Emmanuel S. Nelson, ed. Westport, CT: Greenwood Press, 2000, 29–33.

CARLOS BULOSAN
(1911–1956)

Aiping Zhang

◆ BIOGRAPHY

A Filipino American short story writer, novelist, poet, and labor activist, Carlos Bulosan was born in Binalonan, Pangasinan, Philippines on November 24, 1913 (though his baptismal papers list November 2, 1911 as the birth date). The son of a farmer, Bulosan grew up in poverty. At the age of seventeen, he went aboard a ship for America and arrived in Seattle on July 22, 1930.

Despite his lack of English proficiency and money, Bulosan came with a belief that he would have a better life in America. The shocking discovery of the harsh realities, such as inequality, injustice, and hatred due to racial discrimination, did not diminish the great expectations in his heart. To survive, he worked at all kinds of menial jobs for years, from hotels and produce farms up and down the West Coast to the Alaskan fish canneries. In his constant search for employment, he encountered numerous obstacles and brutalities that were commonly directed at immigrants like him during those years and learned firsthand about the paradoxical nature of America, the "land of opportunity."

His years of experience as a farm worker led him to the role of a labor activist during the 1930s, mobilizing his fellow workers into unions against labor exploitation, wage cuts, unbearable working conditions, and racist violence against immigrants. The hardship in his life and the intense involvement with the labor movement severely affected his health. In 1936, he had several lung operations for tuberculosis at Los Angeles County Hospital and spent two years in a convalescent ward. While recuperating from his illness, Bulosan, who had only three years of formal schooling in the Philippines, became an avid reader and gradually educated himself into one of the first Filipino writers to write in English in America. The more he wrote, the more he discovered that writing was a powerful weapon in dealing with adversity, confusion, frustration, and pain because it helped him to regain his long-suppressed voice.

His literary career started with letter writing, but he soon ventured into other genres. His first book of poems, *Letter from America*, was published in 1942 and a second, *Voice of Bataan*, followed the next year. His stories first appeared in the *New Yorker* and other magazines, and his first collection, *The Laughter of My Father*, was published in 1944. It was an unexpected success for him, as it was translated into several languages and excerpts were read over wartime radio. Two years later, he tried his hand at novel writing and published his masterpiece, *America Is in the Heart: A Personal History*. In spite of his poor health, Bulosan stayed actively involved with the labor movement and kept working diligently on his manuscripts for a novel and many stories until he collapsed and soon died of pneumonia in September 1956 at the age of forty-four.

Thanks to the excellent efforts of a Bulosan scholar, E. San Juan, Jr., many of Bulosan's manuscripts have been sorted, edited, and published since the late 1970s. Bulosan's novel, *Power of the People*, which follows a group of Filipino guerillas in the Huk Rebellion of 1949–1952, appeared in 1977 (later released as *The Cry and the Dedication* in 1995); a collection of his short stories, *The Philippines Is in the Heart*, was published in 1978; a collection of miscellaneous writings, *On Becoming Filipino: Selected Writings of Carlos Bulosan*, appeared in 1995. In addition, the University of Washington Press has kept his *America Is in the Heart* in print over the years.

◆ MAJOR WORKS AND THEMES

Though best known for his autobiographical novel, *America Is in the Heart*, Bulosan is also a talented and versatile short story writer. Like other immigrant writers of his time, he was keenly aware of the fact that he was writing in an adopted language as an outsider for an American audience, and therefore it was imperative to tell his stories with an authentic but enticing native voice. In his essay, "How My Stories Were Written," reprinted in San Juan, Jr.'s *If You Want to Know What We Are* (21–26), Bulosan describes how he obtained the material for his stories from a mysterious old man of the mountains during his childhood. His attempt to establish a credible Filipino voice, which recurs in both his short stories and novels, is mostly executed through mixing fact and myth and alternating between his nativist perspective and his new concepts derived from the U.S. colonial discourse.

Some of the twenty-four stories in *The Laughter of My Father* had been printed in the *New Yorker, Town and Country*, and *Harper's Bazaar*. All the stories in the book are autobiographical reminiscences, representing experiences similar to those of the Bulosan family, its relatives, and neighbors in the village of Binalonan, on the island of Luzon, featuring the same narrative voice and maintaining a common thread in plot development. In most stories, the rich and the Americanized are lauded as the "civilized" and therefore receive a glorifying treatment, while the poor and the indigenous are degraded as the "savage" and are hence cast in exoticizing, if not demeaning, rendition. Occasionally, nevertheless, Bulosan seems to hint that people's definition of savagery could be very arbitrary, that the civilized and uncivilized might easily switch sides, and that both could become targets of exotic spectacles for their similar barbarian attributes. He offers the reader a perfect example in "My Mother's Boarders" when he describes the Americanized schoolteachers from the city as a hilarious spectacle for the uncivilized villagers. The teachers dance in front of the curious villagers, making "ugly gestures with their bodies," and "jumping up and down like monkeys" (22). The narrator's father, along with others, "stood around looking at their hard, pointed breasts sticking out of their tight blouses and sweaters" (22). In this scene, at least, it is the Americanized and therefore "civilized" teachers who appear to be "savages."

Another common trait in this collection is the recurrent image of the sordidness and violence in the Filipino peasants' life. The narrator in "The Gift of My Father" tries to show his cousin Porton's Americanized refinement by contrasting it with the unbearable image of the naked children who follow him around in admiration, "smelling and licking his shoes" (27). The narrator in "The Death of My Father" recounts, with graphic details, his uncle's uncontrollable rage after discovering his wife's promiscuity. His uncle catches his wife nude in bed with a man, beats him with a dead cock, and then throws the headless cock on her stomach. By creating a recurrent narrative voice in all stories that carries views of both sides "in" and "back," Bulosan might be implying that the distinction between the civilized and the savage is subject to self-definition, and that cultural contempt is often reversible, but horrible scenes like these seem to have a sensational effect that catered well to and perhaps further aggravated the widespread perception toward the Filipinos among the American readership at the time.

The Philippines Is in the Heart is a collection of Bulosan stories edited by San Juan, Jr., published in 1978. Many of the stories represent Bulosan's view of the social stratum in the Philippines. Although his narrative is full of favorable remarks for the United States' superior power, Bulosan often leaves traces of doubts and even resentments toward it in his stories, either deliberately or inadvertently. In "Really, a Ghost?" the narrator is an American woman who believes that as an American citizen, a civilized person, she has nothing to fear from any supernatural threat. "This was the twentieth century," she insists, "and I was an American and here was someone who needed help" (129). Her intention might be selfless and noble, but her tone, as Joel Slotkin observes, "shares the patronizing quality of U.S. colonial rhetoric" (847). The irony is that the American woman turns out to be the one who needs help from the "ghost," a rebel of the revolution against the Spanish. The same irony is reinforced by Bulosan's reference to the "little brown children" in two other stories, "The Bandit and the Tax Collector" and "The Wisdom of Uncle Sator," revealing, once again, the condescending undertones of the colonial benevolence.

In some stories, Bulosan attempts to define "civilization," "religion," and the murky connection between the two by stressing two seemingly contradicting perspectives of the Filipino peasants toward Western civilization and Christianity. In "Dinner with a King," the narrator retorts to Alfonso who makes fun of their "savage" lifestyle, "We don't wear shoes and store clothes" as the "civilized" people do, "[b]ut we mind our own business and we go to church once a year to see the beautifully decorated altar" (47–48). Here, the narrator underscores his own definition of "civilization," a definition that deems superficialities irrelevant. The point becomes more poignant and even satiric when Bulosan reveals that Alfonso is not a "civilized" man as he claims to be; he is only the narrator's own brother in disguise. Later, the narrator refers to his uncle, a priest, as a "swindler" who takes advantage of the people he is serving. It is worth noting, though, that priests in several other stories are also portrayed in a negative light. In "The Angel in Santo Domingo," Padre Ruiz has various ways to solicit favors from people, including "frightening people into giving him these things" (141). In "My Father Goes to Church," the narrator's father is warned to bring the priest a gift when he is going to church, even though the priest "is already very fat and rich" (148). In other stories, Bulosan displays the Filipino peasants' ignorance of, disdain for, and opposition to Christianity by implying the deeply rooted presence of an indigenous culture and a pagan religion among the "uncivilized" Filipino peasants. In "The Amorous Ghost Came to Town," the narrator introduces a witch doctor in such a casual way that no specific information is given to the reader regarding his real identity and role in the village. Bulosan's omission of such information is a subtle strategy in his narrative because every villager in the story knows who the witch doctor is and what he does for the village. Clearly, what is implied is that the villagers are far from ready to completely embrace Christianity.

On Becoming Filipino: Selected Writings of Carlos Bulosan, published as part of Temple University Press's Asian American History and Culture series, is a collection of Bulosan's short stories, essays, poems, and letters. The focus in all selections is his growth in "becoming Filipino" in America. The nine short stories reveal the mixed emotions of growing up, exile, alienation, the loss of family, and the fear of death while confronting a lingering colonialism and widespread racism. By tracing the key events in the first fourteen years of Allos's life, the first story, "Passage into Life," depicts the boy's rough initiation into a chaotic world of poverty, greed, violence, and death. With his unyielding trust in nature and people and his hope for a better future, Allos manages to survive after the devastating loss of his parents and learn his lesson: "there in the known world he must go to seek a new life" (59). In "Be American," Bulosan presents a chilling story about how painful seeking a new life in a new country can be. The narrator's cousin, Consorcio, struggles for fifteen years and gives up so many things before receiving "his most cherished dream: American citizenship" (72) shortly before his death. "The Thief" portrays a similar character, Cesar Terson, who dreams the American Dream and struggles in hardship and drudgery until his death. In "Homecoming," Bulosan tells about a man's unpleasant return to the Philippines after years of searching for a new life in America. The man is astonished to realize that his native land has changed so radically since his departure for America that he feels like a stranger in a strange place. Stories like "The Story of a Letter" and "As Long as the Grass Shall Grow" suggest national oppression as another key reason—in addition to class disadvantage and racial discrimination—for the sufferings of Filipinos in America. All the stories seem to have perfectly manifested Bulosan's own bumpy passage into life, first in the Philippines and then in America, and captured his own acute sense of double exile.

◆ CRITICAL RECEPTION

For decades, neither the reading public nor mainstream critics took Bulosan seriously. While his novel *America Is in the Heart* became required reading in ethnic studies classes on college campuses, his short fiction has not generated much quality scholarship. Only after two posthumous publications, *The Philippines Is in the Heart* and *On Becoming Filipino*, have Bulosan's short stories become a frequent subject for journal articles, dissertations, and books.

The Laughter of My Father won rave remarks from some reviewers, but others dismissed the stories as comic-satiric fables with cheap humor and "exotic" color. In recent studies, however, the collection has been praised for its wit, sensibility, and originality, and it has been well explored by critics on a wide range of themes, issues and stylistic features. L. M. Grow calls the collection "a handbook for peasant survival" and its humor "dark rather than hilarious." In Grow's view, "It is unsurprising that the stories are serious, even bitter, since Bulosan intended them to be both" (35).

While there seems to be a consensus to designate this collection as another major work in the Bulosan canon, a few scholars have voiced reservations about Bulosan's portrayal of the Igorots in *The Laughter of My Father*. Slotkin's essay "Igorots and Indians" offers a forceful analysis of this issue. In addition to the derogatory hints of the narrator's Igorot-like attributes, Bulosan often places the "savage" Igorots in scenes where they have no real function other than to represent the bottom of the savagery of Filipino peasants. A telling example can be found in a scene from "The Gift of My Father," in which the rich and Americanized Porton and his wife were received by his poor and envious family while three Igorots, "headhunters from the mountains of Luzon," who "wore G-strings and carried bows and poisoned arrows," sat "under the house with their dogs and talked among themselves" (29). Slotkin believes that Bulosan's portrayal of the Igorots is far from adequate and fair, and that "Bulosan's most unfortunate omission is his failure to provide an Igorot perspective on the hierarchy" that he delineates in his stories, thus denying "the reader access to the interiority of his Igorots, so they remain an incomprehensible Other" (848).

Since its publication in 1978, *The Philippines Is in the Heart* has received only scanty and mixed comments from critics. Comments on this collection are mostly scattered either in news briefs or included as side notes in discussions of Bulosan's fiction writing as a whole. One feature that several critics have deemed as a strong element in the collection is Bulosan's characterization. His characters fall into four basic categories: Americans, Filipino city people and landowners, poor peasants, and the Igorots (the tribal people from the mountains of Luzon who are considered even more "uncivilized" than the poor peasants). Their attitudes toward each other are consistently based on class status. The rich show contempt toward their poor relatives and neighbors. By rendering the Filipino peasants as "uncivilized" but anxious to appear "civilized," Bulosan manages, as Slotkin points out, "to deepen his satire and enrich his investigation of what it means to call oneself civilized" (845). To some critics, however, such a move puts the author at risk of sounding condescending toward his own people.

The interest in Bulosan's short story resurged after *On Becoming Filipino* came out. In his introduction to the volume, San Juan, Jr. sets up a helpful framework for appreciating all the selections in the book. Citing stories like "Be American," "Story of a Letter," and "As Long as the Grass Shall Grow" as representative texts, he suggests "Bulosan tracks the vicissitudes of migrant alienation and analyzes the predicament of return/self-recovery of the sojourner *manqué*" (17).

Some critics have pointed out Bulosan's insights into the differences between the historical experiences of Filipinos and other Asian American ethnic groups. How the voice, identity, and perspective of Bulosan's characters is shaped by the fact that the Philippines used to be under the direct colonial control of the United States has been debated extensively. Jimin Han sees the collection as a full display of Bulosan's evolving political and social views and "a stark testimony to the lives of Filipino migrants" (65). Roland Guyotte considers it "an amplification to *America Is in the Heart*," reflecting "the developing self-consciousness of a young intellectual in a colonial situation at home and, to his disappointment, in the United States" (72). The stories represent a time in history when racial discrimination was rampant and being "different" was like being haunted by a curse. "As a result," Tomio Geron suggests, "Bulosan writes from the perspective of 'exile' rather than the traditional Asian American 'immigrant,' " denouncing American imperialism in his country "as the cause of his family's dismemberment and dislocation," and revealing his "unmistakable passion for his homeland" (13).

Other critics have noted that on the one hand, Bulosan overly exaggerated his family poverty and his lack of education in order to justify the authority of his Filipino peasant identity; on the other hand, his fiction and stories often cast poor Filipino peasants in a negative light and use condescending labels such as "uncivilized" and "savage" to describe them. The reader constantly runs into all kinds of ambiguity in Bulosan's perception of both the poor and the rich and in his assessment of Filipino heritage and American values. Sometimes one is unable to distinguish between an "appealing humor" and a "bitter satire" in his stories. Nevertheless, one can always discover much more than ambivalence in his stories. More than half a century later, Bulosan's spirit of optimism and tenacity as embodied in his short stories is still as inspiring as ever.

◆ BIBLIOGRAPHY

Works by Carlos Bulosan

Short Story Collections

The Laughter of My Father. New York: Harcourt, Brace and Company, 1944.
The Philippines Is in the Heart, ed. E. San Juan, Jr. Quezon City, Philippines: New Day, 1978.

Novels

America Is in the Heart. New York: Harcourt, Brace and Company, 1946.
The Cry and the Dedication, E. San Juan, Jr., ed. Philadelphia: Temple University Press, 1995; first published posthumously as *Power of the People*. Ontario, Canada: Tabloid Books, 1977.

Poetry

Letter from America. Prairie City, IL: The Press of J. A. Decker, 1942.
The Voice of Bataan. New York: Coward-McCann, 1943.

Miscellaneous

On Becoming Filipino: Selected Writings of Carlos Bulosan, E. San Juan, Jr., ed. Philadelphia: Temple University Press, 1995.

Studies of Carlos Bulosan

Geron, Tomio. "Filipino Prophet: The Writings of Carlos Bulosan Re-emerge with a Contemporary Relevance." *Asian Week: The Voice of Asian America* 16.49 (August 4, 1995): 13.
Grow, L. M. "The Laughter of My Father: A Survival Kit." *MELUS* 20.2 (Summer 1995): 35–46.

Guyotte, Roland L. "Generation Gap: Filipinos, Filipino Americans and Americans, Here and There, Then and Now." *Journal of American Ethnic History* 17.1 (Fall 1997): 71–75.

Han, Jimin. "Home of the Brave." *A. Magazine: Inside Asian America* (January 31, 1996): 65.

Ma, Sheng-mei. *Immigrant Subjectivities in Asian American and Asian Diaspora Literatures.* Albany: State University of New York Press, 1998.

Morantte, P. C. *Remembering Carlos Bulosan: His Heart Affair with America.* Quezon City, Philippines: New Day, 1984.

San Juan, E., Jr., ed. *If You Want to Know What We Are: A Carlos Bulosan Reader.* Los Angeles: West End Press, 1983.

———. "Introduction." In *On Becoming Filipino*, 1–44.

Santiago, Maria Katrina Stuart. "Carlos Bulosan in the History of the Philippine Short Story in English." *Diliman-Review* 47.3–4 (1999): 54–63.

Slotkin, Joel. "Igorots and Indians: Racial Hierarchies and Conceptions of the Savage in Carlos Bulosan's Fiction of the Philippines." *American Literature* 72.4 (December 2000): 843–66.

JEFFERY PAUL CHAN
(1942–)

Fu-jen Chen

♦ **BIOGRAPHY**

Born in Stockton in 1942 and raised in Richmond, California, Jeffery Paul Chan is a third-generation American of Chinese ancestry. A grandson of a Nevada railroad worker and a son of a successful dentist, young Jeffery was weary of doing what his elders expected him to do, once claiming that "In a way I was tired of being Chinese. . . . I was tired of following the crowd, because all the Chinese students I knew were pursuing such scientific, technological careers as medicine and engineering" (Hsu and Palubinskas 76). Changing his undergraduate major at the University of California at Berkeley, Chan disappointed his father when he quit his study at the prestigious university and went to Spain's University of Barcelona where he tutored in English and studied Spanish culture. Earning his bachelor's degree in English, he continued his graduate study in creative writing at San Francisco. Later he also studied folklore at the University of California because folklore to him serves as access to "know more about different people" by "opening up many doors to the different cultures" (Hsu and Palubinskas 77). His strong interests in literature as well as various cultures were rooted in his desire to know more about his own ethnic heritage, one that his totally Americanized father was never willing to share.

Chan is currently a professor in the Department of Asian American Studies and English at San Francisco State University. The founding director of the Combined Asian-American Resources Project, Inc., as well as the founding member and former chairperson of the Asian American Studies Department at San Francisco State University, Chan has long championed the inclusion of Asian American literature in the study of American literature. In addition, he was an Asian American consultant to Harcourt Brace Jovanovich and a member of the National Council of Teachers of English, Task Force on Racism and Bias, Textbook Review Committee. More important, as a significant scholar of Asian American Studies, Chan has contributed short stories and essays and coedited two groundbreaking anthologies of Asian American literature. Also a drama critic of Marin County's newspaper, *The Independent Journal*, he had a play, *Bunny Hop*, produced by the East/West Players in Los Angeles. At present, he lives in Marin County, north of San Francisco, with his wife, Janis, and his children, Jennifer and Aaron Bear.

◆ MAJOR WORKS AND THEMES

Though currently he is more recognized as a critic as well as an editor of Asian American literature than as a creative writer, Jeffery Paul Chan has contributed five short stories to journals particularly interested in publishing Asian American writing, including *Aion, Amerasia, Yardbird Reader*, and *Bamboo Ridge*. Three of his short stories are anthologized: "Auntie Tsia Lays Dying" appeared in *Asian-American Authors* (1972), "The Chinese in Haifa" in *Aiiieeeee!* (1974), and "Cheap Labor" in *The Big Aiiieeeee!* (1991). These and two other stories—"Jackrabbit" and "Sing Song Plain Song"—are interestingly narrated in the voice of a boy or a male speaker with a child's consciousness. Typically unfolding through the lens of a boy or an adult male, Chan's short stories mainly explore the issues of Chinese American male identity, the ambivalent connection between immigrant Chinese and American-born Chinese, and a sense of alienation from the "Motherland"—either America or China.

"Jackrabbit" describes young protagonist Frank's tragic pursuit of a masculine identity in a society where his efforts are doomed to fail simply because of his ethnic origin—his Chineseness. Embodying the Chinese heritage, another character, Old Pete, is a Chinese immigrant in the bachelor society of Chinatown, a place described as a "human zoo" filled with "the feeling of hunger and despair and the loneliness" (227). Such an "immigrant's prison" offers no hope to young Frank or other aging Chinese bachelors. Old Pete recalls a life deprived of manhood:

> [H]uddled with their legs drawn to their tight scrotums, talking of women, imagining the idylls of an afternoon spent under the warm quilt of a perfumed sing-song girl, imagining enough for the months and years spent in America. All the little grunts and squeals they remembered, a kind of helpless awe at their own strength, each alone, taking a long piss in the wind. (227)

As imagination can no longer alleviate one's suffering from a forced bachelorhood, death becomes the only outlet for one's sexual urge. Refusing a life of forced celibacy, a Chinese immigrant hanged himself shortly after arriving in America:

> "I think he had a wife in China and someone told him that only merchants can bring their wives here."
> "How can that be?"
> "It's true. I helped clean the cell. He was still hard and he had a big one too. He died with his hand wrapped around his cock. It's true. I saw it." (222)

As Chinatown offers no hope and fellowship with other bachelor Chinese does not help recover a sense of manhood, young Frank tries to establish his masculine identity by first abandoning his Chinese *male* identity, leaving Chinatown, and then assuming a different ethnic identity. Young Frank claims, "Mebbe next year I'm going to be an Indian around here. Hunt rabbits and scalp the Chinese. Mebbe raise mustangs in Las Vegas" (225). In the end, insulted by a white man, Frank stands up for his manhood even at the expense of his life.

Whereas "Jackrabbit" connects the issue of Chinese American manhood to a sense of Chinese heritage and tradition, "The Chinese in Haifa" (1974) depicts the identity of the Chinese American man only with a trace of *Chineseness*. The title is misleading. "The Chinese in Haifa" is not about a Chinese in Israel's Haifa, but an American in Los Angeles who only looks Chinese. An American of Chinese descent, the protagonist, Bill Wong, is a teacher, smokes marijuana, enjoys blintzes, and lives in the suburbs. Wong's only relation to Jewishness is not the seaport in northwest Israel, but a secret romance with his Jewish neighbor's wife. An assimilationist living in the calm and bourgeois façade, Wong regards his Chinese heritage as dreamy Chinese antiques, ridicules his sister-in-law's house in Chinatown as "The Chickencoop," and equates Chinese education for his children with "Chinese torture" (14). The difference of his viewpoints from those of his Chinese American wife on Chinese heritage partly explains their impending divorce. After his children were sent by his wife to Hong Kong to live with their grandmother so that they can keep their Chinese heritage and learn a language their father cannot understand, Wong expresses his resentment on the phone to his sister-in-law:

> "Mamie, this is none of your goddamned . . . oh, shit . . ." How in the hell would they accomplish that? Horrible Chinese tortures? A water cure? Prefrontal lobotomy?
> "You know they're learning to write Chinese? By Christmas, they can write to you in Chinese."
> "Gee, that's terrific, Mamie. How am I supposed to read it?"
> "Now don't you be selfish, Bill. You let your own ignorance rob your kids of their heritage. That's your way." (14)

Wong's marital discord and his antipathy toward his ethnic origin is finally soothed by Ethel, a Jewish woman with green eyes and blond hair, who "offers the prospect not merely of sexual gratification but also of psychological acculturation" (Ma 74).

Both "Auntie Tsia Lays Dying" and "Sing Song Plain Song" express an alienation from the *mother*land, China, in the view of Asian Americans. In "Auntie Tsia Lays Dying" the narrator recalls his childhood memories of Auntie Tsia as he now watches her lying on her deathbed. Through a child's consciousness, the narrator depicts Auntie Tsia as a puzzling figure, her tall tales, and her exotic fish store. Auntie Tsia is pictured vividly: her feet had been bound since she was a child, her maroon sweater had been passed down from her father, and her "musty sweet smell [reminded him] of kept and secret possessions" (79). Her face, forehead, lips, and dress repeatedly catch the boy narrator's eyes. In addition to Auntie Tsia's appearance, her memories of her life in Old China develop several versions of stories that once fascinated the boy, but now the adult narrator suspects that her "Peh River fishing song" might be a fraud and regards her reasons as "slightly ridiculous" (80). He is not quite different from those expectant Chinatown tourists who always spot something exotic and eagerly believe the stories Auntie makes up at random, since Chinatown and the Chinese American experience are still beyond his understanding. As he watches Auntie Tsia dying, he unaccountably "feel[s] lost" and "very guilty" (85). He can only sense that "there is something to this Chinese dying, and the nonsense of Ho Tai, and the colors: silver, red, yellow . . . her brownness. The fish. Kites. Her dying is endless" (85).

Likewise, "Sing Song Plain Song" begins with scenes from the narrator's childhood and expresses his alienation from the ancestral country. The *mother*land is accessible only in dreams and imagination. The boy narrator first describes his dream of starving children in Asia (the scene also appears in "The Chinese in Haifa"). He imagines himself "a care package on the quay of some Far Eastern harbor" and he has "enough rice to feed a family of sixteen" (23). As he is estranged from his ancestral country, he is also limited to Chinatown in the land of his nativity. Joining the celebration of the end of World War II, the boy narrator has a chance to "swagger beyond the neighborhood in their company, beyond the broad red silk ribbons figured with calligraphy, the death-white butcher paper spread over the pavements weighed down with flower pots" (27). He recognizes that "there was a world beyond the boundaries of [his] neighborhood" (27–28). Immediately after the scene of the celebration, the rest of the story shifts to the voice of the adult narrator at the age of thirty-five and focuses on his relationship with his stepmother and his affair with a Chinese widow. Interestingly, despite the shift in perspective, these are still mostly detailed in the setting of Chinatown—his world does not expand and a sense of alienation prevails.

Not only do the American-born Chinese suffer from a sense of alienation from the United States, China, or Chinatown but so do the immigrant Chinese Americans (or what is called "the overseas Chinese"), who feel alienated from their homeland from the day they first step into the new world. In Chan's latest story "Cheap Labor," Fat Adam is pictured exotically as from the far eastern country. An American-born Chinese girl, Eva, describes him as "mentally retarded," "a wetback," "a rice Christian," "a bandit," and a guy who "eats bugs" and "live[s] out of garbage" (106, 107). As the news that China declared war on Japan is announced on the radio, Fat Adam, once a soldier in China who fought the Japanese, reacts agitatedly, swearing that "wha' kinna war will China make? No guns, no bombs. I was a sojer inna Kwantung ah'mee. We fight six months. S'ore wit' spear and lotsa flag. Eat plenty h'awsheet. Dass aw" (112). Although "China is matter of heart, not just a matter of the skin" (116) for him and other "overseas Chinese," living in the new world has inevitably alienated them from China. Uncle Pius says that "everybody wants to go back to fight. Wah Gay and Mee Kee left camp walking because they couldn't wait," but he also adds: "Wouldn't be surprised, though, if they stopped for look for gold" (115). The story ends with Fat Adam's still presence in Marysville during the Bomb Day celebration, "debating strategy with two strangers who held equal shares of second position at a *pai gow* table" (116).

◆ CRITICAL RECEPTION

Little criticism of Chan's work focuses on his short fiction; instead, his essays and anthologies he coedited with other Asian American writers have received much more critical attention. His name is usually mentioned together with Frank Chin, with whom he coauthored an often-cited essay "Racist Love," and with two other Asian American writers with whom he coedited the groundbreaking anthologies, *Aiiieeeee!* and *The Big Aiiieeeee!* In "Racist Love" Chan and Chin argue,

> The white stereotype of the Asian is unique in that it is the only racial stereotype completely devoid of man-hood. Our nobility is that of an efficient housewife. At our worst we are contemptible because we are womanly, effeminate, devoid of all the traditionally masculine qualities of originality, daring, physical courage, creativity. We are neither straight talking or straight shooting. (68)

They equate the racial oppression of Asian Americans with emasculation, the stripping of Asian American manhood. And it is "racist love" that contributes to the stereotype of Asians as submissive and compliant. In response to the feminization of Asian American subjectivity, they turn to celebrating Asian American male voices to authenticate Asian American writing. Heroism or machismo is elevated to a sacred index in Asian American expression. Some Asian American scholars, however, suspect that their fight against racism does not undermine the dominance of the white male but further reproduces the same underlying patriarchal structure. King-Kok Cheung claims, "To reclaim cultural traditions without getting bogged down in the mire of traditional constraints, to attack stereotypes without falling to their binary opposites, to chart new topographies for manliness and womanliness, will surely demand genuine heroism" ("The Women Warrior" 246).

◆ BIBLIOGRAPHY

Works by Jeffery Paul Chan

Short Stories

"Auntie Tsia Lays Dying." *Aion* 1.2 (1971): 82–87. Rpt. in *Asian-American Authors*. Kai-yu Hsu and Helen Palubinskas, eds. Boston: Houghton Mifflin Company, 1972, 77–85.
"The Chinese in Haifa." In *Aiiieeeee! An Anthology of Asian American Writers*. Frank Chin, Jeffery Paul Chan, Lawson Fusao Inada, and Shawn Hsu Wong, eds. Washington, DC: Howard University Press, 1974, 11–29.
"Jackrabbit." *Yardbird Reader* 3 (1974): 217–38. Rpt. in *Yardbird Lives!* Ishmael Reed and Al Young, eds. New York: Grove, 1978, 71–93.
"Sing Song Plain Song." *Amerasia Journal* 3.2 (1976): 23–37.
"Cheap Labor." *Amerasia Journal* 9.2 (1982): 99–116. Rpt. in *Bamboo Ridge* 17 (1982–83): 51–67. Rpt. in *The Big Aiiieeeee! An Anthology of Chinese American and Japanese American Literature*. Jeffery Paul Chan, Frank Chin, Lawson Fusao Inada, and Shawn Wong, eds. New York: Meridian Books, 1991, 563–79.

Articles

"Racist Love." (with Frank Chin). In *Seeing through Shuck*. Richard Kostelanetz, ed. New York: Ballantine, 1972, 65–79.
"The Mysterious West." *New York Review of Books* (April 28, 1977): 41.
"A Response to Diane Johnson's Review." *New York Review of Books* (April 28, 1977): 41+.
"Introduction." In *Eat a Bowl of Tea*, by Louis Hing Chu. Seattle: University of Washington Press, 1979, 1–5.
"Resources for Chinese and Japanese American Literary Traditions." *Amerasia Journal* 8.1 (1981): 19–31.
"An Introduction to Chinese-American and Japanese-American Literature." In *Three American Literatures*. Houston Baker, ed. New York: MLA, 1982, 197–228.
"Asian-American Literary Traditions" (with Marilyn Alquizola). In *A Literary History of the American West*. J. Golden Taylor and Thomas J. Lyon, eds. Fort Worth: Texas Christian University Press, 1987, 1119–28.

Edited Works

Aiiieeeee!, Chin et al., eds.
The Big Aiiieeeee!, with Chin et al., eds.

Studies of Jeffery Paul Chan

Cheung, King-Kok, ed. *An Interethnic Companion to Asian American Literature*. New York: Cambridge University Press, 1997.

———. "The Woman Warrior versus the Chinaman Pacific: Must a Chinese American Critic Choose between Feminism and Heroism?" In *Conflicts in Feminism*. Marianne Hirsch and Evelyn Fox Keller, eds. London: Routledge, 1990, 234–51.

Fischer, Michael M. J. "Ethnicity and the Post-Modern Arts of Memory." In *Writing Culture: The Poetics and Politics of Ethnography*. James Clifford and George E. Marcus, eds. Berkeley: University of California Press, 1986, 194–233.

Hsu, Kai-yu, and Helen Palubinskas, eds. *Asian-American Authors*. Boston: Houghton Mifflin, 1972.

Kim, Elaine H. *Asian American Literature: An Introduction to the Writings and Their Social Context*. Philadelphia: Temple University Press, 1982, 175–94.

Li, David Leiwei. *Imagining the Nation: Asian American Literature and Cultural Consent*. Stanford, CA: Stanford University Press, 1998.

Ma, Sheng-mei. *Immigrant Subjectivities in Asian American and Asian Diaspora Literatures*. Albany: State University of New York Press, 1998.

Wong, Sau-ling. *Reading Asian American Literature: From Necessity to Extravagance*. Princeton, NJ: Princeton University Press, 1993.

G. S. SHARAT CHANDRA
(1938–2000)

Robert D. Sturr

♦ **BIOGRAPHY**

Chandra was born in Nanjangud in the southern Indian State of Karnatak (known as Mysore under the British). His father, a prosperous lawyer, provided his son with a Western-oriented education. After earning a bachelor's degree in English in 1953 and a law degree in 1958 (both from the University of Mysore), Chandra briefly pursued the legal career that was expected of him. Marriage plans were suggested, but he balked. He revealed in a later interview that he was "inspired by reading and movies," and while his father tried to find him a suitable Indian wife, he "was secretly planning to leave the country to pursue a literary life" (Vasudeva and Bahri 11).

Chandra came to the United States and Canada in the early 1960s to pursue advanced degrees in secondary education and labor law, but his studies were ruses to conceal his desire to become a writer. Signaling a complete break with his family's plans, Chandra married Jane Ronnerman (a teacher) in 1966, the same year he entered the prestigious writing program at the University of Iowa. He completed an M.F.A. in 1968, the same year his first book, *Bharata Natyam Dancer and Other Poems*, was published. Three more volumes of poetry followed shortly thereafter: *Will This Forest* (1968), *Reasons for Staying* (1970), and *April in Nanjangud* (1971). Establishing a lifelong pattern of involvement in an international range of literary communities, these first four books were published, respectively, in India, the United States, Canada, and England.

Chandra also began a long and distinguished teaching career. He noted in a 1999 *Contemporary Authors* profile that " 'I was probably the only Indian writer teaching creative writing on a Western campus' " (63). He taught at Iowa, Iowa Wesleyan College, Washington State University, and the University of Missouri at Kansas City. He was actively involved in academic and cultural organizations and was an occasional lecturer or visiting professor at schools in the United States, India, England, and other countries. Throughout this time, Chandra remained prolific, contributing poems, short stories, essays, and reviews to dozens of newspapers, magazines, journals, and anthologies. He produced four more volumes of poetry from the mid-1970s to the mid-1990s and received numerous awards and honors, including a T. S. Eliot Poetry Prize for *Immigrants of Loss* (1993), and a Pulitzer Prize nomination for *Family of Mirrors* (1993). His best short fiction—produced over three decades—was finally collected in his last book, *Sari of the Gods* (1998).

◆ MAJOR WORKS AND THEMES

Chandra's life was marked by major transitions involving not just his country of residence or citizenship but also his family life and career choices. In his poems and short stories he repeatedly explores the perspective of the individual caught in the middle, in liminal spaces between more certain yet conflicting (and even oppressive) identities. He was particularly aware of contradictions in the construction of Indian identity. He observed that "[w]e all led a double life within India. We were Indians but our tastes were Western." Coming to the United States exacerbated this sense of disconnection and filled him with a deep sense of loss. He stated that "[t]his pain and loss became a special force for me and without falling into imbecilic sentimentality, I've kept exploring this" (Vasudeva and Bahri 14).

As an immigrant in the United States, Chandra felt as though he was never allowed (nor did he wish) to forget his foreignness. The examination of a divided self is one of the hallmarks of his writing. In the afterward to the poem "Overland Park, KS," Chandra observed that "[m]y work deals with my bicultural self, memory of an Indian Past, the Midwestern way of life and the common humanity that we all share" (358). This division of self into three parts—Indian, American/Midwestern, and universal—is reflected in the organization of the stories in *Sari of the Gods*. Section one is called "Here," and includes five stories that chart the often painful but sometimes humorously absurd experience of Indian immigrants in the United States. Section two, "There," offers ten stories all set in the small southern Indian town where Chandra grew up. They present portraits of difficult and tenuous lives that seem completely different from those of Chandra's immigrant characters. Finally, the four stories of the last section, "Neither Here Nor There," depict Indian Americans who find that as much as they yearn to return "home" they are unable to adjust to an India that, through their Americanized eyes, seems hopelessly backward and ignorant.

The first story in "Here" dramatizes the frustration and loss experienced by immigrants. In "Sari of the Gods," Prapulla becomes angry when her husband, Shekar, suddenly invites his American coworkers and their wives to dinner. Nervous about making the proper impression, she struggles to prepare the right foods. After an awkward meal, her husband serves brandy that they cannot afford and one of the wives spills her glass on Prapulla's wedding sari, an irreplaceable heirloom that is intricately decorated with Indian deities. Later, as her husband sleeps, she mourns both the loss of her sari and her familiar Indian life.

A more dramatic crisis arises in "Dot Busters," which concerns the harassment of Indian women by a group of skinheads. Radha complains to her husband, Dev, but he is afraid to complain. Radha becomes pregnant around the same time that Dev suffers a sudden stroke and eventually dies. Glo, a lesbian neighbor, helps Radha to assimilate more thoroughly into American culture and they eventually become lovers. Although grateful, Radha feels uncertain of both her true sexuality and of the changes in her life. She "felt hesitant and unsure, as if she had bifurcated into distinct halves, one seeking the new, the other longing to linger in tranquil waters" (32). Radha's long-term future is not made clear in the closing scene; however, during a brutal attempted rape by one of the skinheads, she uses her Shivaji claw—a miniature copy of the weapon used by the famous Indian warrior-king—to stab his penis. The source of her coolheaded courage is not definitely rooted in either her Indian or American identities, but is instead a product of both.

Other stories in the first section also dramatize immigrants who, out of both necessity and desire, quickly become Americanized in their dress, behavior, and thinking. They stand in contrast to the figures who appear in the stories of the second section. In a brief foreword, Chandra writes that his characters "are representative of the timeless beliefs and customs that prevail in the hearts and minds of most traditional Indians" (76). Accordingly, those pieces are more like allegorical tales than intricately plotted narratives, particularly in the use of simpler (or stereotypical) characters and sudden (or fantastical) twists of fate. Because of their setting in a small southern Indian town, comparisons to R. K. Narayan's Malgudi stories are natural, but Chandra's tone is typically more ironic than moral.

Most often, these stories present ordinary but bewildered characters who skirt disaster and even thrive, but who generally have no idea how they came to be so lucky. For example, Linga, the protagonist of "Demon," is fortunate enough to get a job in construction when his mango farm fails because of drought. When a demon inhabits the construction site, he is drawn into a strange, dream-like attraction because it appears as a beautiful woman. Although he does nothing heroic to earn a boon, the demon still lets him go, along with his pregnant wife, with the promise of a rainy season that will return them to their former agrarian lives. Similarly, Pandu, a poor train singer in "This Time Goat; Next Time Man," earns a living from the offerings of pilgrims riding to a holy place. In the span of one day, he is arrested when he unwittingly insults a local politician, but then is elevated to dizzying heights as a popular leader when his friend, the train conductor, embarrasses the elitist Congress Party man who had persecuted Pandu. His rise from poverty to political power is a mystery to everyone, including himself, and woven into the comic absurdity of the situation is the hint that he might fall just as quickly and suffer the same fate as a beloved local goat who is killed in the story.

These examples point to Chandra's general portrayal of traditional Indian life as strange, alternately charming and horrifying, and ultimately fictitious, at least to the highly complex and realistic characters presented in the first and third sections of the book. The town of Nanjangud is primarily a place of memory inspired by Chandra's direct recollection as well as the literary creations of mythmakers like Narayan. It is part of the fantasy of return cultivated by Indian American immigrants; however, Chandra suggests in his third section that such fantasies lead to rude awakenings. "Bhat's Return" focuses on a character who, like Chandra, gave up a good job that his father might have arranged to go to America to study and live. He marries Becky, a midwestern girl, and at the behest of his father, he eventually takes her back to India for a proper Hindu ceremony. While Becky is initially overwhelmed, she comes to understand and even appreciate India. Ironically, it is Bhat who cannot readjust to his mother country. He complains that "No one had heard of David Letterman" and feels frustrated that he can't get a hamburger (208). In a comic twist, Becky runs away to follow a guru while Bhat returns "home" to America. As he romances a "blonde from Kansas" on the flight, he kisses her "gently on the brow as he had seen his father kiss the holy cow" (214). With this strange image, Chandra plants his readers firmly in the middle ground—literally in the air between countries—so that the uncertainties, absurdities, fears, and even excitement of not being neither "here" nor "there" are felt.

◆ CRITICAL RECEPTION

Chandra's reputation rests mainly on his extensive work as a poet and thus his short fiction awaits serious scholarly attention. Reviews of *Sari of the Gods* were generally favorable. In *Studies in Short Fiction*, Robbie Clipper praises the first-person narratives as the strongest in the collection and notes that Chandra reproduces the questioning immigrant persona that is so effective in his poetry. In *World Literature Today*, A. L. McLeod suggests that Chandra's portrayal of Indian life (from the perspective of a diasporic author) has "the ring of honest reevaluation." However, he complains that Chandra's prose style is too disjointed and that he too often gives way to "poetic qualities." McLeod notes similarities in setting to Narayan's fiction and appears to resent the fact that Chandra does not tell his stories in the same style (212–13). Other reviewers did not cite the quick (yet intriguing) transitions as a significant problem.

Disorientation is, in fact, one of the chief effects that Chandra seeks to create. He plunges readers into the minds of both Indian American immigrants and traditional Indian villagers, who serve as the long-lost alter-egos of the more Americanized characters. Philip Miller's assessment of the poems in *Immigrants of Loss*—which are also about being both "here" and "there"—best sums up the thematic intent of *Sari of the Gods*:

> The narrator/poet immigrant has discovered that immigration is the human "state of being." For his eyes to be fully opened, he has had to "deport" himself back to Asia, to re-immigrate before he can genuinely return "home." Yet in rediscovering the past, he reclaims a present, learning that he will always live in both, in two places. By accepting the ordinariness of human isolation and confronting the "blank page" of his life, he can reconnect to what he has become and successfully "immigrate from loss." (338)

Sari of the Gods opens with a story about Prapulla's grief over the loss of her Indian identity and it closes with the narrator of the last story, "Encounter," who, in returning to India after many decades, discovers that he cannot even imagine what it would have been like if he had stayed. All that is left is "an unfamiliar middle, an illusory passage" that, in a small way, helps to lessen his sense of loss.

◆ BIBLIOGRAPHY

Works by G. S. Sharat Chandra

Short Story Collection

Sari of the Gods. Minneapolis, MN: Coffee House Press, 1998.

Poetry

Bharata Natyam Dancer and Other Poems. Calcutta: Writers Workshop, 1968.
Will This Forest. Milwaukee, WI: Morgan Press, 1968.
Reasons for Staying. Toronto: Coach House Press, 1970.
April in Nanjangud. London: Alan Ross, 1971.
Once or Twice. Sutton, England: Hippopotamus Press, 1974.
The Ghost of Meaning. Lewiston, ID: Confluence Press, 1978.
Heirloom. Delhi: Oxford University Press, 1982.
Family of Mirrors. Kansas City, MO: BkMk Press, 1993.
Immigrants of Loss. Sutton, England: Hippopotamus Press, 1993.
"Overland Park, KS." *The Midwest Quarterly* 36.4 (Summer 1995): 357–58.

Translations

Offsprings of Servagna. Calcutta: Writers Workshop, 1975.

Studies of G. S. Sharat Chandra

"Chandra, G. S. Sharat." *Contemporary Authors,* vol. 171. Detroit: Gale Group, 1999, 60–63.

Clipper, Robbie. Rev. of *Sari of the Gods. Studies in Short Fiction* 35.2 (Spring 1998): 205–6.

Gurleen, Grewal. "Indian-American Literature." In *New Immigrant Literatures in the United States.* Alpana Sharma Knippling, ed. Westport, CT: Greenwood Press, 1996, 91–108.

Lawrence, Keith. "G. S. Sharat Chandra." In *Asian American Poets: A Bio-Bibliographical Critical Sourcebook.* Guiyou Huang, ed. Westport, CT: Greenwood Press, 2002, 59–69.

Masello, David. Rev. of *Sari of the Gods. New York Times Book Review* (May 3, 1998): 20.

McLeod, A. L. Rev. of *Sari of the Gods. World Literature Today* 73.1 (Winter 1999): 212–13.

Miller, Philip. "Immigrants of Loss: The Pleasures of Mixed Prosodies." *The Literary Review* 40.2 (Winter 1997): 336–38.

Rev. of *Sari of the Gods. Publishers Weekly* (February 23, 1998): 50.

Vasudeva, Mary, and Deepika Bahri. " 'Swallowing for Twenty Years/The American Mind and Body': An Interview with G. S. Sharat Chandra." *Journal of Commonwealth and Postcolonial Studies* 5.1 (Fall 1997): 9–17.

Williams, Janis. Rev. of *Sari of the Gods. Library Journal* (April 15, 1998): 117.

Wuinn, Mary Ellen. Rev. of *Sari of the Gods. Booklist* (April 1998): 1302.

DIANA CHANG
(1934–   )

Janet Hyunju Clarke

◆ BIOGRAPHY

Diana Chang was born in New York but raised in China. She and her parents, an American mother of Chinese-Irish heritage and a Chinese father who was an architect, lived in Beijing, Nanking, and Shanghai, where she attended American schools. She then returned to New York to finish high school. After graduating from Barnard College, she worked as an editor in several publishing houses in New York. Chang taught in the English Department and the Program in the Arts at Barnard College for ten years, where she developed her interest in writing short stories.

Chang is a prolific writer who has published in several genres including the novel, short story, short-short story, poetry, and essay. In addition, one of her short stories, "Falling Free," was adapted into a radio play by American Public Radio in 1989. Another, "In the Purple Shade," won the best short story award in the *Hampton Shorts* collection of stories in 1997. Chang is the recipient of a John Hay Whitney Fellowship and a Fulbright Fellowship. She served as an editor of *The American Pen* for several years.

Chang is also a painter who has had solo as well as group exhibitions at galleries on Long Island, New York. Her artistic sensibilities inform her poetry and fiction: "That I am a painter is reflected in my writing, I believe, which is imagistic" ("Diana Chang" 16). By writing, Chang has said, "I purchase my citizenship in this land of life from which I feel estranged. Others claim their rightful place simply by virtue of being born. But I must earn it like an illegitimate child, a stateless person, and so, by some exacting game of industry and imagination, I create something in order to become all that I was meant to be" ("Why Do Writers Write?" 3).

◆ MAJOR WORKS AND THEMES

As with her novels and poetry, Chang's short stories deal with a wide range of subject matter: mortality, love, sexuality, alienation, and identity. While some of her published short stories explore Chinese American or biracial subjectivities, many characteristically do not. Chang has been conscious of avoiding the exoticism that can be limiting to cultural expressions, deliberately "[slipping] in and out of identities—Chinese, Caucasian. I don't produce only Chinese American or minority/ethnic stories exclusively" (pers. com.). And while she is "never totally unaware of an otherness" (Medwick 109), Chang is interested in other cultural workers whose oeuvre includes "ethnic" as well as "non-ethnic" characters and narratives, such as David Henry Hwang, Ang Lee, and Kazuo Ishiguro (Hamalian 37, 40).

Indeed, Chang explores various manifestations of otherness in several short stories. In "Falling Free," the 79-year-old Chinese American narrator, Kiki Kuo, reflects on her decision to live out her old age in the United States and her husband's decision to return to China, saying, "A man must die in his native land" (70). This literal separation from her husband who had a successful career as a respected physicist nevertheless reveals Kiki's psychic "bicultural, sitting on the cusp" existence even while her biracial grandson thinks of the family as "oh so Westernized." Kiki muses that her husband, Ying, "who often sounded like a Rotarian when it suited him here, is now Peking man." As for herself, Kiki feels "broken [in] two, which may be my natural condition" (68). When she declares, "I'm at the border" (69), there are several borders that might apply: she is at the border of "Americanness" as a racial other, at the border of active living as a senior citizen, and at the border of mortality as a human being.

"The Oriental Contingent," perhaps Chang's best-known short story, explores a different aspect of racial otherness. The two main characters, Lisa Mallory and Connie Sung, are both accomplished Chinese Americans who meet occasionally at various "culturati" gatherings (171). Each thinking that the other is more authentically Chinese because of her Chinese birth or rearing, each woman secretly feels inferior to the other for being too American, too assimilated. The situation suggests a double-edged sword for these women. Not only are they imperfectly "American" (though thoroughly assimilated, they are instantly referred to as the "Oriental contingent" by a white guest), but they are also imperfectly other (Lisa was raised by adoptive white parents, Connie is third-generation American); imperfect, that is, because there is a hegemonic imperative to position themselves in one racial category or the other.

Since Chang herself has diligently worked against this kind of imperative, many of her stories are conspicuously absent of Chinese American or Asian American characters, themes, or settings. For example, in "A Hospital Fable," the characters' ethnicities are neither mentioned nor essential to the "fable" of a man whose inability to come to terms with death in general, and his own wife's in particular, is signified by his pathological fear of hospitals. This story, along with "Getting Around," "The Appearance . . . of an Uninvited Presence," and "Once Upon a Time," is an example of narratives that tackle themes of mortality, belonging, male/female relations, and existential dilemmas in Chang's short fiction. Their settings are anonymous and urban, possibly New York City, possibly not.

Chang's poetic and painterly sensibilities are reflected in the themes and formal styles of several stories. In "Still Points," described as "a kind of impressionistic memoir" of Chang's childhood in China, the narrator's erasures of memories make her think of "certain Rauschenbergs, Larry Riverses," who used a technique of erasing parts of their paintings (33). The memories of what was once there suggest "A wide-open compositional scheme. This summer I think of those summers—water, land, sky being earthly everywhere. Flowers beginning to wilt, the expected meal, dressing and undressing—these incidents make up shapes, colors, strokes. As easily as anyone crossing a bridge, I can move among hamlets of time" (33). This kind of poetic imagery is also evident in other stories, such as "In the Purple Shade," "Present Self," and "The Nap." Chang's short-shorts, or sudden and flash fiction, also are indicative of her "imagistic" style of writing.

◆ CRITICAL RECEPTION

Chang is best known for her novels and poetry. Indeed, most of the scholarly and critical attention has been focused on her poetry and novels rather than on her short stories. During the 1970s, she was considered one of the most widely published Chinese American poets in the United States (Wand 141). Her first novel, *The Frontiers of Love*, was published in 1956, making it the first novel by an American-born Chinese writer. For this reason alone, Chang has a solid place in Asian American literary history. While the novel is set in wartime Shanghai and has no direct American context, the characters grapple with bicultural and biracial subjectivities in a diasporic framework that make it relevant to Asian American cultural criticism. Thus, this and other works that deal with the Chinese diaspora or Asian American themes make her work important to the Asian American literary canon as well. That Chang's stories are "capable of passing in and out of Asian and American fields of reference without self-consciousness or awkwardness" (Lim, "Introduction" xxii) is a testament to her strengths and sensibilities as a writer.

◆ BIBLIOGRAPHY

Works by Diana Chang

Short Stories

"The Nap." *Ararat* 16.1 (Winter 1975): 12–13.
"A Heretic of Twenty-One-Eighty-Four." *Pulp* 3.1 (1977): 8.

"Wide Awake." *Gallimaufry* 14 (1979): 141–45.

"Present Self." *Greenfield Review* 12 (1984): 113–16.

"The Story That Swallowed Itself." *Confrontation* 30–31 (1985): 81–86.

"Falling Free." *Crosscurrents: A Quarterly* 5.3 (1985): 55–72. Rpt. in *Charlie Chan Is Dead: An Anthology of Contemporary Asian American Fiction*. Jessica Hagedorn, ed. New York: Penguin Books, 1993, 60–75, *Intersections of Aging: Readings in Social Gerontology*. Elizabeth Warren Markson and Lisa A. Hollis-Sawyer, eds. Los Angeles: Roxbury Press, 2000, 167–75, and *Asian American Literature: A Brief Introduction and Anthology*. Shawn Wong, ed. New York: HarperCollins, 1996, 134–46.

"Soundings." *Long Pond Review* 10 (1985–1986): 65–68.

"The Appearance . . . of an Uninvited Presence." *Pulpsmith* 6.1 (Spring 1986): 30–31.

"Getting Around." *North American Review* 27.1 (December 1986): 46–49.

"He Flew." *Magazine of Paragraphs* 4 (Summer 1988): 6.

"The Hat." *North Atlantic Review* 1.1 (Summer 1989): 123–26.

"The Oriental Contingent." In *The Forbidden Stitch: An Asian American Women's Anthology*. Shirley Geok-lin Lim, Mayumi Tsutakawa, and Margarita Donnelly, eds. Corvallis, OR: Calyx Books, 1989, 171–77.

"Still Points." *Ararat* 30.3 (Summer 1989): 33–34.

"For Cows." *Magazine of Paragraphs* 8 (Summer 1990): 29.

"A Hospital Fable." In *Vital Lines: Contemporary Fiction About Medicine*. Jon Mukand, ed. New York: St. Martin's Press, 1990, 24–28.

"Once Upon a Time." *North American Review* 276.1 (March 1991): 50–51.

"A Road Not Taken." *Libido* 3.2 (Spring 1991): 22.

"The Face on the Screen." *Caprice* (June 1991): 27.

"The Pang." *Caprice* (June 1991): 29.

"Their Dad." *Caprice* (June 1991): 28.

"Things." *Caprice* (June 1991): 26.

"Fighting the Cold." *Ledge* 14 (1992): 42–50.

"Maybe." *Caprice* (June 1992): 51–53.

"A Reason for Flowers." *Caprice* (July 1992): 53.

"Sleeping Together." *Caprice* (July 1992): 51.

"True Love." *Caprice* (July 1992): 55.

"Carried Away." *Caprice* (July 1994): 53–54.

"Excusing Herself." *Magazine of Paragraphs* 13 (Fall 1994): 32.

"Onto Something." *Shanti* 10.1 (Winter/Spring 1995): n.p.

"What People Knew." In *On A Bed of Rice: An Asian American Erotic Feast*. Geraldine Kudaka, ed. New York: Anchor Books, 1995, 3–10.

"Try to Imagine." *Magazine of Paragraphs* 16 (Spring 1996): 16.

"What's the Story, Luv?" *Asian Pacific American Journal* 5.2 (Fall–Winter 1996): 130–31.

"In the Purple Shade." In *Hampton Shorts*. Barbara Stone, ed. Water Mill, NY: Hampton Shorts, 1997, 65–71.

Drama

"Falling Free." Radio play adapted from short story of same name. American Public Radio. 1989.

Novels

The Frontiers of Love. New York: Random House, 1956; Seattle: University of Washington Press, 1994.

A Woman of Thirty. New York: Random House, 1959.

A Passion for Life. New York: Random House, 1961.

The Only Game in Town. New York: Signet, 1963.

Eye to Eye. New York: Harper and Row, 1974.

A Perfect Love. New York: Grove, 1978.

Poetry

The Horizon Is Definitely Speaking. Port Jefferson, NY: Backstreet Editions, Street Press, 1982.

What Matisse Is After. New York: Contact House, 1984.

Earth, Water, Light: Poems Celebrating the East End of Long Island. Brentwood, NY: Binham Wood Graphics, 1991.

Articles

"Why Do Writers Write?" *American Pen* 1.1 (1969): 1–3.

"Wool Gathering, Ventriloquism, and the Double Life." *American Pen* 3.1 (1970–1971): 23–30. Rpt. in *The Third Woman: Minority Women Writers of the United States.* Dexter Fisher, ed. Boston: Houghton Mifflin, 1980, 453–58.

"Diana Chang." In *Breaking Silence: An Anthology of Contemporary Asian American Poets.* Joseph Bruchac, ed. Greenfield Center, NY: Greenfield Review Press, 1983, 16.

Studies of Diana Chang

Cheung, King-Kok, ed. *An Interethnic Companion to Asian American Literature.* New York: Cambridge University Press, 1997, 297, 299.

Hamalian, Leo. "A MELUS Interview: Diana Chang." *MELUS* 20.4 (1995): 29–43.

Lim, Shirley Geok-lin. "Exotics and Existentials: The Course of Asian American Writing." *Homegrown 2: Asian American Experiences* (Winter 1984): 26–31.

———. "Introduction." In *The Frontiers of Love.* Seattle: University of Washington Press, 1994, v–xxiii.

———. "Twelve Asian American Writers in Search of Self-Definition." *MELUS* 13.1–2 (1996): 57–77.

Ling, Amy. "Writer in the Hyphenated Condition: Diana Chang." *MELUS* 7.4 (1980): 69–83.

———. *Between Worlds: Women Writers of Chinese Ancestry.* New York: Pergamon Press, 1990.

Lowe, Lisa. *Immigrant Acts: On Asian American Cultural Politics.* Durham, NC: Duke University Press, 1996, 63–64.

Medwick, Lucille. "The Chinese Poet in New York." *New York Quarterly* 4 (1970): 94–115.

Roh-Spaulding, Carol. "Diana Chang." In *Asian American Novelists: A Bio-Bibliographical Critical Sourcebook*. Emmanuel S. Nelson, ed. Westport, CT: Greenwood Press, 2000, 38–43.

Spaulding, Carol Vivian. "Blue-Eyed Asians: Eurasianism in the Work of Edith Eaton/ Sui Sin Far, Winnifred Eaton/Onoto Watanna, and Diana Chang." Ph.D. diss., University of Iowa, 1997.

Wand, David Hsin-Fu. "The Chinese-American Literary Scene: A Galaxy of Poets and a Lone Playwright." In *Ethnic Literatures Since 1776: The Many Voices of America*, vol. 1. Wolodymyr T. Zyla and Wendell M. Aycock, eds. Lubbock: Texas Tech Press, 1978, 121–46.

Wong, Sau-ling Cynthia. *Reading Asian American Literature: From Necessity to Extravagance*. Princeton, NJ: Princeton University Press, 1993, 98–99.

Wu, Kitty Wei-hsiung. "Cultural Ideology and Aesthetic Choices: A Study of Three Works by Chinese American Women: Diana Chang, Bette Bao Lord, and Maxine Hong Kingston." Ph.D. diss., University of Maryland, 1989.

FRANK CHIN
(1940–   )

Aiping Zhang

◆ BIOGRAPHY

A Chinese American short story writer, novelist, playwright, and editor, Frank Chin was born to a young Chinese couple in Berkeley, California, on February 5, 1940. His father was an immigrant and his mother was a fourth-generation resident of Oakland Chinatown. Chin's parents abandoned him shortly after his birth. During the first six years of his life, Chin lived with an elderly white couple near an abandoned gold mine in California. At the age of six, his parents reclaimed him. He grew up in Chinatowns in Oakland and San Francisco.

Chin studied at the University of California, Berkeley, between 1958 and 1961 before attending the Writer's Workshop at the University of Iowa between 1961 and 1963 on a scholarship. Then, he worked as a clerk for the Southern Pacific Railroad for almost three years before finishing up the remaining requirements for his B.A. degree at the University of California, Santa Barbara, in 1965. Starting from the following year, he worked for a Seattle TV station for three years until he got a chance to teach Asian Studies at San Francisco State University and the University of California, Davis. A vanguard that helped shape modern Asian American literature since the 1960s, Chin, as Benjamin Tong recollects, "taught the very first college course in Asian American literature, following the famous student-faculty strike at San Francisco State University" (S6). Chin helped launch the Combined Asian-American Resources Project with a group of Asian American writers and scholars. While serving as a playwright-in-residence at the American Conservatory Theater, Chin established the Asian American Theater Workshop in 1972. He also taught courses in Asian American literature at several colleges.

Chin's literary career started with play writing. His play *The Chickencoop Chinaman* was the first by a Chinese American produced on the New York stage in 1972. Another play, *The Year of the Dragon*, premiered in 1974. In the same year, Chin edited, along with a few other writers, the first major anthology of Asian American literature, *Aiiieeeee! An Anthology of Asian American Writers*. His first collection of short stories, *The Chinaman Pacific & Frisco R.R. Co.*, appeared in 1988. Seventeen years after the publication of *Aiiieeeee!*, Chin and his same editorial team brought out a sequel, *The Big Aiiieeeee! An Anthology of Chinese American and Japanese American Literature*. In 1991, Chin's first novel, *Donald Duk*, was published. *Gunga Din Highway*, his second novel, appeared in 1994. His latest work, *Bulletproof Buddhists, and Other Essays*, a nonfiction book with six essays, came out in 1998. His new book, *Born in the U.S.A.: A Story of Japanese America, 1889–1947*, was published in 2002.

Chin is also an author of many teleplays and several comic books; his writings have been selected for numerous literary magazines, collections, and anthologies. He is the recipient of numerous awards and grants, including the James T. Phelan Award in short fiction, 1966; East-West Players Playwriting Award, 1971, for *The Chickencoop Chinaman*; three National Endowment for the Arts Creative Writing Grants; American Book Award from The Before Columbus Foundation, 1982, for *The Chickencoop Chinaman* and *The Year of the Dragon*, and 1989, for *The Chinaman Pacific & Frisco R.R. Co.*; Rockefeller American Generations Grant, 1991; The Lannan Literary Fellowship, 1992; The Lifetime Achievement Award from The Before Columbus Foundation, 2000. Chin lives in Los Angeles.

◆ MAJOR WORKS AND THEMES

Chin's prose—short stories, novels, and editorial contributions to anthologies—has followed more or less the same concerns, tones, patterns, and sensibilities that he demonstrated in his early plays. While he had a few brief tales and stories published here and there in his early career, his first major book of prose is an anthology, *Aiiieeeee! An Anthology of Asian American Writers*. The first of its kind, it is a foundational anthology of Asian American literature. It begins with an editorial essay, "Fifty Years of Our Whole Voice," to define the Asian American identity and literary voice; it features complete works and excerpts by Chinese, Japanese, and Filipino American writers. The major concern of Chin and his fellow editors is the emasculating effect of those stereotypes directed toward Asian Americans.

His first collection of short stories, *The Chinaman Pacific & Frisco R.R. Co.*, contains eight short stories written between 1970 and 1978. Most of the stories are autobiographical in tone. The main line of the stories is the Chinese American experience, involving both the youngsters who grow up with the Charlie Chan tales and the old generation of immigrants who try to hang on to their

Chinese roots in any way they can. No one seems happy, but everyone is indulged in a frenzied search for some kind of identity. All actions are staged in fantasy and slapstick through bawdy dialogues and movie scenes, reinforced by wily twists and ironies. Despite a few humorous moments, the perspective in all these stories is at once gloomy and mordant. All male characters—usually aspiring writers—indulge themselves in masochistic self-loathing. The monologue is the dominant mode of narration.

A key to all the stories that has often been overlooked is Chin's use of the railroad as a symbol to exemplify both the historical experience of Chinese Americans and the stereotypical portrayal of them as a "passive model minority" in America. In fact, the railroad has been a consistent referent in Chin's work. From his early plays and stories in the 1970s to his recent fiction and essays, Chin has employed the railroad as a reminder of the Chinese American heritage and as a touchstone for any misrepresentation of it. In his view, the railroads were key to the creation of Chinatowns. As time went by, the history of that creation has gradually been pushed into oblivion, because those who lived through that history are gone, and people do not talk about it any more.

In the first story of this collection, "Railroad Standard Time," the railroad is featured prominently through the railroad watch given to the narrator, Dirigible, by his mother. At the outset of the story, Dirigible receives the watch at his grandmother's funeral; at the end of the story, he drives back to Oakland Chinatown to attend his mother's funeral. Such a corresponding structure of the narrative enriches the implication of the story, because the "passing" of the watch is coincided with the "passing" of the old generations in Dirigible's family. Since the watch once belonged to his maternal grandfather, one of the first Chinese men to work for the Pacific Railroad, the "passing" of the watch is like the "passing" of the family and, by extension, the Chinese American heritage. In Dirigible's eyes, this marker of time has become the marker of history. He "held it one hand and then the other, hefted it, felt out the meaning of the 'best' " (2) that his ancestors could offer.

But all the symbolic value of the watch instantly vanishes when his mother fails to recall his grandfather's Chinese name. With "the solemnity of the moment gone," the watch in Dirigible's hand "turned to cheap with the mumbling of a few awful English words" (2). He feels that his connection with the grandfather he never knew and the masculine origin of his heritage is now broken, if not entirely lost. Dirigible's struggle to understand his heritage is further complicated by an American pop culture that at once lures and despises him. For the reader, what rings loud and clear through this incident is Chin's warning of the disruption in the "passing" and the eventual loss of Chinese American heritage. The consequence, as Chin shows through Dirigible's long struggle, is to be trapped forever in the dilemma of dangling between two cultural identities and yet belonging to neither.

Although Dirigible is the dominant figure in the collection, Chin does shift the narrative focus to other characters from time to time. In "The Only Real

Day," the portrait of Dirigible's father, Yuen, is essential to staging the dramatic moments in the story. Weak, silent, and paralyzed, Yuen yields his role as the head of the household to his wife, Rose, who is strong and does not care very much about Chinese culture. He wishes his son, Dirigible, could speak Cantonese better and assume his Chinese identity, but he cannot offer himself as his son's model. He receives a letter from the immigration office, asking for his fingerprints and police record in order to confirm his legality in America. To Yuen, this is humiliating, and more so if he complies with the INS order in the presence of his son. Chin's description delineates his confusion and fear so precisely that he is able to create more than a few light moments in an otherwise sad story.

The structure of the stories is diverse. Some are more realistic and more carefully crafted, while others are written in a freer form. "The Eat and Run Midnight People" is a typical example of the latter. Even though the speaker is constantly struggling with the pain of his past, he does not fixate on the same obsessions as other characters do. Furthermore, the story is not replete with bizarre and violent images. Chin's use of wit and humor works equally well in "A Chinese Lady Dies." The narrator is deeply stressed by his problematic relationship with his mother. In a series of dream-like passages, he imagines himself as a funny old-Western hero. Such comic relief in a tense story on touchy issues is not just witty; it also carries an amusing effect. By comparison, the last story in the collection, "The Sons of Chan," is a more highly fictionalized fantasy about the search for Charlie Chan. As the implication of the story depends heavily on the stereotypes from the Charlie Chan movies, the narrative does not have much room for subtlety, even the Freudian overtones cannot make any difference. Besides, it is too long and too self-indulgent.

Like his two early plays, stories in this collection are all set in the ghetto of Chinatown. As a creation of the racial discrimination and exclusionary injustice in late nineteenth- and early twentieth-century America, Chinatown has always been depicted, according to Viet Thanh Nguyen, "as a geographic and cultural body that is separate from the civil body of the city and as a site where the individual body may degenerate physically and morally" (141). Living in such a place, the male characters in these stories feel as if they had been forgotten, confined, and ultimately doomed. Many of them believe that they are too incompetent, insufficient, and inadequate to function as brothers, lovers, husbands, and fathers because they are infinitely caught between the predominantly masculinity-based expectations from their traditional Chinese heritage and the emasculating treatment from their adopted culture. Any attempt to redefine or reinvent them will surely be futile.

The Big Aiiieeeee! An Anthology of Chinese American and Japanese American Literature is a collection of poems, essays, short stories, excerpts from plays and novels, commentaries, and even captioned drawings from a picture book. But, notably, the work of Maxine Hong Kingston and Amy Tan is not included. Though not a collection of Chin's own short stories, the anthology certainly sheds some light on Chin's notions of short story writing and fiction writing. The anthology begins with Chin's angry ninety-two-page vitriolic essay, "Come All Ye Asian American Writers of the Real and the Fake," in which he attacks Chinese American writers Kingston, Tan, and David Henry Hwang, who impose fake variations upon the real Chinese culture. He blasts them for being "the first writers of any race, and certainly the first writers of Asian ancestry, to so boldly fake the best-known works from the most universally known body of Asian literature and lore in history" (3). Incomplete and even arbitrary as they were at the time, both *Aiiieeeee!* anthologies were pioneering works that established the presence of Asian American literature on the contemporary scene.

Bulletproof Buddhists, and Other Essays is Chin's only non-fiction collection so far. All the six essays in it are funny and erudite, and they read like travelogues and short stories about his adventures and discoveries on the road, from parts of southern California to Seattle, Tijuana, Cuba, and Asia. Four of them focus on the Chinese and Asian American experience in California; one recounts Chin's trip to Cuba in 1962; another records Chin's impressions during his trip to a writers' conference in Singapore in 1994. In most of the essays, Chin nicely combines his quick wit, his sharp observation, and his storytelling gift, mixing the personal stories of youthful gangs and early immigrants, mostly drawn from interviews, with his philosophical reflections on various issues and problems in and beyond America. Each essay is self-contained, but when read as a whole they are nothing less than Chin's continuous attempts to search for the inspirations of the "real" Chinese myths and values that he has cherished so dearly all his life.

◆ CRITICAL RECEPTION

Over the years, Chin has been an influential but controversial figure in Asian American literature. While writers like Ishmael Reed see Chin as a critic who "forces Asian Americans to confront their devils" and "tells the truth" (qtd. in Iwata, 1), Chin's bitter argument with Kingston and others seems to have brought him unwarranted notoriety and isolation. The acrimonious tone is apparent in many reviews of his work. It is true that his views are often shocking and disagreeable, but it is hard to deny that the significance of his role as a pioneering writer, critic, and literary historian has undoubtedly secured him a prominent place in the canon of Asian American literature.

With only one collection of short stories and a couple of other short pieces in obscure publications so far, Chin's short stories are by no means a major component of his writing. Therefore, they have not garnered as much scholarship as his novels, plays and editorial work have. The reception of his stories has been registered mostly in the form of book reviews, rather than scholarly articles.

Assessment of the stories in *The Chinaman Pacific & Frisco R.R. Co.* is a split. Douglas Sun notes in the *Los Angeles Times* that "Chin's rhetoric is often sharp and funny, but he also rides the high horse of racial bitterness for more than it's worth" (6). By far, "Railroad Standard Time" has received more critical analysis than other stories in the collection. It was selected in a popular Penguin collection of multiethnic short stories, *Growing Up Ethnic in America: Contemporary Fiction about Learning to Be American* (Gillan and Gillan, 1999). In Jeannie Chiu's view, the story serves as an example of "the Asian American gothic" (93).

Most of the reviews of the collection are brief and have no in-depth comments on all the stories. Douglas Sun's review, however, offers a comprehensive and objective reading of the whole collection. He defines "the alienation of Chinese America from the America of white skin and Wonder Bread" as the "essential subject" for all the stories in the collection" (6). He lists the first two stories as "the weakest of the bunch" because they "read like meandering stream-of-consciousness memoirs" (6). He does not like the last story either, because it is "a tiring screed on growing up with stereotypes." For Sun, the other five stories represent the best in Chin's collection: "two considerably writerly virtues" (6). The first, which is particularly showcased in "A Chinese Lady Dies," is "a wicked sense of humor" that often transforms from "whimsy" to "satire"; the second is Chin's "considerable skill as a storyteller," the kind of "genuine gift for bringing characters and their predicaments alive." Through a close-knit narrative structure and credible characterization, Chin manages to filter his message subtly in "The Only Real Day" and "Yes, Young Daddy"—the need to forge a Chinese American identity—without leaving any trace of "didactic harshness" (6). But in the essay "Daddy, I Don't Know What You're Talking About," Fiona Cho questions Chin's treatment of this issue in "The Only Real Day": "The necessity of forging a Chinese-American identity is indeed urgent. Chin's notion of finding this identity in the example of ancient heroic tales needs to be re-evaluated, however" (60).

Chin's portrayal of dysfunctional male characters in his stories is not well taken by some critics. All of them are chronically weak, desperate, and unable to take control of their own lives. They are constantly in fear of losing their masculinity and self worth. Sheng-mei Ma asserts, "This phobia of debility is manifested as the anxiety over the male body" (30) in Chin's stories. Similarly, other critics, especially those who take offense to Chin's attack on Asian American "ethnographic feminism," consider Dirigible and other male characters as a bunch of men who are externally angry and contentious, but internally insecure and vulnerable.

Some reviewers find the writing style in the collection quite problematic. They believe that the prose is frequently difficult and overly anxious to strive for the effect of the exotic diction from ethnic vernacular. In Sun's view, "Chin's prose style tends toward a looseness vaguely reminiscent of William S. Burroughs." In addition, "He also enjoys playing fast and loose with temporal shifts in his stories, with the result that memory, present experience, anticipation and pure fantasy often overlap." The problem is that "the reader may have some trouble keeping things sorted" (6).

Given their groundbreaking nature and their lasting impact upon the development of Asian American literature, the two *Aiiieeeee!* anthologies that Chin and his friends produced have become the focus of scholarship on Chin in the last twenty-five or so years. It is hard to find one commentary on Chin in which there is no reference to the two anthologies or his arguments with other Asian American writers. In a sense, all the debates regarding Chin and his two anthologies have generated a critical history of the Asian American literary movement that began in the late 1960s. Since he is the leading editor of these anthologies and the central figure in all the controversies that they incurred, the critical reception of the two anthologies naturally touches up Chin's concepts of literature and offers insight into his short story writing.

People seem to endorse his call on Asian Americans to learn their true history rather than the bias and fabricated myths, but they just do not agree with his hard-driven approach to promote his idea. Qun Wang considers Chin's criticism "too judgmental and arbitrary" (81). Vince Schleitwiler thinks that Chin's "grouchy defense of cultural authenticity is too tactless for current intellectual debates" (133). For instance, Chin repeatedly attempts to show the deeply rooted stereotypes toward Asian Americans by lashing out at other Asian American writers for catering their writing to the mainstream society at all cost, including distorting and faking cultural myths. Toming Jun Liu, who takes issue with Chin's definition of what is "fake" and "true" Chinese cultural heritage, claims that "Chin and the *Aiiieeeee!* group are among those who spearheaded early Asian American cultural criticism by following a culturally nationalist and masculinist agenda" and presented "a stagnant vision of Chinese culture" (18).

Other critics, however, argue that this anthology can help move the debate among Asian American writers to a new stage. "The purpose of an anthology like this," as Merle Rubin explains, "is to allow us to hear Asian-Americans speaking for themselves, in their own voices" (15). Hout Sze calls it "a great anthology of authentic Asian American works," but warns that "Asian American literature cannot exist as a Western construction—an assortment of ignorance and half-patched myths like the chop suey that Chinese restaurants serve their white customers" (19). J. K. Hom notes that "With the appearance of *The Big Aiiieeeee!* the reading public now has an opportunity to see another side of the Asian American psyche" (20). In recent years, Chin's positions, presented in his long essay, "Come All Ye Asian American Writers of the Real and the Fake," for *The Big Aiiieeeee!* seem to have won a few more supporters. David James, for one, likes the way in which "Frank Chin attacked the historical distortions and fabrications" of certain writers, "especially their denigration of Chinese manhood, which, he argued, parlayed their work into popularity with the white racist hegemony" (162).

The review for *Bulletproof Buddhists, and Other Essays* is not as negative as the reception that Chin usually gets. One interesting phenomenon is that more reviewers read the book as a collection of stories, rather than pure non-fiction essays. Vince Schleitwiler enjoys the unique mixture of the book because in it "Chin gathers lost legends, children's stories, personal histories, tall tales, and polemics and cobbles them together into a startling, comprehensive theory of Asian American culture with an ancient past and a global reach" (133). Benjamin Tong finds a new power in Chin's discourse, and he asserts that "Frank Chin has given contemporary word to a complex and profound sensibility that has weathered the onslaught of bigotry, cultural genocide and wholesale assimilation sellout" (S6). Of course, the book has not entirely escaped critical scrutiny. Kitty Chen Dean likes its "hip, fluent, fast-paced style," but she complains that Chin's "rantings about various topics (bigotry, storytelling, Chinese American authors, stereotyping, Singapore, malls, etc.) often seem mean-spirited and incomplete" (108). Since the Chin-Kingston battle started in the early 1990s, there has been hardly any well-balanced and objective scholarship on Chin's critical and fictional work. Some have challenged his highly charged rhetoric from a few introductory essays in defense of the popular writers that Chin considers "fake," but soon afterwards they brushed him off into oblivion—except when they needed a villainous "Other" as the easy target of their argument against him—and have not paid much attention to Chin's own fiction and playwriting since then. Recently, however, a few critics have called upon their colleagues to give Chin's writing some serious scholarly attention that he deserves. In his persuasive and timely essay, "Frank Chin Is Not a Part of This Class," John Goshert proposes "the opening of a space in which we may be able to revisit not only Chin's critical and fictional work, but the field of Asian American studies itself" (Paragraph 1).

◆ BIBLIOGRAPHY

Works by Frank Chin

Short Story Collection

The Chinaman Pacific & Frisco R. R. Co. Minneapolis: Coffee House Press, 1988.

Novels

Donald Duk. Minneapolis: Coffee House Press, 1991.
Gunga Din Highway. Minneapolis: Coffee House Press, 1994.

Plays

Gee, Pop! . . . A Real Cartoon, produced in San Francisco, 1974.

America More or Less, with Amiri Baraka and Leslie Marmon Silko, produced in San Francisco, 1976.

Lullaby, with Silko, produced in San Francisco, 1976.

The Chickencoop Chinaman and *The Year of the Dragon*. Seattle: University of Washington Press, 1981.

American Peek-a-Boo Kabuki, World War II, and Me, produced in Los Angeles, 1985.

Edited Works

Aiiieeeee! An Anthology of Asian American Writers. Ed. with Jeffery Paul Chan, Lawson Fusao Inada, and Shawn Hsu Wong. Washington, DC: Howard University Press, 1974.

Yardbird Reader, vol. 3. Ed. with Shawn Wong. Berkeley, CA: Yardbird Publishing Co-operative, 1974.

The Big Aiiieeeee! An Anthology of Chinese American and Japanese American Literature. Ed. with Jeffery Paul Chan, Lawson Fusao Inada, and Shawn Wong. New York: New American Library/Dutton, 1991.

Essays

Bulletproof Buddhists, and Other Essays. Honolulu: University of Hawaii Press, 1998.

Studies of Frank Chin

Chiu, Jeannie. "Uncanny Doubles: Nationalism and Repression in Frank Chin's 'Railroad Standard Time.' " *Hitting Critical Mass: A Journal of Asian American Cultural Criticism* 1.1 (Fall 1993): 93–107.

Cho, Fiona. "Daddy, I Don't Know What You're Talking About." *Hitting Critical Mass: A Journal of Asian American Cultural Criticism* 1.1 (Fall 1993): 57–61.

Davis, Robert Murray. "West Meets East: A Conversation with Frank Chin." *Amerasia Journal* 24.1 (1998): 87–103.

Dean, Kitty Chen. "Book Reviews: Arts & Humanities." *Library Journal* 123.10 (June 1, 1998): 108.

Gillan, Maria Mazziotti, and Jennifer Gillan, eds. *Growing Up Ethnic in America: Contemporary Fiction about Learning to Be American*. New York: Penguin Books, 1999.

Goshert, John. " 'Frank Chin Is Not a Part of This Class!': Thinking at the Limits of Asian American Literature." *Jouvert: A Journal of Postcolonial Studies* 4.3 (Spring–Summer 2000): 39 paragraphs. http://social.chass.ncsu.edu/jouvert/v4i3/gosher.htm

Hom, J. K. "New Anthology Would Make a Great Stocking Stuffer." *Asian Week: The Voice of Asian America* 13.18 (December 20, 1991): 20.

Huang, Guiyou. "Frank Chin." In *Asian American Novelists: A Bio-Bibliographical Critical Sourcebook*. Emmanuel Nelson, ed. Westport, CT: Greenwood Press, 2000, 48–55.

———. "Frank Chin." In *Asian American Playwrights: A Bio-Bibliographical Critical Sourcebook*. Miles X. Liu, ed. Westport, CT: Greenwood Press, 2002, 24–32.

Iwata, Edward. "Word Warriors," *Los Angeles Times* (June 24, 1990): View Section, 1.

James, David. "Tradition and the Movies: The Asian American Avant-Garde in Los Angeles." *Journal of Asian American Studies* 2.2 (1999): 157–80.

Liu, Toming Jun. "The Problematics of Kingston's 'Cultural Translation': A Chinese Diasporic View of *The Woman Warrior*." *Journal of American Studies of Turkey* 4 (Fall 1996): 15–30.

Ma, Sheng-mei. *Immigrant Subjectivities in Asian American and Asian Diaspora Literatures.* Albany: State University of New York Press, 1998.

Moran, Edward. "Frank Chin." *Current Biography* 60.3 (March 1999): 17–20.

Nguyen, Viet Thanh. "The Remasculinization of Chinese America: Race, Violence, and the Novel." *American Literary History* 12.1–2 (Spring–Summer 2000): 130–57.

Rubin, Merle. "Angry Asian-American Anthology." *The Christian Science Monitor*, Books (September 19, 1991): 15.

Schleitwiler, Vince. "Books." *Village Voice* 43.36 (September 8, 1998): 133.

Sun, Douglas. "Memories of a Chinese-American Boyhood." *Los Angeles Times*, Book Review (January 1, 1989): 6.

Sze, Hout. "The Genuine Article." *Asian Week: The Voice of Asian America* 14.29 (March 12, 1993): 19.

Tong, Benjamin. "A Transcendent Chinaman Pagan Heathen Barbarian on the Road." *International Examiner*, Supplement (August 19, 1998): S6.

Wang, Qun. "The Dialogic Richness of *The Joy Luck Club*." *Paintbrush: A Journal of Poetry and Translation* 22 (Autumn 1995): 76–84.

SUSAN CHOI
(1969–   )

Joonseong Park

◆ BIOGRAPHY

The daughter of a Korean immigrant father and a Russian-Jewish mother, Susan Choi was born in Indiana and raised in Texas. Her father's stories of life in Korea and of his experiences as a newly arrived immigrant in the American South would later inspire her own stories and her first novel, *The Foreign Student*, which was chosen by Richard Eder of the *Los Angeles Times* as one of the Top Ten Books of 1998, and which won the Steven Turner Award for best first work of fiction in 1999. The recipient of a grant from the National Endowment for the Arts and a fellowship to the Fine Arts Center in Provincetown, Choi makes her home in Brooklyn, New York. She attended Yale University, where she majored in literature, and went on to earn an M.F.A. in fiction at Cornell University. A former fact-checker at the *New Yorker*, a teacher as well as a writer, her short fiction has appeared in journals including the *Iowa Review* and *Epoch* magazine.

◆ MAJOR WORKS AND THEMES

Susan Choi published several short stories in literary journals prior to her first novel, *The Foreign Student*. Through a couple of her short stories, "The Runner" and "Memorywork," both published in *Iowa Review*, Choi offers a glimpse of the marriage of her parents. The narrator does not inform that it is an interracial marriage, but the reader can tell that at least the father in "The Runner" is an immigrant whose voice has "his accent and his failed conjugation" (128). "The Runner" is about an immigrant father (who left his daughter for a decade after a divorce) and his renewed relationship with his now grown-up daughter, who visits him every winter. The father has taken up jogging in his late years and Choi beautifully describes the aging father. The Jewish mother in "Memorywork" reminds the reader of Choi's mother and her marriage to a Korean man even though the narrator never reveals that the father is Korean—he was a student like Chang, a Korean exchange student in *The Foreign Student*. Bettina, the daughter, drags herself and her mother out of her mother's enforced amnesia and insists upon having a past when she says that she needs a picture of her parents as young lovers, taken before she was born, for a school project. The narrator of the story, the mother, shows snapshots of her failed marriage before the birth of Bettina, including an X-ray picture of Bettina as a fetus.

Alternately set in wartime Korea during the early 1950s and in Sewanee, Tennessee, in the years following the Korean War, Choi's debut novel, *The Foreign Student*, is a love story between a young Korean man scarred by war and a deeply troubled daughter of a wealthy American southern family. The main character in the novel, Chuck Ahn, a Korean refugee and scholarship student at the University of the South, is based loosely upon Choi's father who had survived torture and prison camps during the Korean War. "[I]t just blew my mind," said Choi in a *Newsday* interview. "I've never known that kind of experience of extremity at all" (B11). Chuck's love interest, Katherine Monroe, has spent half her life in love with the most prominent professor on campus, Charles Addison, a man twenty-eight years her senior and a friend of her parents, who first seduced her when she was fourteen. A short story, "The Dark Ages," which was separately published in *Epoch Review*, deals with the beginning of the long affair Katherine started at fourteen with Charles Addison. Another short story, "The Way to Live Wisely," is set in a college town, like *The Foreign Student*. A college student undergoes an abortion and struggles from its impact.

◆ CRITICAL RECEPTION

Susan Choi has not yet published a collection of short stories, so critical response is limited to her first novel, *The Foreign Student*. Reviewers are generally not taken by the love story itself. For example, the reviewer for *Kirkus Reviews* writes that "the love story never seems all that credible or affecting" and that "the affair never crackles with convincing tension" (913). The reviewer for *Publishers Weekly* agrees, saying that "their eventual relationship at times seems somewhat contrived" (47). However, Choi's attempt to create a love story between Chang and Katherine, who have dramatically different cultural backgrounds, is praised as ambitious.

Shirley N. Quinn writes in her review for *Library Journal* that "when the story lines shift, the individual reader is left with a sense of confusion and disconnection" and "is unable to gain a strong sense of a single character before being moved to the next" (129). Even though Richard Eder admits that "Choi's narrative roughness [caused by the alternation of setting between Sewanee and Korea] is most evident in her account of Chang's wartime ordeal, where her ellipses, sudden juxtapositions and the occasional arrival of an effect before its cause can be confusing" (2), he suggests that "whether intended or not, the roughness is a stylistic match to the book's theme: the awkwardness with which two estranged people—Chang and Katherine, a young American—come zigzag together" (2) and despite the narrative bumpiness, these juxtapositions remain fascinating to him.

The novel's character development also is not seen as a prominent achievement. Don Lee notes that "Chang's 'delicate courtesy' too often makes for a passive, opaque character" (194) and Charlie Dickinson complains about a paucity of Chuck's interactions with others, especially in his first semester at the University of the South in Sewanee, Tennessee. Choi's prose style, on the other hand, has been widely praised for its poetic language, and has been described as "graceful," "cinematic," and "clear-eyed." "Like so many current debut novels," *Kirkus Reviews* says, "the writing here is stronger than plot or character" (913).

◆ BIBLIOGRAPHY

Works by Susan Choi

Short Stories

"The Way to Live Wisely." *Epoch* 41.2 (Spring 1992): 180–86.
"Memorywork." *The Iowa Review* 23.2 (Spring–Summer 1993): 83–94. Rpt. in *Hard Choices: An Iowa Review Reader*. David Hamilton, ed. Iowa City: University of Iowa Press, 1996, 420–33.
"Heir." *Documents* 4/5 (Spring 1994): 99–112.
"Seven." In *Writing Away Here: A Korean-American Anthology*. Hyun Yi Kang, ed. Oakland, CA: Korean American Arts Festival Committee, 1994, 107–26.
"The Runner." *The Iowa Review* 25.1 (Winter 1995): 127–31.
"The Dark Ages." *Epoch* 47.1 (Fall 1998): 179–96.
"Harbor Deep." *Shankpainter* 38 (Spring 1999): 9–15.

Excerpt in Anthology

From *The Foreign Student*. In *Kori: The Beacon Anthology of Korean American Fiction*. Heinz Insu Fenkl and Walter K. Lew, eds. Boston: Beacon Press, 2001, 147–68.

Novel

The Foreign Student. New York: HarperCollins, 1998.

Interview

"Talking with Susan Choi: Factual Fictions." With Liza Featherstone. *Newsday*, Currents (September 6, 1998): B11.

Edited Work

With David Remnick. *Wonderful Town: New York Stories from the New Yorker*. New York: Random House, 2000.

Studies of Susan Choi

Dickinson, Charlie. Rev. of *The Foreign Student*. *Savoy Magazine* (September 26, 1998). http://www.savoymag.net/onb/brev0007.htm. Accessed February 17, 2002.

Eder, Richard. "Crossing Borders." Rev. of *The Foreign Student*. *Los Angeles Times Book Review* (August 30, 1998): 2.

Fitzpatrick, Elizabeth. "Susan Choi." In *Asian American Novelists: A Bio-Bibliographical Critical Sourcebook*. Emmanuel S. Nelson, ed. Westport, CT: Greenwood, 2000, 60–67.

Lee, Don. Rev. of *The Foreign Student* by Susan Choi. *Ploughshares* 25.1 (Spring 1999): 193–94.

Marlowe, Kimberly B. "Chang Chuckified." Rev. of *The Foreign Student*. *New York Times Book Review* (October 18, 1998): 29.

Quinn, Shirley N. Rev. of *The Foreign Student*. *Library Journal* 245.13 (September 1998): 129.

Rev. of *The Foreign Student*. *New Yorker* 74 (October 5, 1998): 109.

Rev. of *The Foreign Student*. *The Sewanee Review* 107.1 (Winter 1999): xx–xxii.

Rev. of *The Foreign Student*. *Washington Post Book World* 28 (September 6, 1998): 13.

Rev. of *The Foreign Student*. *Kirkus Reviews* 66 (July 1, 1998): 913.

Rev. of *The Foreign Student*. *Publishers Weekly* (July 6, 1998): 47.

Smolowe, Jill. Rev. of *The Foreign Student*. *Time* 152.10 (September 7, 1998): 83.

"Susan Choi." *Contemporary Literary Criticism* 119 (1999): 41–45.

CHITRA BANERJEE DIVAKARUNI

(1956–   )

Rocío G. Davis

◆ BIOGRAPHY

Chitra Banerjee Divakaruni was born in 1956 in Calcutta, India. She attended the Loreto School and the University of Calcutta. In 1976, she immigrated to the United States and earned a Master's degree from Wright State University in Dayton, Ohio, and a Ph.D. in English from the University of California at Berkeley. She has taught creative writing at Foothill College and the University of Houston. In 1991, she founded MAITRI, a helpline for South Asian women who are victims of abuse. At present, she lives in San Francisco with her husband, Murthy, and two sons, Anand and Abhay.

Divakaruni's first published works were books of poetry, *Dark Like the River* (1987), *The Reason for Nasturtiums* (1990), and *Black Candle* (1991). Her first collection of short stories, *Arranged Marriage* (1995), was awarded the PEN Oakland Josephine Miles Prize for Fiction, the Bay Area Book Reviewers Award for Fiction, and a 1996 American Book Award from the Before Columbus Foundation. This collection was followed by her first novel, *The Mistress of Spices*, in 1997, which was shortlisted for the Orange Prize in England and was named one of the best books of 1997 by the *Los Angeles Times*. The same year, she also released another book of poems, *Leaving Yuba City*, parts of which have won a Pushcart Prize and an Allen Ginsberg Prize. The novel *Sister of My Heart*, which grew out of the short story "The Ultrasound," from *Arranged Marriage*, was published in 1999 and its sequel, *The Vine of Desire*, in 2002. Her second collection of stories, *The Unknown Errors of Our Lives*, was published in 2001. She was awarded a California Arts Council Award in 1998. Divakaruni's work has been included in over thirty anthologies, including *Best*

American Short Stories and *The Pushcart Prize Anthology*, and translated into eleven languages, including Dutch, Hebrew, and Japanese.

◆ MAJOR WORKS AND THEMES

Divakaruni's stories reflect her continuing concern with the situation of Indian immigrants in the United States, particularly Indian women torn between the values of the old world and those of the new. Linking the physical and psychological landscapes of India and America, she explores the experiences of women who enact strategies of survival in changing cultural contexts. As Roshni Rustomji-Kearns points out, the pervasive imagery in *Arranged Marriage* is of "physical landscapes—of homes, gardens, fields, rivers, cities, villages—where the women live out their lives, and of clothes—the colors, textures, the saris, *shalwar kameez*, dresses, skirts and blouses—worn by women" (224). Divakaruni uses these images to suggest psychological conflicts, longing, and choices. In "Clothes," Sumita's development is traced through suggestive stages of clothing: from her traditional saris to her clandestine posing in American clothes for her husband Somesh, and eventually to her widow's white sari. Picturing herself in a mirror at the end of the story, dressed in a blouse and skirt, symbolizes her decision to remain in the United States and become a teacher.

At the center of many of the stories are important juxtapositions that symbolize the ambiguities in the lives of the Indian women who immigrate to America. In "A Perfect Life" Meena has a yuppie job, yet finds fulfillment when she begins to take care of a runaway boy; the wife's ostensible dutifulness in "Disappearance" covers up her "radical emancipatory actions" (Fludernik 278); in "Doors" the doors Preeti insists on closing in her house will be eventually closed on her. Significantly, many characters dream of the perfect life but must face the realization that it does not exist. Meena's relationship with Krishna makes her see that her vision of a perfect life was profoundly flawed; Abha, in "Meeting Mrinal," believes that her childhood friend Mrinal is the successful one and lies to her about her family life, her divorce, and estrangement from her teenage son. When Mrinal confesses to the emptiness of her own life, Abha is shocked: "What would I live on, now that I knew perfection was only a mirage?" (296). The conclusion of this story, where Abha and her son sit in the kitchen toasting with *pista* milk "to our precious, imperfect lives" (300), makes explicit an important psychological moment that many of the other characters experience—the women's lives are imperfect, but their victory lies in living.

In spite of the book's title and the central role of marriage in the stories, the representation of relationships between the women in the stories is more noteworthy than that of men, which is often presented in generalized, even stereotypical, terms. Through these relationships, women discover a sense of self and begin to exercise their ability to choose: learning about her best friend

Mrinal's affair makes Abha reconsider her own marriage; Mrinal's confession allows Abha to confront the realities of her own life; Anju's and her cousin Runu's simultaneous pregnancies in "The Ultrasound" only strengthen the bonds between them; Jayanti in "Silver Pavements, Golden Roofs" is shocked out of her fantasy of life in America when she experiences violent racism and witnesses the compromises her Aunt Pratima has had to make. The relationships between mothers and daughters are similarly complex. In "The Bats," the young daughter wonders at her mother's simple belief that her father will change, realizing that her mother "just didn't *know* the way I did" (14), condemning both of them to a life of more abuse; in "The Maid Servant's Story," the most narratologically complex tale, the protagonist hears of the tragic episode in her mother's life that changed her, which allows her to understand her mother's distance. The story within a story becomes a cautionary tale, as the protagonist thinks: "I wonder if the story (though not intended as such by my aunt) is a warning for me, a preview of my own life which I thought I had fashioned so cleverly, so differently from my mother's, but which is only a repetition, in a different *raga*, of her tragic song. Perhaps it is like this for all daughters, doomed to choose for ourselves, over and over, the men who have destroyed our mothers" (167).

Divakaruni's use of diverse narrative perspectives is a fascinating exercise at manners of signifying. The child narrator of "The Bats" articulates her father's abuse of her mother in guileless terms: "Things fell a lot when Father was around, maybe because he was so large" (2). The only story narrated from the husband's perspective, "Disappearance," is especially skillful, as the reader begins to unveil the story of the wife's suffering through the husband's blindness to her situation. One of the most poignant moments in the book is when the husband in this story cannot get over his wife's abandonment, even after he remarries. Divakaruni's skillful use of the second-person point of view in "The Word Love" gives the story multilayered meanings on the level of discourse as well, as this narrative strategy allows her to challenge conventional ideas of who the reader of the story is, by conflating the figure of the protagonist and the reader.

The women in these stories are in transition, caught in the border between a traditional patriarchal society and a world of possibilities and choices. Sometimes their choices—or inability to adapt—lead to frustration, as with Preeti in "Doors," whose obsession with privacy alienates her husband, or the mother in "The Bats." Many of the stories end with the woman breaking away—physically and emotionally—from expectations and imposed forms of living and starting again, notably the widowed Sumita in "Clothes," and the protagonists of "The Word Love," "Disappearance," and "Affair." Once the women accept what they often refuse—"It's how we survive, we Indian women whose lives are half light and half darkness, stopping short of revelations that would otherwise crisp away our skins" (167), as one of the women says—the stories become chronicles of hope.

Divakaruni has admitted that the stories in *Arranged Marriage* arose from her awareness of women's issues and her engagement with "women battling and coming out triumphant" (Farmanfarmaian 47). Her second collection, *The Unknown Errors of Our Lives*, demonstrates a shift in Divakaruni's concerns. Though she still privileges the plight of immigrant women, these stories widen her negotiation with cultural adjustment, toward more general human themes of memory, forgiveness and acceptance, the fear of wrong choices and regret, age, and family. Two stories in particular stand out. The first, "Mrs. Dutta Writes a Letter," anthologized in *Best American Short Stories* (1999), recounts the plight of what Divakaruni has called "reluctant immigrants," parents of children who have settled in the United States, who are brought over by their children. Mrs. Dutta cannot answer her friend Mrs. Basu's question, "Are you happy in America?" (5), because she cannot articulate—even to herself—her contradictory situation: she feels lonelier and more useless with her son and family in the States than she did alone in India. When she decides to return to India, she writes a letter, not of defeat, but of wisdom and serenity: "I cannot answer your question about whether I am happy, for I am no longer sure I know what happiness is. All I know is that it isn't what I thought it to be. . . . If I'm lucky—and perhaps, in spite of all that has happened, I am—the happiness will be in the figuring out" (33–34). For Mrs. Dutta, as for many characters, happiness lies in the process of finding and, more importantly, accepting the consequences of their choices, a process that immigrants are constantly engaged in. The title story engages the process of accepting the errors of one's past. Importantly, though Ruchira admits that she had come to terms with "misjudgements and slippages" (216), knowing they will always be a part of her life, her epiphany comes when she can accept an unknown error in her fiancé Biren's life.

The characters in the stories have to come to terms with the confusing coexistence in their lives and memories of past and present, India and America. As in the earlier collection, many of the women in these stories leave India with the intention of living fuller and freer lives, away from the traditional restricted routines of their mothers and grandmothers, only to find themselves unsure of how to proceed and what to believe in a situation that is more insidious than the one they escaped from. Divakaruni problematizes the characteristics and consequences of Americanization. In "The Lives of Strangers," Leela's visit to India after an attempted suicide leads to her gradual release of the "absurdly American" isolating notion of individual control and her appropriation of her aunt's more interconnected notion of destiny (67). The narrator of "The Blooming Season for Cacti" realizes that her "desperate mythologizing of America" (170) has blinded her to the reality of human suffering. Interestingly, American-born Indians revert to the old ways, as in "The Unknown Errors of Our Lives," where a couple choose to have an arranged marriage because, as he says: "the alternative—it doesn't seem to work that well, does it?" (214). The story "The Names of Stars in Bengali" centers on a

San Francisco wife and mother who visits her village in India with her sons, to try and give them some of her memories. As she listens avidly to stories, "[s]he wanted desperately to believe . . . that through them she was learning back her past, what to pass on to her children. What America has leached away from her" (255).

Divakaruni penetrates into the reality of the emotional dislocation caused by stepping into "a time machine called immigration" that condemns members of the same family to be unable to "inhabit a house together, in the old way" (216). In "The Intelligence of Wild Things," a sister understands the sentiment in her brother's heart after their mother obliged him to leave for America and the reason he will no longer write her: "Abhimaan, that mix of love and anger and hurt that lies at the heart of so many of our Indian tales, and for which there is no equivalent in English" (42). She also recognizes her own guilt, as she has wrapped herself up in her own family life and left her brother alone: "I hated this change in myself, this shrinking of sensibility, this failure of intelligence" (43). This is the sentiment of many of the protagonists in the stories, such as Aparna, in "What the Body Knows," who recovers from her illness when she feels attracted to her white doctor, or Ruchira, who, even at fourteen, stated that "An unexamined life is not worth living" (215). Many of the characters struggle to accept painful realities caused by errors, weakness, or misfortune, even as they understand that "[s]ome illusions are essential. We need them to live by" (52). Mrs. Dutta refuses at first to admit that she is not welcome in her son's home; the sister in "The Intelligence of Wild Things" cannot bring herself to tell her brother their mother is dying; the narrator of "The Forgotten Children" admits that her betrayal led to her brother's leaving. Mona, the protagonist of "The Love of a Good Man," struggles with the memory of her mother's death and the possibility of seeing the father who had abandoned her after many years. "We'd buried our hurts inside our bodies, like shrapnel" (90), and she must learn to forgive her father before she can begin to tell her husband her mother's story.

Asked about the increasing predominance of literature that arises from the story of immigration, Divakaruni explains that she engages this experience because

> the underlying larger issue is of leaving home. Just about all of us have an experience of leaving home, how leaving home changes you and how when you go back, home is changed. It's never the same. And what of the home you carry with you? The sense of self. How do we deal with that as we move into a place where self means something quite different? If you repress your sense of your past and that heritage, that need comes out in other ways. It is a definite need in us, to know who we are in terms of where we come from." (qtd. in Benson 79)

◆ **CRITICAL RECEPTION**

Divakaruni's prose has been consistently praised because of her skilled use of lyrical descriptions, the narrative energy that drives the stories, and her representation of the immigrant experience as well, not as something exotic, but as part of a larger, shared human story. Francine Prose points out that "the chasms her protagonists have to straddle have less to do with the ground beneath their feet than with the gap between past and future, between the heart and the head" (20). Sumana Sen-Bagchee argues that the strengths of Divakaruni's stories lie as much in structure as in theme, highlighting, for example, how the lives of the three women in "The Maid Servant's Story" "telescope into one another" (76), or how the strength of the story "Meeting Mrinal" lies "not only in the positioning of the two women, but also derives from the arrangement of emotions" (76). The manner in which her characters respond intensely to situations is an excellent example of lyricism and understatement. Nonetheless, critics have also pointed out that some stories, particularly in the first collection, may be read as "a stereotyping of the polarized concept of freedom for a woman in America versus loss of freedom for a woman in India" (Rustomji-Kearns 224). The situation of abused mothers or forced abortions, for example, appears "contrived and overdone" (Sen-Bagchee 77), and the author's representation of male characters tends to be superficial. The stories in the second collection, though uneven in quality, have been praised for the author's moving insight into human nature, as well as discursive elegance. Claire Messud signals how Divakaruni "locates the true impossibility of translation, the terrible dislocation between cultures and languages and ways of thought" in apparently insignificant moments (T7). Zarena Aslami praises Divakaruni's "sophisticated narrative structures and the pageant of different perspectives" (10), demonstrations of the importance of Divakaruni's stories in the context of contemporary South Asian American literature.

◆ **BIBLIOGRAPHY**

Works by Chitra Banerjee Divakaruni

Short Story Collections

Arranged Marriage. New York: Doubleday, 1995.
The Unknown Errors of Our Lives. New York: Doubleday, 2001.

Novels

The Mistress of Spices. New York: Doubleday, 1997.
Sister of My Heart. New York: Doubleday, 1999.
Vine of Desire. New York: Doubleday, 2002.

Poetry

Dark Like the River. Calcutta: Writer's Workshop Press, 1987.
The Reason for Nasturtiums. Berkeley: Berkeley Poets Press, 1990.
Black Candle. Corvallis, OR: Calyx, 1991.
Leaving Yuba City: Poems. New York: Anchor Books, 1997.

Edited Volumes

Multitude: Cross-Cultural Readings for Writers. New York: McGraw-Hill, 1996.
We, Too, Sing America: A Reader for Writers. New York: McGraw-Hill, 1997.

Studies of Chitra Banerjee Divakaruni

Aslami, Zarena. "Of Home and Heritage." *Chicago Tribune* (April 30, 2001): 10.
Benson, Heidi. "Poet, Novelist Chitra Banerjee Divakaruni." *San Francisco Chronicle* (April 29, 2001): 79.
Davis, Rocío G. "Everyone's Story: Narrative 'You' in Chitra Divakaruni's 'The Word Love.'" In *Asian American Literature in the International Context: Readings in Fiction, Poetry, and Performance*. Rocío G. Davis and Sämi Ludwig, eds. Hamburg: LIT Verlag, 2002, 173–83.
Farmanfarmaian, Roxane. "Writing from a Different Place." *Publishers Weekly* (May 14, 2001): 46–47.
Fludernik, Monika. "Colonial vs. Cosmopolitan Hybridity: A Comparison of Mulk Raj Anand and R. K. Narayan with Recent British and North American Expatriate Writing (Singh-Baldwin, Divakaruni, Gupta)." In *Hybridity and Postcolonialism: Twentieth-Century Indian Literature*. Monika Fludernik, ed. Tübingen, Germany: Stauffenburg Verlag, 1998, 261–90.
Leach, Laurie. "Conflict over Privacy in Indo-American Short Fiction." In *Ethnicity and the American Short Story*. Julie Brown, ed. New York: Garland Press, 1997, 197–211.
Messud, Claire. "Displaced Persons." *Washington Post*, Book World (June 3, 2001): T7.
Moka-Dias, Brunda. "Chitra Banerjee Divakaruni." In *Asian American Novelists: A Bio-Bibliographical Critical Sourcebook*. Emmanuel S. Nelson, ed. Westport, CT: Greenwood Press, 2000, 87–92.
Prose, Francine. "Life in the Global Village." *Women's Review of Fiction* 12.6 (March 1996): 20.
Rustomji-Kearns, Roshni. "Chitra Banerjee Divakaruni." In *The Columbia Companion to the Twentieth-Century American Short Story*. Blanche H. Gelfant and Lawrence Graver, eds. New York: Columbia University Press, 2000, 223–26.
Sen-Bagchee, Sumana. " 'Mericans,' eh?" *Toronto Review of Contemporary Writing Abroad* 14.3 (Spring 1996): 72–77.
Srikanth, Rajini. "Chitra Banerjee Divakaruni: Exploring Human Nature Under Fire." *Asian Pacific American Journal* 5.2 (1996): 94–101.
Streuber, Sonja H. "Chitra Banerjee Divakaruni." In *Asian American Autobiographers: A Bio-Bibliographical Critical Sourcebook*. Guiyou Huang, ed. Westport, CT: Greenwood Press, 2001, 67–75.

SUI SIN FAR (EDITH MAUDE EATON)
(1865–1914)

Vanessa Holford Diana

◆ BIOGRAPHY

The first Asian American to publish fiction in North America, Edith Maude Eaton was born in Macclesfield, England on March 15, 1865, to a Chinese mother, Grace A. "Lotus Blossom" Trefusis, and an English father, Edward Eaton. Interracial marriage was a taboo in China and England, as well as North America, in the late nineteenth century, a topic about which Eaton would later write in both her short fiction and autobiographical essays. In 1872, the family moved to Montreal, where Eaton took care of her younger siblings—there were eventually fourteen—and occasionally helped supplement the family's meager income by selling lace or her father's paintings door-to-door. As a child, Eaton suffered racist taunts and physical abuse from the white children around her, and the consequences of racism against the Chinese would become a central issue in her writing. Supporting herself as a stenographer, magazine subscription saleswoman, and typesetter at the *Montreal Daily Star*, Eaton began publishing short stories, autobiographical essays, and journalistic sketches of Chinese American communities at the age of eighteen. Throughout her life, Eaton struggled to support herself while finding time to write; at the same time she struggled with various physical ailments, including malaria, rheumatoid arthritis, and rheumatic fever, which contributed to her death from heart disease at age forty-nine.

Eaton signed her publications in Canadian and U.S. periodicals with the *nom de plume* Sui Sin Far, a name her mother called her as a child. As S. E. Solberg notes, she chose this pen name early in her writing career despite being "unacquainted with her mother's native language, except for a few phrases, during her early years" and despite the fact that "she had very little contact with Asians or Eurasians, except for her own large group of siblings" (27). The name has been translated as Water Lily, and Xiao-Huang Yin also suggests that Sui Sin Far's name can mean "narcissus," which "in Chinese culture symbolizes dignity and indestructible love for family and homeland" (54). That she chose a name announcing her allegiance to China and the Chinese when she could easily have "passed" as Anglo American illustrates Sui Sin Far's commitment to giving voice to Chinese American concerns and experiences in North America.

In 1897, Sui Sin Far left Canada, traveling to Jamaica to work as a journalist for one year. After a brief return to Montreal, she moved to San Francisco and eventually joined the Chinese American community there, despite initial struggles to find acceptance because she was not fully Chinese. After another brief return to Montreal in 1900, Sui Sin Far spent her remaining years largely in Seattle, with some brief periods in Los Angeles and Boston. Committed to fighting "the battles" of the Chinese "in the papers" (*Mrs. Spring Fragrance and Other Writings* 223), she published fictional stories, autobiographical essays, and journalistic sketches in such periodicals as *Montreal Daily Witness*, *Westerner*, *Land of Sunshine*, *Overland Monthly*, *Good Housekeeping*, *Independent*, *New England Magazine*, *Boston Globe*, and *Los Angeles Express*. In 1912, she published *Mrs. Spring Fragrance*, a collection of new and previously published short stories. Sui Sin Far was purportedly writing a novel at the time of her death, but the manuscript has never been discovered.

◆ MAJOR WORKS AND THEMES

In a 1909 essay entitled "The Chinese in America," Sui Sin Far laments Western literary depictions of the Chinese that portray them as "unfeeling" and "custom-bound." "[F]iction writers seem to be so imbued with [these] ideas that you scarcely ever read about a Chinese person who is not a wooden peg," she protests (*Mrs. Spring Fragrance and Other Writings* 234). She argues that in general the Chinese "think and act just as the white man does, according to the impulses which control them. They love those who love them; they hate those who hate; are kind, affectionate, cruel or selfish, as the case may be" (234). Through this comparison, Sui Sin Far decenters whiteness as the standard of humanity, a challenging move at the turn of the last century, when sinophobia was rampant in the U.S. and Canada. Resistant representation, then, is a central purpose of her fiction.

Sui Sin Far challenges the depictions of Chinese Americans in popular press and fiction, stereotypes which characterized them as unfair labor competition for white Americans as well as harborers of disease and immorality, which they threatened to "spread" to the white Americans with whom they had contact. In order to disprove these stereotypes, she illustrates the struggles of sympathetic, complex Chinese American characters living with the oppressive immigration laws and violent racism of turn-of-the-century America. The short story collection *Mrs. Spring Fragrance* is a complex composite portrait of Northwest Chinatown communities that centers on non-Christian, non-Western cultural practices, beliefs, and values. Through the multiple characterization that the series of short stories provides, individuals come to illustrate collectively diversity within a supposedly homogenous cultural group.

The title character of the collection illustrates the centrality of self-representation to Sui Sin Far's fictional work. In the story "The Inferior Woman," Mrs. Spring Fragrance is a Chinese American woman who wants to be a writer. Using humor and irony to criticize literary misrepresentation while playfully exoticizing white Americans, Sui Sin Far mimics the conventional reliance on orientalism in literature about the Chinese when her character Mrs. Spring Fragrance determines to write "a book about Americans for her Chinese women friends. The American people were so interesting and mysterious" (*Mrs. Spring Fragrance and Other Writings* 28). After all, reasons Mrs. Spring Fragrance, "Many American women wrote books. Why should not a Chinese?" (28). Elizabeth Ammons notes that in moments like these, Sui Sin Far "blatantly turn[s] on its head the white stereotype of 'mysterious,' exotic Asians" (112).

The collection *Mrs. Spring Fragrance* is divided into two sections: "Mrs. Spring Fragrance" and "Tales of Chinese Children." In 1995, Amy Ling and Annette White-Parks edited *Mrs. Spring Fragrance and Other Writings*, a collection of selected short fiction from the original collection, as well as autobiographical essays and newspaper articles published over Sui Sin Far's career. Of the thirty-seven stories in the original collection, Ling and White-Parks selected twenty-four to be included in *Mrs. Spring Fragrance and Other Writings*.

The stories in the "Mrs. Spring Fragrance" section explore a number of adult themes, including cultural assimilation, racism, and immigration laws. Much of Sui Sin Far's fiction focuses on women's issues such as marriage relations, miscegenation, women's rights, gender roles, family conflict, social reform, and parenthood. For example, "The Wisdom of the New" and "The Americanizing of Pau Tsu" dramatize cultural conflicts between Chinese wives and their more Americanized Chinese husbands. Sui Sin Far examines the women's rights movement and the hypocrisy of white feminist activists who discriminate based on class or race in "The Wisdom of the New," "The Story of One White Woman Who Married a Chinese," and "The Inferior Woman." Cross-dressing scenes in "The Smuggling of Tie Co," "Tian Shan's Kindred Spirit," and "A Chinese Boy-Girl" call into question social definitions of gender roles.

The stories in the section entitled "Tales of Chinese Children" include fictional pieces centered on children and parables featuring animals who play out various human conflicts. Nevertheless, the selections are clearly not all meant for children. This classification, White-Parks argues, suggests instead that the stories therein are "about," or "coming from," Chinese children and offer adults a perspective on the results of adult folly on children. "Through children (the mouths of babes) an adult audience naively accepts what it could not if spoken by its peers," she argues ("We Wear" 15). Amy Ling describes many of the stories in this section, such as "The Banishment of Ming and Mai" or "A Chinese Boy-Girl," as "in the vein of Aesop's fables," often "shaped around a moral" and "embody[ing] . . . familiar maxims" ("Introduction," *Mrs. Spring Fragrance and Other Writings* 14–15). "The Banishment," for example, is a parable that "suggests the possibility of breaking through fixed ideas, the monologic assumptions and ethnocentric prejudices that divide human cultures" (White-Parks, *Sui Sin Far* 211).

A number of the stories in *Mrs. Spring Fragrance and Other Writings* portray intergenerational conflict in Chinese immigrant families resulting from American assimilationist efforts. Many of Sui Sin Far's fictional stories center on a child's estrangement from his or her parents, representing a distancing from Chinese cultural values. For example, in "The Land of the Free," which is just one of her many stories about assimilation and the danger it poses to Chinese American children and families, Sui Sin Far illustrates mainstream American society's willingness to shatter Chinese families in order to control definitions of Americanness and the circumstances under which immigrants are to be permitted access to American rights and opportunities. In this case, the forced removal of a Chinese immigrant couple's infant, who is kept in an orphanage for ten months while the parents must battle an overwhelming and corrupt legal bureaucracy, illustrates the cost of Americanization. At the story's close, when the mother is finally reunited with her son, the child responds to her in fear, not recognizing his mother and instead clinging to the skirts of the white missionary woman in whose care he was kept during their separation. The baby's new allegiance can be read as an allegory of Americanization, the price of which is lost memory of one's cultural origins and a learned fear of the designated "Other." In this story and others related to immigration and parenting, the American Dream for Chinese immigrants is shown to be instead a nightmare of shattered families.

Reminiscent of her autobiography, "Leaves from the Mental Portfolio of an Eurasian," where she recounts childhood "battles" against white children, Sui Sin Far also dramatizes the suffering of children in a racist culture in a fictional story from "Tales of Children" titled "Pat and Pan." The story illustrates the destructive nature of American racial categorization while showing that child rearing is, in dominant U.S. culture, a process of indoctrinating children to accept racial hierarchy. "Pat and Pan" focuses on two young children, named in the title. Pat was born to a nameless white mother who was—for unstated reasons—a social outcast from the white community, and was taken in by the Lum Yooks, a loving Chinese couple (also social outcasts based on their race) who treated him "as their own" and "bestowed upon him equal love and care with the little daughter" Pan (164). This harmonious interracial family presents an image of an idealized national family, where the color line is no barrier to love and nurturing. But this tale ultimately ends in estrangement, suggesting Sui Sin Far's pessimism over most white Americans' willingness to see past the color line or envision a united national family. Anna Harrison, a white missionary woman, alerts the white community to Pat's "unnatural" position as a member of a Chinese family, and Mrs. Lum Yook knows "there are many tongues wagging because he lives under our roof" (164). Public opinion does, of course, win out in the end. The Lum Yooks are powerless to resist Pat's removal, and a white couple adopts the boy, who ultimately grows to accept the racism of his white peers.

Another recurring theme of Sui Sin Far's fiction is biracial identity and bicultural experience. By focusing on biracial characters, she redefines "race" as a category in American thought. For example, in the story "Its Wavering Image," the use of a female character of biracial descent and bicultural experience enables Sui Sin Far to deconstruct ideologies of racial difference while illustrating the intersections between racial and sexual oppression in the character Pan's life. In addition, this Eurasian heroine's romantic relationship with a white man named Mark Carson becomes an allegorical representation of race relations that questions the possibility of a future of racial harmony. In the story, Sui Sin Far also resists assimilationist pressures of the era, challenging popular images of the biracial individual as one who tries to distance herself from the marginalized people whose ancestry she shares, "passing" as white for individual social gain.

The heroine of this courtship story shares a name with Pan, the young Chinese sister of "Pat and Pan." That Sui Sin Far chooses to twin the female characters' names between the two stories suggests some connections between the characters' situations; while the childhood Pan suffers family fragmentation because of racial categorization, the adult Pan suffers personal, internal fragmentation when faced with those same unbending racial categories. Furthermore, the shared name contributes to communal characterization in the collection as a whole by alerting readers to the common systems of belief that cause both Pans to suffer. In writing the story, Sui Sin Far borrows from the conventions of sentimental romance, but in this case there can be no happy ending because the man who woos Pan demands she choose white racial self-identification, and she instead chooses to assert her Chinese identity, a biracial identity being impossible in the dualistic thinking of the time. Carson's character illustrates the role of the mainstream gaze in constructing racial barriers and unequal power relations. Pan's biracial identity is threatening to Carson because she disturbs the racial categorization on which the stability of his own ideas about American identity relies; Pan "puzzles" Carson, who asks, "what was she? Chinese or white?" (61). His confusion is much like Anna Harrison's because he both identifies with her and resists her "difference." As for Pan's self-perception, "It was only after the coming of Mark Carson," the narrator tells us, "that the mystery of [Pan's] nature began to trouble her" (61). Her budding desire for Carson and his demand that she abandon her allegiance to the Chinese create of her identity a "wavering image" that she must actively bring back into focus.

In "Its Wavering Image," Carson becomes a spokesperson for mainstream anti-Chinese sentiment while willing Pan to "be" white. His character functions emblematically, infusing the story's specific details of courtship with the national realities of unequal power relations between Anglo American men and women of color, and thereby reminding readers of the persistent patterns of sexual exploitation that result from those power disparities. Carson responds to Pan's declaration of love for the Chinese people with disgust in an attempt to reassert his control over the situation:

> "Pan," he cried, "you do not belong here. You are white—white."
> "No! No!" protested Pan.
> "You are," he asserted. "You have no right to be here." (63)

The two then debate the nature of Pan's "real self" (63), which—in a move that echoes the young Pan of "Pat and Pan"—she defines in terms of where she was born, raised, and loved, and which he defines in terms of literacy and access to the dominant discourse that connects her to mainstream culture. What connection do the Chinese have, he asks, to "the books you read—the thoughts you think" (63). Insisting upon distinct, mutually exclusive racial categories, Carson demands of Pan, "you have got to decide what you will be—Chinese or white? You cannot be both" (63). Pan clearly will not be forced to give up her Chinese identity or community, despite her desire for Carson: "Hush! Hush! . . . I do not love you when you talk to me like that," she replies (63).

Like the linking of the two stories of Pan, Sui Sin Far once more uses the doubling of a character's name to suggest thematic connections between stories. In "The Story of One White Woman Who Married a Chinese," the white woman referred to in the title, whose name is Minnie, marries a white man fifteen years her senior named James Carson. It is not suggested that this character is biologically related to the Mark Carson of Pan's story, and the two do have unique and individual personalities. Nevertheless, their characterizations share much in common, suggesting that Sui Sin Far is using the characters to represent an emblematic type, an American man in a privileged position who bases his identity on the abjection of others. Like Mark Carson, James is a selfish, manipulative, and racist man of cruel nature. Furthermore, both men share the name of the western American "hero," Kit Carson, whose violent battles against the Navajo and Apache in the mid-nineteenth century represented in mainstream imagination the triumph of "civilization" over "savagery." By evoking the cultural myths of racial superiority and manifest destiny that Kit Carson embodies, Sui Sin Far critically examines the way Anglo Americans define civilization.

Similar to Mark Carson, James Carson fails to live up to the expectations for "civilized" or gentlemanly behavior toward his wife. Though he purports to be a social reformer, he insults and oppresses his wife, simultaneously mocking her and expecting her to fulfill the traditional roles of domestic wifehood. As a result of his cruelty and philandering, Minnie leaves him, taking with her their infant daughter. On the brink of starvation with no money and nowhere to go, she is taken in and cared for by a compassionate and generous young Chinese man named Liu Kanghi, who literally saves her life.

In "The Story of One White Woman Who Married a Chinese," Sui Sin Far juxtaposes Liu Kanghi and James Carson in order to offer a redefinition of manhood that defies the emasculating stereotypes of Chinese men. Minnie addresses James Carson:

> For all your six feet of grossness, your small soul cannot measure up to [Liu Kanghi's] great one. You were unwilling to protect and care for the woman who was your wife or the little child you caused to come into this world; but he succored and saved the stranger woman, treated her as a woman, with reverence and respect; gave her child a home, and made them both independent, not only of others but of himself. (77).

This speech raises a number of important issues in Sui Sin Far's critique of race relations and sexual politics at the turn of the last century. First, in contrasting the souls of the two men, Minnie highlights James Carson's hypocrisy, reminding him, the social reformer, that he has ignored the most basic of family duties. In contrast, Liu Kanghi is an ideal man who respects, protects, and provides for the woman and child, but does so without impinging on their independence. The focus on gender roles is a second important element in this story. Sui Sin Far contrasts the quite traditional desires of this white woman—who wants mostly to be a good wife and make her husband happy—with her extremely untraditional decision to violate the miscegenation taboo and marry a Chinese man. Written at a time when women's rights activists were publicly rethinking women's roles and definitions of marriage, this story suggests that the prohibition against marriage between the races also be rethought because it is based on racist assumptions of difference and hierarchy.

Not surprisingly, the white community reacts to Minnie's marriage with horror. "The Story" reflects the realities of sinophobia and antimiscegenation laws at the time, when, for example, in 1905 the State of California declared interracial marriages "illegal and void" (White-Parks, *Sui Sin Far* 106). Because she chooses to marry a Chinese man, Minnie challenges the racial boundaries defining American identity and suffers from white onlookers the consequences of violating the miscegenation taboo. As a result, white men identify her as a prostitute or loose woman, perceptions that preserve sexual exploitation. Nevertheless, Minnie asserts that she has never regretted marrying Liu Kanghi, "not even when men cast upon me the glances they cast upon sporting women" (77). When Minnie refuses to leave Liu Kanghi, Carson threatens to take their child, asking, "What will the judges say when I tell them about the Chinaman?" (76). As readers have learned in "Pat and Pan," Carson's threat of legal action is realistic. Children were taken away from Chinese families based on the racist American legal structure, and Minnie's interracial marriage to Liu Kanghi would not be legally recognized.

◆ CRITICAL RECEPTION

At the time of its publication, *Mrs. Spring Fragrance* met with positive reviews that recognized the author's challenge to stereotypical portrayals of the Chinese. Contemporary critics agree that Sui Sin Far wrote protest fiction to critique racist discourse in North America at the turn of the last century. "Most of the stories in *Mrs. Spring Fragrance*," argues Amy Ling, "sought to counter the prevailing notions that the Chinese were heathen, unassimilable, hatchet-waving rat eaters and pipe-smoking opium addicts who had no right to live in the United States or Canada" ("Introduction," *Mrs. Spring Fragrance and Other Writings* 13). Carol Roh-Spaulding adds that Sui Sin Far's project was "neither to ennoble her ethnic roots nor to deepen her identification with the Chinese but to reveal the suffering caused by notions of categorical purity for those who find themselves racially, ethnically, or culturally in between" (157). Critical studies of Sui Sin Far's fiction explore the strategies by which she carries out such resistant representation and the success with which she achieves it.

For the most part, criticism of Sui Sin Far's fiction is positive, demonstrating the complexity of her rhetorical strategies and her innovative challenges to dominant racist discourse of her time. Nevertheless, some critics, such as Lorraine Dong and Marlon K. Hom, find fault with what even White-Parks identifies as Sui Sin Far's occasional "exoticizing and orientalizing" of the Chinese characters in her fiction. Ling points to Sui Sin Far's frequent use of the word "quaint" as an example of this problematic descriptive style ("Introduction," *Mrs. Spring Fragrance and Other Writings* 12). In addition, Roh-Spaulding believes Sui Sin Far to be "evasiv[e] regarding Chinese-American identity" (156). That Sui Sin Far, raised an English-speaking woman in England and Canada, may maintain to some degree an outsider's perspective to the Chinese communities she describes is likely. But the majority of her critics agree that Sui Sin Far's revolutionary stand in addressing white readers with sympathetic portraits of the Chinese, Eurasians, and the working classes—and the humor, subtlety, and irony with which she creates those portraits—is ample evidence of the groundbreaking work she carried out in Asian American short fiction. Elizabeth Ammons argues, for example, "That Sui Sin Far invented herself—created her own voice—out of such deep silencing and systematic racist repression was one of the triumphs of American literature at the turn of the century" (105).

Much of the critical response to Sui Sin Far's fiction explores the ways in which she incorporates autobiographical material into her short stories. The most comprehensive study is Annette White-Parks's 1995 *Sui Sin Far/Edith Maude Eaton: A Literary Biography*, a groundbreaking work that bridges the biographical and the literary in Sui Sin Far's life. White-Parks's extensive archival research in Montreal uncovered a great deal of previously uncollected non-fiction work of Sui Sin Far's as well as biographical details about her years in Canada. White-Parks and other critics focus on the ways in which Sui Sin Far explores her own biracial identity and bicultural existence in her fictional stories. Ling and White-Parks note that Sui Sin Far portrays "the between-worlds plight of the racially or culturally mixed person" ("Introduction," *Mrs. Spring Fragrance and Other Writings* 6), and Elizabeth Ammons claims that Sui Sin Far searches for ways to represent "an identity that is both Chinese and Western" (108). Essays by Roh-Spaulding and Vanessa Holford Diana also focus on Sui Sin Far's treatment of mixed race identity and the negotiation of bicultural consciousness. Roh-Spaulding argues that Sui Sin Far resists rigid racial designation "by continually shifting her authorial stance in relation to a Chinese American ethnic *locale*, by creating hybrid motifs and characters, and by depicting Eurasian consciousness as one that wavers between but remains permanently resistant to either culturally-imposed notion of categorical purity, Anglo or Chinese" (156).

Because she was the first Chinese American woman to publish short fiction in North America, Sui Sin Far had to invent ways to address white readers effectively so as to change their minds about the Chinese of whom she wrote. White-Parks calls this strategy "decentering whiteness" in an essay entitled "A Reversal of American Concepts of 'Otherness.' " White-Parks notes when readers encounter "interactions between Chinese and White North Americans across racial borders, . . . Chinese North Americans repeatedly occupy the fictional center, taking on the role of insiders, while White North Americans shift to the periphery, becoming the outsiders, or 'Other' " ("A Reversal" 18). In their discussion of American women regionalists, Judith Fetterley and Marjorie Pryse argue that, like other writers in this tradition, Sui Sin Far creates a narrator whose "stance of careful listening fosters an empathic connection between the reader of the work and the lives the work depicts" ("Introduction," *American Women Regionalists* xvii). This decentering of whiteness while simultaneously foregrounding empathy as a reading stance is necessary because Sui Sin Far's fiction focuses on Americans who had—before she wrote—little voice in American literature. Positing the "Other" as speaking voice, Sui Sin Far dramatizes the injustices that plagued race relations in North America at the turn of the last century; Ling characterizes Sui Sin Far's writing as among one of "the earliest attempts by Asian subalterns to speak for themselves" ("Reading" 70).

One mode of oppositional representation that becomes clear across Sui Sin Far's entire project of resistance writing is her use of what White-Parks calls "trickster strategies." Just as Sui Sin Far suggests links among various short stories by using repeated names or parallel circumstances, as in the twinned characters named Pan or Carson mentioned above, Sui Sin Far also uses repetition across genres. White-Parks notes that Sui Sin Far "shuffles 'facts' between stories and enters or exits at will, . . . anonymously, in masquerade as a character, and invisible to an audience that does not know the difference"; this "shuffling" forms "a common thread among journalism, essays, and short stories across her career" ("We Wear" 7). Complicating the "shuffling" and repetition that characterizes Sui Sin Far's body of work is a shifting of narrative perspective that illustrates the complexity of multiracial identity. Roh-Spaulding explains, "the short story was the perfect genre in which to illustrate a 'wavering' identity, because Eaton could shift her authorial stance quite often, both from story to story and within stories" (173). White-Parks describes the multivoiced *Mrs. Spring Fragrance* as enacting what Mikhail Bakhtin has termed carnivalized discourse, as is evident in the collection's "subversive, anarchic" character (*Sui Sin Far* 204).

Feminist analyses of Sui Sin Far's fiction explore her representation of the interlocking systems of oppression that function in North America, demanding that we consider Sui Sin Far's interest in class conflict and sexual oppression as integral to her analysis of racial oppression. Elizabeth Ammons's "Audacious Words," White-Parks's "Intersections of Gender and Cultural Difference," and Ling's "Reading Her/stories Against His/stories in Early Chinese American Literature" are three such essays. Of the short fiction included in *Mrs. Spring Fragrance and Other Writings*, the "adult" stories in the Mrs. Spring Fragrance section have received most critical attention. But Ling argues that " 'What about the Cat?' and 'The Heart's Desire' may be read as stories of female independence and friendship" ("Introduction," *Mrs. Spring Fragrance and Other Writings* 15).

◆ BIBLIOGRAPHY

Works by Sui Sin Far (Edith Maude Eaton)

Eaton, Edith. *Mrs. Spring Fragrance*. Chicago: A. C. McClurg, 1912.
Eaton, Edith/Sui Sin Far. *Mrs. Spring Fragrance and Other Writings*. Amy Ling and Annette White-Parks, eds. Urbana: University of Illinois Press, 1995.

Studies of Sui Sin Far (Edith Maude Eaton)

Ammons, Elizabeth. "Audacious Words: Sui Sin Far's *Mrs. Spring Fragrance*." In *Conflicting Stories: American Women Writers at the Turn into the Twentieth Century*. New York: Oxford University Press, 1991, 105–20.
Diana, Vanessa Holford. "Biracial / Bicultural Identity in the Writings of Sui Sin Far." *MELUS* 26.2 (Summer 2001): 159–86.

Dong, Lorraine, and Marlon K. Hom. "Defiance or Perpetuation: An Analysis of Characters in *Mrs. Spring Fragrance*." In *Chinese America: History and Perspectives*. Him Mark Lai, Ruthanne Lum McCunn, and Judy Yung, eds. San Francisco: Chinese Historical Society of America, 1987, 139–68.

Doyle, James. "Sui Sin Far and Onoto Watanna: Two Early Chinese-Canadian Authors." *Canadian Literature* 140 (Spring 1994): 50–58.

Ferens, Dominika. "Tangled Kites: Sui Sin Far's Negotiations with Race and Readership." *Amerasia Journal* 25.2 (1999): 116–44.

Fetterley, Judith, and Marjorie Pryse. "Introduction." In *American Women Regionalists 1850–1910: A Norton Anthology*. Judith Fetterley and Marjorie Pryse, eds. New York: Norton, 1995, xi–xx.

Leonard, Shannon T. "Edith Maude Eaton (Sui Sin Far)." In *Asian American Autobiographers: A Bio-Bibliographical Critical Sourcebook*. Guiyou Huang, ed. Westport, CT: Greenwood Press, 2001, 77–81.

Ling, Amy. "Writers with a Cause: Sui Sin Far and Han Suyin." *Women's Studies International Forum* 9.4 (1986): 411–19.

———. *Between Worlds: Women Writers of Chinese Ancestry*. New York: Pergamon, 1990.

———. "Creating One's Self: The Eaton Sisters." In *Reading the Literatures of Asian America*. Shirley Geok-lin Lim and Amy Ling, eds. Philadelphia: Temple University Press, 1992, 305–18.

———. "Reading Her/stories Against His/stories in Early Chinese American Literature." In *American Realism and the Canon*. Tom Quirk and Gary Scharnhorst, eds. Newark: University of Delaware Press, 1994, 69–86.

McCann, Sean. "Connecting Links: The Anti-Progressivism of Sui Sin Far." *Yale Journal of Criticism* 12.1 (Spring 1999): 73–88.

Roh-Spaulding, Carol. " 'Wavering' Images: Mixed-Race Identity in the Stories of Edith Eaton/Sui Sin Far." In *Ethnicity and the American Short Story*. Julie Brown, ed. New York: Garland, 1997, 155–76.

Solberg, S. E. "Sui Sin Far/Edith Eaton: First Chinese-American Fictionist." *MELUS* 8.1 (Spring 1981): 27–39.

White-Parks, Annette. "We Wear the Mask: Sui Sin Far as One Example of Trickster Authorship." In *Tricksterism in Turn-of-the-Century American Literature: A Multicultural Perspecitve*. Elizabeth Ammons and Annette White-Parks, eds. Hanover, NH: University Press of New England, 1994, 1–20.

———. "A Reversal of American Concepts of 'Otherness' in Fiction by Sui Sin Far." *MELUS* 20.1 (Spring 1995): 17–34.

———. *Sui Sin Far / Edith Maude Eaton: A Literary Biography*. Urbana: University of Illinois Press, 1995.

———. "Intersections of Gender and Cultural Difference as Both Impediment and Inspiration to Sui Sin Far, a Canadian/American Writer." In *Intersexions: Issues of Race and Gender in Canadian Women's Writing*. Coomi S. Vevaina and Barbara Godard, eds. New Delhi: Creative, 1996, 197–218.

Yin, Xiao-Huang. "Between the East and West: Sui Sin Far—The First Chinese American Woman Writer." *Arizona Quarterly* 7 (Winter 1991): 49–84.

Yu, Ning. "Fanny Fern and Sui Sin Far: The Beginning of an Asian American Voice." *Women and Language* 19.2 (Fall 1996): 44–47.

WINNIFRED EATON
(1875–1954)

Jean Lee Cole

♦ **BIOGRAPHY**

Winnifred Eaton (née Lillie Winnifred) was born in Montreal, Canada, the eighth of fourteen children of an English father, Edward, and Chinese mother, Grace Trefusis. Although she received only a cursory formal education, she embarked on her writing career at a young age, publishing her first short story, according to her own report, in the Montreal *Metropolitan Magazine* in her teens. In the mid-1890s, she briefly worked as a reporter for the Jamaican newspaper, *Gall's News Letter*, and by the end of the decade she was living in Chicago, writing for major magazines such as *Ladies Home Journal*, and had published her first novel, *Miss Nume of Japan* (1899), using the pseudonym that she would use, off and on, throughout her career: Onoto Watanna.

The first decade of the twentieth century was Eaton's most prolific. During this time, she published eight of her sixteen known novels, the vast majority of her short stories, and numerous magazine articles on Japanese subjects. By the middle of the decade she had become something of a literary celebrity. She achieved her greatest popular success with her second novel, *A Japanese Nightingale* (1901), which went through multiple editions, was eventually translated into at least four languages, and was adapted for the Broadway stage (1903) and the screen (1918).

In New York, she met and married her first husband, Bertrand Babcock, and had four children. By mid-decade, the marriage had soured, and she divorced him in 1917. Eaton married her second husband, Frank Reeve, less than two months after her divorce from Babcock was finalized, and with him she moved to a farm outside of Calgary, Alberta. Although she embraced her new role as the farmer's (and later, rancher's) wife, Eaton continued writing, publishing several stories in Canadian magazines and writing scenarios for the nascent New York film industry; between 1921 and 1925, she received her first screenwriting credit and published her last three novels.

In 1924, weary of the isolation of the ranch, she moved with her three surviving children (leaving Frank behind) back to New York, where she actively pursued a career writing for film. Eventually, she was hired as a scenario editor at Universal Pictures, who moved her to their new Hollywood studios in 1925. She received credit for only five films, even though her collected papers contain stories, adaptations, scenarios, and dialogue for dozens, if not hundreds, of others, written for MGM and Twentieth-Century Fox as well as Universal, with whom she had an on-again, off-again relationship. By 1931, her Hollywood career had played out, and she moved back to Calgary, where she lived the life of "Mrs. Frank Reeve," a society maven and supporter of Canadian art and artists, until her death in 1954.

Eaton's stories, never collected or anthologized during her lifetime, nevertheless received a wide readership. They were published in American mainstream periodicals that included *Ladies Home Journal*, *Frank Leslie's Popular Monthly*, *Harper's Monthly*, *Century Magazine*, *The Saturday Evening Post*, and *Lippincott's*, as well as Canadian magazines such as *Maclean's*. She continued to publish short stories in American and Canadian magazines through the 1920s; it is assumed that only a small portion of her total short story output has been recovered. A selected anthology of her short stories and magazine articles is currently being reissued by the University of Illinois Press.

◆ MAJOR WORKS AND THEMES

Eaton adopted the pseudonym Onoto Watanna early on and wrote under it for the bulk of her career (twelve of her novels, and almost all of her short stories, were written as Onoto Watanna; *Me* and *Marion* were published anonymously, and *Cattle* and *His Royal Nibs* were published under her real name). As Watanna, Eaton posed as a Japanese-born, half-Japanese descendent of samurai, even though she was in fact half-Chinese, had never been to Japan, and did not speak the Japanese language. In this guise, Eaton achieved popularity writing in the "Japoniste" style made popular by Pierre Loti (*Madame Chrysanthemum*, 1887) and John Luther Long (*Madame Butterfly*, 1898), who depicted flighty and flirtatious Japanese heroines in love with white Western men.

Eaton's Japanese heroines, however, were marked by several differences: for one, a significant proportion of her heroines were of mixed race (in *Sunny-San* [1922] the title character is only one-eighth Asian, and has blue eyes and blond hair), and more significantly, they resist the image of the exotic sex-toy promulgated by Long and, especially, Loti. Interestingly, many of Eaton's short story heroines were named "Kiku," the Japanese word for chrysanthemum, thus directly connecting her work to Loti's. Perhaps her strongest statement against the geisha stereotype occurs in one of her earliest stories, "A Half-Caste" (1899). The Kiku in this story is a half-Japanese tea-house girl who catches the eye of a middle-aged American man, Hilton. Unbeknownst to him, she is, in fact, his daughter—a daughter he has never seen, since he abandoned his then-wife before Kiku's birth (following the plot lines of both *Madame Chrysanthemum* and *Madame Butterfly*). When she discovers the truth, Kiku decides to encourage Hilton's interest, and then reject him, in order to avenge her mother: she wants to "mek [him] suffer lig her" (496). When she reveals to Hilton the incestuous nature of his "love" for her, he is duly shocked and repentant. Despite his remorse, however, she leaves him "with the same still look of despair on his face and the pitiless sun beating on the fields" (496).

Here and elsewhere in her short stories, Eaton probed themes that she tended to treat obliquely in her novels. Whereas a number of her novel heroines, like Kiku, were "half-castes," none of them confronted so directly the tragic repercussions of miscegenation. Other stories, including "Two Converts" (1901), "Kirishima-San (1901), "A Contract" (1902), "Miss Lily and Miss Chrysanthemum" (1903), "The Loves of Sakura Jiro and the Three-Headed Maid" (1903), and "An Unexpected Grandchild" (1909), explored other aspects of Anglo-Asian intermarriage and biraciality. To be sure, her characterizations of Asians did not always transcend racist stereotyping. In "Two Converts" and "An Unexpected Grandchild," for example, the female Japanese characters deviously manipulate the gullible, well-meaning white characters for their own ends, and in "Lend Me Your Title" (1919), the sole Japanese character, Count Ichi, is depicted in singularly demeaning terms even though he provides the story's hero with the means to marry his beloved. In all of these stories, the speech of nearly all of the Japanese characters is rendered in an exaggerated pidgin dialect that strikes modern ears as alienating, if not downright offensive or even ludicrous.

Another complication in assessing Eaton's career and her relationship to other Asian American writers is the fact that she did not always write about Asians or about racial themes. In "Delia Dissents" (1908), for example, she takes the perspective of an Irish domestic, whose coarsely rendered brogue is just as exaggerated as the pidgin of her Japanese heroines. And in other stories she does not use dialect at all. In "Margot" (1901), she tells the poignant story of an isolated mountain girl who discovers her talent for music; in "Eyes That Saw Not" (1902), the story centers on a blind writer whose wife, through sheer love of him, replaces his stilted, turgid prose with her own, to the great advantage of his career; "Elspeth" (1923) depicts a hard-working mother's anguish when her headstrong daughter elopes at the age of sixteen. Taken in sum, women's empowerment—in romantic and sexual relationships, as working women, or as artists—as well as a critical approach to class are in fact themes more consistent across Eaton's work than race and ethnicity.

Generically and stylistically, Eaton's work also lacks consistency. As a writer working in popular genres, Eaton moved with apparent ease between melodrama, domestic farce, historical fiction, sentimentalism, realism, and torrid romance. Although her stylistic versatility enabled her to support herself and her family solely through the income she received for her writing, it has made it difficult for scholars to place her within a distinctly Asian American literary tradition.

◆ CRITICAL RECEPTION

Eaton, along with her sister Edith, was, in effect, "rediscovered" during the late 1970s by Asian American literary scholars Amy Ling and S. E. Solberg. Ling in particular did much to generate interest in the two sisters, especially Edith, whose Chinese pseudonym, Sui Sin Far, and Chinese-American-centered subject matter did not cause the same concerns with ethnic and literary authenticity that Winnifred's work did. In an early article, Ling described Winnifred as an "ethnic chameleon" who capitalized on the literary market to succeed—if at the expense of her Chinese identity. Ling and others also described Eaton as a "trickster" figure who subverted her Japanese role to comment critically on American attitudes toward the Japanese and Asians in general (Ling, *Between Worlds*; Matsukawa; Honey; Birchall).

More recently, scholars have considered Eaton's work outside of traditional ideas regarding ethnic and authorial authenticity that clearly do not apply to Eaton's work. Tomo Hattori, for example, argues that Eaton's autobiographical novel, *Me*, is valuable precisely because of Eaton's adoption and manipulation of a multiplicity of identities. In the two published book-length studies of her work, Dominika Ferens examines Eaton in relation to the discourse emerging from the developing field of ethnography, while Jean Lee Cole discusses Eaton's work in relation to turn-of-the-century American literature and history.

Within the criticism, Eaton's novels have received far more attention than her short stories, in large part because of their inaccessibility. However, as Ferens, Cole, and Birchall have shown in their work, the stories provide different and important contexts for Eaton's work that will be well worth exploring by future scholars.

◆ BIBLIOGRAPHY

Works by Winnifred Eaton

Short Stories

"A Poor Devil." *Metropolitan Magazine*, clipping, n.d. (1890s) Box 14, Winnifred Eaton Reeve Fonds, Special Collections, University of Calgary Library, Calgary, Alberta, Canada.

"A Half-Caste." *Frank Leslie's Popular Monthly* (September 1898): 489–96.

"Two Converts." *Harper's Monthly* (September 1901): 585–89. Rpt. in *Nineteenth-Century American Women Writers: An Anthology.* Karen L. Kilcup, ed. Cambridge, MA: Blackwell, 1997, 571–76.

"Kirishima-san." *The Idler* (November 1901): 315–21.

"Margot." *Frank Leslie's Popular Monthly* (December 1901): 202–9.

"A Contract." *Frank Leslie's Popular Monthly* 54.4 (August 1902): 370–77.

"Eyes That Saw Not." With Bertrand Babcock. *Harper's Monthly* (June 1902): 30–38.

"Miss Lily and Miss Chrysanthemum." *Ladies Home Journal* (August 1903): 11–12.

"The Loves of Sakura Jiro and the Three-Headed Maid." *Century Magazine* (March 1903): 755–60. Rpt. in *Nineteenth-Century American Women Writers*, Kilcup, ed., 576–81.

"The Wrench of Chance." *Harper's Weekly* (October 20, 1906): 1494–96, 1505; (October 27, 1906): 1531–33.

"Manoeuvres of O-yasu-san." *Saturday Evening Post* (January 25, 1908): 9–11, 22.

"Delia Dissents." *Saturday Evening Post* (August 1908): 22–23.

"A Daughter of Two Lands." *Red Book Magazine* (November 1909): 33–48.

"An Unexpected Grandchild." *Lippincott's Monthly* (December 1909): 689–96.

"The Marriage of Okiku-San." *Red Book Magazine* (June 1910): 254–63.

"The Marriage of Jinyo." *Red Book Magazine* (February 1912): 740–44.

"Lend Me Your Title." *Maclean's Magazine* (February 1919): 13, 14, 72–74; (March 1919): 16, 18–19, 66–69.

"Other People's Troubles: An Antidote to Your Own." *Farm and Ranch Review* (February–August 1919): n.p.

"Elspeth." *The Quill* (January 1923): 23–30.

"Because We Were Lonely." *True Story* (April 1933): 28–30, 92–96.

Novels

Miss Nume of Japan. Chicago: Rand, McNally, 1899. Rpt. Baltimore, MD: Johns Hopkins University Press, 1999.

A Japanese Nightingale. New York: Harper and Brothers, 1901. Rpt. New Brunswick, NJ: Rutgers University Press, 2002.

The Wooing of Wistaria. New York: Macmillan, 1902.

Heart of Hyacinth. New York: Harper and Brothers, 1903. Rpt., Seattle: University of Washington Press, 2000.

The Love of Azalea. New York: Dodd, Mead, 1904.

Daughters of Nijo. New York: Harper and Brothers, 1904.

A Japanese Blossom. New York: Harper and Brothers, 1906.

Tama. New York: Harper and Brothers, 1910.

The Diary of Delia. New York: Doubleday, Page, and Co., 1907.

The Honorable Miss Moonlight. New York: Harper and Brothers, 1912.

Miss Spring Morning. Serialized in *The Blue Book* (January 1915): 666–720.

Marion (originally serialized in *Hearst's Magazine*, 1916). New York: W. J. Watt, 1916.

Sunny-San. New York: Doran, 1922.

Cattle. New York: W. J. Watt, 1924.

His Royal Nibs. New York: W. J. Watt, 1925.

Autobiographical Pieces and Selected Non-fiction

"The Japanese in America." *Eclectic Magazine* 148.2 (February 1907): 100–104.
"A Neighbor's Garden, My Own, and A Dream One." *Good Housekeeping* 46.4 (April 1908): 347–53; 46.5 (May 1908): 485–90.
A Chinese-Japanese Cookbook. With Ara Bosse. Chicago and New York: Rand, McNally, 1914.
Me: A Book of Remembrance (originally appeared in *Century Magazine*, 1915). New York: The Century Co, 1915. Rpt. Jackson: University Press of Mississippi, 1997.
"Starving and Writing in New York." *Maclean's Magazine* (October 15, 1922): 66–67.
"Butchering Brains: An Author in Hollywood Is as a Lamb in an Abattoir." *Motion Picture Magazine* (1928): 28–29+.

Film Scripts, Adaptations, and Scenarios

Adaptation for *False Kisses* (Universal), 1921.
Dialogue for *The Mississippi Gambler* (Universal) (with H. H. Van Loan), 1929.
Scenario and dialogue for *Shanghai Lady* (Universal) (with Houston Branch), 1929.
Adaptation for *East Is West* (Universal) (with Tom Reed), 1930.
Adaptation and dialogue for *Undertow* (Universal) (with Edward T. Lowe, Jr.), 1930.
Adaption and dialogue for *Young Desire* (Universal) (with Matt Taylor), 1930.

Selected Studies of Winnifred Eaton

Birchall, Diana. *Onoto Watanna: The Story of Winnifred Eaton.* Champaign: University of Illinois Press, 2001.
Cole, Jean Lee. *The Literary Voices of Winnifred Eaton: Redefining Ethnicity and Authenticity.* New Brunswick, NJ: Rutgers University Press, 2002.
Doyle, James. "Sui Sin Far and Onoto Watanna: Two Early Chinese-Canadian Authors." *Canadian Literature* 140 (Spring 1994): 50–58.
Ferens, Dominika. *Edith and Winnifred Eaton: The Uses of Ethnography in Turn-of-the-Century Asian American Literature.* Champaign: University of Illinois Press, 2002.
Hattori, Tomo. "Model Minority Discourse and Asian American Jouis-Sense." *differences* 11.2 (1999): 228–47.
Honey, Maureen, with Heidi L. M. Jacobs and Jennifer Putzi. "Onoto Watanna." In *Dictionary of Literary Biography*, vol. 221: *American Women Prose Writers, 1870–1920*. Sharon M. Harris, ed. Detroit: Gale Group, 2000, 103–12.
Ling, Amy. "Winnifred Eaton: Ethnic Chameleon and Popular Success." *MELUS* 11.3 (1984): 5–15.
———. *Between Worlds: Women Writers of Chinese Ancestry.* New York: Pergamon Press, 1990.
———. "Chinese American Women Writers: The Tradition behind Maxine Hong Kingston." In *Redefining American Literary History.* A. LaVonne Ruoff and Jerry Ward, Jr., eds. New York: MLA, 1990, 219–36.
———. "Creating One's Self: The Eaton Sisters." In *Reading the Literatures of Asian*

America. Shirley Geok-Lin Lim and Amy Ling, eds. Philadelphia: Temple University Press, 1992, 305–18.

Matsukawa, Yuko. "Cross-Dressing and Cross-Naming: Decoding Onoto Watanna." In *Tricksterism in Turn-of-the-Century U.S. Literature: A Multicultural Perspective*. Elizabeth Ammons and Annette White-Parks, eds. Hanover, NH: University Press of New England, 1994, 106–25.

Shea, Pat. "Winnifred Eaton and the Politics of Miscegenation in Popular Fiction." *MELUS* 22.2 (Summer 1997): 19–33.

Solberg, S. E. "Sui Sin Far/Edith Eaton: First Chinese-American Fictionist." *MELUS* 8.1 (Spring 1981): 27–39.

JESSICA HAGEDORN
(1949–   )

Aiping Zhang

◆ BIOGRAPHY

A Filipino American short story writer, novelist, poet, performance artist, and songwriter, Jessica Hagedorn was born in the Santa Mesa section of Manila, Philippines in 1949. She grew up during the chaotic years of the Ferdinand Marcos dictatorship. In 1963, she immigrated to the United States with her mother.

While attending a Catholic school back in the Philippines, Hagedorn was drawn to various aspects of American culture—theater, radio serials, music, Hollywood movies, and literature. Living through her teenage years in San Francisco in the early 1960s, Hagedorn attended San Francisco's Lowell High School, a nationally noted academic institution, and had a real dose of multiculturalism in America. She was interested in rock and roll, black culture, especially black soul music. Such an across-the-board immersion seems to anticipate Hagedorn's long-term passion for a multiple cultural production in her future career. While in high school, though, she often skipped classes to cope with her feeling of alienation. Her English literature teacher somehow nurtured in her a strong passion for art and writing. She graduated from high school in 1967, four years after her arrival in America.

Even though she never went to college, Hagedorn kept writing on her own all along and spent a lot of time with a group of black and Chicana women writers and musicians. Her participation in San Francisco's Kearny Street Writers' Workshop was essential to her pursuit of a literary career. There, she had her first exposure to Asian American history and literature, shared her writing ideas with other writers of color, and got involved in the turmoil, excitement, and changes of the late 1960s. During the 1970s, especially after she formed her band, the "West Coast Gangster Choir," renamed in New York as the "Gangster Choir" in 1978, music consumed most of her time. In the mid-1980s, she realized that she could not lead a band, do theater, be a mother, and write literature all at once. Soon, she gave up her band, but kept her passion for writing, music, and theater. Hagedorn started her writing career with poetry. She had her poetry suite "The Death of Anna May Wong" published in an anthology, *Four Young Women: Poems*, edited by the San Francisco poet Kenneth Rexroth in 1973. Her own collection of poetry, plus one short fiction, *Dangerous Music*, appeared in 1975. A similar collection of both poetry and a prose work, *Pet Food and Tropical Apparitions*, came out in 1981. Despite her busy commitment to family, theater, and music in New York, Hagedorn always managed to find time for her poetry and prose during the 1980s. Her reputation as a writer began to grow because her poetry and short fiction were published in a number of anthologies of Asian American, ethnic, and women's literature.

Her first full-length novel, *Dogeaters*, appeared in 1990. The novel's mordant exploration of poverty, commercialism, rampant corruption, and postcolonial disintegration in the Philippines under the Marcos regime brought Hagedorn instant success. She received a nomination for the National Book Award and won the American Book Award from the Before Columbus Foundation. In 1993, she published *Danger and Beauty*, a collection of twenty-four years' worth of poetry and prose, and edited *Charlie Chan Is Dead: An Anthology of Contemporary Asian American Fiction*. Her second novel, *The Gangster of Love*, came out three years later.

Hagedorn attributes her early inspiration to her mother who was a painter and to a maternal grandfather who was a teacher and an accomplished writer. She writes in her introduction to *Charlie Chan Is Dead*, "Everyone in my family enjoyed books. I had always been encouraged to write. . . . Poems were my way out of isolation. I read anything I could get my hands on" (xxv). For her growth as a writer, she often cites Gabriel García Márquez, James Baldwin, Ishmael Reed, the Beat poets, Bienvenido Santos, and Toni Morrison as her literary heroes and inspirations.

Hagedorn's poems, scripts, essays, and fiction have been anthologized widely. Many of her non-fiction articles, interviews, and reviews have been published in the *New York Times Sunday Magazine*, *Harper's Bazaar*, *USA Weekend*, and the *Village Voice*. She is the recipient of many awards and fellowships, including a 1994 Lila Wallace-Reader's Digest Fund Writer's Award and a 1995 National Endowment for the Arts Creative Writing Fellowship. She has been living in New York since the late 1970s.

◆ MAJOR WORKS AND THEMES

Hagedorn's major accomplishments came from her novels, but despite its relatively low quantity, her short fiction often displays an early glimpse of those distinctive features that the reader would eventually discover in her novels. Her second book, *Pet Food and Tropical Apparitions*, mixes a novella with her seven musical poems, a unique form that Hagedorn continues to use in her later publications. Critics note that this novella, *Pet Food*, contains the basic ingredients for the story in *Dogeaters*, such as the grim voice of the narrator, surreal melodrama, desperate characters, and bizarre scenes.

The novella features a young writer, George Sand, as the first-person narrator. She is an immigrant Filipina who indulges in the "avant garde" lifestyle on the streets of San Francisco and works frantically on a Broadway musical. Her long-time friend, Boggie, is gay but bordering on straight. Since George's family is relatively affluent, they do not feel as "foreign" as people like Boggie do. Boggie laments his father's broken English and his worn-out hands, and he calls his parents "permanent immigrants in this lousy place" (36). George's mother does not like Boggie because he is gay and is an "American born Pinoy with no class" (16). It is a story that encompasses all the common but still horrifying ingredients of life in today's American city: sex, drugs, isolation, exile, violence, and murder. It draws heavily upon Hagedorn's own rough passage into life in San Francisco and her pursuit of a double career in writing and performance art.

Danger and Beauty is a collection of selected poetry and short fiction from her early poetry; poetry and short story from her first published work, *Dangerous Music*; poetry and prose (the novella) originally published in 1981 as *Pet Food and Tropical Apparitions*; and new previously unpublished material written between 1981 and 1992, including a few that Hagedorn called "performance texts." It received rave reviews for its juxtaposition of inspirations and images from diverse literary and pop culture sources. Literary experimentations are both its primary intention and characteristic. One of them is her creative way to bring together mainstream pop culture and ethnic culture.

Hagedorn's major achievement in short story writing is rightly the groundbreaking anthology, *Charlie Chan Is Dead: An Anthology of Contemporary Asian American Fiction*. The first anthology of Asian American fiction published by a major press, it collects the works of forty-eight writers representing a range of cultural and ethnic backgrounds, ages, and literary styles that is wider than any similar anthology of Asian American literature before.

In her introduction to the anthology, Hagedorn mischievously defines the intended scope of the selection herself: "Asian American literature? Too confirming a term, maybe. World literature? Absolutely." She claims, "In this collection, some of us retell familial and cultural mythology, yet we also write out of more personal and terrifying truths" (xxx). She did not "impose" any particular themes on her writers when she solicited submissions. On the contrary, she told them that she "was definitely more interested in 'riskier' work" and "was eager to subvert the very definition of what was considered 'fiction' " (xxx). A reader might notice an excerpt from *Itsuka*, a novel by Joy

Kogawa, a Canadian resident, in the anthology. This selection proves that Hagedorn has even allowed the notion of "Asian American" to be expanded in her anthology.

The selections in the anthology are largely drawn from three representative groups of writers: the old pioneers of Asian American literature, the well-established writers of today, and the emerging young writers who had their stories published in a major collection for the first time. Stories by Jose Garcia Villa, Toshio Mori, Bienvenido Santos, and Carlos Bulosan capture their heart-wrenching tales of struggle, bewilderment, discrimination, and disillusionment; stories by popular writers like Maxine Hong Kingston, Amy Tan, David Mura, Bharati Mukherjee, and Gish Jen represent their share of the pain, frustration, and triumph in breaking into the circle of today's American literature; stories by young talents incorporate a new line of ingenuity, diversity, and vitality into the fast growing canon of Asian American fiction.

Glancing through the table of contents, one will surely be struck by the absence of a prominent figure in Asian American literature, Frank Chin, who produced the first major anthology of Asian American literature, *Aiiieeeee!*, in 1974. According to Hagedorn, Chin declined to be included in her anthology due to his continuous attempt to distance himself from what he called "fake" Asian American writers who are in the practice of distorting facts through myth fabrication. Yet, Hagedorn still mentions Chin's story "Goong Hai Fot Choy" as one of her first favorable readings, and cites Chin's anthology as her source of influence.

Hagedorn has one story of her own, "Film Noir," in the anthology. It is, as she indicates right under its title, "an excerpt from a novel-in-progress" (122). The story starts with a scene on a hot and humid day, in which Marlon Rivera, a dancer in a show group, greets his neighbor, Isabel L'Ange, who is an old "B-movie temptress," a "reclusive widow" of a famous director, and Marlon's "fantasy mother" (125). Marlon and Isabel drink and get high together whenever he is not on the road. Ostensibly, the story might seem simple in language and fragmentary in plot, but its thematic implications are quite intricate. It offers much more than just the empty chats over rum between the two characters: Marlon's niece, Raquel, and her boyfriend are dreaming of living in Malibu; Marlon himself is trying to come to terms with his breakup with his lover, Stephen; having outlived her husband and daughter, Isabel is anxiously seeking a little more companionship than her five cats can offer. By shifting the narrative focus between Marlon, Raquel, and Isabel, Hagedorn delineates a detached and desolate world in which three generations of Filipinos attempt to make some sense out of their senseless life. The story is characteristic of Hagedorn's poignancy and sensibility in tackling the touchy themes of nostalgia, dislocation, homosexuality, and identity conflict.

Another story by Hagedorn, "Black: Her Story," which appeared in *Ploughshares* in 1993, concerns the same issues. Though sketchy in its stream-of-consciousness narrative, this brief story presents a less subtle, but more cynical, inquiry about the purpose of being an undesirable Filipino in America and challenges the true nature of the American Dream. The first-person narrator raises a series of questions: "What is a Filipino?" "Does America live up or down to my expectations? Is it the Hollywood of our colonized imaginations?" "Where do we live now? Here or there? Are you disappointed? Have your dreams and ways of speaking become too precise and American?" (174). Given the monologue-like structure of the story, these questions are mostly rhetorical; they sound more like pleas, laments, and even denunciations.

◆ CRITICAL RECEPTION

Most, if not all, of Hagedorn's stories are urban-centered and set in America or the Philippines. Her stories, as Susan Evangelista comments on *Dogeaters*, carry "a strong sense of magic realism, of bizarre characters and strange co-incidences, of real life gone unreal with a sudden verbal twist" (41). Some critics believe that Hagedorn is often too extreme in dramatizing the dilemma of having a dual cultural heritage and stretching the immigrants' life into disjuncture and irrelevance in a world of chaos, indifference, bias, and cruelty. Hagedorn herself, though, insists that her theme calls for such a seemingly disjointed narrative form. In a conversation with Jessie Mangaliman, a reviewer of *Dogeaters* for *Newsday*, Hagedorn explains, "I wanted the form to capture that chaos, that fragmented feeling . . . which I completely understand. It's not weird to me. I straddle two worlds and I do so happily. All of that feeds the art. It enriches your imagination and your understanding of people. It makes your world bigger" (3).

Hagedorn's *Pet Food and Tropical Apparitions* and *Danger and Beauty* have not attracted much attention from critics. Those who reviewed these two collections, however, offered very positive assessments on her daring move to project herself as an "eclectic" and "experimental" artist. In analyzing the narrative structure of the novella, which is included in both collections, Oscar V. Campomanes praises the way in which the story is "driven by two memorable cinematic moments": a starlet's recounting of a sordid sexual spree and the protagonist, George Sand's "morbid desire for patricide and suicide." Such a cinematic technique gives the story an effect of what critics called "cinematext" by creating a series of "character sketches" and an "ensemble of deftly-spliced 'rushes.' " "The cinematic metaphors," Campomanes suggests, "are apt since Hagedorn has acknowledged Manuel Puig as an influence and has now moved into video- and filmmaking" (371).

Other reviewers find some comparable features between Hagedorn's novels and short stories. As a short story writer, they believe, she has a sharp and credible vision, and her language is strong and visceral. Ellen Finnie Duranceau notes that "Hagedorn's major theme in *Danger and Beauty* is the disillusionment of immigrants," but it is "less penetrable" (114). Jean C. Fulton's review of *Danger and Beauty* gives high remarks to Hagedorn's novella, *Pet*

Food, for representing "an amalgam of Filipino roots and urban American experiences that never fully blends." Also, Fulton offers her keen observation on the musicality of Hagedorn's language. She eloquently declares, "music pulses here in her [Hagedorn's] language. The unconventional melodies may not suit everyone, but words rise boldly off the pages none the less, demanding to be heard."

As editor, all Hagedorn's concepts of and wishes for Asian American fiction have gone into the making of her anthology, *Charlie Chan Is Dead*. The anthology might not look as formal and massive as other standard anthologies for mainstream literature, but critics agree that its short length belies not only its two distinctive features, range and inclusiveness, but also its profound impact upon the future development of Asian American fiction. While the preface by Elaine Kim invites the reader to revisit the history and glory of Asian American literature, Hagedorn's introduction draws up a transparent framework for the reader to appreciate the rich traditions and the new inventions in Asian American fiction. As inventive as her other pieces of literature, Hagedorn's introduction often does not sound like one, yet it delivers much more than any conventional introduction can. It is witty, informative, and insightful; it is also personal, sincere, and engaging. It is, above all, an enlightening story about Hagedorn's growth as a writer and the growth of Asian American fiction as well.

Interpretations of the cryptically chosen title differ among the critics. Some see it as a bad idea, because they fear that it might invoke the long forgotten stereotypes against Asian Americans; others, such as Greg Choy, like it because it signifies the start of a new era for Asian American literature, an era "When the gaze is reversed and the stereotype deconstructed, then the creative possibilities, the contingencies of experience, and the agencies for self-expression and self-definition become boundless" (10).

Gerard Lim commends Hagedorn for constructing "a daring compilation which strikes the right balance between safe and dangerous, chummy and unfriendly, tame and thought-provoking" and for inventing "a self-determined banshee, hell-bent on enlarging the American consciousness so that Asian Pacific Americans are treated and appreciated as equals" (28). A few critics, however, have mixed views of her ambitious undertaking. Sven Birkerts, a reviewer for the *New York Times Book Review*, dislikes Hagedorn's selection from a broad spectrum of writers, accusing Hagedorn of turning "Asian American" into "a term so hospitable that half the world's population can squeeze in under its banner" (17).

Many critics believe that with this anthology Hagedorn wishes to take Asian American literature in a new direction. As she says in her introduction, she sees the anthology as a book that she "wanted to read that had never been available" to her (xxx), but she has no intention to put any didactic content in it. Hagedorn once said to Somini Sengupta, "You don't go to literature and say I need to feel good about my race. . . . I hate preaching" (C1).

Her aim is to produce an anthology that accurately reflects the long growth of Asian American fiction. Writers before the 1970s wrote their stories primarily from a historical perspective, lamenting their ill fortunes as outsiders and exploring their ways of fighting racism. Since then, Hagedorn insists, Asian American literature has evolved and changed drastically. More and more writers have represented the emotional and philosophical entanglements in individual lives not necessarily exclusive to Asian Americans. In doing so, their writing has ventured beyond the realm of the traditional Asian American fiction. Clearly, this is the rationale behind her anthology's emphasis on the diversity of perspective, voice, plot, characterization, and style. The difference, or gap, among the selections might seem a little extreme, but it is a top quality that Hagedorn intends to achieve.

◆ BIBLIOGRAPHY

Works by Jessica Hagedorn

Short Story

"Black: Her Story." *Ploughshares* 19.4 (Winter 1993–1994): 173–78.

Novels

Dogeaters. New York: Pantheon, 1990.
The Gangster of Love. Boston: Houghton Mifflin, 1996.

Poetry

Dangerous Music. San Francisco: Momo's Press, 1975.
Pet Food and Tropical Apparitions (including the novella, "Pet Food"). San Francisco: Momo's Press, 1981.
Danger and Beauty (the novella, "Pet Food," reprinted). New York: Penguin, 1993.

Edited Anthology

Charlie Chan Is Dead: An Anthology of Contemporary Asian American Fiction. New York: Penguin, 1993.

Play

With Thulani Nkabinad and Ntozake Shange, *Where the Mississippi Meets the Amazon*, produced in New York City, 1977.

Other

Burning Heart: A Portrait of the Philippines. Photographs by Marissa Roth. New York: Rizzoli Books International, 1999.

Studies of Jessica Hagedorn

Ancheta, Shirley. Rev. of *Danger and Beauty*. *Amerasia Journal* 20.1 (1994): 197–202.

Birkerts, Sven. Rev. of *Charlie Chan Is Dead*. *New York Times Book Review* (December 19, 1993): 17.

Bonetti, Kay. "Jessica Hagedorn." In *Conversations with American Novelists: The Best Interviews from The Missouri Review and the American Audio Prose Library*. Kay Bonetti, Greg Michalson, Speer Morgan, Jo Sapp, and Sam Stowers, eds. Columbia: University of Missouri Press, 1997, 217–33.

Campomanes, Oscar V. "Jessica Hagedorn." In *The Oxford Companion to Women's Writing in the United States*. Cathy N. Davidson and Linda Wagner-Martin, eds. New York: Oxford University Press, 1995, 370–71.

Campomanes, Oscar V., and N.V.M. Gonzalez. "Filipino American Literature." In *An Interethnic Companion to Asian American Literature*. King-Kok Cheung, ed. New York: Cambridge University Press, 1997, 62–124.

Casper, Leonard. "Bangungot and the Philippine Dream in Hagedorn." *Solidarity* 127 (July–September 1990): 152–57.

Choy, Greg. "Bursting from and into the Borders: *Charlie Chan Is Dead* Offers Wide Range of Stories from the Other Side." *International Examiner* 21.1 (January 18, 1994): 10.

Duranceau, Ellen Finnie. Review of *Danger and Beauty*. *Library Journal* 118.1 (January 1993): 114.

Evangelista, Susan. "Jessica Hagedorn and Manila Magic." *MELUS* 18.4 (Winter 1993/1994): 41–52.

Fulton, Jean C. "*Danger and Beauty*." *Magill Book Reviews* (February 1, 1994): n.p. Available at "EBSCO Database: "Academic Search Elite."

James, Caryn. Rev. of *Danger and Beauty*. *New York Times Book Review* (March 13, 1993): 12–13.

Lee, Rachel C. *The Americas of Asian American Literature: Gendered Fictions of Nation and Transnation*. Princeton, NJ: Princeton University Press, 1999.

Lim, Gerard. "Jessica Hagedorn Is Not Dead: *Charlie Chan Is Dead* Packages 48 Voices in Asian America," *Asian America: The Voice of Asian America* 15.36 (April 1, 1994): 28.

Mangaliman, Jessie. "Revenge of the Anti-Imelda." *Newsday*, Part II (April 10, 1990): 3.

Sengupta, Somini. "Cultivating the Art of the Mélange." *New York Times* (December 4, 1996): C1.

Uba, George. "Jessica Hagedorn." In *Asian American Poets: A Bio-Bibliographical Critical Sourcebook*. Guiyou Huang, ed. Westport, CT: Greenwood Press, 2002, 101–11.

GISH JEN
(1956–   )

Shuchen Susan Huang

◆ **BIOGRAPHY**

"Gish" is a pseudonym that Jen invented in high school. She sees her creation of the pen name "Gish Jen" as "a way of having [her] own identity" (Pearlman 45). Her real (first) name is Lillian. Born in Yonkers and growing up in Scarsdale, New York, Jen is the second of five children, all of whom attended Ivy League schools. She graduated from Harvard University in 1977 and went to the Stanford business school in 1979 but dropped out a year later. After returning from China where she taught English for a year, she entered the writing program at the University of Iowa and received her M.F.A. in 1983.

Becoming a writer is not an easy path for those with Asian immigrant parents who expect their children to pursue more "practical" careers. Jen is no exception. She tried pre-med and pre-law in college and later also studied toward an M.B.A. for a year. Her decision to attend an M.F.A. program and to pursue a writing career was at first greeted with strong disapproval from her parents. But her parents' objection was not the only challenge for the writer-to-be. Generally speaking, before the commercial success of Amy Tan's *Joy Luck Club* (1989), it was not easy for Asian American writers to have their works accepted by major publishers. As Jen started her writing career in the early 1980s, she had to tackle the problem of the publishers' preconception of what an Asian American writer should produce. When studying at Iowa, Jen did not think that her stories would "be published in a commercial magazine," because she was told that her stories were not "exotic" enough (R. Lee, "Gish Jen" 227).

Yet, Jen continued to write against all odds and her works have gradually met with increasing recognition. Before her first book, *Typical American* (1991), she had already won many awards for her short fiction, including the Henfield Foundation *Transatlantic Review* Award (1983), Massachusetts Artists Foundation Fellowship (1988), National Endowment for the Arts Award (1988), as well as prizes from the Katherine Ann Porter Contest (1987) and the Boston MBNA Urban-arts Project (1988). In addition, she received fellowships from the Guggenheim Foundation, the Bunting Institute of Radcliffe College, the MacDowell Colony, and other sources. When her novel *Typical American* was published, the *New York Times* named it "the Notable Book of the Year." Her second novel *Mona in the Promised Land* (1996) was listed by the *Los Angeles Times* as one of the top ten best books of 1996. Both of her novels were finalists for the National Book Critics' Circle Award. In 1999 she received a Lannan Literary Award for fiction.

Although her first short story collection *Who's Irish? Stories* (1999) appeared after the two novels, Jen has been writing short stories since the beginning of her writing career. Before *Typical American*, Jen had published many short stories in various literary magazines, including *Iowa Review, Fiction International, Yale Review, Southern Review, Nimrod, Atlantic Monthly*, and *New Yorker*. Many of her short stories have been included in numerous anthologies and college textbooks. For instance, "In the American Society" appears in books such as *New Worlds of Literature* (1989), *Imagining America: Stories from the Promised Land* (1991), and *The Oxford Book of Women's Writing in the US* (1995). "What Means Switch" appears in numerous anthologies, including *Growing up Asian American: Anthology* (1993), *Growing Up Female: Stories by Women Writers from the American Mosaic* (1993), and *Growing Up Ethnic in America: Contemporary Fiction about Learning to Be American* (1999). Moreover, "The Water Faucet Vision" and "Birthmates" are anthologized in *Best American Short Stories: 1988* and *Best American Short Stories: 1995*, respectively. Recently, "Birthmates" was canonized by John Updike in *The Best American Short Stories of the Century* (1999). The variety of these anthologies clearly attests that Jen is not seen merely as an ethnic writer or a woman writer but as an important contemporary American author.

◆ MAJOR WORKS AND THEMES

Jen established herself in the literary arena first as a novelist, not as a short story writer. She is best known for her two novels, *Typical American*, which chronicles a Chinese American family's pursuit of the American dream, and *Mona in the Promised Land*, which continues the saga of the family but focuses on the younger daughter Mona's attempt to convert to Judaism. Jen's short stories do not all deal with the Asian American subject or Asian American experiences. "Bellying Up" (1981) and "Eating Crazy" (1985) are two short tales that feature only white American characters. "The Small Concerns of Sparrows" (1982), on the other hand, is set in the People's Republic of China in 1958 and comprises only Chinese characters. Another early piece titled "The

White Umbrella" (1984), cast with the same characters as Jen's novels, portrays how the children respond to their mother's taking on a job to support the family.

"The White Umbrella" is not the only story that has the same characters as the novels. "In the American Society" and "The Water Faucet Vision," both of which are collected in *Who's Irish?*, are also cast with the same characters—the immigrant parents Ralph and Helen Chang, and their American-born children Callie and Mona. In these two stories, both told in the voice of the elder daughter Callie, the two children act as mediator and witness of the conflicts occurring between the father and mother, and between their parents and the "American" society. "In the American Society" consists of two parts: the first recounts how Ralph wants to run his pancake house like his "kingdom" in which he gives personal favors to his employees, hoping to win their loyalty in return; the second describes how the family, particularly Helen, endeavors to gain admittance to the elitist town country club. However, the Changs' application is given the same politely dismissive treatment as the African Americans'. While "In the American Society" concerns societal and cultural clashes, "The Water Faucet Vision" focuses on a marital conflict. The parents argue in Shanghainese, a Chinese dialect, which the children do not understand. As the marital cacophony evolves into physical violence, the elder daughter Callie, who is attending a Catholic girl's school and is fascinated by Catholicism, starts to practice ostentatious piety and prays for a miraculous reconciliation between her parents.

Like her novels, the majority of Jen's short fiction explores the themes of assimilation, identity, displacement, generational conflict, interracial relationships, and the American dream. In the short story collection *Who's Irish?* a particular thematic refrain runs through the eight pieces: Chinese immigrants and Chinese Americans are constantly measured against stereotypical notions of what Chinese (Americans) should be and how they should behave. On the other hand, though many of her stories focus on Chinese immigrants and Chinese American experiences, Jen's characters are not limited to Chinese immigrants and their American-born children. *Who's Irish?* comprises a wide range of characters, such as Irish American, African American, Latino American, Japanese American, Scandinavian American, and Hawaiian American. The eight stories in the book also vary in length, structure, and narrative perspective.

The title story "Who's Irish?" told in the voice of a feisty Chinese grandmother, focuses on the conflicts between the narrator and her Americanized daughter and Irish American son-in-law. The grandmother is in charge of babysitting her granddaughter Sophie while her daughter Natalie goes to work because her son-in-law John, though unemployed at home, finds childcaring demeaning to his manhood. The narrator is contemptuous of her son-in-law because he is unemployed and seems to be unmotivated to find and keep a job. She also differs with her daughter and son-in-law regarding how to discipline the "wild" Sophie. On the other hand, Natalie thinks that her mother is not "supportive" and John suggests that the grandmother be sent back to China. The familial frictions finally reach a crisis when the willful Sophie defies her grandmother, hiding from her in a playground foxhole. The incident is mistaken for an instance of child abuse by Sophie's parents. The grandmother is subsequently asked to move out. However, a tragic ending is spared. The grandmother goes to live with the mother of her son-in-law, whom she admires and with whom she can commiserate, and who calls her "honorary Irish" (16).

The story "Just Wait," consisting of five mini-sections, also deals with a domestic subject. The writer probes the possibility and problematic of forming a non-nuclear family. At their baby shower party, Chinese American Addie and her Japanese American husband Rex learn that Addie's mother Regina, recently divorced, plans to come to live with them in their small two-bedroom apartment. As the couple tries to reconfigure their home to accommodate the two new additions—Regina and the baby—they cannot help but wonder if they should have chosen other careers, such as researchers and surgeons, as their friends "with immigrant parents" (102) have done. Addie and Rex, an "artisan" and an innercity housing project office worker, respectively, having tried to lead a life without their parents' "influences," now find themselves financially too constrained to afford a house.

The longest piece of the collection, "House, House, Home," narrated in the third person, also portrays a character who defies the expectations of her immigrant parents. Chinese American Pammie drops out of college in her senior year to marry a cynical, eccentric, self-absorbed and twice-her-age "art professor" Sven Anderson. The relationship becomes strained as they run out of money and realize how different they are. Sven despises anything bourgeois and refuses to work for money. Pammie wonders if Sven, "an elective outsider [can] ever know what it [is] like to be the other kind of outsider?" (189). She eventually goes back to school to become an architect. When she finds herself pregnant with their third child, Sven takes off to live in his Maine cabin alone. As the protagonist examines her failed marriage and struggles to sustain the single-parent household, she meets a Hawaiian named Carver at "the children of color lunch" (133). Pammie's new friend instills confidence in her and new perspectives about how she has been "wifed" and treated as "Orientalia" by Sven.

Told in the voice of an (Italian?) American teenage boy, the story titled "Chin" is another text concerning domestic issues. Although the narrative focuses on the title character Chin, Chin's immigrant father plays an important part. The father used to be a doctor in China, but now works as a taxi driver in America. It is his insecurities and cultural and financial difficulties that govern his son's problems. The father's desire for his son's future success turns into frequent beatings. Consequently, the boy grows so tolerant of his father's ill treatment that he also endures abuses meted out by his peers and teacher at school. Through the narrator, Chin's neighbor and classmate, assumptions and stereotypes about the Chinese (American) and their culture are exposed.

Although many of Jen's stories concern familial issues, not all of them take place in domestic settings. In "Birthmates," the forty-nine-year-old salesman Art Woo finds himself accidentally booked into a welfare hotel during a sales convention, a result of his attempt to budget the travel expenses for his company. Art likes to "[maintain] a certain perspective" (22), which has cost him a better career opportunity and his marriage and leads to his inability to grieve. He finally comes to realize these losses through his displacement in the welfare hotel and his encounter with its denizens.

In "Duncan in China," the thirty-seven-year-old Duncan Hsu, an American dropout, sets off on a journey to see "the China of the ineffable nobility and restraint" (49) as embodied in Sung dynasty porcelains he sees in museums. However, in China, regarded as a "foreign expert" (49) and teaching English in a remote coal-mining town, he discovers that the "China" of the early 1980s is a place of physical discomfort and mysteries, in which every appearance is misleading to him. His lovable students could be spies; the woman he falls in love with plans to marry her daughter to him; his Chinese cousin, impoverished and physically broken by the Cultural Revolution, is pathetic and gratingly importuning. "China" makes Duncan realize how "American" he is.

In summary, although Jen is generally viewed as a Chinese American woman writer, her works are by no means limited to Chinese American experiences. *Who's Irish?* encompasses a variety of characters and subjects. Narrated in a humorous vein, Jen's stories are very complex and involve various critical issues. For instance, many of her stories reflect serious strains of modern American life, such as interracial marriages, interracial misunderstandings, working mothers and childcare problems, women's career aspirations, aging elders, domestic discord between married couples and in-laws, and children's reactions to domestic stress. In her stories, Jen does not take sides or impose any moral lessons, but simply stitches these themes or issues into the plot with humor and compassion.

◆ CRITICAL RECEPTION

By and large, like her two novels, Jen's *Who's Irish?* has been received favorably by book reviewers. The collection is praised by many for its diverse characters and themes. Alix Wilber comments that Jen differs from other ethnic writers precisely in "the wide-angle lens she turns not only on her own Chinese American ethnic group, but on Jewish Americans, African Americans, Irish Americans, and just about any other hyphenated you'd care to name" (*Amazon.com*). Moreover, the collection is acclaimed for "[transcending] the genre of immigrant fiction" (Changnon 12L) and its "unequivocally American perspective" (M. Lee B11). Some reviewers even recatalog her. For instance, distinguishing Jen from Amy Tan, Greg Changnon states that, while Tan "offers a taste test of her culture's exotic fable," Jen "shoves readers past sight-seeing and into the territory of self-discovery" (12L). Donny O'Rourke also remarks that Jen's works are "more emphatically American" than Tan's (22). Amy Blair associates Jen with "mainstream" American writers such as Updike, Oates, and Cheever (27). Jen is also applauded for her "deft way of turning stereotypes on their heads" (James), uncovering "the effect of isolation and racism inside families" (Homes 11), subverting the myth of Asian Americans as the model minority (Wynn O71), and "quieting much of the orientalizing rhetoric that was in danger of overwhelming and thoroughly marginalizing Asian American writers in the early 1990s" (Blair 27).

Unlike her novels, however, Jen' short fiction has received little critical attention (even though she has been publishing short fiction since the early 1980s). In "A Quartet of Voices in Recent American Literature," Gerald T. Burns points out that Jen's "What Means Switch" (first published in *Atlantic Monthly* in 1990 and later incorporated into *Mona in the Promised Land*) marks a departure from Maxine Hong Kingston's *The Woman Warrior* in that Jen's "cultural encounter . . . turns out not to be the clash of bewildered traditional Asians with incomprehensible modern Americans" (4), but that between different Asian Americans. In "From Story to Novel and Back Again: Gish Jen's Developing Art of Short Fiction," R. C. Feddersen maintains that Jen is as deft a short story writer as a novelist. Reading "Birthmates," Feddersen notes that "venturing into the novel has sharpened, not diminished, [Jen's] sense of symbolic structure, ironic resonance, and narrative complexity in the limited third-person short story" (351). In "Asian American Short Fiction: An Introduction and Critical Survey," Rachel Lee notes that Jen's short stories, like other Asian American short stories published in the 1990s, "deliberately [resist] the narrow ways 'real' Asian American literature has been defined" (269). Although there are only a few critical studies on Jen's short fiction, they were written before the publication of *Who's Irish?* Perhaps the book will finally draw more critical attention to Jen's short stories.

◆ BIBLIOGRAPHY

Works by Gish Jen

Short Stories

"Bellying-up." *Iowa Review* 12.4 (Fall 1981): 93–94.
"The Small Concerns of Sparrows." *Fiction International* 14 (1982): 47–55.
"The White Umbrella." *Yale Review* 73.3 (April 1984): 401–9.
"Eating Crazy." *Yale Review* 74.3 (April 1985): 425–33.
"In the American Society." *Southern Review* 22 (1986): 606–19.
"The Water Faucet Vision." *Nimrod* 31.1 (1987): 25–33.
"What Means Switch." *Atlantic Monthly* (May 1990): 76–84.

"Grover at the Wheel." *New Yorker* (December 31, 1990): 32–37.
"Birthmates." *Ploughshares* 20.4 (Winter 1994): 81–97.
"Who's Irish?" *New Yorker* (September 14, 1998): 80.

Short Story Collection

Who's Irish? Stories. New York: Random House, 1999.

Novels

Typical American. Boston: Houghton Mifflin, 1991.
Mona in the Promised Land. New York: Vintage, 1996.

Essays

"Challenging the Asian Illusion." *New York Times* (August 11, 1991): B1+.
"Our Luck: Chips, but No Breast." *New York Times* (November 28, 1991): B4.
"An Ethnic Trump: They Always Said They Didn't Want Their Young Son to See Himself as More Chinese Than Irish. But Is That Possible?" *New York Times Magazine* (July 7, 1996): 50.
"Who's to Judge? Identity Politics v. Inner Lives." *New Republic* (April 21, 1997): 18–19.
"Wen Ho Lee, Still Not So Very Free." *New York Times* (September 15, 2000). Available at http://www.crimelynx.com/wenho.html.
"Inventing Life Steals Time: Living Life Begs It Back." *New York Times* (December 4, 2000): E1.

Studies of Gish Jen

Blair, Amy. "Mastery of Love." *Boston Book Review* 6 (July 1999): 27.
Burns, Gerald T. "A Quartet of Voices in Recent American Literature." *Philippine American Journal* 3 (1991): 1–8.
Changnon, Greg. "Subtler View of Immigrant Life in Remarkable Debut of Stories." *The Atlanta Journal and Constitution* (June 20, 1999): 12L.
Cryer, Dan. "Peeling Away the Layers of Ethnicity." *Newsday* (June 7, 1999): B8.
Feddersen, R. C. "From Story to Novel and Back Again: Gish Jen's Developing Art of Short Fiction." In *Creative and Critical Approaches to the Short Story.* Noel Harold Kaylor, Jr., ed. Lewiston, NY: The Edwin Mellen Press, 1997. 349–58.
Gates, David. "On Being Hyphenated." *Newsweek* (June 7, 1999): 75.
Gilbert, Matthew. "Gish Jen, All-American: The Cambridge Novelist Doesn't Like to Be Labeled—Except as a Bigmouth." *Boston Globe* (June 4, 1996): 53.
Heung, Marina. "Windows of Opportunity." *Women's Review of Books* 16 (July 1999): 41.
Homes, A. M. "Discoveries." *Los Angeles Times* (June 6, 1999): 11.
James, Jamie. "Who's Irish? In Her First Collection of Stories, Chinese American Novelist Gish Jen Turns Stereotypes on Their Heads." *Salon.com* (June 4, 1999). Available at http://www.salon.com/books/review/1999/06/04/jen.

Kakutani, Michiko. "Free and Confused by Infinite Possibility." *New York Times* (June 4, 1999): E40.

Kobylarz, Philip. "Rich, Humor-Tinged Tales: New Americana." *The Commercial Appeal* (August 8, 1999): H3.

Lee, Margaret Juhae. "Talking with Gish Jen." *Newsday* (July 11, 1999): B11.

Lee, Rachel. "Asian American Short Fiction: An Introduction and Critical Survey." In *A Resource Guide to Asian American Literature.* Sau-ling Cynthia Wong and Stephen H. Sumida, eds. New York: Modern Language Association, 2000, 252–84.

———. "Gish Jen" (interview). In *Words Matter: Conversations with Asian American Writers.* King-Kok Cheung, ed. Honolulu: University of Hawaii Press, 2000, 215–32.

Liu, Calvin. "Who's Chinese American? Gish Jen Adds a New Dimension to APA Literature." *AsianWeek* 20.43 (June 24, 1999). Available at http://www.asianweek.com/062499/ae.gishjen.html.

Matsukawa, Yuko. "*MELUS* Interview: Gish Jen." *MELUS* 18.4 (Winter 1993/1994): 111–20.

O'Rourke, Donny. "Chinese To Go." *The Herald* (Glasgow) (July 15, 1999): 22.

Pearlman, Mickey. "Gish Jen" (interview). *Listen to Their Voices: Twenty Interviews with Women Who Write.* New York and London: W. W. Norton & Co., 1993, 36–46.

Satz, Martha. "Writing About the Things That Are Dangerous: A Conversation with Gish Jen." *Southwest Review* 78.1 (Winter 1993): 132–40.

Smith, Ali. "Brief Tales of Love and Culture." *The Scotsman* (August 28, 1999): 10.

Trudeau, Lawrence J. "Gish Jen." In *Asian American Literature: Reviews and Criticism of Works by American Writers of Asian Descent*, Lawrence J. Trudeau, ed. Detroit and London: Gale Group, 1999, 176–86.

Wilber, Alix. Rev. of *Who's Irish? Stories.* Accessed at *Amazon.com*.

Wynn, Judith. "Educating Asia Innocents—Jen Examines Stereotypes of 'Model' Group." *Boston Herald* (May 16, 1999): O71.

HA JIN
(1956–   )

Wenxin Li

◆ BIOGRAPHY

Xuefei Jin, who writes under the name of Ha Jin, was born on February 21, 1956, in Liaoning, China, into a privileged "military family." His father, Danlin Jin, was an army officer, and his mother, Yuanfen Zhao, a factory worker. Growing up during a period of extreme political upheaval in China's modern history known as the Cultural Revolution (1966–1976), Ha Jin joined the Chinese Army when he was fourteen and served six years, first stationed on the Sino-Soviet border and later trained as a telegraph operator. When higher education was formally restored in 1977, Ha Jin became a member of the first class to be admitted to a university. After graduating from Heilongjiang University with a B.A. in English in 1981, he went on to Shandong University for his M.A. in English, writing a thesis on Robert Penn Warren. He married Lisha Bian in 1982. His life took a drastic turn in 1985 when he came to the United States for further education, earning a Ph.D. in English from Brandeis University in 1992 with a dissertation entitled, "The Universalization in Modern English and American Poetry: With Particular Reference to China." He became an assistant professor of English at Emory University in 1993.

Even before receiving his doctorate, Ha Jin had published a book of poetry, *Between Silences*, in 1990, marking the beginning of a prolific and distinguished career. In just over a decade, he has published two more collections of poetry, three books of short stories, and two novels, which won numerous awards, including the PEN/Hemingway Award, the PEN/Faulkner Award, the National Book Award, and a Guggenheim Fellowship. In 2000, he resigned as Young J. Allen Professor of English and Creative Writing from Emory to join the Creative Writing Program at Boston University, where he first honed his skills as a fiction writer from 1991 to 1993 under the tutelage of Leslie Epstein.

◆ MAJOR WORKS AND THEMES

Although Ha Jin started his career as a poet and has continued to write poetry, it is his fiction that has earned him major critical acclaim. He has published three collections of short stories so far, *Ocean of Words* in 1996, *Under the Red Flag* in 1997, and *The Bridegroom* in 2000. Like his poetry and novels, Ha Jin's short stories portray the extraordinary social upheaval of the Cultural Revolution. His prevalent theme is the excruciating struggle for survival of a nation dominated by a dogmatic Communist ideology and harsh material conditions. Set in Ha Jin's native Northeast provinces, the three collections of short stories each consist of twelve stories, carefully planned for their unity of theme and setting.

Ocean of Words, the first collection, is based on his six-year experience as a PLA (People's Liberation Army) soldier. Set along the Sino-Soviet border in the 1970s, these stories portray, as the *New York Times Book Review* calls it, an "achingly human" drama:

> Whether nurturing lifelong grudges against enemy soldiers, aiding vagabond neighbors who once betrayed them or witnessing the slaughter of an ox, these men isolated in a forbidding landscape are brought together to form a group portrait that suggests how an entire people struggles to keep its basic humanity within the stiff, unnatural confines of Maoist ideology. (Solomon 21)

Speaking of his first collection of stories, Ha Jin offers his assessment as well as the purpose of its creation:

> There is very little bitterness . . . in *Ocean of Words*. . . . I had a lot of affection for the soldiers, men and women both, whom I was writing about. Most of them were as innocent as I once was, full of potential but never having the opportunity to develop. The human loss touched me, and I meant to preserve some of the loss on the page. (61)

Featuring a broad section of army life during a period of elevated tension across the border with the Soviet Union, these stories explore the collective "revolutionary psychology" (Montgomery) of individuals trapped in a remote world of climatic austerity and spiritual deprivation. Some of these stories, such as "Too Late," "Love in the Air," "My Best Soldier," and "Ocean of Words," deal with the forbidden subject of love, whether it is for women or books, which finds various and unexpected expressions under inhospitable circumstances. Other stories reflect on the unpredictability of life as well as human frailty for those caught between the two Communist giants sparring over the authenticity of their respective versions of Marxism. "Dragon Head" and "The Russian Prisoner" are good representatives of this category.

Its title taken from the Maoist cliché, "Born in the New China, raised under the red flag," *Under the Red Flag*, set in a fictitious town called Dismount Fort, continues to examine the stark social realities of the same period in rural China. However, *Under the Red Flag* differs significantly from *Ocean of Words* in tone. While *Ocean of Words* exposes the revolutionary fervor and its curb on individual freedom and desire, its narrative voice is tinged nevertheless with a sense of ambivalent nostalgia. *Under the Red Flag*, on the other hand, presents a social landscape that is increasingly bizarre and grotesque. Ha Jin's castigating stance in *Under the Red Flag* results from his anger at and disillusionment with the Chinese government after the June 1989 Tiananmen crackdown, which is his defining event while living in America. "My Best Soldier" from *Ocean of Words* and "Resurrection" from *Under the Red Flag*, two stories dealing with the theme of repressed sexual desires, help demonstrate the point. In the first story, a soldier who visits a prostitute is disciplined, so he takes to having sex with a mule instead. In the second story, a farmer castrates himself to atone for an affair with his sister-in-law. Although the stories are similar in that they both illustrate resistance to what Ha Jin calls "the government['s] control of sexual energy" (Montgomery), his handling of these two characters invites very different reactions from readers. While the soldier's sexual frustration is more of a result of his inability to reconcile his desire with army discipline, the farmer's desperation is blamed more on the part of the Party apparatus. More important, "Resurrection" takes on allegorical implications for Ha Jin, who intends to show "how the Chinese neutered themselves in order to live a 'normal' life" (*Under the Red Flag* 62).

Other stories in the collection also appear to exhibit more violence, aggression, and chaos. For example, "In Broad Daylight" depicts the horrific suicide of a woman who is accused of prostitution. "Man to Be" portrays an impotent old man who invites his fellow villagers to gang rape his young wife to punish her for suspected infidelity. Many other stories, such as "Sovereignty," "Again, the Spring Breeze Blew," "The Richest Man," and "Emperor," all include scenes of bloody fighting or violent death. In "Sovereignty," a fight between two boars mirrors the violent nature of society. "Again, the Spring Breeze Blew" opens with a rape scene, although the surprise twist comes after the victim kills her attacker: the Party uses her actions for its own propaganda. "Emperor" features juvenile gang wars and "The Richest Man" highlights the persecution of a man whose only fault was his inadvertent dumping of a Mao button. These and other stories in the collection paint a vivid picture of a nation in mindless obedience to Mao's radical attempts to leapfrog Chinese society into Communist utopia.

The Bridegroom, Ha Jin's latest collection, brings the reader from the last years of the Cultural Revolution to the present. Set in a small town called Muji, these stories portray a nation emerging from the dark and menacing turmoil to face the new realities of modernization that began in the late 1970s when China opened its doors to the West. Despite the shifted social scene, Ha Jin's theme remains the strenuous struggle of a people yet unable to free themselves from the haunting past. "Saboteur," which portrays a victim of judicial abuse bent on revenge with no regard to the rights of others like himself, represents another testimony of the dehumanizing effect of an authoritarian system. "Alive" tells the transformation of a man's life through a temporary memory loss brought on by the devastating Tangshan Earthquake in 1976. "In the Kindergarten" depicts the predicament of a teacher, who coerces her kindergarteners to pick purslanes for her dinner in order to save money to pay off the bill for her secret abortion.

The rest of the stories in the collection deal with more contemporary subject matter. "A Tiger-Fighter Is Hard to Find," "The Bridegroom," "An Entrepreneur's Story," and "A Bad Joke," feature post–Cultural Revolution themes: the reviving of a classic martial artist's heroism, male homosexuality, the impact of wealth on marital fortunes, and political satire. Although the themes are clearly post-Maoist, these stories continue to reflect the lingering mentality of a bygone era: individuals are no more masters of their own fate than in the past and still very much the inconsequential chips on an ideological agenda. "The Woman from New York" and "After Cowboy Chicken Came to Town" introduce the long awaited American connection in Ha Jin's work, although the setting of the stories is still China, not the United States. Both stories explore society's deep ambivalence toward American influence: on the one hand, the Chinese are tempted by the allures of U.S. capitalism; on the other, they remain suspicious and resentful of those deemed "sold out" to America.

◆ CRITICAL RECEPTION

The critical response to Ha Jin's work has been overwhelmingly positive, as nearly every work of his fiction has garnered a major literary award. The publication history of his work points to an astounding success for a man working in his second language. The University of Chicago Press published his first collection of poetry, *Between Silences*, when he was still a graduate student. *Ocean of Words*, featuring the Pushcart winning "My Best Soldier," won the PEN/Hemingway Award for first fiction. Jin's second collection, *Under the Red Flag*, won the Flannery O'Connor Award. "In Broad Daylight" won a second Pushcart and is anthologized in *Norton Introduction to Fiction* and *Norton Introduction to Literature*. Another story in the collection, "Man to Be," is also a Pushcart winner. *Waiting* (1999), his second novel and by far his most well-known work to date, garnered both the PEN/Faulkner

Award and the National Book Award. In addition, three stories from his third collection, *The Bridegroom*, were reprinted in *The Best American Short Stories* ("Saboteur," 1997; "In the Kindergarten," 1999; and the title story "The Bridegroom," 2000).

Critics have accorded Ha Jin with lavish praises. Andy Solomon calls *Ocean of Words* "a compelling collection of stories, powerful in their unity of theme and rich in their diversity of styles" (21). Also commenting on *Ocean of Words*, Jocelyn Lieu calls Ha Jin's prose "laconic, luminous" and "a nearly flawless treasure" (6). A review for *Publishers Weekly* points to Ha Jin's "genuine talent for humor" in *Ocean of Words*, and concludes that "the author is at his best when telling the stories of soldiers forced to choose between ideology and love" (98). In a review of *Under the Red Flag*, Paul Gray explores the reasons behind Ha Jin's miraculous success and suggests that it was due to the author having "had the good luck to be born outside the U.S. and hence be protected from the homogenizing and potentially trivializing influences that afflict so many U.S.-born aspiring authors." Gray concedes that "[a]n exotic subject matter helps, but narrative talent proves victorious" (94). Verity Ludgate-Fraser praises *The Bridegroom*'s "seamless narration" and "inconspicuous" voice, adding, "[This] is an absorbing work by a deeply gifted writer, spare yet rich, witty yet heart-rending. Despite the pain these characters endure, Jin rejoices in the humanity he so aptly depicts" (21).

However, there are some mixed opinions on Ha Jin's literary style. Peter Bricklebank is disappointed with *Under the Red Flag* for its lack of sophistication and depth: "Unfortunately, these sorts of political exigencies seem awfully familiar, especially when used in the service of well-worn themes. And Ha Jin's narrative style isn't much of a help. As plain and stiffly serviceable as a Mao uniform, it lacks expressive elegance and leaves the reader wishing for greater psychological richness, for colors other than red" (14). Wenxin Li argues that while Ha Jin's narrative style appears "plain and unassuming," his work is "always captivating and rewarding." "Working in the tradition of the classic Chinese story," Li adds, "he strongly prefers a well-spun yarn to elaborate stylistic experimentation" (25). Commenting on *The Bridegroom*, Claire Messud is critical of Ha Jin's language, but is full of admiration for his narrative talent:

> It is impossible to escape the impression that for Ha Jin, the English language—potentially so pliable, so complex—is ultimately an unwieldy tool that merely suffices for his purposes. His literary vision, like his subjects thus far, is Chinese, and the English language not his calling, but his arbitrary fate. But his eye for detail, his great storytelling talent—these universal gifts suffuse his work and make "The Bridegroom" a genuine pleasure. (9)

◆ BIBLIOGRAPHY

Works by Ha Jin

Short Story Collections

Ocean of Words: Army Stories. Cambridge, MA: Zoland, 1996.
Under the Red Flag: Stories. Athens: University of Georgia Press, 1997.
The Bridegroom: Stories. New York: Pantheon, 2000.

Novels

In the Pond. Cambridge, MA: Zoland, 1998.
Waiting. New York: Pantheon, 1999.

Poetry

Between Silences. Chicago: University of Chicago Press, 1990.
Facing Shadows. New York: Hanging Loose, 1996.
Wreckage. New York: Hanging Loose, 2001.

Studies of Ha Jin

Bricklebank, Peter. Rev. of *Under the Red Flag*. *New York Times Book Review* (January 11, 1998): 14.
Carlile, Jennifer, and Joyce Bell. "The Cost of Honesty: Writing in Exile." *Emory Report* (October 22, 1993): n.p. Available at www.emory.edu/EMORY_REPORT/ erarchive/1993/.
Gray, Paul. "Modern-Day Folktales That Show the Real China." Rev. of *Under the Red Flag*. *Time* (December 1, 1997): 94.
Jin, Ha. "An Interview with Liza Nelson." *Five Points* 5.1 (2000): 53–67.
Li, Wenxin. "Searching for a Good Man among the Crimson Mountains and Rivers of the Motherland." Rev. of *Under the Red Flag*. *Ten Magazine* 4.2 (1998): 22–25.
Lieu, Jocelyn. "Beating the Odds." Rev. of *Ocean of Words*. *Chicago Tribune Books* (December 24, 1996): 6.
Ludgate-Fraser, Verity. Rev. of *Bridegroom*. *Christian Science Monitor* (November 2, 2000): 21.
Messud, Claire. Rev. of *Bridegroom*. *New York Times Book Review* (October 22, 2000): 9.
Montgomery, Matt. "Xuefei Jin Discusses the Research of the Fiction Writer." *Emory Report* (April 10, 1995): n.p. Available at www.emory.edu/EMORY_ REPORT/.
Quan, Shirley N. Rev. of *Bridegroom*. *Library Journal* 125.14 (2000): 254.
Rev. of *Ocean of Words*. *Publishers Weekly* (February 26, 1996): 98.
Solomon, Andy. Rev. of *Ocean of Words*. *New York Times Book Review* (June 2, 1996): 21.
Thomas, John D. "Across an Ocean of Words." *Emory Magazine* 74.11 (1998): n.p. Available at www.emory.edu/EMORY_MAGAZINE/spring98/hajin.html.

LONNY KANEKO
(1939–   )

Kyoko Amano

◆ BIOGRAPHY

A sansei (a third-generation Japanese American), Lonny Kaneko was born in 1939 in Seattle, Washington. At the outbreak of World War II, the family was first sent to an assembly center in Puyallup, Washington, and then to the Hunt Relocation Center (a.k.a. Minidoka Relocation Center) in Idaho. His poems and short stories are shaped by his internment camp experience; he published a collection of poems titled *Coming Home from Camp* and his masterpiece, a short story titled "The Shoyu Kid," set in Minidoka Camp.

Kaneko studied under Theodore Roethke and received an M.A. in English from the University of Washington in 1963. His thesis was titled "Catchcan of Chicken Feathers in an Old Roost," a collection of poems. In 1974, a whimsical short story, "The Wife and the Kappa," was published in *Playboy*. He was a recipient of the National Endowment for the Arts fellowship in 1982, which resulted in his publication of *Coming Home from Camp* in 1986. In 1999, he published a short story, "Old Lady," in the *Seattle Review*. With playwright Amy Sanbo, he wrote two plays, *Lady Is Dying* and *Benny Hana*. *Lady Is Dying* won the Henry Broderick Playwright Prize at the Pacific Northwest Writers Conference and was performed at the Asian American Theatre Workshop in 1977. He is also the recipient of a fiction prize from *Amerasia Journal*. Currently, Kaneko teaches English at Highline Community College in Washington.

◆ MAJOR WORKS AND THEMES

Despite the fact that Kaneko considers himself first a teacher and second a poet, not a short story writer, he is known for his short story, "The Shoyu

Kid." The story, like his collection of poems in *Coming Home from Camp*, is drawn from his years growing up in Minidoka internment camp during World War II. The internment camp experience is described from the point of view of a young boy, Masao, who, along with his friends, Jackson (Hiroshi) and Itchy (Ichiro), chases the title character in order to find out where the Shoyu Kid gets the chocolate bar he eats every morning. In the background, the detained Japanese Americans chase a nondescript creature. By the end of the story, both the Shoyu Kid and the animal are trapped, and the Kid confesses that he just plays with the soldier's *chimpo* (penis). The title character turns out to be triply victimized: he is detained in a camp for being an American of Japanese ancestry; he is bullied by Japanese American kids; the Caucasian soldier takes advantage of the Kid's alienation to fulfill his perverse desires. Multilayered images of chase and trap complicate the story of power and authority in a Japanese American internment camp, and despite the fact that the narrator presents his friends with the images of predominant American culture, he ultimately finds them as powerless and entrapped as other Japanese American internees. The theme of betrayal (of self and of community) is also prominent, as Sau-ling Cynthia Wong points out in *Reading Asian American Literature*.

"Nobody's Hero" is also set in Minidoka Camp during the war and is told from the point of view of Masao. It deals with the question of Japanese American identity and loyalty. Characters similar to those in "The Shoyu Kid" appear in "Nobody's Hero": Hiroshi, Jackson, Itchy, and Masao (Mas), the narrator. While Jackson is Hiroshi's nickname in "The Shoyu Kid," here Jackson and Hiroshi are two separate characters. Their plan is to steal some candies and cigarettes from a canteen before Mitch and Toru get there and to let them be responsible for the theft. While this plan would be considered a childhood prank in any other circumstances, Hiroshi considers it heroic because it might make the War Relocation Authority (WRA) officers' lives miserable. They succeed in the robbery and hide their booty under the tar paper on the back of the outhouse. They become camp heroes for showing the WRA that they would not bow to them. At the end of the week, their glory is shattered because the WRA publishes the incident in the camp newspaper and calls it "the work of bored children" (156).

Both "The Shoyu Kid" and "Nobody's Hero" deal with the themes that arise from the historical situation of internment of Japanese Americans during the war. They draw young boys in camp as a community of their own, separate from their parents, and the loyalty among boys as interned Japanese Americans is the central issue, as they witness and challenge the power of the U.S. government represented in the figures of soldiers and WRA officers.

◆ CRITICAL RECEPTION

Critical evaluations of Kaneko's works center around "The Shoyu Kid." In her *Reading Asian American Literature*, Sau-ling Cynthia Wong labels "The

Shoyu Kid" as "a microcosmic reproduction of the racial stratification in the larger society" (48) and a "meticulously wrought moral allegory" (101). David Eng finds "something queer in the world of Kaneko's Minidoka concentration camp" and suggests in his article, "Primal Glances: Race and Psychoanalysis in Lonny Kaneko's 'The Shoyu Kid,'" that Kaneko's short story provides "some primary but provocative answer" to the question of how the Asian American male is often portrayed as an emasculated, effeminate homosexual (67). In "The Minority Self as Other: Problematics of Representation in Asian-American Literature," David Palumbo-Liu calls "The Shoyu Kid" "an intensely visual text that openly and explicitly problematizes the representation of Self via the mediation of the Other" (91).

Eng focuses on Kaneko's use of images, which he identifies as the images of "the white male heterosexual." For example, the characters have American nicknames; the narrator portrays their actions, using images drawn from American popular culture, such as John Wayne, a soldier in a war movie, an Indian, and the cavalry colonel. While the camp bullies, including the narrator, imitate the image of the privileged, the title character is coerced "to play the role of the abject" (70). However, in the scene where Itchy witnesses the red-headed soldier's molestation of the Kid, Eng maintains that Itchy's choice becomes homosexual whether he identifies himself as the soldier or the Kid. Eng also asserts that "the moment of heterosexual foreclosure is . . . attached to an inaugural moment of racial difference" (75) because the color of the Kid's snot, the narrator realizes, comes from the chocolate that he receives for his sexual favor to the soldier, not from his frequent use of soy sauce, an essential ingredient in Japanese cooking.

Palumbo-Liu, likewise, analyzes the narrator's language and images and points out, "nearly every trope and figure rhetorically links the boys to America" (92). While the narrator attempts to identify his friends and himself as the empowered, like Americans through images, Palumbo-Liu finds the characters fail to claim their power and authority because no one in the camp recognizes them in the way they portray themselves.

◆ BIBLIOGRAPHY

Works by Lonny Kaneko

Short Stories

"The Wife and the Kappa." *Playboy* (June 1974): 157.
"The Shoyu Kid." In *The Big Aiiieeeee! An Anthology of Chinese American and Japanese American Literature*. Jeffery Paul Chan, Frank Chin, Lawson Fusao Inada, and Shawn Wong, eds. New York: Penguin, 1991, 304–13.
"Nobody's Hero." In *Asian American Literature: A Brief Introduction and Anthology*. Shawn Wong, ed. New York: Harper, 1996, 147–56.
"Old Lady." *Seattle Review* 21.1 (1999): 66–72.

Poetry

"Renewal: Algona, Washington." In *Ayumi: A Japanese American Anthology*. Janice Mirikitani, ed. San Francisco: Japanese American Anthology Committee, 1980, 192.

"Requiem for John Kazuo Yamamoto, Sr." *Amerasia Journal* 9.2 (1982): 117–20.

Coming Home from Camp. Waldron Island, WA: Brooding Heron Press, 1986.

"Wild Light," "Balley Gatzert: The First Grade, 1945," and "Beasts from the Heart." In *An Ear to the Ground: An Anthology of Contemporary American Poetry*. Marie Harris and Kathleen Aguero, eds. Athens: University of Georgia Press, 1989, 141–44.

"Song for Lovers." In *On a Bed of Rice: An Asian American Erotic Feast*. Geraldine Kudaka, ed. New York: Doubleday, 1995, 274–75.

Essays

"Of Rice and Bread." *Daily Fare: Essays from the Multicultural Experience*. Kathleen Aguero, ed. Athens: University of Georgia Press, 1993, 174–84.

"Journey to Minidoka." In *Where the Morning Light's Still Blue: Personal Essays about Idaho*. William Studebaker and Rick Ardinger, eds. Moscow: University of Idaho Press, 1994, 144–49.

Drama

With Amy Sanbo. *Benny Hana. Lady Is Dying*. Asian American Theater Company, San Francisco. October 21, 1977.

Studies of Lonny Kaneko

Eng, David L. "Primal Glances: Race and Psychoanalysis in Lonny Kaneko's 'The Shoyu Kid.' " *Hitting Critical Mass: A Journal of Asian American Cultural Criticism* 1.2 (Spring 1994): 65–83. http://socrates.berkeley.edu/~critmass/v1n2/engprint.html.

Nimura, Tamiko. "Lonny Kaneko." In *Asian American Poets: A Bio-Bibliographical Critical Sourcebook*. Guiyou Huang, ed. Westport, CT: Greenwood Press, 2002, 159–63.

Palumbo-Liu, David. "The Minority Self as Other: Problematics of Representation in Asian-American Literature." *Cultural Critique* 28 (Fall 1994): 75–102.

Wong, Sau-ling Cynthia. *Reading Asian American Literature: From Necessity to Extravagance*. Princeton, NJ: Princeton University Press, 1993.

ALEX KUO
(1939–   )

Doug Sugano

◆ **BIOGRAPHY**

Alex Kuo was born in 1939 while his father was teaching psychology at Harvard. During World War II, from 1942 to 1945, Kuo's family moved to China, living in Chongqing and Shanghai. Kuo completed his primary and secondary education in Hong Kong, receiving a General Certificate of Education from London University at the age of 16. In 1955, his family moved to Windsor, Connecticut. He went on to complete his B.A. degree in writing at Knox College (Galesburg, Illinois) in 1961. Kuo studied alongside Frank Chin and Lawson Inada at Iowa's M.F.A. program under Donald Justice and Philip Roth.

After completing his M.F.A., Kuo taught creative writing and literature at South Dakota State University for a year and received tenure at the University of Wisconsin at Oshkosh, where he taught for five years until 1969. Kuo resigned his position to protest the expulsion of African American students from the university. He moved on to direct the Creative Writing Program and the Fine Arts Division at Roger Williams College and the Communications Program at Northern Illinois University. Kuo came to the Pacific Northwest in 1971 to direct the Ethnic Studies Program at Central Washington University, a position he held for three years. During the next five years he served as vice chancellor for academic affairs and taught in the Black Studies and English programs.

In 1979, disenchanted with academics, Kuo worked for the U.S. Forest Service. Later that year, he resumed teaching at Washington State University, where he established the Comparative American Studies Program in 1984 and still teaches for the Creative Writing and Comparative American Cultures programs. In 2001, Kuo was appointed Writer-in-Residence at Washington State University.

Since 1989, Kuo has traveled three times to China: the first time to teach at Beijing University and Beijing Forestry University; the second occasion as a Senior Fulbright Scholar at Jilin University, 1991–1992; and, in 1997–1998, as the Lingnan Visiting Scholar in American Studies at Hong Kong Baptist University. Since the 1960s, over eighty of Kuo's poems and over twenty short stories have appeared in journals. Kuo's *The Window Tree* (1971) was the first volume of poetry published by an Asian American. *Chinese Opera*, his first novel, was published in 1998, while his first collection of short stories, *Lipstick and Other Stories*, appeared in 2001 and was nominated for the American Book Award.

◆ MAJOR WORKS AND THEMES

We can see Kuo's influence upon Sherman Alexie's work. Many of Alexie's trademarks such as postmodern histories, absurdist anachronism and allusions, self-conscious humor and gnomic sayings are first found in Kuo's shorter fiction. His short stories sometimes blur the line between prose poetry and fiction: many of the stories are brief, lyrical sketches with pithy and imagistic resolutions. His first published short story, "Where Are You Really From?" which appeared in 1975, describes America's failure to acknowledge multicultural identities. Many of Kuo's short stories from the 1980s reflect his move to the Northwest. Hence, these stories also display a pioneering spirit that attempts to reconcile rural Western American culture with ecological concerns, pacifism, and popular culture.

With his travels to China that began in 1989, Kuo's short stories deepen with new referential layers. Most of his stories published in the 1990s allude to his experiences during World War II, the Communist revolution of 1949, the Cultural Revolution, the students' protest in Tiananmen Square, and life in contemporary China. Many of the stories contain vignettes from Kuo's childhood and his recent past: Chongqing in 1944, Mao's affect on China and upon global popular culture, and the students' protest at Tiananmen Square. These newer themes have been grafted onto his familiar topoi of the American West, European painters, and ecological crises. One of his stories from 1990, "Eggs," contemplates our relationship to the flow of history:

> We are here for the duration, carefully balanced between address and rumor, carefully watching those who are siphoning from our pain, allowing us to go on. In the early morning our children will thrust from our thighs and float away from us, like chilled stars. (81)

Kuo's short prose explores the people and the memories that disappear from our lives. In subsequent stories, Kuo reexamines this notion of disappearance, but playfully invites us to view the effects of myth-making institutions (governments, politicians, official histories) on our notions of reality.

Lipstick and Other Stories meticulously weaves sixteen older pieces with fifteen new ones. It is divided into three sections: the first (all previously published stories) contains stories about Kuo's childhood in China during World War II; the second section concerns the paradoxes of contemporary China; and the last section incorporates themes and ideas from the previous two sections, but adds more layers of Chinese and American multiculturalism and events with global implications. One of the most delightful creations from the new material is Ge, a Chinese everyman who understands the multicultural sham of Bizet's *Carmen*, engages in "subversive" activities, but also digs his way to the "free" West with a trowel. Kuo's newer stories are rife with irony, political poignancy, metafiction, magic realism, and a trickster's wink because in most of his short stories, as at the end of "The Catholic All-Star Chess Team," Kuo warns us that history cannot be the only way we can approach truth.

◆ CRITICAL RECEPTION

The pre-release reviews of *Lipstick* appreciate Kuo's intelligence, sardonic humor, and absurdist sensibilities, comparing him to Kafka, Borges, Lu Xun, Can Xue, Twain, Lessing, Gorki, and Beckett. The critics also agree on the sustained effort and intelligence that Kuo expects from his readers. But there are also concerns apart from influence and style. Kuo's skeptical views of memory, history, and reality all confront us with the joys and uncertainties of a postmodern world. In sum, Kuo never derides anyone, but realizes that, at best, we all embody a feeble and indefensible humanity. Kuo, instead, chooses to share and to laugh with us (most of the time). Robert Abel believes that Kuo's stories:

> do not show much faith in "realism" to probe with sufficient depth either the chaos of modern life or the complexities of our responses to it, or our efforts even to develop sufficient strategies to keep from being overwhelmed. Perhaps Kuo is not telling stories so much as, through fiction, struggling to discover what, in fact, the real story is, and which stories we can truly say we share. (39)

◆ BIBLIOGRAPHY

Works by Alex Kuo

Short Stories

"Where Are You Really From?" *Greenfield Review* 4 (1975): 99–102.
"Dates/80." *Tin Can Journal* 1 (1980): 5–9.

"Statements/81." *Journal of Ethnic Studies* 10 (1982): 83–84.
"Statements/81.2." *Journal of Ethnic Studies* 10 (1982): 85–88.
"Why He Did What He Did." *Wisconsin Review* 17 (1983): 24–25.
"Did You Not See?" *The Literary Review* 28 (1984): 70.
"It's the Third Embrace." *The Malahat Review* 69 (1984): 59–61.
"Does Anything Come Out Alive?" *Journal of Ethnic Studies* 12 (1985): 65–86.
"A Story." *Journal of Ethnic Studies* 12.1 (1985): 65–86.
"Something's Wrong with This Picture." *Wisconsin Review* 19 (1986): 46–47.
"Absences." *Chicago Review* 36 (1990): 82–83. Rpt. in *Dreamers and Desperadoes: Contemporary Short Fiction of the American West*. Craig Lesley and Katheryn Stavrakis, eds. New York: Laurel, 1995, 290–91, and in *Lipstick and Other Stories*. Hong Kong: Asia 2000, 2001, 19–21.
"Eggs." *Chicago Review* 36 (1990): 80–81. Rpt. in *Dreamers and Desperadoes*, 292–94, and in *Lipstick*, 15–17.
"Cicadas." *Chicago Review* 36 (1990): 85–86. Rpt. in *Dreamers and Desperadoes*, 295–96, and in *Lipstick*, 25–27.
"Growing Tomatoes." *Chicago Review* 36 (1990): 84. Rpt. in *Dreamers and Desperadoes*, 297, and in *Lipstick*, 23–24.
"Morning Stars." *Caliban* 10 (1991): 37–39.
"Past Perfect Tense." *Redneck Review of Literature* 21 (1991): 11–12. Rpt. in *Lipstick*, 29–31.
"Reductions." *Ergo!* 6 (1991): 52–54. Rpt. in *Lipstick*, 79–82.
"Relocation, After the Manhattan Project." *Redneck Review of Literature* 21 (1991): 11. Rpt. in *Lipstick*, 33–34.
"Captured Horses." *Ergo!* 7 (1992): 9–10.
"Exit, a Chinese Novel." *Universe* 5 (1992): 24–25. Rpt. in *Lipstick*, 179–82.
"The Peking Cowboy." *Blue Mesa Review* 4 (1992): 78–81. Rpt. in *Lipstick*, 45–49.
"The Connoisseur of Chaos." In *Charlie Chan Is Dead: An Anthology of Contemporary Asian American Fiction*. Jessica Hagedorn, ed. New York: Penguin, 1993, 201–3. Rpt. in *Lipstick*, 71–74.
"Definitions." *Green Mountains Review* 6 (1993): 47–49. Rpt. in *Lipstick*, 55–59.
"The Catholic All-Star Chess Team." *The Redneck Review of Literature* 29 (1995): 27–32. Rpt. in *Lipstick*, 92–112.
"Lipstick." *Ploughshares* 26.4 (Winter 2000): 27–32. Rpt. in *Lipstick*, 171–78.

Short Story Collection

Lipstick and Other Stories. Hong Kong: Asia 2000, 2001.

Novel

Chinese Opera. Hong Kong: Asia 2000, 1998.

Poetry

The Window Tree. Peterborough, NH: Windy Row Press, 1971.
New Letters from Hiroshima and Other Poems. New York: Greenfield Review, 1974.

Changing the River. Berkeley: Ishmael Reed, 1986.
This Fierce Geography. Boise: Limberlost, 1999.

Studies of Alex Kuo

Abel, Robert. "Telling the Stories of the Disappeared." Rev. of *Lipstick and Other Stories*. *Willow Springs* 50 (June 2002): 37–39.
Grinnell, Jim. "Telling Truth in Art and Freedom in Expression: An Interview with Alex Kuo." *Bloomsbury Review* 22.1. (November–December 1999): 17. http://www.asia2000.comhk/Asia2000/kuorbr.html. Accessed February 18, 2002.
———. Rev. of *Lipstick and Other Stories*. *Bloomsbury Review* 22.1 (January–Feburary 2002): 17.
Huntington, Rebecca. Rev. of *Chinese Opera*. *Seattle Times*, Weekend ed. (September 20, 1998): B5.
"Lipstick and Other Stories." *Asia 2000*. http://www.asia2000.com.hk/Asia2000/lipstick.html#Reviews. Accessed February 18, 2002.
Review of *Chinese Opera*. *International Examiner* (September 2–16, 1998): 17.
Sugano, Douglas. "Alex Kuo." In *Asian American Novelists: A Bio-Bibliographical Critical Sourcebook*. Emmanuel S. Nelson, ed. Westport, CT: Greenwood Press, 2000, 168–71.
Webster, Dan. Rev. of *Chinese Opera*. *Spokane Spokesman-Review* (September 20, 1998): E7, E8.

JHUMPA LAHIRI
(1967–   )

Shuchen Susan Huang

◆ BIOGRAPHY

Of Bengali immigrant parents, Jhumpa Lahiri was born in London in 1967. Two years later, her family immigrated to the United States. She grew up in South Kingston, Rhode Island, where her father worked as a librarian and her mother taught Bengali at a university. Like many children of immigrant households, Lahiri spoke Bengali to her parents at home. Her knowledge of the language made easy her stay in Calcutta, where her parents took her and her younger sister for long visits during her youth. She did not feel like a typical tourist in India in part because she spoke the language and in part because her family always stayed in the homes of their extended families. But she was also aware that she was perceived by the local people to be different. In an interview, Lahiri admits that she is indeed "indebted to [her] travels to India for several of the stories" (Aguiar) in her debut book, *Interpreter of Maladies* (1999). Though Lahiri speaks Bengali, English is really her first language in terms of writing. She started writing fiction when she was seven. In grade school, she collaborated with her friends in writing stories during recess. In high school, she wrote for the school newspaper, but did not compose fiction. In college, although she attended several writing workshops, she did not feel confident in writing stories.

Lahiri took a winding road to become a writer. After receiving her B.A. from Barnard College, she applied to several graduate schools but was rejected by all. While waiting to apply again, she worked as a research assistant at a non-profit institution in Cambridge, Massachusetts. The job gave her full access to a computer, which she discovered to be an excellent tool for writing. She came in early and stayed late in order to write. Eventually, she accumulated enough writing samples to get into the M.F.A. program at Boston University. After finishing the M.F.A. program, she went on to obtain an M.A. in English Literature, an M.A. in Comparative Studies in Literature and the Arts, and a Ph.D. in Renaissance Studies at Boston University. In an interview, Lahiri reveals that she thought that an academic career would be more "practical and secure" (Rhankar) than writing fiction. However, in graduate school, she was always writing fiction and publishing in various journals and magazines, including *Agni*, *Harvard Review*, *Epoch*, *Salamander*, *The Louisville Review*, and *Story Quarterly*. When she finished her dissertation in 1997, she also received a fellowship at the Fine Arts Center in Provincetown, Massachusetts. During her residency at the Fine Arts Center, things really started to look up for her. In 1998 she had three stories published in the *New Yorker* and her first book, a collection of short fiction, was scheduled to appear in the following year. In 1999, she was named by the *New Yorker* one of twenty best American fiction writers under the age of forty. Furthermore, her first short story collection, *Interpreter of Maladies*, garnered the Pulitzer Prize in fiction in 2000. Since the Pulitzer, her book has become a bestseller and has made its way into public/college libraries, book clubs, and even college classrooms. Lahiri has also become a celebrity not only in the United States and the Subcontinent but also elsewhere.

Ever since *Interpreter of Maladies* was published, she has been variously proclaimed to be an "American writer," an "Indian-American author," an "NRI" (non-residential Indian), and an "ABCD" (American born confused desi). Her writings are described as "diaspora fiction" by Indian scholars and "immigrant fiction" by American critics. Lahiri does not mind being so variously cataloged and thinks all of these labels are "accurate" ("To Heaven without Dying"). However, she states that she does not really "identify [herself] with [writers like Chitra Banerjee Divakaruni and Bharati Mukherjee] apart from the fact that [she is] Indian, too" (Uviller B11). She expresses an interest in their works but has "never looked to them as an influence" (Uviller B11). Commenting on her own writings, Lahiri explains that her stories are "less a response to [her] parents' cultural nostalgia, and more an attempt to forge [her] own amalgamated domain" ("To Heaven without Dying"). Indeed, Lahiri's fiction is a unique addition to the existing Asian American literary corpus. When compared with many popular works set in postcolonial South Asia and narrated from immigrant or diasporan perspectives, Lahiri's is a refreshing voice because many of her stories are located in America and written from a second-generation Indian American point of view.

◆ MAJOR WORKS AND THEMES

Interpreter of Maladies is Lahiri's first and only book to date. The collection contains nine stories, most of which appeared previously in different journals and magazines. Writing these pieces individually, Lahiri did not initially have in mind a book. Nonetheless, these nine stories have in common certain themes and motifs, such as exile, displacement, loneliness, difficult relationships, and problems about communication. Her characters range from Indians, Indian émigrés, and American-born Indians to white Americans involved with them. Some of her stories are set in North America while others in South Asia. Although Lahiri's fiction either has a narrative setting of India or features an Indian (American) character, "Indian-ness" is never overemphasized or exaggerated to render her story to be exotic or "ethnic." Her characters do not act as "native informants" or appear to be the embodiment of oriental exotica. In fact, many of her Indian American characters often learn about India from tour guides (e.g., Mr. and Mrs. Das in "Interpreter of Maladies") and history books (e.g., Shukumar in "A Temporary Matter" and Lilia in "When Mr. Pirzada Came to Dine"). In Lahiri's stories, there is no nostalgia for Indian traditions. The writer indulges in neither the exotic nor the historic. She does not exaggerate her immigrant characters' Indian inflection, either. Her Indian American characters appear to be more "American" than "Indian." For instance, in "This Blessed House" Twinkle is writing her master's thesis on an Irish poet. In "When Mr. Pirzada Came to Dine" Lilia is excellent in "American" history. In "A Temporary Matter" Shukumar and Shoba met because they were bored at a Bengali poetry reading. In some of her tales, ethnicity almost seems to be incidental rather than essential to the theme.

Many pieces of the collection treat troubled marriages or problematic relationships. For example, "A Temporary Matter," set in Boston, concerns the gradual dissolution of a marriage. Shukumar is a graduate student in his thirties trying to complete his dissertation and his wife Shoba works as a professional proofreader. The couple has grown estranged from each other since the death of their stillborn child. Shukumar is depressed at home and feels vaguely guilty because he was at an academic conference during his wife's premature labor and the death of the baby. Since the tragic incident, the husband has taken over the role of cooking while his increasingly distracted and remote wife seeks refuge in her job. It is only in the darkness resulting from an electricity repair that the couple can finally communicate. Yet, the reconciliation turns out to be just "temporary." During the power outage, they reveal their secrets, from petty betrayals to true feelings about each other. When the electricity is restored, the wife discloses her plan of moving out into an apartment alone, and the husband unfolds his knowledge about their stillborn child.

"This Blessed House" also focuses on a difficult relationship between a couple. An MIT graduate, Sanjeev is a successful engineer who has his own secretary and "a dozen people working under his supervision" (138) at a firm in Connecticut. Tanima, nicknamed "Twinkle," is writing her master's thesis on an Irish poet at Stanford. They are recently married and have just moved into a suburban house. As Twinkle discovers a hoard of Christian knickknacks left by the house's former owner(s), the couple starts their marital sparring.

As Twinkle becomes increasingly fascinated by the Christian paraphernalia she keeps unearthing in their new house, Sanjeev grows more and more irritated by his wife's discoveries and enthusiasm. Twinkle wants to display the kitschy collection on the mantelpiece, but Sanjeev wants to discard them. He reminds his wife: "We are not Christian" (137). He does not want his colleagues, who will be coming for their housewarming party, to think otherwise. The couple's conflicting attitudes toward the kitschy knickknacks makes Sanjeev realize how different they are and wonder if he has made the right choice of marrying "this woman, whom he had known for only four months" (146) through their parents' arrangement.

In the story titled "The Third and Final Continent," the first-person narrator is looking back upon his arrival in America in 1969. The unnamed narrator journeyed from Calcutta to Boston through London in search of livelihood. He has just married a woman named Mala through their parents' arrangement in India before leaving for America, where he found a librarian job at MIT in Cambridge. He needs to establish himself before sending for his bride who has remained in India after the wedding. At first, he lives in a rented room in a house owned by an eccentric elderly lady whose peculiar habits he gradually comes to accept. The story of his adjustment in the new country is parallel to his own reflection on his arranged marriage—to both of which he is learning how to adjust. He and his bride are awkward with each other and uncomfortable at the beginning of their marital life in the new country. The narrator views Mala as a traditional Indian woman who is steeped in her native customs, which he finds difficult to accept. However, when they visit his former landlady, the latter thinks his bride "a perfect lady" (195). The compliment narrows not only the distances between the couple but also between cultures and continents. The fact that the protagonist arrives in Boston during the 1969 moon landing is more symbolic than coincidental. The new country the protagonist stumbles upon is as foreign to him as the moon, particularly considering his relationship with his eccentric elderly landlady.

Like Mala in "The Third and Final Continent," Mrs. Sen in "Mrs. Sen's" is also a wife of an Indian immigrant in America. This story recounts the difficulties faced by Mrs. Sen who is left at "home" to cope with her new life, without family and friends, while her husband immerses himself in his work that brought them to the United States. Unlike "The Third and Final Continent," the narrative is told in the third-person voice and focuses on the immigrant woman's life rather than her husband's. Mrs. Sen, married to an untenured and anxious math professor and trying to adapt to the lonely life of a housewife, tries to expand her horizon by babysitting a white American boy named Eliot in her apartment in the afternoons. Mrs. Sen misses terribly her "home" and folk in Calcutta. She is trapped in her private world of frustration and despair in a quiet university town on the northeast coast. There are only two things that make her happy in the United States: letters from India and fresh fish sold at the seaside stalls. Not being able to fetch fresh fish as often as she wants frustrates her. Despite her virtuoso displays of cutlery and culinary skills, she freezes whenever she gets behind the wheel of a car. She has been relying on her husband to drive her to the seaside to get her fish. Mr. Sen drives her whenever he can, but more than often his duties at the university prevent him. When Mrs. Sen sets off alone in the car with Eliot, she has an accident, which consequently terminates her job as a babysitter.

The story "When Mr. Pirzada Came to Dine" focuses on a bond between a child and an adult. The ten-year-old Lilia, the first-person narrator, is excellent in "American" history but ignorant and curious about the division of Bengal between Hindus and Muslims. Her Calcutta immigrant parents are usually anxious to hobnob with their compatriots. Mr. Pirzada is sought out by them through the university directory, even though he, speaking the same language, is technically not an "Indian" for he comes from East Pakistan. Lilia and Mr. Pirzada become fast friends. Mr. Pirzada is a botanist visiting New England for his research, whose stay coincides with the Bangladeshi war of independence in 1971. He worries about his wife and seven daughters in Dacca. Lilia prays secretly for the safety of her friend's family in the newly developed war situation in South Asia. As suddenly as he comes, Mr. Pirzada disappears from Lilia's life to find out the fate of his family. However, from her friendship with him, the ten-year-old girl learns a little about human relationships and an idea of what it means for Mr. Pirzada to have been away from his family and home for so long.

"Sexy" is another story about a woman's displacement and loneliness and also features a child character whose innocent words help the female protagonist make sense of her relationship with a married man. Miranda, a twenty-two-year-old woman from Michigan, has come to Boston to work and live alone. She is depicted as a woman with "silver eyes and skin as pale as paper, and the contrast with her hair, as dark and glossy as an espresso bean" (87). She is having an affair with a married Indian American banker named Dev who picked her up by the cosmetics counter in a department store. Miranda's involvement with Dev reminds her of the only Indian American family, the Dixits, that she knew in her youth. She recalls that the Dixits' house, "the only one with the vinyl siding, detracted from the neighborhood's charm" (95). She also remembers that she was frightened by the picture of the goddess Kali hung in the family's living room, so much so that she could not walk on the same side of the street as the Dixits' house. Her relationship with Dev, however, prompts her to learn about India, superficially. Miranda's affair is mirrored by the cousin of her Indian American colleague Laxmi, whose husband met a British girl on an airplane and for whom he has abandoned his wife and seven-year-old son in Montreal and moved to London. Laxmi's cousin is flying to visit her parents in California "to try to recuperate" (100), and has a layover at Boston. Miranda is asked by her friend to babysit the son of Laxmi's cousin named Rohin. After spending an afternoon babysitting Rohin, she finds herself reevaluating her affair with her lover.

In Lahiri's book, cultural clashes can occur in both North America and South Asia. The title story treats cultural clashes between an Indian cabdriver/ tour guide named Mr. Kapasi and an Indian American family from New Jersey touring India. Mr. Kapasi is a gifted linguist but his talent has not got him very far in life. Monstrous doctor's bills for his child with cancer (who has since died) have forced him to abandon his teaching career to work as an interpreter for a doctor's Gujarati patients. On weekends, he acts as a driver cum tour guide for mainly foreign tourists. The narrative focuses on the day when he takes the Das family to see the Sun Temple in Konarak. The Das family may look Indian but are actually very American; the couple bicker; Mr. Das relies too heavily on the tour book; the children constantly snack and have elaborate orthodontia. Yet, Mr. Kapasi identifies himself with Mrs. Das's marital discomfort because he feels the same about his marriage. He is at first fascinated by Mrs. Das's appearance and behavior but then shocked by the secret she reveals to him. While Mr. Kapasi is just looking for a friend or pen pal, Mrs. Das is looking for an "interpreter of maladies" who "could help [her] feel better, say the right thing, [and suggest] some kind of remedy" (65).

"A Real Durwan" and "The Treatment of Bibi Haldar" are two other stories also set in India, but feature exclusively Indian characters. "A Real Durwan" tells the story of a sixty-four-year-old woman named Boori Ma, who has been deported to Calcutta as a result of the Partition. She is a self-appointed door-keeper and stair sweeper of a flat-building, whose residents allow her to sleep on the floor under the letter boxes by the main entrance. She has been looked after by the inhabitants of the building; however, when a theft occurs, she is wrongly accused and subsequently turned out of the building. "The Treatment of Bibi Haldar" recounts the life experience of a young woman, Bibi Haldar, who suffers from an epileptic disease. She has come to live under her uncle and aunt's supervision after her father died. Her uncle and aunt take her in because the family relationship, not compassion, obliges them. Hence, she is much neglected in many ways. Bibi believes that marriage can cure her. Yet, it is precisely because of her ailment that she obtains no marriage proposal. During a fit, she becomes pregnant. Bibi does not remember how it happens, but she is cured from the disease. Her relatives disappear on her after the disgrace. With the help of the neighborhood women, Bibi starts a pharmacy business with her uncle's remaindered stock, and brings up her child.

◆ CRITICAL RECEPTION

By and large, Lahiri's *Interpreter of Maladies* has been favorably received. Reviewers praise the short story collection for its "direct translucent prose" (Shapiro 67), "exquisite language" (Guckenberger), "lucid and clear" tone (Roy-Chowdhury), "details that capture the differences between Indian and American lifestyle" (Uviller 11), and "harsh truth about the politics of borderland existence" (Freeman 37). In *London Review of Books*, Gabriele Annan describes the writer as "funny . . . sharp and ironical" (40). In *Booklist*, Mary Ellen Quinn admires Lahiri for her "ability to use different eyes and voices" (1514). In *World Literature Today*, Ronny Noor says that the author has "a keen eye for observation and an admirable gift for details" (365). In the *New York Times*, Michiko Kakutani calls Lahiri "a writer of uncommon elegance and poise" (E48).

Although Amy Tan and Chitra Banerjee Divakaruni have proffered their compliments to *Interpreter of Maladies*, as seen on the back cover of the book, most reviewers tend to group Lahiri not with the "ethnic" writers like Tan and Divakaruni, but with the more "classic" American authors. For instance, writing in the *Plain Dealer*, Jeff Guinn states that Lahiri's writings can be viewed "as gentle Hemingway" (3E). In *Meghdutam.com*, Kanan K. Purkayastha comments that Lahiri's book recalls Carver, Hemingway, and Isherwood because it also "illuminates human nature." In *India Today*, Sumit Mitra and Arthur Pais describe her as a "quintessentially American" writer like Hemingway, Faulkner, and Mailer (89). Many critics also point out that Lahiri's stories transcend the so-called "ethnic," immigrant or postcolonial literature. For example, reviewing the book for *Amerasia*, Purvi Shah remarks that Lahiri's short story collection is an alternative to "the indulgences of postcolonial magical realism" (186). Tamsin Todd in the *Washington Post* contends that Lahiri's stories recall "more Hemingway than [Arundhati] Roy" (C8). Rani Sinha in *Sawnet* notes that, unlike Bharati Mukherjee and Chitra Divakaruni, who write about "ethnic exotica," "Lahiri writes with a depth and honesty which require no melodrama." Sandip Roy-Chowdhury in *New California Media Online* asserts that Lahiri does not write to "give white suburban women (who apparently are the biggest purveyors of 'ethnic fiction') an easy armchair tour of India."

Nevertheless, a few reviewers have some reservations about Lahiri's "Indian" stories, "A Real Durwan" and "The Treatment of Bibi Haldar," in particular. Victoria Millar in *The Scotsman* thinks that the author is "less confident on all-Indian terrain" (10). In *Meghdutam.com*, Paul Sanjoy Gonsalves maintains that neither of them "rings entirely true" because "her characters appear farcical, the circumstances forced" and her "Bengali colloquialisms . . . end up sounding comical." Erin Stringer in *LiteralMind.com* also finds that the two stories "fall flat, lacking real depth and making the characters appear foreign and untouchable." In *India Today* Mitra and Pais remark that the two stories represent only "a tunnel vision at best of Indians in India" (89). Kakutani in the *New York Times* thinks that "A Real Durwan" and "The Treatment of Bibi Haldar" "suffer from a certain folk-tale contrivance that results in overly neat, moralistic endings" (E48).

In summary, Lahiri has garnered copious accolades for her debut short-fiction collection. Many praise her work for its language, style, subject and theme. Quite a number of reviewers agree that she is truly an American author like other previous Pulitzer winners such as Hemingway. However, some contend that her "American" stories are better than her "Indian" stories on the grounds that the author's vision of "India" is narrow and limited. Apart from numerous reviews, however, no scholarship on Lahiri has been published yet, perhaps because *Interpreter of Maladies* is the author's first book that was just published a couple of years ago.

◆ BIBLIOGRAPHY

Works by Jhumpa Lahiri

Short Story

"Nobody's Business." *New Yorker* (March 12, 2001): 78–95.

Short Story Collection

Interpreter of Maladies. Boston: Houghton Mifflin, 1999.

Essays

"Money Talks in Pakistan: In this Novel, It Speaks Much the Same Language Jay Gatsby Did." *New York Times Book Review* (March 12, 2000): 7.
"To Heaven without Dying." *Feed Books Issue* (July 24, 2000). http://www.feedmag.com/book2/essay-lahiri.html.

Studies of Jhumpa Lahiri

Aguiar, Arun. "One on One with Jhumpa Lahiri." *Pifmagazine.com.* http://www.pifmagazine.com/vol28/i_magui.shtml.
Annan, Gabiele. "Some Kind of Remedy." *London Book Review* (July 20, 2000): 40.
Crain, Caleb. "Subcontinental Drift." *New York Times* (July 11, 1999): 11.
Dwarakanath, Kala. "A New Yorker Is New Arrival on Literary Scene." *India in New York* (June 25, 1999). http://www.indiainnewyork.com/iny062599/women/anewyorker.html.
Flynn, Gillian. "Passage to India: First-time Author Jhumpa Lahiri Nabs a Pulitzer." *Entertainment Weekly* (April 28, 2000): 100.
Freeman, John. "Facing the Sharp Edge." *Bonton Book Review* 6 (June 1999): 37.
Gonsalves, Paul Sanjoy. "Out and Out: A Review of *Interpreter of Maladies*." *Meghdutam.com* (July 2000). http://www.meghdutam.com/2000/july/book.shtml.
Guckenberger, Katherine. "Translation: A Short-Story Collection Decodes Mysteries of Culture." *Boston Phoenix.com* (June 10–17, 1999). http://www.bostonphoenix.com/archive/books/99/06/10/INTERPRETER.html.
Guinn, Jeff. "Pulitzer Committee Uncovers a Treasure." *Plain Dealer* (April 24, 2000): 3E.
"Jhumpa Lahiri Wins Pulitzer." *Rediff.com* (April 11, 2000). http://www.rediff.com/news/2001/jan/11jhump.html.

Johnson, Hillary. "We: The View from the East." *LA Weekly* (October 22–28, 1999). http://www.laweekly.com/ink/99/48/books-johnson.shtml.

Jones, Vanessa E. "Prized Writer: Jhumpa Lahiri's Debut Book Won a Pulitzer. Now What?" *Boston Globe* (November 9, 2000): E1.

Kakutani, Michiko. "Liking America, But Longing for India." *New York Times* (August 6, 1999): E48.

Kenny, Michael. "Names and Faces: Lahiri and Dower Honored at PEN Event." *Boston Globe* (April 10, 2000): B8.

Kipen, David. "Interpreting Indian Culture With Stories." *San Francisco Chronicle* (June 24, 1999): E1.

Millar, Victoria. "Indian Tales Whispering Across Parallel Worlds." *The Scotsman* (August 21, 1999): 10.

Mitra, Sumit, and Arthur Pais. "Jhumpa Lahiri: Boston Brahmin." *India Today* (April 24, 2000): 89.

Noor, Ronny. Rev. of *Interpreter of Maladies*. World Literature Today 74.2 (Spring 2000): 365–66.

Patel, Vibhuti. "The Maladies of Belonging." (Interview) *Newsweek* (September 20, 1999): 80.

Purkayastha, Kanan K. "The Anatomy of *Interpreter of Maladies*." *Meghdutam.com* (July 2000). http://www.meghdutam.com/2000/july/book1p.shtml.

Quinn, Mary Ellen. Rev. of *Interpreter of Maladies*. Booklist (April 15, 1999): 1514.

"A Reader's Guide: Jhumpa Lahiri." http://www.houghtonmifflinbook.com/reader-guides/interpreter-maladies.shtml.

Rhankar, Radhika R. "A Writer Free to Write All Day." *Rediff on the Net* (August 23, 1999). http://www.rediff.com/news/1999/aug/23us2.html.

Roy-Chowdhury, Sandip. "*Interpreter of Maladies*: A Fresh Take on Immigrant Lives." *New California Media Online* (October 8, 1999): http://www.ncmonline.com/arts-and-culture/1999–10–08/books.html.

Shah, Purvi. Rev. of *Interpreter of Maladies*. Amerasia 27.2 (2001): 183–86.

Shapiro, Laura. "India Calling." *Newsweek* (July 19, 1999): 67.

Sinha, Rani. Rev. of *Interpreter of Maladies*. Sawnet. http://www.miacs.umd.edu/users/sawweb.sawnet/books/interpreter2.html.

Stringer, Erin. Review of *Interpreter of Maladies*. LiteralMind.com. http://www.literalmind.com/0045/html.

Taylor, Robert. "A Quietly Powerful 'Interpreter.'" *Boston Globe* (July 14, 1999): F8.

Todd, Tamsin. "At the Corner Delhi." *Washington Post* (October 7, 1999): C8.

Uviller, Daphne. "Talking with Jhumpa Lahiri through the Looking Glass." *Newsday* (July 25, 1999: B11.

ANDREW LAM
(1963–   )

Kim-An Lieberman

Andrew Lam was born May 23, 1963, in Saigon, Vietnam. His father, de-
scended from wealthy landowners in the Mekong Delta, served as a general
in the South Vietnamese Army. His mother, from a small rural village in
northern Vietnam, fled south in 1954 to escape communist rule.

Growing up, Lam enjoyed the privileges of his father's money and status.
The family retained servants and occupied beautiful villas, traveling frequently throughout South Vietnam to accommodate military assignments. The
youngest of three children, Lam was a self-proclaimed bookworm. War, however, remained a constant part of the background. In his essay "A Child's
View," Lam recalls crouching in a bomb shelter during the 1968 Tet Offensive:
"I remember bursts of gunfire and random explosions that left horrible echoes
like thunder, yet they did not drown out the shouts of soldiers and the shrieks
of women and children in other houses."

On April 28, 1975, two days before the North Vietnamese Army took control of Saigon, eleven-year-old Lam escaped with his mother, grandmother,
sister, and brother on a crowded cargo plane. They passed through refugee
camps in Guam and California before settling in the San Francisco Bay Area.
Lam's father, who had stayed behind in Saigon determined to fight off the
communists, finally left Vietnam by boat on April 30. It would be several
months before the family was reunited.

As a teenager, Lam attended public schools in the Bay Area. He then enrolled at the University of California-Berkeley, graduating in 1986 with a bi-
ochemistry degree. After two years working at a cancer research lab, Lam quit
to pursue a writing career. He studied creative writing at San Francisco State

University, where the student magazine *Transfer* published his first short story "Dark Wood and Shadows."

In 1989, Lam joined the Pacific News Service and traveled throughout Asia as a foreign correspondent. He recorded his first return trip to Vietnam in an award-winning series of articles. Back in the United States, Lam covered Vietnamese American community issues for the *San Jose Mercury News* and provided regular commentaries for National Public Radio. In 1995, he coedited *Once Upon a Dream: The Vietnamese-American Experience*, the first collection to focus exclusively on Vietnamese American literature and art. Lam also continues to publish short fiction. He has received numerous honors for his work, including the Storke Excellence in International Journalism Award, a Rockefeller Fellowship, and recognition as one of New Horizon's Top 25 Vietnamese Americans.

◆ MAJOR WORKS AND THEMES

Lam's writing reflects his experiences as a Vietnamese American immigrant. His earliest stories, "Dark Wood and Shadows" and "On the Perfume," describe events from his childhood in wartime Vietnam. Later works are more clearly fictionalized, introducing sustained character studies or elements of magical realism. Still, they retain a strong link to Lam's personal history through protagonists who are also dealing with the memory of war or the challenge of a new life in the United States.

One story that displays Lam's characteristic blend of personal and fictional is "Show and Tell," which D. E. Perushek describes as "the moving portrayal of the introduction of a Vietnamese refugee boy into an eighth-grade class" (86). Like Lam himself, Cao Long Nguyen arrives in an American middle school unable to speak English. Cao's story, however, is relayed from the first-person viewpoint of an American classmate who befriends him. Using this narrative approach, Lam shifts the focus from a replay of his own past to a broader examination of intercultural communication and empathy.

Lam often merges the poignant with the comedic. In "Grandma's Tales," the Vietnamese American protagonist relates the sudden reincarnation of his dead grandmother. Witty and elegant, a new-and-improved Grandma enchants a snooty cocktail-party crowd with tales from her past, then runs off to see the world with a handsome stranger. The reincarnation, while humorous, is also a bittersweet metaphor for the endurance of Vietnamese familial and cultural heritage. Instead of dwelling on her death—"what we had always expected as the tragic ending of things, human frailty, the point of mourning and loss"—the protagonist remembers his grandmother as a source of strength and hope (70).

Throughout his work, Lam stresses a balanced, bicultural perspective. Multifaceted situations challenge both Vietnamese and American stereotypes. For instance, the narrator of "Slingshot" resents U.S. veteran Steve for his patronizing attitude toward her Vietnamese American family: "You two are my favorite Mekong Delta girls. So smart. So filial" (154). But later, when she discovers that Steve has gone to great lengths to retrieve her father's ashes from Vietnam, the narrator finds herself guilty of a similar underestimation of character.

Lam's stories avoid simple prescriptions for ethnic identity. Instead, by placing individualistic characters within culturally complex situations, Lam suggests that interpersonal connection is the key to understanding and bridging difference.

◆ CRITICAL RECEPTION

Lam has been heralded as one "of the most seminal and influential" Vietnamese American writers publishing today (Karlin 1). In many anthologies which include his work, Lam's stories stand out as highlights "not to be missed" (Perushek 86).

Critics note Lam's willingness to grapple with difficult issues such as war and refugee experience. Wayne Karlin commends Lam for touching on "the eternal questions of exile: What is lost, what is kept and what is gained?" (1). Lam is especially skilled at blending these universal themes with a lively writing style. For example, Paul Signorelli describes "Dark Wood and Shadows" as both "an entertaining page-turner and, at a far deeper level, a paean to loss and remembrance."

Even though Lam has not published a self-standing collection yet, his stories have been widely reprinted. His best-known piece, "Grandma's Tales," appears in about ten different anthologies and journals. The story is praised for its mix of witty narration and fairytale atmosphere. Daisy Fried calls it "more than just another sentimental frail-but-wise-and-feisty grandmother story. It's full of good humor and culture-crossing, plus some mythical magic."

Lam is also known for being an outstanding storyteller in person. Many people have commented on the emotional strength of his live readings. One audience member at a reading of "Slingshot" describes how Lam "really brought down the house . . . people were weeping with laughter" (Hanig 6). Lam himself recalls looking up, after presenting an essay to his college writing workshop, to find that "the entire room was in complete silence and everyone, including the professor, was in tears" (Nguyen 56).

Despite Lam's popular acclaim, there are few in-depth studies of his work. Vietnamese American literature as a whole remains greatly underrated. After the United States withdrew from Saigon in 1975, Americans seemed eager to forget that the war had ever happened. Vietnamese immigrants were targets of racism, considered unwelcome reminders of the U.S military defeat. Only recently have readers realized that Vietnamese Americans can offer a fresh perspective on the war's events and aftermath as well as a unique reflection of America's changing demographics. Additionally, the 1995 restoration of U.S.–Vietnam diplomatic ties has helped revise old perceptions of the Vietnamese as "enemies."

Lam represents a new generation of Vietnamese Americans whose literature is not just in greater demand but also more accessible. Most first-generation authors wrote in Vietnamese, and translations of their work have been infrequent. Now, with the English-language efforts of younger authors, Vietnamese American literature is finding its way to a broader audience. As the genre claims more critical attention, there is no doubt that Lam's name will appear at the forefront.

◆ BIBLIOGRAPHY

Works by Andrew Lam

Short Stories

"Dark Wood and Shadows." *Transfer* 57 (Fall 1989): 24–35.
"Grandma's Tales." *Amerasia Journal* 20.3 (1994): 65–70.
"On the Perfume." *Manoa* 6.2 (1994): 132–41.
"She in a Dance of Frenzy." In *The Other Side of Heaven: Postwar Fiction By Vietnamese and American Writers*. Wayne Karlin, Le Minh Khue, and Truong Vu, eds. Willimantic, CT: Curbstone, 1995, 322–26.
"Requiems in Blue." *Vietnam Review* 2 (Spring/Summer 1997): 449–53.
"Show and Tell." In *Watermark: Vietnamese American Poetry and Prose*. Barbara Tran, Monique T.D. Truong, and Luu Truong Khoi, eds. New York: Asian American Writers' Workshop, 1998, 111–21.
"Slingshot." *ZYZZYVA* (Winter 1998): 151–63.
"The Shard, the Tissue, an Affair." *Manoa* 12.2 (2000): 64–67.
"Fire." In *Of Vietnam: Identities in Dialogue*. Jane Winston and Leakthina Ollier, eds. New York: Palgrave, 2001, 130–41.

Essays and Articles (Selected)

"My Vietnam, My America." *The Nation* (December 10, 1990): 724–26.
"Goodbye, Saigon. Finally." *New York Times*, National ed. (April 30, 1993): A17.
"Love, Money, Prison, Sin, Revenge." *Los Angeles Times Magazine* (March 13, 1994): 24+.
"To Be Viet Kieu Is to Be Santa Claus." In *New to North America: Writing by U.S. Immigrants, Their Children, and Grandchildren*. Abby Bogomolny, ed. Oakland, CA: Burning Bush, 1997, 73–75.
"A Child's View: Watching Bombs, Hearing Bombs in Memory." *Jinn Magazine* (January 5, 1999) http://www.pacificnews.org/jinn/stories/5.01/990105-bombs.html. Accessed December 21, 2001.

Collections

Editor and contributor. *Once Upon A Dream: The Vietnamese-American Experience.* Ed. with De Tran and Hai Dai Nguyen. San Jose, CA: San Jose Mercury News, 1995.

Contributor. Pacific News Service. http://www.pacificnews.org/contributors/lam/. Accessed February 22, 2002.

Writer. *Alsop Review.* http://www.alsopreview.com/lam/alam.html. Accessed February 22, 2002.

Studies of Andrew Lam

Christopher, Renny. "Transgressive Humor in Recent Vietnamese American Fiction: Andrew Lam and Khoi Luu." *Abstracts of the 1998 AAS Annual Meeting.* http://www.aasianst.org/absts/1998abst/seasia/se196.htm. Accessed January 10, 2002.

Fried, Daisy. "Get Your Shorts in a Bunch." Rev. of *Sudden Fiction (Continued): 60 New Short Stories. Philadelphia CityPaper.Net Book Quarterly.* Robert Shepard and James Thomas, eds. (September 26–October 3, 1996). http://www.citypaper.net/articles/092696/article011.shtml. Accessed November 10, 2001.

Hanig, Ross. "Author Andrew Lam Gives Personalized Book Reading." *California Aggie* (March 15, 1999): 1+.

Karlin, Wayne. "Hot Damn Vietnam: Twenty-Five Years Later, A Literature of War and Remembrance." *Los Angeles Times,* Book Review (April, 23, 2000): 1.

Nguyen, Phuong Madison. "Andrew Lam: Beyond the Fountain Pen." In *New Horizon/ Chan Troi Moi: 25 Vietnamese Americans in 25 Years, 1975–2000.* Nguyen Thi Diem Huyen and Nguyen Thi Thuy, editors-in-chief. San Jose, CA: 2000, 55–59.

Perushek, D. E. Rev. of *Watermark: Vietnamese American Poetry and Prose.* Tran, Truong, and Khoi, eds. *Library Journal* (May 15, 1998): 86.

Signorelli, Paul. "Armchair Tales: Vietnam Brings the Journey Home." Rev. of *Vietnam: A Traveler's Literary Companion.* John Balaban and Nguyen Qui Duc, eds. *San Francisco Bay Guardian Lit* (March 27, 1996). http://www.sfbg.com/lit/reviews/armchair.html. Accessed January 10, 2002.

Turks, Victor. "Making Good in the Land of Milk and Honey." *AsianWeek.com.* (June 22–28, 2000). http://www.asianweek.com/2000_06_22/ae2a_andrewlambio.html. Accessed January 10, 2000.

EVELYN LAU
(1971–   )

Nikolas Huot

♦ **BIOGRAPHY**

Born the second of July 1971 in Vancouver, British Columbia, Evelyn Lau has always known she wanted to be a writer. Unfortunately, the path to her writing career was strewn with many obstacles. As the oldest daughter of ambitious Chinese immigrants, she was expected to follow the wishes of her parents and become either a doctor or a lawyer. Her writing, which she perceived to be her sole talent, was considered by her parents to be a nuisance and a distraction from her studies and, accordingly, was forbidden at home. Despite her parents' efforts, Lau wrote in secret and managed to publish some poems and short stories at the age of twelve. Constantly pressured to excel at school and incessantly forced to study, Lau ran away from her repressive parents early in 1986. With only ten dollars in her pocket, the fourteen year old was soon forced to turn to prostitution to support herself. During her life on the streets, Lau was raped, interned in a psychiatric ward, tried twice to commit suicide, became bulimic, and turned to drugs; through it all, Lau kept a diary, "the one thread by which [she] could keep alive" (Condé 106). A condensed form of this journal was published in 1989 under the title of *Runaway: Diary of a Street Kid*. The success of her autobiography—it stayed on the Canadian best-seller list for more than thirty weeks—propelled Lau out of the streets and social institutions.

Merely a year after the publication of *Runaway*, Lau published her first volume of poetry, *You Are Not Who You Claim* (1990), for which she was awarded the Air Canada/Canadian Author Association's Award for Most Promising Writing Under 30 and the Milton Acorn People's Poetry Award for a work that sustained the tradition of a people's literature in Canada and internationally. With her second collection of poetry, *Oedipal Dreams* (1992), Lau became the youngest nominee for the most prestigious award in Canadian literature, the Governor General's Award. Following her two volumes of poetry, Lau published a widely acclaimed collection of short stories, *Fresh Girls and Other Stories* (1993), another collection of poems, *In the House of Slaves* (1994), and a novella, *Other Women* (1995). Other than her frequent contributions to *Vancouver Magazine*, Lau has more recently published her second collection of short stories, *Choose Me* (1999), and a compilation of autobiographical essays, *Inside Out: Reflections on a Life So Far* (2001). Despite her success and her acclaim, Lau still finds herself fighting for recognition as a serious writer; to this day, many critics continue to label her as the teenage prostitute who can write or condescendingly try to help her as if her writing were a form of public therapy. Regardless of the labels and the patronizing critics, Evelyn Lau continues to produce distinguished and outstanding work from her condo in Vancouver.

◆ MAJOR WORKS AND THEMES

In her first collection of short stories, *Fresh Girls*, Lau presents young women searching for a physical and psychological place where they will find love, comfort, and contentment. Far from being "fresh girls," Lau's characters are seen mostly as sexual objects that married boyfriends or "johns" can visit any time they choose. Most of the characters are longing for a man to declare his love and for him to tell them that "he wants them to go out on real dates: movies, dinners, walks around the seawall" (*Fresh Girls* 92). That declaration never arrives, however, since after sex the man invariably leaves to meet his wife for dinner or tells her to leave his apartment while shoving money in her coat pocket. By the end of their respective stories, the dominatrixes, prostitutes, and masochists are left with the realization that tomorrow will bring the same unfulfilling violence and disappointing loneliness.

While *Fresh Girls* mostly deals with prostitutes and dominatrixes, *Choose Me* centers on women who are not associated with the sex industry. Although the main characters are from different social spheres, the theme of longing to be chosen by a man is still prevalent. Stories of women who are attracted to men and yearn to connect with them in a sustained and meaningful relationship are not uncommon in this collection. Unfortunately for the young women, their choices of men (invariably older and occasionally married) are revealed as unwise as the latter prove to be almost repulsive once intimacy is achieved.

In *Choose Me*, Lau also presents the consequences of the choices women have made in their relationships. Nobody chooses well, and nobody finds comfort in Lau's stories. Through their choices and their attempts to find a substantial relationship, the women struggle to define themselves and to create personal identities that would transcend their images as sexual objects.

However, too often in Lau's stories, "the images of women [prove to] be stronger than the women themselves" (Wong, "Varied" 197). Through the psychological abuse of failed relationships, the women are "caught in a confusion of images where they misrecognize themselves and cannot make out a whole from the pieces" (Gray 46). As a result, the characters in *Choose Me* find themselves alone and psychologically shattered.

Whether physical or psychological, pain constantly surrounds the young women in Lau's fiction. In order to survive the violence and the loneliness, the first-person narrator detaches herself from her environment and observes objectively what she is doing and what is being done to her. Lau's characters are active participants and aloof observers at the same time. Even when the voice of the narrator does not belong to the main character, Lau still writes with an icy detachment that lets the reader inside the mind of the woman who yearns for comfort and love in the midst of all her pain. This quality in Lau's writing makes for a realistic and, in some cases, difficult reading.

Among some of the notable stories written by Evelyn Lau are "Glass," a story where the detached self expresses her worries about the young woman (herself) who has just put her fist through a window; "Pleasure," where the narrator explains matter-of-factly how a woman chained and blindfolded comes to enjoy masochism as the only time that "she could not be held responsible for anything that happened next" (*Fresh Girls* 41); "Roses," where an eighteen year old removes herself mentally from the beatings suffered at the hands of her client by remembering the physical and sexual abuse of her father; "Mercy," a first-person narrative about a dominatrix who realizes that "each time your face wrenches with pain . . . you are killing me and not the other way around" (*Fresh Girls* 85); "The Apartments," a story about a prostitute who desperately hopes to live a normal life with her client, but who comes to realize the hollowness of her dream; "Family," where a young writer stays for a weekend in her lover's house while he and his family are away; "A Faithful Husband," which deals with a young wife who decides to stay in her marriage despite her infidelity and her disgust over her aging husband; and "In the Desert," where an impotent husband's attempt at sex leads his revulsed younger wife to look "at the wall beyond his shoulder and [wish] herself far away from this" (*Choose Me* 152).

Although candidly dealing with sex in all its forms, Lau's stories are not erotic. Not only because she delves mostly into the psychological rather than the physical realm but also because her descriptions of sex are rarely graphic. Moreover, as Lau explains, she perceives eroticism as a matter of desire: "If I read something that's erotic, the person in it is wanting something sexual, and it is genuine and heartfelt," she told Misao Dean. "In my work," Lau continues, "these women aren't wanting what is happening to be happening to them" (qtd. in Dean 24). Sex, in Lau's stories, is not an expression of love, but a detached and sometimes violent act empty of affection.

◆ CRITICAL RECEPTION

Lau's fiction, as well as her poetry, has usually been received by critics with a mix of enthusiasm and curiosity. If the enthusiasm reflects the quality of her work, the curiosity typically arises from the main themes presented in her fiction and from suspicions that her stories and poems are autobiographical.

Nonetheless, the majority of critics highly praise Lau's fictional debut. Calling *Fresh Girls* "a beautifully crafted collection of short stories," Joel Yanofsky's review echoes the majority of those who see Lau's poetic gift in her stories ("Hooking" J2). The most recurrent praise surrounding *Fresh Girls* centers on Lau's prose and realistic vision. Fellow fiction writer Irene Wanner considers Lau's prose to be "spare and eloquent, her observations deep and perceptive" (M2); as for critic Rita Wong, she acknowledges that "Lau has a brilliant ability to describe subtle emotional shifts with uncanny accuracy ("Varied" 196). Erika Taylor applauds the authenticity of Lau's writing, while Keith Nickson writes that her prose, "tight as a drum and laced with arresting images, is wonderfully free of creative writing school tics. You'll find no cliches [and] no deadpan minimalism in the American style" (J17).

If *Fresh Girls* is seen as a "brilliant fiction debut," Lau's second collection of short stories was not as well received (Nickson J17). *Choose Me* is mostly read as a bleak book with few redemptive qualities. With the exception of Linda Richards and Heather Mallick, the detached, "foolish and morally suspect" characters involved in doomed relationships make some critics uncomfortable with the book (Yanofsky, "Writer" J3). In addition, many reviewers have assumed that the stories about older men and younger women were largely based on her relationship turned sour with fellow Canadian writer William P. Kinsella. Mostly interested in the seemingly autobiographical aspect of her stories, critics have berated Lau for what they perceive to be a tell-all book. Calling these assumptions "distressing," Lau defends herself by explaining that although she writes "about older men and younger women, drawing aspects of [her] own experience and life into [her] stories, [it] doesn't mean [she is] writing exactly about [her] life" (Page C1).

Readers, mostly women, have also criticized Lau's detachment toward violence done to women and her apparent lack of condemnation of abusive men in her work. "Horrified and outraged" that as a female writer she would be expected to "write about things from a feminist perspective," Lau is determined to stay apolitical and to write about what she knows (qtd. in Dean 26). Lau has also been reproached for not writing about Chinese Canadians. However, removed from her family and the Chinese community at an early age, Lau feels that her ethnicity has little impact in her work: "If I think of being different from other people, I think of being different in terms of my background. That leaps to mind much sooner than being Chinese" (qtd. in Dean 26). Her background and her personal experiences indeed differentiate Lau from most other people; however, that difference is responsible for making Evelyn Lau one of the most engaging and provoking writers on the Canadian literary scene.

◆ BIBLIOGRAPHY

Works by Evelyn Lau

Short Stories

"California." *Canadian Forum* 73.829 (May 1994): 30–34.
"If Wishes Were Horses." *The Capilano Review* 2.14 (Fall 1994): 5–11.

Short Story Collections

Fresh Girls and Other Stories. Toronto: HarperCollins, 1993.
Choose Me: A Novella and Stories. Toronto: Doubleday, 1999.

Novel

Other Women. Toronto: Random House, 1995.

Poetry

You Are Not Who You Claim. Victoria, BC: Porcépic Books, 1990.
Oedipal Dreams. Victoria, BC: Beach Holme, 1992.
In the House of Slaves. Toronto: Coach House Press, 1994.

Autobiography

Runaway: Diary of a Street Kid. Toronto: HarperCollins, 1989.
Inside Out: Reflections on a Life So Far. Toronto: Doubleday, 2001.

Essays

"Global Exchange." Rev. of *Gold by the Inch* by Lawrence Chua. *Village Voice*, Literary Supplement (April 7, 1998): 13.
"Father Figures." In *Desire in Seven Voices*. Lorna Crozier, ed. Vancouver: Douglas and McIntyre, 1999, 43–61.

Studies of Evelyn Lau

Asimakopulos, Anna. "Dark Eroticism with Ring of Truth." Rev. of *Fresh Girls*. *Gazette* [Montréal], final ed. (October 2, 1993): J2.

Cockburn, Lyn. "A Laudable Life." Rev. of *Inside Out*. *Herizons* 15.1 (Summer 2001): 15–17.

Condé, Mary. "An Interview with Evelyn Lau." *Études Canadiennes/Canadian Studies* 21.38 (June 1995): 105–11.

Dean, Misao. "Reading Evelyn Right." *Canadian Forum* 73.837 (1995): 22–26.

Fitzgerald, Judith. "Fear and Self-Loathing in Vancouver." Rev. of *Choose Me*. *Toronto Star*, Entertainment (March 21, 1999): 1.

Furtsch, Stephanie. "Book Reviews: Fiction." Rev. of *Fresh Girls*. *Library Journal* 120.2 (February 1, 1995): 102.

Girard, Daniel. "Life, Love and the Evolution of Evelyn Lau." Rev. of *Choose Me*. *Toronto Star*, Entertainment (March 20, 1999): 1.

Glasser, Perry. "Good Stories, Well-Written, 4 Sale, Cheap." Rev. of *Fresh Girls*. *North American Review* 281.1 (January–February 1996): 44–48.

Goldstein-Jackson, Kevin. "The Runaway's Progress." *Financial Times* (London), Perspectives (July 26, 1997): 3.

Gray, Robert. "Coffee with Someone Who Shares Too Much." Rev. of *Choose Me*. *Canadian Forum* 78.877 (May 1999): 45–47.

Hluchy, Patricia, and Rob Howatson. "The Pen Is Mightier Than the Sordid." *Maclean's* 106.41 (1993): 72–73.

Huot, Nikolas. "Evelyn Lau." In *Asian American Poets: A Bio-Bibliographical Critical Sourcebook*. Guiyou Huang, ed. Westport, CT: Greenwood Press, 2002, 195–200.

Mallick, Heather. "Evelyn Lau Exploits Real Life." Rev. of *Choose Me*. *Jam! Books* (April 18, 1999). http://www.canoe.ca/JamBooksReviewsC/choose_lau.html.

Nathan, Paul. "Rising Star." Rev. of *Fresh Girls*. *Publishers Weekly* 242.7 (13 Feb. 1995): 18.

Ng, Maria Noelle. "A Woman's Place." Rev. of *Fresh Girls*. *Canadian Literature* 145 (Summer 1995): 147–48.

Nickson, Keith. "The Dark Side of Desire." Rev. of *Fresh Girls*. *Toronto Star*, final ed. (October 16, 1993): J17.

Page, Shelley. "Untangling Evelyn Lau." *Ottawa Citizen*, final ed. (April 18, 1999): C1+.

Parsons, Tony. "The Arts: Her True Life Is Stranger Than Fiction." *Daily Telegraph* (London) (November 17, 1994): 14.

Richards, Linda. "*January Magazine* Interviews Evelyn Lau." *January Magazine* (October 1999). http://januarymagazine.com/profiles/lau.html.

Seaman, Donna. "Adult Books: Fiction." Rev. of *Fresh Girls*. *Booklist* 91.13 (March 1, 1995): 1179.

Taylor, Erika. Rev. of *Fresh Girls*. *Los Angeles Times*, Book Review (September 3, 1995): 6.

Wanner, Irene. "*Fresh Girls* Wiser Than It Appears." *Seattle Times*, final ed. (April 23, 1995): M2.

Wong, Rita. "Market Forces and Powerful Desires: Reading Evelyn Lau's Cultural Labour." *Essays on Canadian Writing* 73 (Spring 2001): 122–40.

———. "Varied Stories." Rev. of *Choose Me*. *Canadian Literature* 163 (Winter 1999): 195–97.

Yanofsky, Joel. "From Hooking to Three-Book Deal; Evelyn Lau Has Seen It All and Writes to Tell about It." *Gazette* [Montréal], final ed. (October 9, 1993): J2.

———. "A Writer Too Much in Spotlight: Evelyn Lau's Misadventures Make Her Object of Fascination in Media." *Gazette* [Montréal], final ed. (May 15, 1999): J3+.

CHANG-RAE LEE
(1965–   )

Joonseong Park

◆ BIOGRAPHY

Chang-rae Lee was born in Seoul, Korea, in 1965 and immigrated with his family to the United States at the age of three. Lee's father was a physician who built a prosperous psychiatric practice in Westchester County, New York. Lee grew up there in a bilingual household and was graduated from Phillips Exeter Academy, from Yale University with a degree in English, and from the University of Oregon with an M.F.A. in creative writing. Upon graduation from Yale, Lee analyzed stocks on Wall Street for a year before fully devoting himself to his passion for writing. Lee has received numerous prestigious awards for his two novels, *Native Speaker* and *A Gesture Life*, which explore the modern Asian immigrant experience. He has also written stories and articles for the *New Yorker*, the *New York Times Magazine, Granta*, and other magazines. Lee was a Guggenheim Foundation Fellow in 2000–2001; was named a finalist for *Granta*'s Best American Novelists Under 40 in 1996; and was selected by the *New Yorker* as one of twenty best American writers under forty in 1999. He currently serves as director of the M.F.A. Program at Hunter College of CUNY, where he teaches writing workshops and seminars in literature and is working on his third novel, about a group of U.S. soldiers in Korea during the Korean War. He lives in New Jersey with his wife and daughter.

◆ MAJOR WORKS AND THEMES

Chang-rae Lee's fiction explores the modern Asian immigrant experience. Though not particularly autobiographical, Lee's novels and short stories and essays draw from the author's own experiences as a Korean immigrant. A short story, "My Low Korean Master," which has a similar structure and theme with an essay, "The Faintest Echo of Our Language," is about the narrator's recollections of a Korean immigrant father, a grocery store owner, who struggles to adapt to a new life. Lee beautifully describes the relationship between a father and son. "The Volunteers" is a story within a story in the novel, *A Gesture Life*. As a paramedic in an army camp in the final days of the Pacific war, the main character, Hata, is put in charge of the so-called "comfort women," Korean women (often teenagers) whom the Japanese Imperial Army forced into sex slavery during World War II. Hata is required to examine the five "female volunteers" servicing 200 officers and men in the "comfort house" stalls; VD is known to deplete whole battalions. Hata thus witnesses a psychotic soldier kill one of the comfort women.

The central characters in Lee's novels experience a paradox: although successful, even affluent in their adoptive land, they feel alienated from both American culture and the cultures they left behind in the Far East. Identity and assimilation are central themes in Lee's debut novel *Native Speaker*. For its exploration of cultural identity, *Native Speaker* has drawn comparisons to Ralph Ellison's classic *Invisible Man*. Korean American Henry Park is forever uncertain of his place, a perpetual outsider looking at American culture from a distance. A man of two worlds, he is beginning to fear that he has betrayed both—and belongs to neither. Like *Native Speaker*, his second novel, *A Gesture Life*, elaborates his themes of identity and assimilation through the character of Hata. As the book opens, the narrator, Franklin "Doc" Hata, the retired owner of a surgical supply store, is looking back on his life, his relations and his own assimilation. Like the character Henry Park from *Native Speaker*, Hata has thoughtfully grappled with his assimilation into American life, though for Hata that drama is in the past. He is a man who has traveled vast seas of identity: from native Korean to Japanese soldier to American storekeeper. Korean by birth, Hata was adopted by a Japanese family, and emigrated to this country as a young man. In *Native Speaker* Lee grafts a domestic spy drama onto a novel of assimilation. With *A Gesture Life* he delves into happenings more lurid and graphic than the reader would expect from such a stately narrative. It addresses the issue of Korean "comfort women."

◆ CRITICAL RECEPTION

Chang-rae Lee has not yet published a collection of short stories, so critical response is limited to his novels, *Native Speaker* and *A Gesture of Life*. His debut novel, *Native Speaker*, is the first Korean American novel published by a major American publishing house and has generated a well-deserved critical buzz. It received numerous prizes and citations, including the PEN/Hemingway Award, the American Book Award, the Barnes and Noble Discover Award, the QPB New Voices Award, and the Oregon Book Award. It was also a finalist for the PEN West Fiction Prize and was an ALA Notable Book of the Year. *Time* magazine named *Native Speaker* one of the Year's Best Books of

1995, and it was translated into Korean and Italian. *Vogue* said that "With echoes of Ralph Ellison, Chang-rae Lee's extraordinary debut speaks for another kind of invisible man: the Asian immigrant in America . . . a revelatory work of fiction" (qtd. in "Chang-Rae Lee," *Asian American Literature* 244).

His second novel, *A Gesture Life*, reaped even higher critical praise than its predecessor. It won the Anisfield-Wolf Prize, Myers Outstanding Book Award, NAIBA Book Award, Asian American Literary Award for Fiction, and was a *New York Times* Notable Book of the Year, *Talk* magazine's Best Book of 1999, a finalist for the *New Yorker* Book Award, a *Publishers Weekly* Best Book of the Year, and an ALA Notable Book of the Year. The *New York Times* (August 31, 1999) said *A Gesture Life* is even more of an achievement than *Native Speaker* and called the novel "wise and humane." Leslie Brody, in the *Los Angeles Times Book Review* (September 19, 1999), describes Lee as "an original." *A Gesture Life* already has been compared to Kazuo Ishiguro's *The Remains of the Day* for the careful tone of its narrator.

◆ BIBLIOGRAPHY

Works by Chang-rae Lee

Short Stories

"My Low Korean Master." *Granta* 49 (Winter 1995): 121–32.
"The Volunteers." *New Yorker* (June 21, 1999): 150–55. Rpt. in *The Beacon Best of 2000: Great Writing by Women and Men of All Colors and Cultures*. Edwidge Danticat, ed. Boston, MA: Beacon Press, 2000, 62–82.

Novels

Native Speaker. New York: Putnam/Riverhead, 1995.
A Gesture Life. New York: Riverhead, 1999.

Essays

"The Faintest Echo of Our Language." *New England Review* 15 (Summer 1993): 85–92.
"Coming Home Again." *New Yorker* (October 16, 1995): 164–68. Rpt. in *The Best American Essays, 1996*. Geoffrey C. Ward and Robert Atwan, eds. Boston: Houghton Mifflin, 1996, 227–37, and *The Best American Essays*. Robert Atwan, ed. Boston: Houghton Mifflin, 1998, 115–26.
"Mute in an English-Only World." *New York Times*, late ed. (April 18, 1996): B21.
"Uncle Chul Gets Rich." *New York Times Magazine* (May 12, 1996): 44.
"My Suburb: Ridgewood, N.J." *New York Times Magazine* (April 9, 2000): 66. Rpt. in *The Beacon Best of 2001: Great Writing by Women and Men of All Colors and Cultures*. Junot Diaz, ed. Boston: Beacon Press, 2001, 100–101.

Excerpts in Anthologies

From *Native Speaker*. In *On a Bed of Rice: An Asian American Erotic Feast*. Geraldine Kudaka, ed. New York: Anchor Books, 1995, 271–73.
From *Native Speaker*. In *Kori: The Beacon Anthology of Korean American Fiction*. Heinz Insu Fenkl and Walter K. Lew, eds. Boston: Beacon Press, 2001, 45–56.

Interviews

"Interview: Adopted Voice." By Dwight Garner. *New York Times* (September 5, 1999): 6.
"Chang-rae Lee." By Pam Belluck. *New York Times* (July 10, 1995): B1.
"Talking with Chang-rae Lee: A Cultural Spy." With James Marcus. *Newsday*, Newspapers & Newswires 26, (March 26, 1995): 34.
"Talking with Chang-rae Lee: Speaking in Tongues." With Bill Vourvoulias. *Newsday*, Currents (September 26, 1999): B13.

Studies of Chang-rae Lee

"Chang-Rae Lee." *Contemporary Literary Criticism* 91 (1995): 53–58.
"Chang-Rae Lee." In *Asian American Literature: Reviews and Criticism of Works by American Writers of Asian Descent*. Lawrence J. Trudeau, ed. Detroit: Gale Research, 1999, 241–49.
"Chang-Rae Lee." *Contemporary Authors New Revision Series* 89 (2000): 224–26.
Engles, Timothy David. " 'Visions of Me in the Whitest Raw Light': Assimilation and Toxic Whiteness in Chang-Rae Lee's *Native Speaker*." *Hitting Critical Mass: A Journal of Asian American Cultural Criticism* 4.2 (1997): 27–48.
Huh, Joonok. " 'Strangest Chorale': New York City in *East Goes West* and *Native Speaker*." In *The Image of the Twentieth Century in Literature, Media, and Society*. Will Wright and Steven Kaplan, eds. Pueblo, CO: Society for the Interdisciplinary Study of Social Imagery, University of Southern Colorado, 2000, 419–22.
Hurst, Mary Jane. "Presidential Address: Language, Gender, and Community in American Fiction at the End of the Century." *Southwest Journal of Linguistics* 17.1 (1998): 1–13.
Kich, Martin. "Chang-rae Lee." In *Asian American Novelists: A Bio-Bibliographical Critical Sourcebook*. Emmanuel S. Nelson, ed. Westport, CT: Greenwood Press, 2000, 175–79.
Millard, Kenneth. "Chang-rae Lee: Native Speaker." In *Contemporary American Fiction*. Oxford and New York: Oxford University Press, 2000, 163–69, 185.
Park, You-me, and Gayle Wald. "Native Daughters in the Promised Land: Gender, Race, and the Question of Separate Spheres." *American Literature* 70.3 (1998): 607–33.

DON LEE
(1959–   )

Seiwoong Oh

A third-generation Korean American and son of an officer who served the U.S. State Department for thirty-eight years, Don Lee was born in 1959 and spent most of his childhood in Seoul and Tokyo. In the first two years at the University of California, Los Angeles, he majored in engineering while occasionally taking English and creative writing classes. Finding these occasional English courses fulfilling his need for a "verbal outlet," he "frightened" his parents by switching to an English major in his junior year (Rutten 2). After graduating in 1982 with a B.A. in English from UCLA, he went on to study creative writing and literature at Emerson College and received his M.F.A. degree in 1986. After a brief career as an adjunct faculty member at Emerson College, he has worked since 1988 as the editor of *Ploughshares*, a literary journal. Lee has occasionally published his short stories in *GQ*, *New England Review*, *American Short Fiction*, and other periodicals.

After resisting the idea of a book for fear of failure, Lee, approaching forty, decided to put together his stories into a volume. Interestingly, "The Lone Night Cantina," "Widowers," and "Casual Water" were originally written with white characters but were revised to render a sense of community in his fictional town. Lee says the revision made him understand "more of why the characters behaved as they did in the stories" (qtd. in Rutten 3). According to an interview, Lee had two contradictory agendas within the collection: to make Asian American characters "just as sexy, artsy and screwed up as everyone else in America," but also to "educate people about the kind of prejudice Asian Americans face everyday" (Rutten 2).

Many of the stories in the collection *Yellow* contain autobiographical elements. For example, "Yellow," a novella written while he was confined in his room for ten weeks after breaking his foot while running, reflects his own struggle with his ethnic identity. Lee became aware of his "Asianness" after he moved to Boston, saying that the racial epithets in the story are the ones "actually thrown" at him (qtd. in Rutten 3). His expertise as a certified wind-surfing instructor also appears to have found its way into his detailed description of surfing in such stories as "Voir Dire" and "The Possible Husband."

Besides the short stories which make up his debut collection, *Yellow*, Lee has written numerous book reviews and interview articles. Living in Boston, this admirer of F. Scott Fitzgerald is currently working on a novel tentatively entitled *There Once Was a Country*, an offshoot of his short story "Domo Ari-gato," to be published by Norton in 2004. He still considers himself primarily an editor with writing as a hobby (Liu 33).

◆ MAJOR WORKS AND THEMES

Mostly set in the fictional town of Rosarita Bay, California, the short stories in *Yellow* are loosely connected by the same setting and shared characters, many of whom are second- or third-generation Korean Americans like the author. In these stories about contemporary, post-immigration Asian America, Lee explores the issues of identity, race, love, family, and ambiguities inherent in human experiences.

The first of the eight stories, "The Price of Eggs in China," is a quasi-crime story revealing the irrational nature of love: a Japanese American chair maker, caught in the rivalry between his girlfriend and her former college friend, goes to great lengths to win his girlfriend back. "Voir Dire," the second story, is a court drama, in which a Korean American lawyer wrestles with the question of ethics when he is assigned to defend a drug addict who killed his girl-friend's son. "Widowers" features a middle-aged Japanese American, a com-mercial charter-boat owner, who is led into a relationship with a young Korean American widow. In "Lone Night Cantina," a Korean American da-tabase programmer tries the identity of a cowgirl in a bar. "Casual Water" investigates the father-son relationship between two mixed-race children and their white father, who abandons them to pursue his dream as a pro golfer. "The Possible Husband" narrates the love life of a forty-one-year-old Korean American, a retired stock analyst, who goes through several women of dif-ferent ethnicities and vocations to find someone to share his appreciation of nature. "Domo Arigato" develops the theme of interracial love by depicting a Korean American medical student's affair with a white girl as they travel to meet her racist parents staying in Japan. In "Yellow," Lee looks into the impact of racism on the psyche of a Korean American boy; denying his ethnicity, the boy takes up boxing and dates white girls. "Imperialistas," the only published short story that is not included in *Yellow*, describes the musings of a young

Korean American woman on a vacation in Mexico with her rich English boyfriend, who displays imperialistic attitudes toward the natives and her.

◆ **CRITICAL RECEPTION**

Yellow has been reviewed favorably by both regional and international publications. Reviewers credit Lee for moving Asian American literature out of the diasporic Asia and into post-immigration Asian America. Lee is also praised for humor, narrative control, and realistic character development. Most reviewers consider the title story the best piece.

Calling Lee's book an "elegant and engrossing collection" and "a triumph of the artful over didactic," Tim Rutten, for example, praises the author for "shrewdly" exhibiting new possibilities for ethnic literature and for "stunningly" transcending its limits (1). In this "rich and unusually complete portrait of contemporary Asian America," Rutten continues, memorable American characters of various ethnic backgrounds and vocations display deep complexities of human life (1). Jean Charbonneau offers a similar assessment of *Yellow*. Lee—"a melange of intelligence, humor, and candor"—does not preach, says Charbonneau; rather he is "particularly adept" at showing various ways racism hurts the minorities (1). Charbonneau adds that Lee's style in his "fine collection" is "fluid and easygoing" (2). Peggy Barber, reviewing for *Booklist*, also praises Lee's "compelling, beautifully written collection," in which each of the "achingly vulnerable characters deals with totally believable fears, plus an added layer of racial awareness" (1447). Wingate Packard writes for the *Seattle Times* that Lee's "lively and relevant" stories are "powerful, well-crafted and provocative" (1-2). He also notes how Lee "manages to pack in a lot of humor of gender and ethnic projections without drawing clichéd characters" and how Lee shows a "marvelous organizing technique that produces the effect of a grapevine through a community" (1).

For Andrew Sun of *Asiaweek*, *Yellow* is "mature and complex in its emotional dynamics," and the stories are "elegant, almost Chekhovian, meditations on people trying to pick up the pieces of their lives" (2). For John Freeman, writing for the *Dallas Morning News*, Lee's collection captures the rich and complicated nature of Asian American experience "beautifully, wisely and with winning economy" (7). Jinhee Kim, writing for the *Korea Times*, goes as far as to call the anthology "arguably one of the best works by an Asian American writer" (3).

While most reviewers share similar views, there have been mixed reviews as well. In his generally positive review, Will Blythe, for example, criticizes the "forced" connection between the stories and the few characters who seem "spawned from a thesis" (2). Jan Alexander, while praising Lee's development of male characters, finds his female characters painted in "quick, flippant strokes" (2).

◆ BIBLIOGRAPHY

Works by Don Lee

Short Story

"Imperialistas." *North American Review* 284.3, 4 (May–August 1999): 64–67, 71.

Short Story Collection

Yellow. New York: Norton, 2001.

Studies of Don Lee

Alexander, Jan. "Variations on Asian States of Mind." Rev. of *Yellow* and others. *Chicago Tribune* (July 8, 2001): 5 pages. (July 9, 2001) http://chicagotribune.com.

Barber, Peggy. Rev. of *Yellow*. *Booklist* 97.15 (April 2001): 1447.

Blythe, Will. "Tales from Both Sides of the Hyphen." Rev. of *Talking in the Dark* by Laura Glen Louis and *Yellow* by Don Lee. *New York Times* (July 15, 2001): 4 pages. http://www.nytimes.com/2001/07/15/books/review/15BLYTHET .html.

Charbonneau, Jean. "Editor Tries on Short Stories." Rev. of *Yellow*. *DenverPost.com* (May 20, 2001): 4 pages. http://www.denverpost.com/Stories. Accessed February 8, 2002.

Freeman, John. "Another Place Where Life's Not Always Black, White." Rev. of *Yellow*. *Dallas Morning News* (July 3, 2001): 7 pars. http://www.dallasnews.com. Accessed November 21, 2001.

Johnston, Hillary. "The Short Story." Rev. of *Yellow* and others. *LA Weekly* (September 21, 2001): 5 pages. http://www.laweekly.com. Accessed November 21, 2001.

Kim, Jinhee. "Voice from Afar: Moving Beyond Diasporic Trauma: 'Yellow' by Don Lee." *Korea Times* (September 16, 2001): 11 pars. http://www.hankooki.com/ kt_culture. Accessed November 21, 2001.

Liu, Dana. "On Being Yellow: Don Lee." Review of *Yellow*. *10* 7.1, 2 (2001): 33.

Packard, Wingate. "Provocative Stories of Asian Americans." Rev. of *Yellow*. *Seattletimes.com*, Arts and Entertainment (May 6, 2001): 2 pages. http:// www.seattletimes.com. Accessed November 21, 2001.

Rev. of *Yellow*. *AsiaWeek.com*, Arts and Entertainment (March 30, 2001): 3 pages. http://www.asiaweek.com/2001_03_30/ae3_litpicks.html. Accessed February 8, 2002.

Roca, Elizabeth. "Short Stories." Rev. of *Yellow*. *Washington Post* (April 8, 2001): BW13.

Rutten, Tim. "Don Lee's Revealing Visit to Rosarita Bay." Rev. of *Yellow*. *Los Angeles Times* (May 1, 2001): 5 pages. http://www.latimes.com/living/20010501.

Sun, Andrew. "Beyond Racial Melodrama." Rev. of *Yellow*. *Asiaweek.com* (September 21, 2001): 6 pars. http://www.asiaweek.com/asiaweek/magazine/life. Accessed February 8, 2001.

Zaleski, Jeff. Rev. of *Yellow*. *Publishers Weekly* 248.14 (April 2, 2001): 38.

MONFOON LEONG
(1916–1964)

Amy W. S. Lee

◆ **BIOGRAPHY**

Monfoon Leong was born on January 14, 1916 in San Diego's Chinatown, the eldest of four brothers and two sisters. When he was fourteen, his father's death made him, the number one son, the head of the family, and he took the job of a houseboy to support the family. Because of his status, he came to associate easily with people of his mother's generation, and that gave him a chance to observe carefully the traditional customs and beliefs of the Chinese.

While attending La Jolla High School, he was particularly active in drama and writing. His poem "Ode to a Worm" appeared in the school paper. But Leong's interest was not limited to schoolwork; he was also a leader in the church and actively participated in sports. Later he became the first Chinese to be employed by Convair Aircraft and Naval Air Station at North Island as a patternmaker and draftsman. During World War II, he worked very hard to be accepted into the U.S. Army Air Force for training as a ferry pilot. It was said that Leong did lots of stretching exercises to fulfill the height requirement and consumed carrot juice to improve his night vision. But shortly before the end of the war the program was cancelled.

By the time the pressure to support his family eased a little, he moved to northern California to attend San Jose State College. There his interest and talent in writing was recognized by his teachers, who encouraged him to specialize in this field. He went to study at Stanford University and majored in English (writing). In June 1951, he married Diana Ming Chan, just a few days before he was awarded his B.A. degree.

Leong continued his pursuit of knowledge. In 1953 he completed his Master's degree in American Studies at the University of Minnesota, and the following year he got his teaching credentials from the University of California at Berkeley. All this time Leong had been working on his writing, but it was not possible to make a living just by writing. Therefore he went into teaching and taught at the Merritt Community College and high schools in Oakland and San Francisco.

Leong had two children, Allison and Harrison Leong, with his wife. In 1964, after saving up for a few years, the whole family went on a world tour, and Leong was killed in a car accident in Yugoslavia.

◆ MAJOR WORKS AND THEMES

Monfoon Leong was hailed as a truly "bicultural man" because of his interest in and perceptive understanding of his own Chinese roots on the one hand and adaptive flexibility, which led to his quick Americanization on the other. Being in a position to have "inside knowledge" of the Chinese people and access to American representations of these same figures, Leong had wanted to right the wrong done to the unjust misrepresentations of the Chinese. This intention is strongly reflected in the setting, characterization, and themes chosen for his stories, many of which are based on his own experience in Chinatown and his own identity as someone in the crossroads of Chinese and American cultures.

Number One Son, which was posthumously published in 1975, eleven years after his death, is the only published collection of his short stories. The collection contains seven short stories and one longer piece, which would certainly have been a novella had Leong not met his untimely death. "Precious Jade," which shares the main characters with "Golden Mountains," had not gone through the same meticulous editing and polishing as other of Leong's writings because of his death and was meant to be published separately.

Except for a few, the main characters of all the stories are Chinese, the older generation being well immersed in traditional Chinese thoughts and beliefs, and the young generation being born in America facing cultural conflicts in their day-to-day experiences. The stories strive to present, from an insider's perspective, the behavior of Chinese people in a foreign land with an understanding of the hardship and rationale behind seemingly inexplicable decisions. Although situations and problems vary in the stories, they evolve around the difficult life of first-generation Chinamen amidst miscommunication and devaluation, and how second-generation American-born Chinamen had problems coming to terms with what their forefathers had thought and done.

◆ CRITICAL RECEPTION

In the introductory essay of the collection, editor Chuck Chan mentions the difficulty Chinese American writers like Monfoon Leong were facing when they wanted to get their work published. The stories collected in *Number One Son* were all published for the first time because readership and marketability for such intercultural work were major problems in the 1950s and 1960s when Leong was writing. Elaine Kim also noted that it had to be the ethnic journalism media to take up the publication of the stories, which had been rejected by the "national literary magazines" then.

To his friends and supporters, Leong's writing shows keen insight into and sensitivity about the complicated issues of conflicts between the Chinese and American ways of life. The meticulous care Leong took to find the right word for the right effect was noted in the collection, as can be seen in the Chinese terms inserted in the margins to ensure recognition of the original spoken dialects.

Leong's sympathetic representation of Chinatown life has been compared to other works of similar themes. Examining Louis Chu's *Eat a Bowl of Tea*, King-Kok Cheung regards Leong's stories as matching in intention but second in linguistic skills and management of its form.

◆ BIBILOGRAPHY

Works by Monfoon Leong

Short Story Collection

Number One Son. San Francisco: East/West Publishing Company, 1975.

Studies of Monfoon Leong

Cheung, King-Kok, ed. *An Interethnic Companion to Asian American Literature.* Cambridge: Cambridge University Press, 1997.

Kim, Elaine H. *Asian American Literature: An Introduction to the Writings and Their Social Context.* Philadelphia: Temple University Press, 1982.

A Literary History of the American West. http://www.tcu.edu/depts/prs/amwest/html/wl1119.html. Accessed February 18, 2002.

RUSSELL LEONG
(1950–   )

Jie Tian

♦ BIOGRAPHY

Russell Leong is a poet, editor, essayist, documentary filmmaker, and short story writer. Born in Chinatown, San Francisco, California in 1950, Leong was educated in local Chinese and American schools. His parents, brother, and English teacher encouraged him to write from an early age. He took one of the first Asian American writing/literature classes from Jeffery Chan at San Francisco State College, where he also earned his B.A. in 1972. Leong was part of the Kearny Street Workshop, a community-based workshop consisting of writers, poets, and filmmakers of Chinese, Filipino, and Japanese American heritage who linked their artistic creations with social and political activism. Leong pursued graduate study at National Taiwan University in 1973 and 1974 and received an M.F.A. from the University of California at Los Angeles in 1990.

Phoenix Eyes and Other Stories (2000), Leong's first short story collection, includes fourteen stories from a thirty-year span. It won the American Book Award from the Before Columbus Foundation in 2001. Some of the stories in this collection (some under a different name) had appeared in several Asian American literature anthologies: "Thread" in *Asian American Authors* (1972), "Rough Notes for Mantos" in *Aiiieeeee! An Anthology of Asian American Writers* (1974), and "Geography One" in *Charlie Chan Is Dead: An Anthology of Contemporary Asian American Fiction* (1993). Leong's stories, essays, and poems have also been published in numerous journals, magazines, and newspapers, including the *New England Review, Tricycle: The Buddhist Review, Positions: East Asia Cultures Critique, Los Angeles Times, Zyzzyva,* and *Disorient.* Leong's first poetry collection, *The Country of Dreams and Dust* (1993), won the PEN Oakland Josephine Miles Literature Award in 1994.

The poet and short story writer is also a noted editor. Since 1977, Leong has been the editor of *Amerasia*, one of the primary journals in Asian American Studies that reflects an interdisciplinary approach and covers social sciences and humanities research as well as creative expressions. Leong is also the managing editor of publications at the UCLA Asian American Studies Center. He has edited several collected works on Asian American Studies, Asian American literature, media and the arts, and ethnic studies, including *Frontiers of Asian American Studies: Writing, Research, and Criticism* (1989), *Moving the Image: Independent Asian Pacific American Media Arts, 1970–1990* (1991), *Asian American Sexualities: Dimensions of the Gay and Lesbian Experience* (1996), *Los Angeles—Struggle toward Multiethnic Community: Asian America, African America, and Latino Perspectives* (1994).

In an interview with Gale's *Literature Resource Center*, Leong acknowledges his literary influences from diverse origins, from the Chinese inscriptions on Alcatraz Island, generations of students, Chinese writers Lu Xun, Sun Zi, and Mao Zedong, to Asian American playwright Frank Chin, Ethiopian film essayist Teshome Gabriel, Filipino writer N.V.M. Gonzales, Vietnamese master monk Thich Minh Ton, Italian novelist Italo Calvino, Yasunari Kamabata, Frantz Fanon, and early Theravada Pali Buddhist texts.

◆ MAJOR WORKS AND THEMES

Leong's prose is clean, suggestive, impressionistic, meditative, and at times poetic. His stories tend to be episodic, journalistic, ethnographic, or at worst fragmented. Yet, such deviations from the tight structure of traditional novelistic devices serve well for the kind of stories he is telling and for the types of characters he creates. Together, his style and stories express his ultimate fictional preoccupation with dislocation, identity, space, place, gender orientation, and spirituality of Asian Americans, most of whom are single Asian males, gay or otherwise. The lives and worlds of these characters are anything but coherent, connected, purposeful, and organic. Leong's fictional world is like air and dust, like dreams, driven by wind and cloud, by passion and desire, and by the instinct and urge for transcendence.

Space and place play a central role in Leong's stories. In "Bodhi Leaves," the characters are refugees displaced from Vietnam who settled down in Southern California after floating through refugee camps in Southeast Asia. The story centers on the efforts of the Vietnamese Buddhist monk, or Sifu, to find artists to paint the bodhi tree leaves for a temple converted from a suburban tract home in Little Saigon, Orange County. While being instructed to "imagine how a bodhi tree appears under the skies of another county" (3), the first artist's attempt resembles more a banyan tree or a eucalyptus, the second artist paints a tree that lacks spirit, and the third, a nineteen-year-old

Vietnamese in striped surfer shirt and baggy shorts, "transferred the image that existed only in his mind—molecules of light and darkness—onto the canvas" (11). In a poignant sentence, Leong surmises the experience of dislocation, or loss of place, to "distort a person's sense of balance and proportion and alter their perception" (6).

The experience of dislocation that characterizes the Vietnamese community also sets the tone for the sad, chilly, and ironic story of Eddie in "The Western Paradise of Eddie Bin." Eddie comes to San Francisco, the paradise, as a Chinese immigrant, but faces bankruptcy, a broken marriage, and unemployment. Eddie Bin's Western paradise is but an ironic metaphor for the single Asian male character's maladjustment in American society. At the end of the story, Eddie is at the Greyhound bus station, leaving San Francisco for Los Angeles. Leong leaves us with the admonition that Eddie would float in the air and never send down roots (123).

The dislocated ethnic space of the Vietnamese in "Bodhi Leaves" and "The Western Paradise of Eddie Bin" enlarges to encompass broader space and place in Leong's other stories. In "No Bruce Lee," the character's lone bus ride on a Sunday afternoon traverses Santa Monica Boulevard and West Los Angeles to downtown, passing Beverly Hills, the Jewish section, the Korean stores along Olympic Boulevard, the Spanish section, and Armenian bakery. The geographical space is also immediately cultural, ethnic, and racial. In a bar, the narrator sees Asian, black, the Spanish-speaking, a black with Indian blood, and men of undetermined sex. Through the numerous encounters and even a splash of passion and lust, the character still remains a loner, a drifter, and a displaced participant and observer of the culturally and ethnically diverse Los Angeles, a place that remains racially mixed, yet divided, estranged, and strained.

The themes of dislocation, disconnection, and loss take a more complex twist in "Where Do People Live Who Never Die?" and assume a spiritual transcendence that characterizes many of Leong's stories. Andrew Tom, an associate editor of a museum magazine, is, again, a single Asian male, who has been separated from his parents since he was two years old when his parents returned to help build the new China after Liberation. Now on a journey to Chengdu, Sichuan, to learn more about the train wreck that is alleged to have killed his parents, Andrew is presented with complex and contradicting issues. Leong deftly reveals the emotions that Andrew has been burying all his life: his loneliness and displacement, his deprivation of and craving for parental love. The story ends with an illusive yet deep, mysterious, and universal connection that Andrew feels toward his parents: "they had also left traces of their presence, elements of water, fire, wood, metal, and earth that had drawn me back to them" (169). The quest for the truth of his parents' death turns into a spiritual quest, ending with a resolution that embraces the Buddhist and/or Daoist cycle of life and the fusion of the Chinese cosmology of the five elements.

In the culturally marginalized and isolated place and space, Leong's characters also undergo a new kind of displacement as a result of the battle between passion and desire, gender disorientation, deviation from traditional family norms, thus suffering from samsara—desire and rebirth—and driven toward transcendence, spiritual or otherwise. "Geography One" is set in the post–L.A. riots in Los Angeles and Orange County and is one of Leong's most poetic stories about dislocation, desire, passion, and the spiritual journey. It blends rich Vietnamese culture with evocative expressions of physical and sexual desire. With the imminence of death of friends from AIDS and loss of love, the character is engaged in a struggle between the flesh and the spirit, loss and spiritual yearning. At the pivotal point of the story, the character is on his knees, listening to the Buddhist master speaking about sadness, happiness, unhappiness, and detachment. "The Sifu's words resounded, as sound does, in the spaces within me" (23). This story further exemplifies the inclination of Leong's characters to seek shelter, solace, and transcendence in Eastern spirituality while in torment.

Dislocation, isolation, and misconstrued sexual identity take on a metaphysical, philosophical, Buddhist, or fatalist bent in another series of Leong's stories. These stories employ a flashback that constitutes the center of the story and ends at a dramatic moment in the present where the characters are about to abandon their past lives and embrace something new. In "Phoenix Eyes," Terence, the narrator, is to don the gray robe of a layman Buddhist, to take refuge in the five precepts after a life of twenty years seeking pleasure and in the aftermath of the death of a friend from AIDS. "Neither prayer nor desire worked to bring back anyone whom I love" (143). The path of Terence echoes the Buddhist cycle of birth, suffering, death, and rebirth. Something is reborn in Terence when he accepts the five precepts at the end of the story—no lying, no drinking, no stealing, no killing, and no improper sexual relations.

"No Bruce Lee" portrays a gay Asian male, another loner who once had a life as the maitre d' at Flamingo West, the Chinese supper club on the Sunset Strip, and his off-hours service as a masseur for gay western men. Painfully marginalized, misplaced, and disconnected from his own history, tradition, and family, "Bruce" feeds on alcohol and passion. Paradise is an irony, a mark-up for dislocation, not belonging, and homelessness. Unlike Terence who retreats to the Buddhist world, "Bruce" heads for downtown LA with an unknown fate and undefined destiny. In "Samsara," a story about gay love and the loss of love, Leong gives full expression to human life that encompasses all the ranges and dimensions of emotion. The main character Alec voices the cycle of the samsara and of the unknown: "I did not know how would we escape samsara, the cycle of desire and rebirth without end" (116).

These fourteen stories paint a chilly picture of displaced people and cultures; personal, sexual, and cultural identity; place, space, and faith; the multicultural and multiethnic Los Angeles as well as international space—China, Taiwan, Hong Kong, Japan, Thailand, and so on. At the same time, they also reveal Leong's sensitivity to the human experiences and his fictional clinging to transcendence. In an interview with Cynthia Liu, Leong speaks of a worldview that would help explicate his fictional and artistic intention: "Three phrases sum up my affiliation with my view of the world . . . Anima divina—divine spirit. Anima humana—human spirit. Anima mundi—spirit of the world, or universe. Along with the Buddhist Heart Sutra, that talks about form and emptiness" (15).

◆ CRITICAL RECEPTION

The collection of stories in *Phoenix Eyes* has generated significant critical response since its publication in 2000 by the University of Washington Press. Although research articles have not appeared in scholarly journals, book reviews and interviews in major newspapers and magazines as well as in ethnic newspapers present meaningful interpretations of and responses to Leong's first collection of stories. These responses provide both stylistic and thematic insights into the understanding of Leong's work.

Jonathan Kirsch, the book editor of the *Los Angeles Times*, comments on Leong's power of observation and poetic sensibilities. He calls the book "a collection of startling and unsettling short stories" about Leong's take on the Asian experience in America. He regards Leong's style as "rich," "evocative," and "skillful." Kirsch praises Leong's power to shift "from the mundane details of a prostitute's life . . . to an almost mythic scene of crisis and redemption" in "Daughters." In "Bodhi Leaves," "Leong shows us how memory and identity persist even in the melting pot of America." "His acute power of observation and his poet's gift for capturing the experience of transcendence—are given full expression in the pages of *Phoenix Eyes*" (E-1). In his review in the *San Francisco Chronicle*, Leonard Chang also praises Leong's delicate sensibility throughout the collection. Robert Murray Davis compares Leong to Hemingway and Steinbeck in his power to "reveal important traits of character as well as to establish a milieu" (341).

Along with praises for Leong's poetic sensibility and prose, some reviewers examine the form of the stories and note that these stories are loosely structured, jump from one scene to another, and are only slightly held together as a whole. While commenting that Leong succeeds at bringing the reader into "unfamiliar worlds and ways of responding to them," Robert Murray Davis observes that "the volume contains a master narrative that seems to be struggling toward the coherence and weight of a longer form" and that Leong "could have even greater success with a novel" (341). A *Publishers Weekly* reviewer considers the collection as an "impressionistic, uneven collection" and that "some of Leong's stories are slight, but the best of them exploit the stresses of sexual desire and family relationships, and probe the cultural forces shaping the immigrant experience" ("Phoenix Eyes" 61). Cynthia Liu writes that "Leong's fiction could be weighed down with a didactic impulse to show breadth . . . at the expense of depth" (13).

Other reviewers address the thematic concerns of Leong's stories and shed deep insights into Leong's perennial concern for ethnicity, gender, and place. Bob Papinchak, in his *Seattle Times* article, "Story Collections Draw Portraits of Their Different Worlds," states that Leong's book deals "effortlessly with minority groups, people on the fringe and characters on the edge" and that "Leong's collection coalesces into a telling amalgamation of stories of struggle and survival, of displaced persons seeking accommodation through desire and new identification" (M8). Robert Murray Davis affirms that Leong "has presented important issues for Asian America" and "adopts the voices of various ethnicities—Vietnamese, Chinese (Asian and American born), and Filipino—and sexualities to portray a side of that life usually kept from view" (341).

Reviewers also capture another important theme in Leong's stories: faith and transcendence. Robert Murray Davis recognizes Leong's "struggle toward serenity rather than its attainment" in his use of samsara, the Buddhist term for "the world of attachment and the folly of rebirth" (341). Cynthia Liu treats the three sections of the collection as displaying a deliberate thematic pattern for transcendence. She suggests that stories in the first section, "Leaving," "meditate upon separations"; the second section, "Samsara," "sets the irony of sexual and other couplings, visceral and very basic forms of attachment, against the Buddhistic notion of detachment"; and the third section, "Paradise," portrays characters who "search for illusory places" (14).

◆ BIBLIOGRAPHY

Works by Russell Leong

Short Stories

"Thread." In *Asian American Authors.* Hsu Kai-yu and Helen Palubinskas, eds. Boston: Houghton Mifflin, 1972, 89.

"Rough Notes for Mantos." (under the pseudonym Lin, W.) In *Aiiieeeee! An Anthology of Asian American Writers.* Frank Chin, Jeffery Paul Chan, Lawson Fusao Inada, and Shawn Hsu Wong, eds. Washington, DC: Howard University Press, 1974, 197–205.

"Geography One." In *Charlie Chan Is Dead: An Anthology of Contemporary Asian American Fiction.* Jessica Hagedorn, ed.; preface by Elaine Kim. New York: Penguin Books, 1993, 215–29.

"The Painted Branch: A Parable." *New England Review* 15.3 (Summer 1993): 93–98.

Short Story Collection

Phoenix Eyes and Other Stories. Seattle: University of Washington Press, 2000.

Poetry

The Country of Dreams and Dust: Poems. Albuquerque, NM: West End Press, 1993.

Edited Works

A History Reclaimed: An Annotated Bibliography of Chinese Language Materials on the Chinese of America. Written and compiled by Him Mark Lai; Russell Leong and Jean Pang Yip, eds. Los Angeles: Resource Development and Publications, Asian American Studies Center, University of California, 1986.

Frontiers of Asian American Studies: Writing, Research, and Criticism. Gail M. Nomura, Russell Endo, Stephen H. Sumida, and Russell Leong, eds. Pullman: Washington State University Press, 1989.

Moving the Image: Independent Asian Pacific American Media Arts. Ed. with an Intro. by Russell Leong; preface by Linda Mabalot. Los Angeles: UCLA Asian American Studies Center and Visual Communications, Southern California Asian American Studies Center, 1991.

Why Is Preparing Fish a Political Act? Poetry of Janice Mirikitani [videorecording]. Producer/director/writer, Russell Leong. San Francisco: CrossCurrent Media; National Asian American Telecommunications Association, 1991.

Los Angeles—Struggles toward Multiethnic Community: Asian American, African American and Latino Perspectives. Edward T. Chang and Russell C. Leong, eds. Seattle: University of Washington Press, 1994.

On a Bed of Rice: An Asian American Erotic Feast. Geraldine Kudaka, ed.; foreword by Russell Leong. New York: Anchor Books, 1995.

Asian American Sexualities: Dimensions of the Gay and Lesbian Experience. Russell Leong, ed. New York: Routledge, 1996.

The Truth in Rented Rooms. Koon Woon; foreword by Russell Leong. New York: Kaya Production: Distributed by D.A.P. Distributed Art Publishers, 1998.

Studies of Russell Leong

Chang, Leonard. "Rising Phoenix: Arresting New Works from Three West Coast Asian American Writers." *San Francisco Chronicle* (March 18, 2001): 16.

Davis, Robert Murray. "Phoenix Eyes and Other Stories." *World Literature Today* 1 (April 2001): 341.

Kirsch, Jonathan. "West Words Sassy, Sad Tales Draw on Vivid Images of WWII." *Los Angeles Times,* home ed. (August 23, 2000): E-1. *Dow Jones Interactive.* http://nrstg2s.djnr.com/. Accessed April 20, 2002.

"Russell Leong/Interviewed by Robert B. Ito." In *Words Matter: Conversations with Asian American Writers.* King-Kok Cheung, ed. Honolulu: University of Hawaii Press in association with UCLA Asian American Studies Center, Los Angeles, 2000, 233–51.

Liu, Cynthia. "Looking Through the Eyes of Russell Leong." *International Examiner* 27.16 (September 5, 2000): 13+. *Ethnic News Watch.* http://enw.softlineweb.com/. Accessed December 3, 2001.

Papinchak, Bob. "Story Collections Draw Portraits of Their Different Worlds." *Seattle Times* (August 20, 2000): M8. *Dow Jones Interactive*. http://nrstg2s.djnr.com/. Accessed October 30, 2001.

Rev. of "Phoenix Eyes And Other Stories." *Publishers Weekly* (June 19, 2000): 61. *Dow Jones Interactive*. http://nrstg2s.djnr.com/. Accessed October 30, 2001.

"Russell Leong." *Contemporary Authors Online*. Updated August 29, 2001. Literature Resource Center. http://www.galenet.com/. Accessed October 30, 2001.

SHIRLEY GEOK-LIN LIM
(1944–   )

John H. Park

◆ **BIOGRAPHY**

Shirley Geok-lin Lim was born on December 27, 1944 in Malacca, Malaysia, a British subject under the then tripartite estate called the Straits Settlements. The awkward and discordant experience of growing up in a world of Chinese-Malayan traditions with newly injected Western influences marks many of Lim's early experiences, beginning with the selection of her name. "Lim Geok Lin," suggested by her grandfather, was given to her as a conventional name "intended to humble, to make a child common and same" (*White Moon Faces* 2); "Shirley," a name taken after Shirley Temple, was chosen by her father who had a penchant for Hollywood and British films and whose imagination "was possessed by Western images" (21). Her childhood was further complicated by a shifting cultural climate produced from ethnic tensions and imperial occupations by both Britain and Japan: "My birth, at the end of 1944, at the peak of Japanese torturous repression, and of food shortages and mass starvation, could have brought no rejoicing" (38).

Speaking the language and dialect of assimilated Chinese, *baba* Malay, in a community that spoke Hokkien, Lim became sensitive to the effects of language at an early age. Once exposed to English, she eagerly read Western novels and poetry and believed in the "vital connection between language" and her "specific local existence" (76). A precocious child who fell in love with literature at a young age, and inspired by a poem by William Blake, she decided to become a poet at age eleven. Her gift for words also became a means to access fatherly approval, rebel from a domineering Catholic school system, and escape poverty: "Then, as if the only thing between this poverty and myself was that A grade, I set myself to work to escape from my home with an intensity I have seldom felt later in life" (83).

While attending the University of Malaya on a scholarship, she became the first person from the university to be awarded First Class Honors in English, and later won a Fulbright and Wien International scholarship to Brandeis University, where she completed her M.A. (1971) and Ph.D. (1973). She eventually settled in California, where she is currently a Professor of English and Women's Studies at the University of California, Santa Barbara.

Although resistant to the word "prolific" when used to describe her work, Lim has nonetheless produced a staggering amount of creative and scholarly material. Her short stories, poems, reviews, and critical essays have made over 100 appearances in academic journals and in dozens of anthologies; and she has given over thirty television, radio, and other interviews worldwide. Her short fiction first appeared as a collection of fifteen stories in *Another Country and Other Stories* (1982). Four stories were added to the second collection entitled *Life's Mysteries: The Best of Shirley Lim* (1995), and five were added to *Two Dreams: New and Selected Stories* (1997). Her first collection of poems was published under the title, *Crossing the Peninsula and Other Poems* (1980), winning the 1980 Commonwealth Poetry Prize. The four collections of poetry that have since followed are *No Man's Grove* (1985), *Modern Secrets* (1989), *Monsoon History* (1994), and *What the Fortune Teller Didn't Say* (1998); and she is working on a new collection of poetry called *Passports*. Her memoir, simultaneously published in the United States as *Among the White Moon Faces: An Asian American Memoir of Homelands* and in Singapore as *Among the White Moon Faces: Memoirs of a Nonya Feminist* (1996), won an American Book Award in 1996. Her novel, *Joss and Gold*, was published in 2001.

◆ MAJOR WORKS AND THEMES

With the sensibilities of a poet, short fiction writer, novelist, critic, editor, academic, activist, mother, and a woman from a colonized Third World country, Lim draws from all of her roles to inform each area of her writing. As with her novel, her short stories allow the reader to settle easily into the characters' worldviews and formative social and material conditions. Readers who are familiar with Lim's autobiography will find many direct parallels between her stories and her life, particularly with "Hunger" and "All My Uncles." *Two Dreams*, with stories written intermittently between 1969 and 1996, is loosely categorized into three parts: "Girl," "Country," and "Woman." The stories, mostly following the experiences of a young woman, touch on a broad spectrum of issues including poverty, invisibility, colonial and Western influences, sexuality, gender, class, and ethnicity.

The first story in the book, "Hunger," closely parallels a poignant episode in Lim's childhood, including an event where Chai's cousin Ah Lan (Ah Swee in the memoir) steals her doll and claims it as her own, which Chai (and Lim) recognizes by the red mark on its arm. Because Chai is a poverty-stricken eight-year-old girl without the means to change her material conditions, she learns to adjust her internal world and psychology in order to survive. A careful and syntactical placement of metaphors and images reveals Chai's thought processes and the ways she overlaps bodily hunger with the absence of her mother, and also the manner in which she transmutes and deflects this hunger by feeding it with feelings of "freedom" and the "consumption" of books: "She had this secret machine inside her that could eat up books, swallow them whole, then give them back in bits and pieces, as good almost as before she ate them" (7). At the end of the story, Chai skirts the edge of prostitution when an old man offers her food in exchange for illicit fondles, and later a ten cent coin, which she rejects because it "did not make up for the terrible pleasure of ignoring his pleading eyes and wavering hand" (12).

"Two Dreams," the title of the book and also the last story of the collection, is very conscious of the fluidity and movement of both time and memory. The story builds toward the frustrating epiphany of a woman who sees past the illusion of her glorified childhood, which she has projected onto a specific, and mentally cryogenized, cultural and national landscape—a familiar immigrant experience that also lies at the center of Salman Rushdie's paradoxical question: "How can culture be preserved without becoming ossified?" The protagonist, Martha, has recurring dreams that can be described as memories and experiences of three temporal spaces: her childhood Malaysia, her present New York, and her present Malaysia. The story begins with Martha dreaming of an Elysian childhood in Malaysia, where she sits in the carrier basket of a bicycle with her brother cycling along the embankment of a beach. Although on a narrow embankment, the scene evokes a sense of between-ness, but a kind that fits together seamlessly and naturally where on one side "the sea frothed in little breaks" and "On the other side, the grassy and rocky bank rose steeply to the road" (209). Martha's ominous second dream, almost diametrically opposite the first, is of "New York's Grand Central, of dark menacing faces, and of hurrying down long deserted streets shadowed by crumbling buildings" (210). In the course of her vacation she begins to see the discord of Malaysia's politics and witnesses a *kerata* boy (an abandoned or orphaned child living on the streets) bludgeoned by a uniformed guard. As her observations undermine her memory of Malaysia as a blissful place for childhood experiences, she has another dream where she is in "a classroom in New York. Harry was giving a lecture which had many numbers in it, but all his students were leaving because the police were beating them on the head" (214). This final dream, a violent scene mixing images of both Malaysia and the United States, ruptures her comforting binary that neatly splits East and West, leaving her at the end of the story in a state of jarring disillusionment, a painful awakening from intimately held past memories and dreams.

◆ CRITICAL RECEPTION

Having received a Commonwealth Poetry Prize for best first book (1980) for *Crossing the Peninsula and Other Poems*, an *Asiaweek* Short Story Award in 1982, and two American Book Awards, one for coediting *The Forbidden Stitch: An Asian American Women's Anthology* (1989) and the other for *Among the White Moon Faces: An Asian American Memoir of Homelands* (1996), Lim's creative work has been eagerly received on a national scale and continues to grow internationally. Although she admits in an interview with Kirpal Singh that she rarely reads criticism on her writing, though she has been "receiving quite a few articles, chapters of dissertations and books that treat my writing," her work is nonetheless thoroughly embedded in the discourse of Asian American, postcolonial, and women's studies. Zhou Xiaojing writes that her "art enables us to see the extraordinary in the ordinary and to be at once surprised and moved"; and because her professional protagonists more closely reflect the shifting demographics of communities in North America, she also suggests that her immigrant stories are more related to works of a "younger generation of Asian American writers like Gish Jen, Wang Ping, and Chang-Rae Lee, rather than to the stories of Hisaye Yamamoto, Wakako Yamauchi, or Maxine Hong Kingston" (338). Referring to her style of writing, Larry Yu describes her prose as "appealing for its precision and economy, and her narrative voice mixes subtlety with an occasional sense of ironic whimsy" (175).

◆ BIBLIOGRAPHY

Works by Shirley Geok-lin Lim

Short Story Collections

Another Country and Other Stories. Singapore: Times Books International, 1982.
Life's Mysteries: The Best of Shirley Lim. Singapore: Times Books International, 1995.
Two Dreams: New and Selected Stories. New York: The Feminist Press, 1997.

Autobiography

Among the White Moon Faces: An Asian American Memoir of Homelands. New York: The Feminist Press, 1996.
Among the White Moon Faces: Memoirs of a Nonya Feminist. Singapore: Times Books International, 1996.

Poetry

Crossing the Peninsula and Other Poems. Kuala Lumpur: Heinemann Writing in Asia Series, 1980.

No Man's Grove and Other Poems. Singapore: National University of Singapore English Department Press, 1985.

Modern Secrets: New and Selected Poems. Sydney: Dangaroo Press, 1989.

Monsoon History: Selected Poems. London: Skoob Pacifica, 1994.

What the Fortune Teller Didn't Say. Albuquerque, NM: West End Press, 1998.

Novel

Joss and Gold. New York: The Feminist Press, 2001.

Edited Anthologies

The Forbidden Stitch: An Asian American Women's Anthology. Corvallis, OR: Calyx Books, 1989.

Approaches to Teaching Kingston's The Woman Warrior. New York: Modern Language Association, 1991.

Reading the Literatures of Asian America. Coed. with Amy Ling. Philadelphia: Temple University Press, 1992.

One World of Literature: An Anthology of Contemporary Global Literature. Boston: Houghton Mifflin, 1992.

Asian American Literature: An Anthology. Chicago: NTC/Contemporary Press, 1999.

Tilting the Continent: An Anthology of Southeast Asian American Writing. St. Paul, MN: New Rivers Press, 2000.

Critical Studies

Nationalism and Literature: Literature in English from the Philippines and Singapore. Quezon City: New Day Publishers, 1993.

Writing Southeast/Asia in English: Against the Grain. London: Skoob Pacifica, 1994.

Transnational Asia Pacific Gender, Representations, and the Public Sphere. Champaign: University of Illinois Press, 1999.

Power, Race, and Gender in Academe: Strangers in the Tower? New York: Modern Language Association, 2000.

Informing the American Nation: Asia, Genre and Gender. New York: Columbia University Press (forthcoming).

Studies of Shirley Geok-lin Lim

Fox, Timothy. "Just Another Cell in the Beehive: Interview with Shirley Geok-lin Lim Feminist Scholar, Teacher and Poet." *Intersections: Gender, History, and Culture in the Asian Context* 4.43 (September 2000). Online. Available: http://wwwsshe.murdoch.edu.au/intersections/issue4/lim_fox _interview.html.

Gadd, Bernard. Review of *Modern Secrets. World Literature Today* 64.3 (Summer 1990): 533.

Knowlton, Edgar C., Jr. Rev. of *Another Country and Other Stories. World Literature Today* 58 (Winter 1984): 167.

Mandal, Somdatta, ed. *The Diasporic Imagination: Asian American Writing*. New Delhi: Prestige Books, 2000.

Means, Laurel. "The 'Orient-ation' of Eden: Christian/Buddhist Dialogics in the Poetry of Shirley Geok-lin Lim." *Christianity and Literature* 43.2 (Winter 1994): 189–203.

Morgan, Nina. "Locating Shirley Geok-lin Lim, An Interview." In *The Diasporic Imagination: Asian American Writing*. Somdatta Mandal, ed. New Delhi: Prestige Press, 2000, 99–110.

———. "Shirley Geok-lin Lim." In *Asian American Autobiographers: A Bio-Bibliographical Critical Sourcebook*. Guiyou Huang, ed. Westport, CT: Greenwood Press, 2001, 215–20.

———. "Shirley Geok-lin Lim." In *Asian American Poets: A Bio-Bibliographical Critical Sourcebook*. Guiyou Huang, ed. Westport, CT: Greenwood Press, 2002, 213–18.

Singh, Kirpal. "An Interview with Shirley Geok-lin Lim." *Ariel: A Review of International English Literature* 30.4 (October 1999): 135–41.

Wang, Jennie. "Interview with Shirley Geok-lin Lim." In *Speaking of the Short Story: Interviews with Contemporary Writers*. Farhat Iftekharuddin, Mary Rohrberger, and Maurice Lee, eds. Jackson: University Press of Mississippi, 1997, 153–65.

Whitlock, Gillian. *The Intimate Empire: Reading Women's Autobiography*. London: Cassell Academic, 2000.

Yu, Larry. "New and Selected Stories, by Shirley Geok-Lin Lim." *MELUS* 24.4 (Winter 1999): 173–76.

Zhou, Xiaojing. "Introduction." *Two Dreams*, by Shirley Geok-lin Lim. New York: The Feminist Press, 1997.

DAVID WONG LOUIE
(1954–   )

Rocío G. Davis

◆ BIOGRAPHY

David Wong Louie was born in Rockville Center, New York, in 1954, the second of four children of Chinese immigrants who arrived in the United States after World War II. His parents operated a laundry in a Long Island suburb. He has a B.A. from Vassar College (1977) and an M.F.A. in Creative Writing from the University of Iowa (1981). He has received fellowships from the National Endowment for the Arts, the California Arts Council, the Mac-Dowell Colony, Yaddo, and the Lannan Foundation. Louie began publishing in literary journals such as *Kansas Quarterly, The Iowa Review, Quarry West,* and *Ploughshares.* His first collection of stories, *Pangs of Love* (1991), was a *New York Times* Notable Book of 1991 and a *Voice Literary Supplement* Favorite that year. It won the *Los Angeles Times* Art Seidenbaum Award for First Fiction and the *Ploughshares* John C. Zacharis First Book Award for 1991. "Displacement," from that collection, was published in *The Best American Short Stories 1989.* His first novel, *The Barbarians Are Coming* (2000), won the Association for Asian American Studies Award for Prose in 2000. He taught at Vassar College from 1988 to 1992, and is currently Associate Professor of English and Asian American Literature at the University of California, Los Angeles. Louie lives in Venice, California, with his wife.

◆ MAJOR WORKS AND THEMES

The eleven stories in *Pangs of Love* explore the often ambivalent situation of Asian Americans (mostly Chinese and male) in contemporary society and address the question of alienation in highly original ways. Though ostensibly assimilated and successful, many of the characters in the stories occupy liminal positions in their families and in society. This unstable position is exemplified by the otter in "Bottle of Beaujolais": it lives in a tank that replicates the environment of its lakeshore home and is subject to the whims of its caretaker. Louie engages diverse forms of displacement: dislocation, separation from a past history or family. For instance, Mrs. Chow, the aristocratic immigrant in "Displacement," must accept her husband's subservience, and their employer's accusations, as well as a future landlady's callous comments: "I'm willing to take a risk on you. . . . Besides, I'm real partial to Chinese take-out" (29). In stories such as "Birthday," "Pangs of Love," "The Movers," and "Social Science," characters inhabit houses that are not theirs, and their occupation is a physical manifestation of their psychological or social displacement. The narrators of these stories struggle to establish connections—real or imaginary—with family or places, and, in particular, with children. Henry, in "Social Science," for example, watches as a man called David Brinkley (who fakes being the model Christy's husband) begins to appropriate the touchstones of his life—his house, his ex-wife, his students. The obese and unemployed Hank in "Warming Trends" is alienated from his family, his talent for embalming and preparing corpses unused. Many Chinese builders of the Great Wall, in "Disturbing the Universe," die brokenhearted at the loss of home: "After all, ours was never a transient race; we grow thick, deep roots" (182).

Sau-ling Wong notes that an "anxiety over paternity, progeny, extinction" (181) recurs in the stories, many of which also engage unstable, adulterous, or broken relationships. Louie's representation of Asian American men is complex: the servile Mr. Chow in "Displacement," the frustrated Wallace in "Birthday," and the lovesick narrator of "Bottle of Beaujolais" struggle to assert themselves. The issue of fatherhood echoes in many others. Wallace longs to take his ex-girlfriend's son to a baseball game on the child's birthday but is stopped from doing so by the child's biological father; Mrs. Pang, in the title story, wonders why her children, one of whom is gay, do not have children; the narrator in "The Movers" pretends to be a father; in "One Man's Hysteria—Real and Imagined—in the Twentieth Century," Stephen invents a son and concludes a memo to himself with "[d]on't forget Todd, he changes the world" (159). In "Inheritance," the only story with a female narrator, Edna's father is "shaken by the fact that his lone surviving child was . . . opposed to babies" (205), while her husband, Li, having escaped China's one-child policy, joins a father's softball team and dreams of siring a team of his own. Images of the Cold War and the terrors of bellicose conflicts linked to issues of extinction also haunt many characters' imaginations. Ultimately, though, the stories are about love and the search for permanence in relationships with parents, partners, children—significant elements in the process of self-affirmation.

Interethnic relationships are addressed in stories like "Birthday," "Love on the Rocks," and "Social Science," highlighting the precariousness of the Asian

American man's position, caught between cultural expectations and their own desires. Wallace's parents, for example, are against his relationship with Sylvie, and argue in favor of its ending in ethnic terms: "My mother wanted to know if I was eating rice again, now that the girl was gone" (8). Several stories engage the cultural and generational gap between immigrant parents and their American-born children. Importantly, the children are aware that their parents need to believe in the American dream, and stories such as "Pangs of Love" or "Inheritance" recast the parents' "deluded beliefs as necessary, hopeful illusions" (Lee 274). The question of authenticity also figures prominently. "Disturbing the Universe" posits a Chinese origin to baseball; David Brinkely lives stolen identities; the son in "Pangs of Love" works for a company that manufactures synthetic smells and flavors, which he uses to enhance his love life and sweeten their family meal at the end of the story. Women are often required to look or act in culturally prescribed manners. Mrs. Pang tells her son that if he's "going to marry a non-Chinese, she might as well look the part"—which translates into skirt, nylons, high-heeled shoes (80); Edna feels judged by Mrs. Woo as "not quite the real thing, neither Chinese nor American, and wouldn't Li be happier with a culturally pure spouse?" (208).

Louie's prose is erudite and incisive—a dark humor offers ironic insights on situations and characters. He experiments successfully with distinct discursive strategies, constructing a complex multivoiced narrative in "Love on the Rocks," a story that Shirley Lim believes "gestures toward a multiplicity of identities at play in the ethnic subject" (347). "One Man's Hysteria," an exercise in metafiction, explores the limits of invention. Surreal elements abound in "Bottle of Beaujolais" as well as in "Disturbing the Universe." His stories, on both thematic and contextual levels, address crucial issues in contemporary Asian American literary concerns and production, and widen readers' appreciation of possible formulations of the ethnic experience.

◆ CRITICAL RECEPTION

Though the themes Louie addresses are traditional to Asian American literature, his stories are admirable for their innovative and nuanced articulation of the Asian American position. Shirley Geok-lin Lim praises the originality of the characters and the style, which are "fresh with satirical energy, and full of elegantly ironic layerings that disavow conventional sentiment and stale disclosures of ethnic identity" (349). Rachel Lee includes the title story in her overview of emblematic Asian American short stories, highlighting how Louie leaves his reader with a sense of the tension between caring and pain, deception and hope (273). Sau-ling Wong commends the collection's engagement with larger concerns regarding uniquely Asian American identities and asserts that the volume "looks ahead to confront the disturbing possibilities raised by the problematic positioning of Chinese/Asian American men in a racialized and gendered society" (189). Lim also appreciates the manner in which the stories "destabilize" stereotypes of Chinese Americans, and "demonstrate his resistance to the contemporary cultural movement both to fix the Chinese Americans in an orientalist fantasy and to assimilate them into U.S. culture as model minorities" (346). This strategy enacts a necessary revision of the images of Asian Americans, which, as Sheila Sarkar points out, challenges the master narratives of stereotypical Asian men, questioning them through characters who, "by demonstrating their abilities to create alternative stories, show they can be productive even within their oppressed space" (80).

◆ BIBLIOGRAPHY

Works by David Wong Louie

Short Story Collection

Pangs of Love. New York: Alfred A. Knopf, 1991.

Novel

The Barbarians Are Coming. New York: Putnam, 2000.

Studies of David Wong Louie

Lee, Rachel. "Asian American Short Fiction: An Introduction and Critical Survey." In *A Resource Guide to Asian American Literature*. Sau-ling Wong and Stephen Sumida, eds. New York: Modern Language Association, 2001, 252–84.

Lim, Shirley Geok-lin. "David Wong Louie." In *The Columbia Companion to the Twentieth-Century American Short Story*. Blanche H. Gelfant, ed. New York: Columbia University Press, 2000, 345–49.

Partridge, Jeff. "Towards a More Worldly World Series: Reading Game Three of the 1998 American League Championship and David Wong Louie's 'Warming Trends.' " *American Studies International* 38.2 (June 2000): 115–25.

Samarth, Manini. "Affirmations: Speaking the Self into Being." *Parnassus: Poetry in Review* 17.1 (1992): 88–101.

Sarkar, Sheila. "Cynthia Kadohata and David Wong Louie: The Pangs of a Floating World." *Hitting Critical Mass: A Journal of Asian American Criticism* 2.1 (Winter 1994): 79–97.

Wong, Sau-ling Cynthia. "Chinese/Asian American Men in the 1990s: Displacement, Impersonation, Paternity, and Extinction in David Wong Louie's *Pangs of Love*." In *Privileging Positions: The Sites of Asian American Studies*. Gary Y. Okihiro, Marilyn Alquizola, et al., eds. Pullman: Washington State University Press, 1995, 181–91.

DARRELL H. Y. LUM
(1950–   )

Kenneth J. Speirs

♦ **BIOGRAPHY**

Darrell H. Y. Lum is a Chinese American writer born on April 2, 1950, in the Alewa Heights area of Honolulu, Hawaii. Lum's grandfather on his father's side was a provincial government official in Canton, China, before being invited to be a Chinese language teacher in Kaimuki, Honolulu. Although he was later forced to become a butcher, among other jobs, because he could not support his family as a teacher, Lum's grandfather maintained a lifelong interest in writing and reading poetry. Lum's father was born in Canton and came to Hawaii at age five or six. His grandmother on his mother's side moved to Hawaii when she was an infant, and married a Chinese rice-mill manager. His mother was the youngest of seven children and was raised in the Waikane Valley. Currently, Lum lives in Honolulu, Hawaii, with his wife Mae Amy and their two children, Lisa and Daniel.

After graduating from McKinley High School in 1968, Lum left Hawaii to study engineering at Case Institute of Technology in Cleveland. After his freshman year, he transferred to the University of Hawaii at Manoa, where he studied creative writing and graphic design. In May 1972, he received a B.A. in Liberal Studies. He continued his studies at the same university, earning an M.A. in Educational Communications and Technology in 1976. In 1997, Lum was awarded a Ph.D. in Educational Foundations from the University of Hawaii at Manoa; his dissertation is entitled "What School You Went? Stories from a Pidgin Culture." From 1974 to the present he has worked as an academic advisor at the University of Hawaii Student Support Services.

Lum's two short story collections, *Sun: Short Stories and Drama* (1980) and *Pass On, No Pass Back* (1990), have both achieved wide readership in Hawaii and, increasingly, on the mainland. His stories have appeared in numerous publications, such as *Manoa, Bamboo Ridge, Seattle Review, Chaminade Literary Review*, and *Hawaii Review*, and have been reprinted in anthologies of contemporary Asian American fiction, most notably in *Charlie Chan Is Dead* (1993). His much-admired plays—including *Oranges Are Lucky, Fighting Fire, A Little Bit Like You, My Home Is Down the Street*, and *Magic Mango*—have been widely produced by Kumu Kahua, Honolulu Theater for Youth, and other theatrical companies. In addition to his fiction and drama, Lum has published essays and children's books. His children's books—including *The Golden Slipper: A Vietnamese Legend, Hot-Pepper-Kid and Iron-Mouth-Chicken Capture Fire and Wind, The Rice Mystery*, and *Riding the Bullet*—present an informative and respectful representation of various aspects of Asian heritage. His critical writings have been crucial to the establishment and examination of Hawaii's local literature movement.

He is cofounder and coeditor (along with Eric Chock) of the literary magazine *Bamboo Ridge*, an important venue for the publication of Hawaii's literature. Begun in 1978, *Bamboo Ridge* is a non-profit literary and scholarly press devoted to the continued support and further development of works by and about the peoples of Hawaii.

Lum received a National Endowment for the Arts Fellowship in 1989 and the Elliot Cades Award in 1991. For *Pass On, No Pass Back*, Lum was awarded the Outstanding Book Award in fiction by the Association for Asian American Studies in 1992. Both Lum and Chock were awarded the Hawaii Award for Literature in 1996, the state's highest award for literature, for their work on *Bamboo Ridge*. In 1999 and again in 2001 Lum served a term as Centrum Artist in Residency in Port Townsend, Washington.

◆ MAJOR WORKS AND THEMES

The central concerns of Lum's fiction are to preserve Hawaiian culture and, relatedly, to investigate racial and cultural inequities within Hawaiian and American society. Lum's deepest impulse as a writer, then, is to recognize "the responsibility to listen to the land, to the people, to all the voices" (*Quietest Singing* 2).

This project is well served by Lum's innovative use of the pidgin dialect of Hawaii, a striking feature of his writing that is frequently praised by commentators. Asserting that it is the "voice that wants to tell the stories," Lum confesses that despite "the efforts of parents, teachers, and the board of education to eradicate it," pidgin—or Hawaii Creole English—is "part of who I am" ("Pidgin and Children" 298). Often applauded by readers for his use of distinctly individualized first-person narrators, Lum's memorable use of local dialect has helped to structure the taste and shape the style of many younger writers in Hawaii.

"Pidgin English" is the local generic term in Hawaii for what is termed

Hawaii Pidgin English (HPE) by linguists. Spoken natively by the offspring of immigrant plantation laborers and other Hawaii residents, Hawaii Pidgin English evolved as various immigrant groups, such as Chinese, Japanese, Portuguese, Filipino, Spanish, and others, worked to find ways to communicate among themselves and with the white English-speaking plantation owners. Set against this complex historical backdrop, Lum's choice to employ Pidgin English in his writings, while a vehicle for much of the humor that characterizes his fiction, necessarily takes on greater significance.

Certainly Lum's fiction celebrates the commonplace and the everyday absurdities that he sees as a part of island life for many Hawaiians. Seen through the eyes of his characters, who are often young or elderly, the events of daily life take on an absurd and humorous quality. Striving to make sense of their marginalized positions, Lum's characters often approach insights into the self and the world. More likely than not, these insights remain just beyond where Lum's characters can give them voice; this familiar scene, played out in various ways, lends Lum's work an ironic, mildly poignant brand of humor. Yet, beneath the humor and the good fun "talk story" of his work, Lum's fiction encourages readers to consider larger questions and to think more deeply about the ways racial and class issues structure much of Hawaiian and American society. In this way, Lum's use of regional dialect has led some critics to suggest that his work shares similar concerns with important writers in the American literary tradition, such as Mark Twain, Bret Harte, and William Faulkner.

◆ CRITICAL RECEPTION

Although widely recognized and influential in contemporary Hawaiian literary circles, Lum's unfamiliarity to mainland readers has become an area of inquiry for critics. For example, exploring Hawaii's geographic and cultural marginalization from the "main" land, Gayle K. Fujita Sato, in an essay entitled "The Island Influence on Chinese American Writers," both details the ways Lum (and other writers) engages the central themes of Chinese American history and traces the ways his perspective is shaped by Island influences. Sato goes on to argue that the 1978 "Talk Story" conference held in Honolulu provided an important early moment in the growth of an emerging literary consciousness among Hawaii writers—"a consciousness that Hawaii's history and multicultural society needed broader and better representation by the variety of people who actually lived there and had shaped the culture" (17). Coincident to the conference, Sato notes that Darrell Lum and Eric Chock founded *Bamboo Ridge: The Hawai'i Writers' Quarterly*, the seminal journal whose aim is to publish and encourage the development of Hawaii's multiethnic writers. Not merely the outgrowth of the conference, rather, *Bamboo Ridge* has in Sato's mind become the "hub of development" (18) for Lum and other Island writers. As such, *Bamboo Ridge* is, in Sato's estimation, an important starting place for gauging and estimating the range of Island influences on Lum's work. Sato's essay draws into her analysis not only Lum's masterful use of Pidgin English, but also the use of metaphors of recycling in his stories. Through these Sato argues that Lum "represents the understructure of social exchange characterizing Hawaii's local culture" (26), which in turn points to the larger patterns of social exchange that typify American culture.

In a highly compelling essay entitled "Resistance and Reclamation: Hawaii 'Pidgin English' and Autoethnography in the Short Stories of Darrell H. Y. Lum," Gail Y. Okawa explores the various resistances embedded in Lum's fiction. Contextualizing her analysis within Hawaii's social, linguistic, and literary history, Okawa argues that Lum's short stories "reflect in the author's choice of subject, language, and form a growing resistance to the dominant society's stereotypes of and colonial attitudes towards Hawaii's multiethnic people, culture, and language" (179). The term "autoethnography" that appears in Okawa's title is borrowed from Mary Louise Pratt. It refers to the ways in which the Pidgin English–speaking narrators of Lum's stories construct self-representations that complicate, if not contradict, the representations others have made of them. These self-representations are involved in a project of reclamation, effecting a reconnection through Pidgin English to "a language that we continue to use and, in some cases, return to in varying degrees and circumstances to give us our identity and provide a sense of continuity with other speakers and our culture" (193).

◆ BIBLIOGRAPHY

Works by Darrell H. Y. Lum

Short Stories

"No Mistaking." In *Pake: Writings by Chinese in Hawaii*. Eric Chock and Darrell H. Y. Lum, eds. Honolulu: Bamboo Ridge Press, 1989, 169–81.

"J'like Ten Thousand." In *Pake*, Chock and Lum, eds., 182–86.

"Fourscore and Seven Years Ago." In *Charlie Chan Is Dead: An Anthology of Contemporary Asian American Fiction*. Jessica Hagedorn, ed. New York: Penguin, 1993, 287–95.

"Yahk Fahn, Auntie." In *American Dragons*. Laurence Yep, ed. New York: HarperCollins, 1996.

"Giving Tanks." In *Into the Fire: Asian American Prose*. Sylvia Watanabe and Carol Bruchac, eds. New York: Greenfield Review Press, 1996, 113–18.

"Primo Doesn't Take Back Bottles Anymore." In *Asian American Literature: A Brief Introduction and Anthology*. Shawn Wong, ed. New York: Longman, 1996, 215–19.

"Encountering Sorrow." In *The Quietest Singing*. Darrell H. Y. Lum, Joseph Stanton, and Estelle Enoki, eds. Honolulu: Bamboo Ridge Press, 2000, 134–56.

Short Story Collections

Sun: Short Stories and Drama. Honolulu: Bamboo Ridge Press, 1980.
Pass On, No Pass Back. Honolulu: Bamboo Ridge Press, 1990.

Children's Stories

The Golden Slipper: A Vietnamese Legend. New York: Troll Associates, 1994.
Hot-Pepper-Kid and Iron-Mouth-Chicken Capture Fire and Wind. New York: Macmillan/
     McGraw-Hill, 1997.
The Rice Mystery. New York: Macmillan/McGraw-Hill, 1998.
Riding the Bullet. New York: Macmillan/McGraw-Hill, 1999.

Drama

Oranges Are Lucky. Talk Story: An Anthology of Hawaii's Local Writers. Eric Chock, Darrell
     H. Y. Lum, Dave Robb, Frank Stewart, Gail Miyasaki, and Kathy Uchida, eds.
     Honolulu: Petronium and Talk Story, 1978, 139–56. Rpt. in *Sun: Short Stories
     and Drama*. Honolulu: Bamboo Ridge Press, 1980, 44–61.
Kumu Kahua Plays. Dennis Carroll, ed. Honolulu: University of Hawaii Press, 1983, 64–
     82.
Magic Mango. Bamboo Shoots. Dennis Kawaharada, ed. Honolulu: Bamboo Ridge Press,
     1982, 4–13.

Edited Anthologies

Talk Story: An Anthology of Hawaii's Local Writers. Eric Chock, Darrell H. Y. Lum, Dave
     Robb, Frank Stewart, Gail Miyasaki, and Kathy Uchida, eds. Honolulu: Pe-
     tronium and Talk Story, 1978.
The Best of Bamboo Ridge: The Hawai'i Writers' Quarterly. Eric Chock and Darrell H. Y.
     Lum, eds. Honolulu: Bamboo Ridge Press, 1986.
Pake. Chock and Lum, eds.
Growing Up Local: An Anthology of Poetry and Prose from Hawai'i. Eric Chock, James R.
     Harstad, Darrell H. Y. Lum, and Bill Teter, eds. Honolulu: Bamboo Ridge
     Press, 1998.
The Best of Honolulu Fiction: Stories from the Honolulu Magazine Fiction Contest. Eric Chock
     and Darrell H. Y. Lum, eds. Honolulu: Bamboo Ridge Press, 1999.
The Quietest Singing, Lum, Stanton, and Enoki, eds.

Essays

"Local Literature and Lunch." In *The Best of Bamboo Ridge*, Chock and Lum, eds., 3–5.
"Pake: Our Literary Tradition." In *Pake*, Chock and Lum, eds., 10–15.
"On Pidgin and Children in Literature." In *Infant Tongues: The Voice of the Child in*

Literature. Elizabeth Goodenough, Mark A. Heberle, and Naomi Sokoloff, eds. Detroit: Wayne State University Press, 1994, 298–301.

"Local Genealogy: What School You Went?" In *Growing Up Local*, Chock, Harstad, Lum, and Teter, eds., 11–15.

Interview

"Response." Interview. In *Yellow Light: The Flowering of Asian American Arts*. Amy Ling, ed. Philadelphia: Temple University Press, 1999, 93–98.

Studies of Darrell H. Y. Lum

Fujikane, Candace. "Between Nationalisms: Hawaii's Local Nation and Its Troubled Racial Paradise." *HCM: A Journal of Asian American Cultural Criticism* 1.2 (Spring 1994). http://socrates.berkeley.edu/~critmass/v1n2/fujikane1.html.

Okawa, Gail Y. "Resistance and Reclamation: Hawaii 'Pidgin English' and Autoethnography in the Short Stories of Darrell H. Y. Lum." In *Ethnicity and the American Short Story*. Julie Brown, ed. New York: Garland Publishing, 1997, 177–96.

Sato, Gayle K. Fujita. "The Island Influence on Chinese American Writers: Wing Tek Lum, Darrell H. Y. Lum, and Eric Chock." *Amerasia Journal* 16.2 (1990): 17–33.

Sumida, Stephen H. "Sense of Place, History, and the Concept of the 'Local' in Hawaii's Asian/Pacific Literatures." In *Reading the Literatures of Asian America*. Shirley Geok-lin Lim and Amy Ling, eds. Philadelphia: Temple University Press, 1992, 215–37.

———. "Postcolonialism, Nationalism, and the Emergence of Asian/Pacific American Literatures." In *An Interethnic Companion to Asian American Literature*. King-Kok Cheung, ed. Cambridge: Cambridge University Press, 1997, 274–88.

Watanabe, Sylvia. "A Conversation with Darrell Lum and Eric Chock." In *Into the Fire*, Watanabe and Bruchac, eds., 85–98.

Wong, Sau-ling Cynthia. *Reading Asian American Literature: From Necessity to Extravagance*. Princeton, NJ: Princeton University Press, 1993.

———. "Chinese American Literature." In *An Interethnic Companion to Asian American Literature*, Cheung, ed., 39–61.

ROHINTON MISTRY
(1952–   )

Alice D'Amore

◆ BIOGRAPHY

Rohinton Mistry, like many of the characters he draws to life in *Swimming Lessons and Other Stories from Firozsha Baag*, is an Indian of Parsi descent. Born in 1952, he graduated from the University of Bombay with a Bachelor of Arts in Mathematics and Economics before emigrating to Toronto, Canada, in 1975. While working on his second Bachelor of Arts in English at the University of Toronto's Woodsworth College, Mistry began to write short stories that illustrated the cultural dichotomies that separate India from the Western world as well as the tensions that divide generations in postcolonial India.

Mistry's work has achieved great success in Canada and the United States as well as in India. In 1983, his first short story was awarded a Hart House Prize for fiction. He won the award again in 1984, as well as *Canadian Fiction Magazine*'s Annual Contributor's Prize in 1985. His novel *Such a Long Journey* (1991) received Canada's Governor General's Award, the Commonwealth Writer's Prize for Best Book, and the W.H. Smith/Books in Canada First Novel Award. Likewise, *A Fine Balance* (1996) won various merits, including the Giller Prize, the Royal Society of Literature's Winfried Holtby Prize, and the 1996 *Los Angeles Times* Award for fiction. In 2001, Oprah Winfrey chose *A Fine Balance* as her November Book Club selection, thus exposing Mistry's work to a vast new and multicultural audience. His stories have been published in various Canadian anthologies and literary journals. Currently, Mistry is working on a third novel, which is forthcoming from Alfred A. Knopf in the United States and from Faber and Faber in England.

◆ MAJOR WORKS AND THEMES

Mistry's collection of short stories, *Swimming Lessons and Other Stories from Firozsha Baag*, centers on a lower-class community, where the members interact, often comically and poignantly, in a crumbling Bombay apartment complex. In a 1997 interview with Mary Mazzocco, Mistry reflects, "I don't think these people have been represented enough in fiction. . . . Most fiction is about the middle class" (http://lubbockonline.com/news/062697/rohinton.htm.) In each of these stories, Mistry manages to balance the tensions of cultural as well as interpersonal conflict within the struggling blocks of Firozsha Baag.

This novel-like compilation serves as a series of initiations for the maturing Kersi Boyce, who narrates several of the stories. In "Of White Hairs and Cricket," Kersi faces a double strain as he suffers a financial burden caused by his father's inability to gain employment, while at the same time experiencing the emotional depression sparked by the father's inevitable aging. Forced to pull the white hairs from his father's head as the old man shuffles through the classified advertisements, presumably to make him appear younger to employers, Kersi listens as his father makes promises of a "Gas Company stove and cylinder" and a refrigerator for Mrs. Boyce and emigration to America for Kersi when the elder Boyce gets a job. His father reads aloud want ads that seek "Dynamic Young Account Executives," as Kersi describes how "Mummy listened to such advertisements week after week [as] harbingers of hope that ended in disappointment and frustration" (*Swimming Lessons* 112).

The elder Boyce's aging not only affects Kersi's social status but his emotional state as well. Kersi resents the aging of the man who once appeared indomitable to him. He recalls Sunday afternoons of bike riding and cricket games, until "one Sunday, halfway through the game, Daddy said he was going to rest for awhile. Sitting on the grass a little distance away, he seemed so much older than he did when he was batting, or bowling leg breaks. He watched us with a faraway expression on his face. Sadly, as if he had just realized something and wished he hadn't" (*Swimming Lessons* 117). Surprised by his father's groan during the white-hair pulling by the "nimble fourteen-year-old fingers [which] uproot the signposts of mortality sprouting week after week" (*Swimming Lessons* 107), Kersi reflects, "He had taught me to be tough, always," but the signs of his father's failing now depress him.

Struggling to become a man in an environment where his sole mentor is ineffective as the head of the family, Kersi struggles to toughen the image he feels he must portray to the world. When his father suggests sending him to America, Kersi notes, "I felt suddenly like hugging him, but we never did except on birthdays, and to get rid of the feeling I looked away and pretended to myself that he was saying it just to humour me, because he wanted me to finish pulling his white hairs" (*Swimming Lessons* 112–13). He fears the great loss that comes naturally with death and the accompanying and often debilitating emotional release of loss. He further realizes the inevitability of his father's mortality when he visits his best friend Viraf and observes the boy's obese, dying father with his "stone-grey face" and the "lines on his brow, like Daddy's, only Daddy's were less deep" (*Swimming Lessons* 119).

At the end of the story, the torn Kersi falls into his bed, yearning for the tears that fail to come: "I wanted to weep for myself, for not being able to hug Daddy when I wanted to, and for not ever saying thank you for cricket in the morning, and pigeons and bicycles and dreams; and for all the white hairs that I was powerless to stop" (*Swimming Lessons* 120). Where the detached young Jehangir fails to show emotion at the end of "The Collectors" as he merely accepts the crippling lessons of life with a shrug of mute indifference, Kersi struggles with his powerlessness against the natural cycle of life and his innate need to emote, a trait he sees as an obstacle to achieving manhood.

"One Sunday," the story involving the robbery of the self-righteous Najami by the starving Francis, pictures the desperation and humiliation of a grown man through the eyes of the young, sexually-frustrated Kersi. In the story, Kersi experiences the abject brutality of humanity when a crowd in the slums of "Tar Gully," as well as spectators at his home in Firozsha Baag, beat Francis relentlessly. Kersi, the only individual affected by the incident, gazes at his destroyed cricket bat in its "flayed and naked state," learning his first lesson in his turbulent transition to manhood (*Swimming Lessons* 39).

◆ CRITICAL RECEPTION

Much of Mistry's writing deals with complicated societal interactions between first- and second-generation Parsis, a religious sect which, as Robert L. Ross indicates in his article "Seeking and Maintaining Balance: Rohinton Mistry's Fiction," migrated from Persia in the seventh century to escape Islamic rule. He notes that the Parsis make a significant contribution to the business community of India, but,

> they continue to live outside the mainstream and strive to retain their identity in a predominantly Hindu country. Their religious practices, based on tradition, intrude on all avenues of their lives and appear at times to be more the product of the letter than the spirit. The younger residents in Firozsha Baag rebel, and the older ones fear the encroachment of a changing world. This conflict between religious tradition and personal fluidity creates the tension in each of the stories. (5)

Similarly, Jennifer Takhar notes that because Mistry's heritage displays this dual displacement, namely the emigration from Persia and the strict adherence to Parsi tradition in an Indian culture, he "finds himself at the margins of

Indian society, and hence his writing challenges and resists absorption by the dominating and Hindu-glorifying culture of India" (http://www.victorian web.org/post/canada/literature/mistry/takhar1.html). This thorny aspect of Mistry's work is evident most specifically in stories such as "Condolence Visit," where Daulat shocks Najami and Moti by breaking traditional Parsi death rituals, and in "The Ghost of Firozsha Baag," where the Catholic *ayah* "Jaakaylee" comically manages to convince her Parsi employers that *bhoots* (ghosts) truly exist.

Mistry's frank depiction of Parsi life on the border of overwhelming poverty (i.e., Tar Gully) has ruffled the feathers of such visitors to India as Germaine Greer, Australian commentator for BBC-TV, who publicly criticized Mistry's latest novel, *A Fine Balance*, and its portrayal of Bombay prior to his acceptance of the Booker Prize in 1996. Greer states, "I just don't recognize this dismal, dreary city." She contends that, "It's a Canadian book about India. What could be worse? What could be more terrible?" Mistry calls the criticism "asinine" and firmly stands by his twenty-three years of experience in India (*Canoe*, http://www.canoe.ca/JamBooksFeatures/mistry_rohinton.html). In his reflection on the darker side of Mistry's work, Ross notes that Mistry captures "the city's squalid side, the poverty, disorder, filth and ruin, the chaos, but at the same time engages its immense vitality and diversity" (5).

◆ BIBLIOGRAPHY

Works by Rohinton Mistry

Short Stories

"The Collectors." In *Coming Attractions 4*. with Dayv-James French and Lesley Krueger. David Helwig and Sandra Martin, eds. Ottawa: Oberon Press, 1986, 101–28.

"Condolence Visit." In *Coming Attractions 4*. with Dayv-James French and Lesley Krueger. David Helwig and Sandra Martin, eds. Ottawa: Oberon Press, 1986, 62–81.

"Lend Me Your Light." In *Coming Attractions 4*. with Dayv-James French and Lesley Krueger. David Helwig and Sandra Martin, eds. Ottawa: Oberon Press, 1986, 82–100.

"The More Important Things." *The Canadian Fiction Magazine* 65 (1989): 38–56.

Short Story Collections

Coming Attractions 4. With Dayv-James French and Lesley Krueger. David Helwig and Sandra Martin, eds. Ottowa: Oberon Press, 1986.

Swimming Lessons and Other Stories from Firozsha Baag. Boston: Houghton Mifflin Company, 1989.

Novels

Such a Long Journey. New York: Vintage, 1991.
A Fine Balance. New York: Alfred A. Knopf, 1996.

Speech

"A Fable of Lost Dreams." *The Canadian Forum* 75 (1996): 18–20.

Studies of Rohinton Mistry

Albertazzi, Silvia. "Passages: The 'Indian Connection,' from Sara Jeanette Duncan to Rohinton Mistry." In *Imagination and the Creative Impulse in the New Literatures in English*. M. T. Bindella and G. V. Davis, eds. Amsterdam: Rodopi, 1993, 57–66.

Bharucha, Nilufer E. "From Behind a Fine Veil: A Feminist Reading of Three Parsi Novels." In *Margins of Erasure: Purdah in the Subcontinental Novel in English*. Jasbir Jain and Amina Amin, eds. New Delhi: Sterling, 1995, 174–85.

———. " 'When Old Tracks Are Lost': Rohinton Mistry's Fiction as Diasporic Discourse." *Journal of Commonwealth Literature* 30 (1995): 57–64.

Canoe. "Mistry Calls Criticism of His Book 'Asinine.' " (2002). http://www.canoe.ca/JamBooksFeatures/mistry_rohinton.html.

Cooke, Hope. "Beehive in Bombay." Rev. of *Swimming Lessons and Other Stories from Firozsha Baag*. *New York Times* (March 5, 1989): 26.

Craig, T. L. "Fiction." *University of Toronto Quarterly* 62.1 (1992): 21–53.

Dodiya, Jaydipsinh, ed. *The Fiction of Rohinton Mistry*. London: Sangam, 1998.

Heble, Ajay. " 'A Foreign Presence in the Stall': Towards a Poetics of Cultural Hybridity in Rohinton Mistry's Migration Stories." *Canadian Literature* 137 (1993): 51–61.

Malak, Amin. "Insider/Outsider Views on Belonging: The Short Stories of Bharati Mukherjee and Rohinton Mistry." In *Short Fiction in the New Literatures in English*. J. Bardolph, ed. Nice: Faculté des Lettres et Sciences Humaines de Nice, 1989, 189–96.

Malieckal, Bindu. "Rohinton Mistry." In *Asian American Novelists: A Bio-Bibliographical Critical Sourcebook*. Emmanuel S. Nelson, ed. Westport, CT: Greenwood Press, 2000, 219–28.

Mazzocco, Mary. "Rohinton Mistry Became an Author Almost by Chance." *Knight-Ridder/Tribune Information Services for Contra Costa Times*. (1997). http://lubbockonline.com/news/062697/rohinton.htm.

Mitchell, Tom. "Rohinton Mistry." Online. (2000). http://www.emory.edu/ENGLISH/Bahri/Mistry.html.

Ross, Robert L. "Seeking and Maintaining Balance: Rohinton Mistry's Fiction." *World Literature Today* 73 (1999): 5. Online. *EBSCOHost*. Accessed April 30, 2002.

Shostak, Elizabeth. Rev. of *Swimming Lessons and Other Stories from Firozsha Baag*. *Wilson Library Bulletin* 63.9 (1989): 128–29.

Singh, Amritjit. "Rohinton Mistry." In *Writers of the Indian Diaspora: A Bio-Bibliographical*

Critical Sourcebook. Emmanuel S. Nelson, ed. Westport, CT: Greenwood Press, 1993, 207–18.

Steinberg, Sybil. Rev. of *Swimming Lessons and Other Stories from Firozsha Baag. Publishers Weekly* (December 9, 1988): 43.

Takhar, Jennifer. "Mother and Son: Oedipus Wrecks in Rohinton Mistry." *Canadian Literature & Culture in the Post-Colonial Literature and Culture Web.* (2000). http://65.107.211.206/post/canada/literature/mistry/takhar2a.html.

SHANI MOOTOO
(1958–)

Chandrima Chakraborty

◆ BIOGRAPHY

Shani Mootoo, writer, visual artist and video maker, was born in Ireland in 1958 to parents of Indian origin and grew up in Trinidad. She immigrated to Canada at the age of nineteen and began her career as a visual artist. Her photos and videos have been exhibited in the United States and Canada and at a number of international film festivals. Her writing has appeared in many anthologies and her first book was a collection of short stories, *Out on Main Street and Other Stories*. Her novel, *Cereus Blooms at Night*, which won the Chapters/Books in Canada First Novel Award, was short-listed for the Giller Prize and the Ethel Wilson Fiction Prize. Her most recent publication is a collection of poems, *The Predicament of Or*. She has lived in Vancouver, British Columbia, since 1981.

◆ MAJOR WORKS AND THEMES

Shani Mootoo's *Out on Main Street* voices the experience of women, particularly of the diasporic community constantly battling with the internalization of gendered upbringing alongside their struggle to create a home in the metropolis. As Mootoo's female characters try to conform to or resist the conventional paradigms of the good wife/daughter, they demonstrate their hybridized, diasporic subjectivities. Mootoo's personal experiences as a girl child, lesbian, and brown immigrant in Canada emerge as central themes in *Out on Main Street*. It validates her statement that "being lesbian/of colour is the foundation or world view" from which all her works "undoubtedly arise" (Dhaliwal 24). The identities that are presented here are symptomatic of the author's multiple national/ethnic (Indian-Trinidadian-Irish-Canadian) and sexual identities. The first story of the collection, "A Garden of Her Own," focuses on the repression of female desires, the resilience and power of tradition, and the expectation of a patriarchal family back home. The male character in this story is simply called "the husband." The woman/wife is given a name, a political strategy that individualizes her and interrogates traditional narrative techniques that use a husband's name or profession to define a wife. Having moved to North America after her marriage of six months, Vijai represses her sexual desires while her husband "slams himself against her, from behind grunting. She holds her breath taut against his weight and the pain, but she will not disturb the moment" (23). Having grown up seeing her mother wait for her father for dinner every night she asks: "Mama, why did you wait to eat? If I were to eat now would you, Papa, think I am a bad wife? Why did you show me this, Mama?" (14).

The hegemonic power of tradition and the feminine struggle with memories of gendered upbringing that requires a woman to be "her mother's daughter" (16) are very well brought out in "Wake Up"—a similar tale of a wife waiting for her husband to return home. Angenie, a 14-year-old girl awakened by her mother every other night to share her anxieties and her pain poignantly narrates it. This story is packed with elements from Mootoo's childhood experiences of her father's extramarital relationships, her mother's call to her "for advice and support," the demands on her that she dress and "behave like a girl" and her admiration for her father ("Photo Parentheses" 114, 108). Angenie, like Mootoo, is envious of the freedom she sees "inherent" in her father's maleness—"the freedom to work, to go to meetings, . . . to smoke, to drink, to have adventures" (42). She articulates Mootoo's childhood fears of having to spend "a lifetime trapped by the body of a female" (43) as she is "expected as a girl, to grow up to be just like her [mother]" (42). "The Bright New Year's Eve Night" dramatizes Angenie's fears. Tanya's experiences of domestic violence and abuse make her realize that she is "living the same hell" like her parents. She muses: "This is how Mama's head must have felt every time Papa banged it onto the wall" (74).

Memory functions as the chain, which connects various characters in *Out on Main Street* to their disrupted history and colonial "placing." In "Sushila's Bhakti" the kneading of mehndi triggers memories of Sushila's Brahmin grandmother and the religious festivals practiced in Trinidad. In "Nocturnals" a late night phone call from the narrator's aged mother reminds her of her forgotten Trinidadian neighbors. In "A Garden of Her Own" Vijai's reminiscences of "home"—the Trinidadian climate, the neighbors who talked over the fence and the cheerful shouts of children playing outdoors—position her as "a foreigner" in Canada. The memory of an "original" and ancestral heritage makes Mootoo's characters undertake a journey into the past. It is these (re)memberings and recollections that help to constitute their identity as Caribbeans. In "Sushila's Bhakti" the protagonist's upbringing as "a good-

Brahmmin girl" precludes her from taking part in carnival, an important component of Trinidadian culture. She is hemmed in through various kinds of restrictions and admonishments and is denied the possibility of being "properly Trinidadian (she could not sing one calypso, or shake down her hips with abandon when one was sung—the diligence of being a good Brahmin girl" (60). Yet, Indians from India "insist defiantly that she is in fact not truly Indian" (61).

In "Out on Main Street," the Indo-Trinidadian butch lesbian narrator uses Trinidadian English to relate her experiences while shopping with her girlfriend in an Indian area of Vancouver. She explains: "I used to think I was a Hindu *par excellence* until I come up here and see real flesh and blood Indians from India" (47). The Indians cannot accept the narrator's Caribbean identity or her lack of femininity and regard her with derision and contempt. The pressure to emerge as "the real" Indian leads the narrator in "The Upside-downness of the World as it Unfolds," like Mootoo, to buy cookbooks to learn something about Indian cooking and Sushila to embark on a search for an "authentic" Indian past—the land from where her ancestors were brought to Trinidad as indentured labourers—her "diluted" roots ("Sushila's Bhakti").

The Indo-Trinidadians are variously described as "watered-down Indians," "kitchen Indians: some kind of Indian food everyday," "cultural bastards" ("Out on Main Street"), or "cultural orphan" ("The Upside-downness of the World"), which is a reflection of their uncentered and inauthentic existence. The irony of the situation is explicit in the title of the story, "The Upside-downness of the World as It Unfolds," where the Indo-Trinidadian narrator meets two white women "genuine in their desire to be Indians" (115). They invite the narrator to a Krishna worship ceremony to enable her to "learn a little about your culture" (117). The seemingly Indian-looking narrator feels "shown-up as a cultural ignoramus" (119) in her T-shirt and slacks accompanied by two white women wearing elaborate saris. At the temple, the narrator finds the "Brown folk on the periphery of the room, not at all central to the goings-on" (120). She recognizes her "familiar" "urgent rage" at the racism that underlies this affected Indian-ness when midway through the sermon a young man comes to fetch women to help serve the food. He heads for the "Brown women," crossing over the white women worshippers. Her white friends comment on this sexist gesture unaware of their complicity in this blatant display of racism, not sexism. The author's emphasis on skin colors throughout the story alludes to the underlying tensions involved in the lesbian narrator's feelings of community and belonging in the company of the white lesbian couple. The different readings of the incident in the temple at the end of the story hint at the temporal nature of such a communion and foreground the complexities of creating a home for the queer cultural hybrid.

Recently there has been some crossover between queer and postcolonial studies and many of the stories in *Out on Main Street* demonstrate the nexus between queer and postcolonial positions. The Indo-Trinidadian butch lesbian narrator and her girlfriend Janet in "Out on Main Street" challenge the societal construction of sexuality and identity. Janet's appearance contradicts society's expectations of what a lesbian should act and look like. The waiters in the shop frown over Janet, who is "pretty fuh so" (48), while the narrator is treated in a condescending manner because of her unfeminine looks, androgynous clothes and loss of the Indian tongue.

Many of Mootoo's female narrators are openly lesbian. The narrative voice of the stories is female and the subject position assigned to the reader/auditor is also female. By giving the subject position and speaking voice to peripheral characters (immigrants/females/lesbians) Mootoo successfully moves them to the center. Her use of oral modes of storytelling makes the female voice in the written text more personal and intimate. For instance, "Out on Main Street," written in the structure of an oral narration, ends with the narrator asking the hearer/reader to tell her whether she is jealous or possessive about her girlfriend: "So tell me, what yuh think 'bout dis nah, girl?" (57). Such techniques make the readers believe that the narrators are taking them in their confidence and thereby evoke the readers' sympathy for the dilemmas, pain, and anger articulated by the hybrid and diasporic female/lesbian subjects.

All Mootoo's characters are linked to the Indian subcontinent, but in a way that registers the limitations of this link. Mootoo's use of omnipresent narration and Trinidadian English in some of the stories registers the characters' distance from all points of origin and explores the historically contingent contours of the composite identity that has resulted from the loss of origins. The transcultural exchange brought about by colonization has created their identity so that their syncretic identity seems less dependent upon roots (but migratory routes), not consolidation of one but (con)fusion of many.

In "The Upside-downness of the World," "Out on Main Street," and "Sushila's Bhakti" the female subjects strive for a definitive termination of their hybridized condition of postcoloniality but they soon realize that the core of their identity lies in the act of voicing and carving an identity and place in North America in the midst of many floating and rootless, diasporic communities of the world. Mootoo's short stories successfully emphasize the need for the new generation of Indo-Canadians/Indo-Caribbeans (and other immigrant communities) to create new languages and new narratives in order to grapple with their complex histories.

◆ CRITICAL RECEPTION

Mootoo's fictional works have received scant critical attention. Her own comments about the reviews of her novel can be applied to *Out on Main Street* as well: "Reviewers have been acutely aware of brownness in the book, of the author's skin, of the heat of the sun" (22). Virginia Gillese argues that the use of Trinidadian English, although "quirky enough to prove interesting, . . . is not sufficient to sustain the tension necessary for a short piece of fiction" (132).

She finds Mootoo's protagonists inadequate in expressing what she identifies as the central motif of this book, isolation. She also expresses her dissatisfaction with the "internal musings or the recounting of dreams" of the female characters and critiques "the absence of complex characterization" of male characters (132). Heather Smyth applauds Mootoo's use of "the flexibility of queer identity as a decolonizing tool" through her "both/and" approach to sexuality (151).

◆ BIBLIOGRAPHY

Works by Shani Mootoo

Short Story Collection

Out on Main Street and Other Stories. Vancouver: Press Gang Publishers, 1993.

Novel

Cereus Blooms at Night. Vancouver: Press Gang Publishers, 1996.

Essay

"Photo Parentheses." In *Desire in Seven Voices*. Lorna Crozier, ed. Vancouver: Douglas and McIntyre, 1999, 105–24.

Poetry

The Predicament of Or. Vancouver: Raincoat Books, 2000.

Studies of Shani Mootoo

Dhaliwal, Sarinder. "Shani Mootoo: Shifting Perceptions, Changing Practices." *Fuse Magazine* 22.2 (Spring 1999): 18–25.

Ghosh, Dipti. "Baigan Aloo Tabanka Bachanal: Writer, Artist, Filmmaker Shani Mootoo in Her Own Words." *Trikone Magazine* 9.4 (1994): 5–6.

Gillese, T. Virginia. "Isolation as Existence." Rev. of Kristjana Gunnars' *The Guest House and Other Stories* and Shani Mootoo's *Out on Main Street and Other Stories*. *Canadian Literature: A Quarterly of Criticism and Review* 145 (Summer 1995): 131–32.

Misrahib Barak, Judith. "Beginners' Luck among Caribbean-Canadian Writers: Nalo Hopkinson, Andre Alexis and Shani Mootoo." *Commonwealth Essays and Studies* 22.1 (Autumn 1999): 89–96.

Saul, Joanne. "Home Free?" Rev. of Shani Mootoo's *Cereus Blooms at Night* and Constance Rooke's *Writing Home: A PEN Canada Anthology. Canadian Literature* 164 (Spring 2000): 166–67.

Smyth, Heather. "Sexual Citizenship and Caribbean-Canadian Fiction: Dionne Brand's *In Another Place, Not Here* and Shani Mootoo's *Cereus Blooms at Night.*" *A Review of International English Literature* 30.2 (April 1999): 141–60.

TOSHIO MORI
(1910–1980)

Sarah Catlin Barnhart

◆ **BIOGRAPHY**

Toshio Mori was born in San Leandro, a community now overcome by the sprawling metropolis of Oakland, California, on March 20, 1910. He was the American son of Japanese parents, Hidekichi and Yoshi (Takaki) Mori. Upon arrival in America, his parents worked in plant nurseries, a profession which Mori would adopt as an adult. In an interview with Russell Leong, he credits an early affection for dime novels for his eventual infatuation with writing (Leong 93). Mori attended public schools, eventually earning a high school diploma. Although he did not receive additional formal schooling, he continued to educate himself, frequenting bookstores and libraries. He read French and Russian writers such as de Maupassant, Balzac, Chekhov, and Gorki, as well as Americans such as Katherine Mansfield, Stephen Crane, and Sherwood Anderson (Leong 93). At night, after a full day of work at the nursery, he wrote. Beginning in 1932 and up until 1942, he held himself to a strict four-hour-a-day writing schedule, 10:00 P.M. until 2:00 A.M., including Sundays (Leong 101). Eventually his hard work and perseverance began to produce results. In 1941, Mori's first book, *Yokohama, California*, was accepted for publication; however, the book was set aside by the publisher during World War II due (at least in part) to anti-Japanese sentiment. Because a Japanese American wrote the book, it was suspect. In the mid-1940s, Mori and his family were relocated to Topaz Camp, Millard County, Utah, by the War Relocation Authority, Department of the Interior. Mori was named "camp historian." Ironically, Mori had a brother who had been serving voluntarily in the U.S. Army before the war broke out. He was later injured in Europe while defending the very country that had incarcerated his family. On June 29, 1947,

Mori married Hisayo Yoshiwara. They had one son, Steven. By 1949 Mori had returned to his native Oakland, and *Yokohama, California* was finally being published after a seven-year postponement with one difference: two stories had been added to the already complete manuscript.

After the war, the majority of American readers no longer cared to read stories written by a Japanese American, but in 1985 renewed interest in Asian American writers spurred the publication of a new edition of *Yokohama, California* with a second introduction. Mori published two other books in his lifetime, *Woman from Hiroshima*, a novel, and *The Chauvinist and Other Stories*, both in 1979. Both books were largely ignored by critics and are now out of print. Mori also published short stories in anthologies such as *Speaking for Ourselves* (1969), *Japanese Americans: Untold Story* (1971), *Asian-American Authors* (1972), *Asian-American Heritage* (1974), *Aiiieeeee! An Anthology of Asian American Writers* (1974), and *Counterpoint* (1976). In 2000, a posthumous collection of stories, letters, photographs, an interview, and a short novel, *Unfinished Message: Selected Works of Toshio Mori*, was released.

◆ MAJOR WORKS AND THEMES

Toshio Mori introduced himself to the reading public with the publication of his first book, *Yokohama, California*, in 1949. Although he wrote two other books, this is the one that most often receives critical attention; this is the one for which he is known and remembered. The book is comprised of several sections that are often described as vignettes instead of short stories. The volume is unified as a whole by its focus on a specific time, place, and people, making it read more like a novel than a collection of unrelated stories.

Mori's tales are set in either his own California hometown or in the Topaz Center, a World War II detention camp. The original manuscript of the book was entirely set in Yokohama, California, but two stories were added to the collection after World War II and before the book was published, one of which is set in a relocation camp. In the introduction to the 1985 edition, Lawson Fusao Inada best captures the reigning tone of the original stories in the collection:

> There is . . . a burnished glow to the book which simply reflects the actual atmosphere of the time, the way the people felt, saw, and lived. Not that the book is gilded with goodness from cover to cover; on the contrary, the people and incidents portrayed are very real, with more aspirations than outright successes. But there are no failures, no real losers and victims. This was, after all, a time of hope and optimism, of established communities, of flourishing culture, of the new generation getting on with America. This was a time of pride and accomplishment. The people quite obviously believed in themselves, in what they could do, were doing, in America. (ix–x)

The book is infused with hope, hope that is often unfulfilled but continues, unchecked. Inada goes on to argue that this "continuing and extending" of tradition is the main theme of the entire work, especially as found in the story "Nodas in America." Inada is describing the general tone of the book, one that is drastically altered by the two post–World War II stories. Critics agree that the two added stories change the tone of what was already a complete work in important ways. The first additional story, "Tomorrow Is Coming, Children," was added at the very beginning of the book. It attempts to orient the reader in Japanese America and is set in one of the camps. The story was first published in *Trek*, the Topaz Camp magazine, in 1943. Because the rest of *Yokohama, California* was written pre–World War II, the inclusion of this new story at the beginning of the book adds a whole new dimension to the collection, not the least being the relocation camp setting. What had once been an uplifting book of stories about Japanese Americans was now forced to reconfigure itself in the aftermath of the war. This new story features a grand-mother recounting her history to her two grandchildren. The grandmother speaks of her pride in being a part of America and seems to be telling the children to "forgive and forget." However, in recounting her history, she is clearly instilling in her grandchildren a sense of their heritage and asking them to remember. The second added story, "Slant-Eyed Americans," deals with a family seeing their son off to war. One reading this story cannot help but remember that this family will soon be relocated to the camps just as Mori's family was. Unlike the sincere, hopeful, and often funny stories of the original collection, both added stories are tainted by the war. The collection as a whole was affected by this inclusion, as well.

Several critics have noted the influence of Sherwood Anderson's *Winesburg, Ohio* on Mori's work, particularly *Yokohama, California*. Mori's title pays tribute to a work that was so important to Mori and his contemporaries, as does the way he centers his work around one specific community and its inhabitants. Mori includes a story called "Akiro Yano" that features an aspiring author who can write in the style of Anderson. Although Mori begins in the tradition of Anderson, locating his stories in a small community, his style and subject are all his own. Gayle Sato notes the main difference between Anderson and Mori is the importance of *amae*, a term describing the feeling of wanting to be "passively loved in order to avoid the necessity of negotiating for the satis-faction of desires" (130). According to Sato, *amae* as a communicative act can be a key to unlock the relationships between the characters in *Yokohama, Cal-ifornia*, whereas Anderson's characters suffer from "a failure to speak to and be heard by other people" (135). The only story in the collection whose nar-rator lacks a listener, titled "Toshio Mori," may at first seem to be the only failure of *amae* between characters in the collection, but Sato points out that in this story, the desire for indulgence is directed at the reader instead of another character (140–41). Sato's reading of *Yokohama, California* is crucial in understanding where Mori's homage to Anderson ends and his own culture and artistry begin. Mori never reaches into Anderson's realm of the "grotesque." His portraits of characters are rendered with humility, sweetness, and, often, humor, and he chooses rather ordinary people for his subjects—ordinary, that is, in the little Asian American community of Yokohama.

This original style and subject are partially responsible for Inada's proclamation, "This is the book—the first real Japanese-American book. . . . This is the book—by the first real Japanese-American writer. . . . This is more than a book. . . . This is the enduring strength, the embodiment of a people" (Introduction v). Mori chronicles a particular set of people in a particular time and place, Japanese Americans in his hometown of California in the late 1930s and early 1940s.

Mori does write about a particular set of people, Japanese Americans. There are rarely any white characters in Mori's books, although his son, Steven, reveals that his father was "far more complex than most people realize. He also wrote stories about other cultures, but they never sold" (Mori, *Unfinished* ix). Inada theorizes, "it is crucial to note that these are not 'minority stories' in the negative sense but 'majority' stories told from the perspective of the full self and self-determining community" ("Of Place" 256). In reading the original stories of *Yokohama, California*, one does not get the impression that the characters are working in opposition to the white community because the white community is absent. These Japanese Americans do not define themselves in relation to whiteness, nor do they depend on the white community for assistance. Yokohama is a self-contained community.

Mori's community is peopled with characters whose essences Mori effortlessly (or so he makes it seem) captures. There is the grandmother in "Tomorrow Is Coming, Children." There is Motoji Tsunoda, a laundryman who fancies himself a philosopher. There is Tom Fukunaga of "Japanese Hamlet," who passes his young adult life studying for a role he will never play despite his Uncle Bill's attempts to dissuade him. There is Hatsuye, who is in love with Clark Gable, who "is hopeful in spite of the fact she is hopeless" (165). There is "The Woman Who Makes Swell Doughnuts," a section that has no plot, character development, or movement of any kind. Inada labels this story a "tribute" or an "anthem" to the woman's way of life. This unusual narrative move is only one of many noteworthy artistic experiments in Mori's works.

One theme that is particularly pervasive in Mori's short stories is intergenerational tension. Stories like "Between You and Me," "Miss Butterfly," "Through Anger and Love," "Strange Bedfellows," and many more explore the rewards and problems encountered between first-, second-, and third-generation Asian Americans who are struggling to balance assimilation to American culture and honoring their families' traditional beliefs and practices with varying success. This theme is pervasive in Mori's only published novel, *Woman from Hiroshima*, as well. The novel is one long lesson in assimilation as a grandmother recounts to her grandchildren her experiences upon arriving in San Francisco from Japan. She tells them of her tentative enjoyment of these new experiences, which is tainted by the racism she encounters.

The particular and even peculiar style of Toshio Mori is difficult to describe, as various critics have discovered. To be sure, one cannot help but notice Mori's pervasive humor. In the new introduction to *Yokohama, California*, Inada writes, "It might be said that this book is in the time-honored shibai tradition of folk drama and humorous skits" (vi). The humorous situations serve to stimulate learning; through showing in a humorous manner how various characters fail to communicate, for instance, Mori teaches the reader how to communicate. Inada continues, "Toshio Mori is an exemplary teacher, and a writer of great compassion. There is not a mean bone in all of *Yokohama, California*. His is the gentle humor of respect, not the cynical laughter of ridicule" (vi). All critics agree that humor is key to Mori's writing, but that there is something else, something inexplicable, that runs deeper than the humor to create sincere and poignant moments for the reader.

One of the most exciting developments in Mori studies is the publication of a short novel, *The Brothers Murata* (*Unfinished* 138–212). Set in Topaz relocation camp, Inada notes, "the representational realism has been distorted to an angular expressionism verging on surrealism. . . . And most striking of all, there are no people depicted in this 'mural,' but thousands upon thousands of five-digit numbers, like '19228' " (*Unfinished* 7). Future scholars will surely find the historical circumstances and artistic departures of the novel enlightening.

♦ CRITICAL RECEPTION

As a Japanese American writer after World War II, Toshio Mori faced insurmountable obstacles; no one wanted to read works written by and about Japanese Americans. Mori's first collection of short stories was accepted for publication in 1941, but it was not published until after the war. As Lawson Fusao Inada notes in the introduction to the 1985 edition, "By its very nature, [*Yokohama, California*] was destined for obscurity; it had to be one of the most unwanted books in history" (xx). One could see the fact that it overcame the obstacle of anti-Japanese sentiment and was ever published at all as testament to its unquestionable literary merit. Even in the aftermath of World War II, the publisher could not deny that Mori had something unique and valuable to offer. *Yokohama, California* was finally printed in 1949 and reprinted in 1985, but it received scant attention until the early 1990s. Only after critics began reclaiming "lost" authors who were once marginalized for one reason or another but now are valued for their unique qualities did Mori begin to receive notable critical attention. In the face of an unmoved and unmoving readership, Mori continued to write.

Mori was never widely reviewed. In fact, contemporary reviewers tended to ignore him completely. Once interest in "lost" authors arose, most critics were concerned with reclaiming Mori and offering him belated membership in the canon of American literature. The majority of critics champion Mori, painting him as a wronged man who deserves attention both for the quality of his writing and as a sort of recompense for allowing him to live and die in obscurity. Strangely, one of the few critics who outwardly criticizes Mori is William Saroyan, Mori's friend and champion. In his introduction to the first edition of *Yokohama, California*, written long before the collection was published, he wrote: "It will be better for [Mori] when [he] learns to be more lucid" (1). Later critics have questioned exactly which aspect of Mori's writing Saroyan is responding to. Some, such as Inada, suggest that Saroyan is merely treating Mori as he, himself, was treated when he appeared on the literary scene (Introduction xxvi).

Not only was Mori ignored by critics, but he was ignored by the very people he wrote for and about, as well. In the new introduction, Inada chides,

> There is a very expensive lesson to be learned here. It might have been funny to some that Toshio Mori, the nurseryman down the street, spent all of his spare time, spent his entire life, actually, trying to be, of all things, a legitimate American writer. He considered himself to be a writer, but his writing career was pathetic, a noncareer; his own people ignored, rejected the art that he produced. . . . No one took him seriously; he died as he lived—in obscurity. . . . His literature is Japanese-American; he was committed to his people, he lived up to his people, he saw his people as the stuff of great art. He took the responsibility of founding and maintaining the tradition of Japanese-American literature. Toshio Mori did not fail; others failed him. (viii)

Inada's response is representative of the general feeling among recent critics. Such stirrings spurred the October 2000 publication of the long-awaited *Unfinished Message: Selected Works of Toshio Mori*. The collection pulls stories from *Yokohama, California* and *The Chauvinist and Other Stories*, and it makes available for the first time a novella called *The Brothers Murata*, set not in Yokohama but in Topaz, the Central Utah Relocation Camp. Lawson Fusao Inada believes it was written around 1944, and in his introduction to *Unfinished Message* he claims that it "may very well be the only such work to be written in an American concentration camp" (*Unfinished* 6).

In the foreword to *Unfinished Message*, son Steven Mori notes that in the early 1970s, "college students began to discover my father's stories. He started speaking at college campuses and struck up lasting friendships with the newer generation of Asian American writers. Despite failing health, he was finally gaining recognition for all of his hard work, after years of neglect. Thanks to all his friends and fans, his final years were among his best" (*Unfinished* x).

Surely it is only a matter of time before his second collection of short stories and his only novel, *Woman from Hiroshima*, are again made available to the public. Based on his previous efforts and his obvious dedication to the art of writing, one can only guess what Mori, given the full support of readers, critics, and publishers, might have accomplished.

◆ BIBLIOGRAPHY

Works by Toshio Mori

Short Story Collections

Yokohama, California. Caldwell, OH: Caxton Printers, 1949, 2nd ed. Seattle: University of Washington Press, 1985.
The Chauvinist and Other Stories. Los Angeles: Asian American Studies Center, University of California at Los Angeles, 1979.
Unfinished Message: Selected Works of Toshio Mori. Berkeley, CA: Heydey Books, 2000.

Novels

Woman from Hiroshima. San Jose, CA: Isthmus Press, 1979.

Studies of Toshio Mori

Bedrosian, Margaret. "Toshio Mori's California Koans." *MELUS* 15.2 (1988): 47–55.
Horikoshi, Peter. "Interview with Toshio Mori." In *Counterpoint: Perspectives on Asian America.* Emma Gee, ed. Los Angeles: Asian American Studies Center, 1976, 472–79.
Inada, Lawson Fusao. "Of Place and Displacement: The Range of Japanese-American Literature." In *Three American Literatures: Essays in Chicano, Native American, and Asian-American Literature for Teachers of American Literature.* Houston A. Baker, ed. New York: Modern Language Association, 1982, 254–65.
———. "Standing on Seventh Street." Introduction. In *Yokohama, California*, by Toshio Mori. Seattle: University of Washington Press, 1985, v–xxvii.
———. "Introduction." In *Unfinished Message: Selected Works of Toshio Mori*, by Toshio Mori. Berkeley, CA: Heydey Books, 2000, 1–10.
Leong, Russell. "Toshio Mori: An Interview." *Amerasia Journal* 7.1 (1980): 89–108.
Mayer, David R. "The Short Stories of Toshio Mori." *Fu Jen Studies: Literature and Linguistics* 21 (1988): 73–87.
———. "Akegarasu and Emerson: Kindred Spirits of Toshio Mori's 'The Seventh Street Philosopher.' " *Amerasia Journal* 16.2 (1990): 1–10.
———. "Toshio Mori: Chronicler of Japanese-American Oakland." In *Door Stoops and Window Sills: Perspectives on the American Neighborhood Novel.* Nagoya: Nanzan University, 1992, 55–77.
———. "Toshio Mori and Loneliness." *Nanzan Review of American Studies* 15 (1993): 20–32.
———. "Toshio Mori's Neighborhood Settings: Inner and Outer Oakland." *Fu Jen Studies: Literature and Linguistics* 23 (1993): 100–115.

———. "The Philosopher in Search of a Voice: Toshio Mori's Japanese-Influenced Narrator." *AALA Journal* 2 (1995): 12–24.

Palomino, Harue. "Japanese Americans in Books or in Reality? Three Writers for Young Adults Who Tell a Different Story." In *How Much Truth Do We Tell Children? The Politics of Children's Literature*. Betty Bacon, ed. Minneapolis, MN: Marxist Educational Press, 1988. 125–34.

Palumbo-Liu, David. "Toshio Mori and the Attachments of Spirit: A Response to David R. Mayer." *Amerasia Journal* 17.3 (1991): 41–47.

———. "The Minority Self as Other: Problematics of Representation in Asian-American Literature." *Cultural Critique* 28 (1994): 75–102.

———. "Universalisms and Minority Culture." *Differences: A Journal of Feminist Cultural Studies* 7.1 (1995): 188–208.

Saroyan, William. "Introduction." *Yokohama, California*, by Toshio Mori. Caldwell, OH: Caxton Printers, 1949, 1–4.

Sato, Gayle K. "(Self) Indulgent Listening: Reading Cultural Difference in *Yokohama, California*." *The Japanese Journal of American Studies* 11 (2000): 129–46.

Yamamoto, Hisaye. "Introduction." In *The Chauvinist and Other Stories*, by Toshio Mori. Los Angeles: UCLA Asian American Studies Center, 1979, 1–14.

BHARATI MUKHERJEE
(1940–   )

Leela Kapai

◆ **BIOGRAPHY**

Bharati Mukherjee was born on July 27, 1940, in Calcutta to Sudhir Lal and Bina Mukherjee. Her childhood was spent in a traditional Brahmin extended family where members of several generations lived together. Her father's business took the family abroad in 1948, giving his children an occasion to be schooled in England and then in Switzerland. On their return to India, Bharati Mukherjee attended the Loretto Convent School in Calcutta where she received a good grounding in English and Western thought. She earned a B.A. in English Honors from Calcutta University in 1959 and an M.A. in English and ancient Indian culture from Baroda University in 1961.

Mukherjee's upbringing had a tremendous influence on her development as a writer. In fact, the lack of privacy in her household during her early childhood turned her into an avid reader, for the books provided an escape for a shy girl. Long before she was ten, she knew she was going to be a writer. Traditional families like the Mukherjees would not have dreamed of sending girls to college, let alone sending them across the seas to a foreign land. However, breaking with tradition, her parents sent their three daughters to the United States for further education. For once, being a female worked to her advantage when she decided to be a writer. A son of the family would have been expected to choose a useful occupation, but since she was not being groomed for a career, she was allowed to enroll in the Iowa Writers' Workshop at the University of Iowa to get an M.F.A. in creative writing. She was expected to return, after getting her degree, to get married. As it turned out, after she received her M.F.A degree, she stayed on to earn a Ph.D. in 1969.

It was in Iowa that Mukherjee met and married Clark Blaise, a fellow Canadian student, in 1963. This event marked an end to any possibility of her returning home for good. In her own words, she became an "accidental immigrant." The family moved to Montreal where Blaise and Mukherjee began their teaching careers. She became a Canadian citizen and rose in the academic ranks to become a professor in 1978 at McGill. Yet she was never at home in the Canadian environment. She felt that the Canadian immigration policy encouraged ethnic ghettos in the guise of encouraging multiculturism and discouraged the non-Europeans from assimilating in the mainstream. After the influx of Asians fleeing from Uganda and later from South Asia, conditions in cities like Toronto grew worse. All people of color, professionals and laborers alike, were subjected to mistreatment and insults. Relinquishing their tenured positions at McGill, she and her husband decided to return to the United States in 1980. After teaching at various universities in the United States, Mukherjee has been a distinguished professor of English at the University of California, Berkeley since 1989.

◆ MAJOR WORKS AND THEMES

Bharati Mukherjee's entire fiction is characterized by variations on the themes of immigration, displacement, and re-creation of identities. The characters, their locale, and quests vary, but in each case she is concerned with what she calls the "making of Americans." *The Tiger's Daughter* (1972), like most first novels, is autobiographical in nature. The protagonist Tara, an Indian student from Calcutta, marries an American and returns home for a visit. Life in Calcutta, beset by labor unrest and political upheavals, is no longer what she remembered. Her experiences lead her to shed the romantic vision of India that had sustained her during her periods of homesickness. Realizing that she no longer fits in the old environment, she longs to return to her adopted land.

In 1973, Mukherjee and her husband spent a year in India. They kept separate journals recording their experiences which were published as *Days and Nights in Calcutta* in 1977. While Clark Blaise was truly an outsider in India, Mukherjee, too, was a stranger in her homeland after years spent abroad. The stay provided a wealth of material for the novelist in Mukherjee as she observed the lives of women with whom she had grown up and who were now busy socialites living in the shadow of their husbands.

In the next novel, *Wife* (1975), the locale shifts from Calcutta to New York. The novel is essentially a biting critique of the upbringing of girls from middle-class traditional Indian families. While waiting for her parents to arrange her marriage, Dimple, the protagonist, immerses herself in idyllic visions of romance gleaned from cheap women's magazines. After she emigrates with her husband to the United States, Dimple finds life in New York nowhere close to her dreams of the land of plenty. The newspapers and television are filled with tales of violence. Despite her knowledge of English, she cannot follow the American accent, and she has no friends. Cooped up in a small apartment, she cannot overcome the culture shock. It is hard for her to reconcile being a submissive wife with the barrage of images offering a life of freedom on the television screen, and in a fit of depression and desperation, she stabs her husband.

Mukherjee's third novel, *Jasmine*, published in 1989, is the story of Jyoti, a young woman from Punjab, who, after her husband's murder at the hand of the separatist Sikh terrorists, resolves to come to Florida where she and her husband were planning to go together. The tortuous journey of being smuggled into the United States transforms Jyoti into Jasmine and later to Jane. The protagonist, an illegal immigrant, is a survivor, who is willing to change with the times in order to find a place for herself in the new world.

The Holder of the World (1993) marks a shift in Mukherjee's fiction from depiction of the immigrants' lives to a tale spanning two continents in the nineteenth century, yet the theme of displacement prevails. The narrator is Beigh Masters whose research leads her to Hannah, a seventeenth-century Puritan woman, who journeyed from New England to the Coromandel Coast in India. In this intricate tale swinging between the twentieth and seventeenth centuries, Hannah's adventures land her eventually in an Indian prince's palace. After the Raja is vanquished by the Moghul emperor's army, Hannah, expecting a child, returns to New England, and the reader learns that she is no other than Hester Prynne of Hawthorne's *The Scarlet Letter*.

Leave It to Me (1997) is the tale of Debbie DiMartino, a young woman adopted as a baby by an Italian-American family, who now yearns to find her biological parents. She steps out of her safe, sheltered environment, gives up a budding career, and christens herself as Devi Dee. She assumes the persona of the goddess of revenge and leaves a trail of violence and destruction in her wake. Mukherjee's latest novel, *Desirable Daughters*, was published in 2002.

Between the writing of *Wife* and *Jasmine*, Mukherjee focused on short stories, which were later published in two collections. *Darkness* (1985) has twelve stories and *The Middleman and Other Stories* (1988) has eleven. *Darkness* has an important place in the new literatures of America for its portrayal of Indian immigrants, a group that had never been written about. In *The Middleman and Other Stories*, Mukherjee says she made "another sort of breakthrough" by speaking in the voices of immigrants from other countries (Vignisson). The stories are about the hardships endured by the immigrants and the ongoing conflict between the desire to adapt to the new country and the reluctance to change. A common theme that runs through these stories is that letting go of old culture is perhaps essential for surviving in the new country and need not arouse a feeling of guilt.

The "Introduction" to *Darkness* provides an account of the writing of these stories. Most of them, Mukherjee tells us, were written in a three-month burst of energy in 1984 when she was a writer in residence at Emory University. Until this period, she had considered herself an expatriate in the tradition of

V.S. Naipaul and had seen the immigrants as "lost souls, put upon and pathetic." She describes her fiction "as stories of broken identities and discarded languages, and the will to bond oneself to a new community, against the ever-present fear of failure and betrayal" (3). Most of the stories are indeed sad, but the writer feels confident of her direction: "It's possible—with sharp ears and the right equipment—to hear America singing even in the seams of the dominant culture." Ready to claim her place in the American tradition of Whitman, she gradually moved away from "the aloofness of expatriation to the exuberance of immigration" (3). Three of the twelve stories in *Darkness*, "The World According to Hsu," "Isolated Incidents," and "Tamurlaine" are about Indian immigrants in Canada. In the first story, we see the turmoil in the mind of Ratna Clayton, on a holiday with her husband Graeme. The vacation on an island off the coast of Africa is planned as Graeme is considering a move to Toronto. While her husband, an Englishman, would find relief in moving away from the separatist Quebec, Ratna dreads the prospect of facing blatant racism in Toronto: "In Montreal she was merely 'English' . . . in Toronto, she was not Canadian, not even Indian. She was something called, after the imported idiom of London, a Paki. And for Pakis, Toronto was hell" (41).

"Isolated Incidents" reveals the attitude of the Canadian government toward the immigrants through the consciousness of Ann, a mid-level employee of the office of Human Rights in Toronto. Ann's job is to deal with complaints from immigrants about discrimination. Her idealism has gradually given way to indifference: "Now she saw problems only as a bureaucrat. Deal with the sure things. Pass the other off. Get documentation. Promise nothing" (81). The contrast between her life and that of an old school friend, now a pop star, makes her disassociate herself further from the immigrants that batter on her door constantly. She rationalizes her attitude toward their complaints of assaults and unfairness by treating them as "isolated incidents." The "human drama" has lost its power to touch her. "Tamurlaine," narrated by an illegal restaurant worker from India, describes another encounter with the Canadian system. The busboy and the waiter, without valid visas, hide behind the sacks of rice and flour when the place is raided periodically. We come to know that the cook walks with a limp because he had lost his legs when some Canadian hoodlums had thrown him in front of a subway train. On one of these frequent raids, the Canadian Mounties, acting on a tip, find the hiding men. Gupta, the chef, who has been present all along in the kitchen, is also taken into custody. When he protests that he cannot leave the premises unattended, the Mounties become obnoxious. Gupta picks up a cleaver, and the narrator describes the next scene: "Gupta managed to sit straight. He held his Canadian passport in front of his face. That way he never saw the drawn gun, nor did he try to dodge the single bullet" (125).

The other stories in *Darkness* take place in the United States and depict the confusion and uncertainty faced by the displaced women, men, and young adults. Nafeesa, "The Lady from Lucknow," is a sophisticated, well-traveled young Pakistani woman married to an IBM employee, now stationed in At-lanta. While the husband works hard to "arrive" in the new world, Nafeesa, a homemaker, distracts herself by having an affair with Jim Beamish, a re-puted doctor at the Centers for Disease Control. Nafeesa is lost in an alien environment where people like her husband, "not quite" there, have to work harder than others "to set the standards." She is still like a traveler who "feels at home everywhere, because she is never at home anywhere." When Mrs. Beamish finds out about them, it is not the discovery of the affair but the wife's attitude toward her that shatters Nafeesa; she realizes she was "just another involvement of a white man in a pokey little outpost, something that 'men do' and then come to their senses while the *memsahibs* drink gin and tonic and fan their faces" (33).

Vinita in "Visitors" also comes from a similar background. She is younger, newly married to a successful Wall Street investment broker. Having just re-cently arrived from India, she is not sure of the rules of the new society. So when a young graduate student she had met at a party arrives unannounced, she does not know what to do. In Calcutta, she would never have allowed a man to enter her house if she was alone; in New Jersey, she is uncertain of the rules. When the young man, seizing the moment of her hesitancy, steps inside and closes the door, she swiftly shifts into the role of a gracious hostess, offering him a cup of tea. His declaration of love for Vinita disturbs her but also awakens her sexuality; she knows her husband is a good man, that he will be a millionaire some day, and that he loves her. But she wonders as she lies awake, "Why then is she moved by an irresistible force to steal out of his bed in the haven of his expensive condominium, and run off into the alien American night where only shame and disaster can await her?" (176).

Other stories deal with men who react to the new environment in different ways. There is Mr. Bhowmick in "A Father" who still feels insecure despite a graduate degree in engineering from Carnegie and a well-paid job in Chicago. While his wife and daughter seem to have adjusted well to life in the new country, Mr. Bhowmick needs the blessing of goddess Kali every morning to pull him through each day. When he discovers accidentally that his unattrac-tive, unmarried engineer daughter is pregnant, he talks himself into accepting the shameful situation. However, the revelation that the baby's father is "a bottle and a syringe" brings out all the latent anger and frustration as he brings down the rolling pin on his daughter's stomach.

In "Nostalgia," it is Dr. Manny Patel, a psychiatrist employed in a state hospital, who loses his cool. The sight of an attractive young girl in an Indian store brings back nostalgic memories of his years in India. He arranges a date with her and later takes her to a seedy hotel, only to find out that he had been set up for blackmail. The story ends with the cornered Manny Patel losing his self-control and acting like a demented man but then ready to resume his dreary life once again.

"Angela," "Saints," and "The Imaginary Assassin" depict young lives in turmoil. "Angela" is narrated by a young girl from Dhaka, who was adopted by the Brandons two years ago. As Delia Brandon lies in a coma following an automobile accident, Angela wonders why she has survived, whereas her sister by adoption, responsible for rescuing her from the orphanage, probably will not. The Brandon family is kind to Angela, but she is still imprisoned in her "bony, scarred body and plain face." She is being wooed by Dr. Menezies, an unmarried immigrant nearing forty, who also comes from "the same subcontinent of hunger and misery." Dr. Menezies hides behind his stethoscope and leaves the "frolicking to natives" but Angela and Kim, the other adopted child of the Brandon family, are forced to assimilate. Surrounded as she is by love and attention, marveling constantly about her luck, she is still haunted by the phantoms of her childhood.

Dr. Manny Patel's son, Shawn, is the narrator of "Saints." It comes as no surprise that the teenaged bicultural son of dysfunctional, now divorced parents, is a lost soul. In his secret life, he and his friend Tran, a boat person, make pornographic calls to strangers. Often he wanders alone at night, like the saint in a book sent by his father with whom he has no emotional bond. "The Imaginary Assassin" has another maladjusted young man who feels cheated because he has nothing while "the Californian boys had their rock stars and their movie stars and their cute sexy girlfriends who went all the way" (190).

The Middleman and Other Stories, published in 1988, won the prestigious National Book Critics Circle Award for Fiction. These stories are no longer limited to just Indian immigrants; Mukherjee includes characters from other backgrounds that range from a "middleman" in the jungles of Latin America to a Vietnam veteran, angry to see his hometown now taken over by strangers from other lands. The characters in these stories are outsiders, either newcomers from another continent or those pushed to the peripheries of their society. Among this rich array of characters are Indians, a Vietnamese, a Filipino, Americans, and even Europeans. Though violence permeates many of these stories, there is a glimpse of optimism as well.

The women protagonists in these stories are capable of adjusting to the changed environment. The wife in the "Wife's Story" is Panna Bhatt, a woman away from her husband in India, doing graduate studies in New York. Her stay is gradually changing her: the truth dawns on her when the husband comes to visit her. During this period, Panna takes charge as her husband feels ill at ease in the new environment, a role that she could never have assumed in India. As he is preparing to return, Panna realizes that she has come too far in her journey of discovering herself as an individual to ever recede into the role of a traditional wife.

"The Tenant" looks at another woman, Maya Sanyal, a professor who has just accepted a university faculty position in Iowa. No newcomer to the country, she has earned her degrees in the United States and has taught at other institutions. She is lonely but hesitates to connect with the local Indian community because as a divorcee, she knows she will be an easy target for men. Her fears are justified as Dr. Chatterji, a physics professor, makes a pass at her when he is taking her back home after her visit to meet his family. Unable to connect with her feminist colleagues and equally a misfit in the Indian circle, she settles in a relationship with her landlord, a man without arms, who describes them as "two wounded people." His joke shocks her: "This assumed equivalence with a man so strikingly deficient. She knows she is strange, and lonely, but being Indian is not the same . . . as being a freak" (112). It is obvious at the end that she will leave Iowa to start afresh.

"Jasmine" is named for the protagonist of the story, who also enters the country illegally. Like many others, she too has left her comfortable life in Trinidad in search of better prospects. When she finds employment as a nanny, Jasmine is enthralled by the infinite possibilities that lie ahead. As she assumes more and more responsibility at home while the wife, a performance artist, goes on tours, she is drawn closer to the husband. If she is being exploited by her employers, she too seems ready to exploit the coming split in the family.

In "Orbiting," Mukherjee captures the baffling meeting of the old and the new world. The narrator, Renata deMarcos, chooses the family's Thanksgiving gathering to introduce her Afghan lover to her American family. It is an interesting mix: her parents came from Italy, her sister has married a mainstream American, and her lover is from a world that her family knows nothing about. Ro, the Afghan who talks of revolutions, of the Soviets in Afghanistan, of torture of dissidents, of his own escape, baffles them. The father does not know how to deal with a man who does not share their passion for sports and someone who won't drink. Brent, Renata's brother-in-law, has never been exposed to people like Ro: "He thought only Americans had informed political opinions—other people staged coups out of spite and misery. It's an unwelcome revelation to him that a reasonably educated and rational man like Ro would die for things that he, Brent, has never heard of and would rather laugh about" (72–73). Seeing her lover amidst this group of Americans, Renata realizes the depth of her love for him, "her chance to heal the world."

The gallery of characters in other stories includes Blanquita, a young woman from the Philippines, seen through the eyes of her lover Griff, a young executive in "Fighting for the Rebound." He is unwilling to make any commitment to her; for him Blanquita is "a Third World aristocrat, a hothouse orchid you worship but don't dare touch" (83). He finds the exotic appealing, but "real foreign is a little scary" for him. Marshall in "Loose Ends" and Jason in "Fathering"—both Vietnam veterans, are displaced persons, threatened by the immigrants. Jeb Marshall is a professional hit man, who finds Florida no longer the place he remembers. He resents the strange people from nowhere who seem to have taken over the state and seem to ignore him. When he encounters a young Indian girl working in the family-run motel, he feels insulted by her look of disgust, of distaste for people like him. He pounces on the girl "and take[s] America with her" (54). Jason is trying to atone for his irresponsible Vietnam years by bringing his love child into the country long after the damage to her is irreversible.

Perhaps the most moving story in *The Middleman* is "The Management of Grief." It is based on the research that Mukherjee and her husband did for their book *The Sorrow and the Terror* about the Air India tragedy. The plane, carrying over three hundred Indian-Canadians, exploded near the coast of Ireland leaving no survivors. Shaila is one of the many left to mourn the loss of her entire family in this act of terrorism. Because of her stoic attitude, Judith, the social worker, seeks her help in communicating with an old illiterate Sikh couple whose sons were also in the doomed plane. Shaila accompanies Judith and in the course of the meeting realizes the futility of her efforts. She does not know how to bridge the difference between the Canadian and the couple's way of thinking. The old couple would not sign any papers to receive help, for doing so would mean admitting their sons were dead, and keeping hope alive, they feel, is their duty—an attitude beyond Judith's grasp. Shaila pulls herself out of her state of numbness and resolves to move on with her life.

These stories, with a rich canvass of characters from different parts of the world, illustrate Mukherjee's mission to show readers an America they may have never seen and make them realize how post-Vietnam America has been changed by the interaction with the new immigrants.

◆ CRITICAL RECEPTION

Mukherjee's short stories have drawn widespread acclaim. Since *Darkness* was published in Canada and not widely distributed, it received few, but all favorable, reviews. Peter Nazareth, writing in *Canadian Literature*, admires the literary style of the writer. Anita Desai in writing for *London Magazine* sees Mukherjee's portrayal of "the outcasts" honest and appealing. Mahnaz Ispahani calls her "Henry Roth with a subcontinental twist." He refers to several stories and shows how Mukherjee "skillfully mixes history with fantasy, real violence with felt violence, the seeming straightforwardness of American life with the continuing tussle with themselves that inevitably characterizes such divided people" (36).

The Middleman has received a wider range of reviews and has drawn even more attention after it won the American Critics Circle Award. Jonathan Raban, in the *New York Times Book Review*, gives a glowing tribute to Mukherjee's depiction of the new arrivals, "their guiltlessness, bounce, sexual freedom, their easy money and the lightness of their footsteps on the American landscape" (22). He refers to Mukherjee's acknowledgment of her debt to Bernard Malamud and concludes that she has hijacked the "whole tradition of Jewish-American writing and flies it off to a destination undreamed of by its original practitioners" (23).

Elizabeth Ward, in her review in the *Washington Post Book World*, admires

Mukherjee's grasp of the language and culture of America. She singles out "Orbiting," "Loose Ends," and "The Management of Grief" to illustrate the writer's skill in depicting the lives of her characters. She admires Mukherjee's ability to capture American culture in a few terse phrases and concludes that "first and foremost a very fine fiction writer, funny, intelligent, versatile, and on occasion, unexpectedly profound," Mukherjee is "herself the most valuable kind of Middleman, bridging disparate worlds" (9). Uma Parameswaran is, however, critical of *The Middleman* in her review and introduces a strain that many postcolonial critics level against Mukherjee in later years. Even as she admires "the curious mix of voices and experiences," she notes, "these characters may be full-blooded Americans racing with both hands grabbing all that life has to offer, but what they grasp is rather obnoxious all the way" (363).

By the early 1990s, Mukherjee's works had established her reputation as a writer of fiction as well as non-fiction. A spate of books, dissertations, articles, and interviews followed. The numerous interviews she has granted over the years are a valuable source of information about the intent and philosophy underlying her creative work. Though the focus has mainly been on the novels, her short stories have merited considerable attention. Arvindra Sant-Wade and Karen Marguerite Radell discuss several stories focusing on the women, who are "reborn" as they fashion a new identity for themselves. They point out that Mukherjee weaves "contradiction into the very fabric of the stories: positive assertions in interior monologues are undermined by negative visual images; the liberation of change is undermined by confusion and loss of identity; beauty is undermined by sadness."

C. Sengupta's discussion revolves around four of Mukherjee's stories that deal with the effect of cultural encounters: "A Wife's Story," "Danny's Girls," "Buried Lives," and "The Tenant." These stories show that a foreign culture is "a catalyst, not an impediment in a person's coming to terms with oneself" and that alienation is a part of the make-up of these characters (148). Deborah Bowen applies the observation of Salman Rushdie that postcolonial people are "translated" in the process of dislocation to "The Management of Grief." She provides the context of the story and then focuses on Shaila's transformation after the Air India tragedy in which she loses her husband and two sons. Bowen offers an insight into the "gaps in cultural constructions" (53) and the negotiations to traverse them. In short, the story suggests that "embracing of hybridity can actually be empowered by the experience of grief, because grief first exposes an inner world irrevocably divided and estranged by loss, . . . and then acts as a form of energy to enable the dislocated mourner in the task of management, reconstruction, and translation into acceptance" (5).

Critics may occasionally find fault with her portrayal of some of her characters or with her preoccupation with violence, but Mukherjee's ability to give voice to a wide range of individuals outside the mainstream remains uncontested and establishes her as a pioneer charting unknown territories.

◆ BIBLIOGRAPHY

Works by Bharati Mukherjee

Short Story Collections

Darkness. New York: Penguin, 1985.
The Middleman and Other Stories. New York: Fawcett Crest, 1988.

Novels

The Tiger's Daughter. Boston: Houghton Mifflin, 1972.
Wife. Boston: Houghton Mifflin, 1975.
Jasmine. New York: Grove Weidenfeld, 1989.
The Holder of the World. Toronto: HarperCollins, 1993.
Leave It to Me. New York: Knopf, 1997.
Desirable Daughters. New York: Hyperion, 2002.

Non-fiction

Days and Nights in Calcutta. Coauthored with Clark Blaise. New York: Doubleday, 1977.
The Sorrow and the Terror: The Haunting Legacy of the Air India Tragedy. Coauthored with Clark Blaise. Markham, ON: Viking, 1987.
Political Culture and Leadership in India: A Study of West Bengal. New Delhi: Mittal Publications, 1991.
Regionalism in Indian Perspective. Calcutta: K.P. Bagchi, 1992.

Selected Essays

"An Invisible Woman." *Saturday Night* (Ontario) 96 (March 1981): 36–40.
"Immigrant Writing: Give Us Your Maximalists!" *New York Times Book Review* (August 28, 1988): 29.
"A Four-Hundred-Year-Old Woman." In *The Writer on Her Work*, vol. 2. Janet Sternburg, ed. New York: Norton, 1991, 33–38.
"American Dreamer." *Mother Jones*, (January–February 1997). http://www.mother jones.com/mother_jones/JF97/mukherjee.html.

Studies of Bharati Mukherjee

Alam, Fakrul. *Bharati Mukherjee*. New York: Twayne Publishers, 1996.
Bannerji, Ranee Kaur. "Singing in the Seams: Bharati Mukherjee's Immigrants." In *No Small World: Visions and Revisions of World Literature*. Michael Thomas, ed. Urbana, IL: NCTE, 1996, 189–201.
Bowen, Deborah. "Spaces of Translation: Bharati Mukherjee's 'The Management of Grief.'" *ARIEL: A Review of International English Literature* 28.3 (July 1997): 47–60.

Bradbury, Patricia. "Mukherjee Draws Tales from Fear in the Streets of Toronto." *Quill And Quire* 51.8 (August 1985): 43.

Carchidi, Victoria. " 'Orbiting': Bharati Mukherjee's Kaleidoscopic Vision." *MELUS* 20.4 (Winter 1995): 91–101.

Chen, Tina, and S. X. Goudie. "Holders of the Word: An Interview with Bharati Mukherjee." *Jouvert: A Journal of Postcolonial Studies.* (1997). http://social.class. ncsu.edu/jouvert/vlil/bharati.html.

Connell, Michael, Jessie Grierson, and Tom Grimes. "An Interview with Bharati Mukherjee." *Iowa Review* 20.3 (1990): 7–30.

Desai, Anita. "Outcasts." *London Magazine* 25.9–10 (December 1985–January 1986): 143–46.

Desai, Shefali, and Tony Barnstone. "A Usable Past: An Interview with Bharati Mukherjee." *Manoa* 10.2 (1998): 130–47.

Doerkson, Teri Ann. "Bharati Mukherjee." In *Dictionary of Literary Biography*, vol. 218. *American Short Story Writers Since World War II Second Series*. New York: The Gale Group, 1999, 228–34.

Fruchter, Barry. "Bharati Mukherjee." *Asian American Autobiographers: A Bio-Bibliographical Critical Sourcebook.* Guiyou Huang, ed. Westport, CT: Greenwood Press, 2001, 257–72.

Ispahani, Mahnaz. Rev. of *Darkness. The New Republic* (April 14, 1986): 36. http:// web2.infotrac.gale.../purl=rc1.

Knippling, Alpana Sharma. "Towards an Investigation of the Subaltern in Bharati Mukherjee's *The Middleman and Other Stories* and *Jasmine.*" In *Bharati Mukherjee: Critical Perspectives.* Emmanuel S. Nelson, ed. New York: Garland, 1993, 143–59.

Low, Gail Ching-Liang. "In a Free State: Post Colonialism and Postmodernism in Bharati Mukhejee's Fiction." *Women: A Cultural Review* 4.1 (Spring 1993): 8–17.

Nazareth, Peter. "Total Vision." *Canadian Literature* 110 (Fall 1986): 184–91.

Parameswaran, Uma. Rev. of *The Middleman and Other Stories. World Literature Today* 64.2 (Spring 1990): 363.

Pati, Mitali R. "Love and the Indian Immigrant in Bharati Mukherjee's Short Fiction." In *Bharati Mukherjee: Critical Perspectives.* Emmanuel S. Nelson, ed. New York: Garland, 1993, 197–211.

Raban, Jonathan. Rev. of *The Middleman and Other Stories. New York Times Book Review* (June 19, 1988): 1, 22–23.

Sant-Wade, Arvindra, and Karen Marguerite Radell. "Refashioning the Self: Immigrant Women in Bharati Mukherjee's New World." *Studies in Short Fiction* 29.1 (Winter 1992): 11–17. Literature Resource Center. Prince George's Community College Library Online Databases. http://www.galenet.com/servl.

Sengupta, C. "Asian Protagonist in Bharati Mukherjee's *The Middleman and Other Stories.*" *Language Forum* 18 (January–December 1992): 148–56.

Vignisson, Runar. "Interview with Bharati Mukherjee." *SPAN: Journal of the South Pacific Association for Commonwealth Literature and Language Studies* 34–35 (1992–1993). http://www.eng.fju.edu.tw/worldlit/india/mukherjee_interview.html.

Ward, Elizabeth. "Notes from a New America." *Washington Post Book World* (July 3, 1988: 3, 9.

FAE MYENNE NG
(1956–   )

Su-ching Huang

◆ **BIOGRAPHY**

Fae Myenne Ng's parents immigrated to the United States from Guangzhou, China. Ng's father worked as a merchant seaman and as a cook at a University of California, Berkeley, fraternity house, and her mother was a seamstress. Their jobs supported Ng and her brother. Ng grew up in San Francisco's Chinatown, and as a child she went to Chinese school every day after her regular school day. She spoke Cantonese at home and helped her mother with the sewing. She received her B.A. in English from the University of California at Berkeley and her M.F.A. from Columbia University. Since 1989, she has lived in Brooklyn, New York, where she worked as a waitress and in other temporary jobs to support herself while working on her first novel, *Bone*. It took her ten years and many drafts to complete that novel. She is currently working on a second novel, tentatively titled *The Cat King*, the Cantonese/Chinese name for Elvis Presley.

Ng received many awards and writing grants for *Bone*, including the Pushcart Prize, a National Endowment for the Arts Award, a Fellowship in Literature from the American Academy of Arts and Letters, and so forth. In 1996, Ng was named by *Granta*, the London-based literary magazine, as one of the top twenty "Best of Young American Novelists of 1996." *Bone* was translated into Spanish (*Un padre de papel*) and published in Barcelona in 1995. Ng's short story "A Red Sweater," has been included in several anthologies, including *Charlie Chan Is Dead: An Anthology of Contemporary Asian American Fiction*, *Forever Sisters: Famous Writers Celebrate the Power of Sisterhood with Short Stories, Essays, and Memoirs*, and *The Bedford Introduction to Literature: Reading, Thinking, Writing*.

◆ MAJOR WORKS AND THEMES

Ng's stories published so far are all set in Chinatown. Growing up in San Francisco's Chinatown, she is acutely aware of the detrimental effects of U.S. legislation against Chinese immigration; up to the 1940s Chinese communities in North America had been "bachelor societies," as male immigrants could not save enough money for a glorious homecoming or send for their wives from China due to immigration restrictions. In an interview Ng remembers fondly the "grandfathers" in Chinatown—the old-timers, who were "very wonderful, very generous and giving because they knew they would die and they wanted to give life somehow" (Schoof 01C). She honors their memories by writing about their delights and tribulations, not only paying tribute to their perseverance but also exposing structural inequalities in U.S. society.

Drawing on her own experience, Ng has set all her stories in a San Francisco Chinatown family where the husband works as a merchant seaman and the wife as a seamstress. The recurrent theme is the passing of old-timers' way of life and the new generation's negotiation between old-world and mainstream American values. Read together, Ng's short stories and her novel *Bone* form one work about the hardships and endurance of immigrant parents and the physical and psychological impacts on their children. Like Faulkner, she has constructed a region-specific community, which has its own particular socio-historical context but could also serve as a microcosmic representation of America's race/class/gender structure in general.

The story "The First Dead Man" presents a slice of Chinatown life from the perspective of a schoolgirl, Mai-bo. Mai-bo's parents own a Chinatown grocery store, which the mother tends and where she also manages to do piece-work sewing for a sweatshop; her father is a merchant seaman. Mai-bo attends Chinese School daily after the American school. She runs on a tight schedule after school: tending the grocery store, helping her mother sew garments, and delivering the sewing consignments back and forth between home and the sweatshop. Her only diversion is window shopping at a local department store, browsing the Hong Kong starlet magazines, examining the fabrics and sewing patterns, and dreaming of making a fashionable dress of her own. Her daily routines are concentrated in Chinatown. Always running from one errand to another, she treasures a forty-minute break between Chinese school and the grocery store. In the beginning of the story, Mai-bo savors the rare time off: "Forty minutes was a long time, and all of the next 40 minutes were hers. Mai-bo smacked her tongue. She could almost taste it. Forty minutes! She felt rich" (10). A daughter of immigrant laborer parents, she can hardly afford any commodity but time, which seems free to her but on closer analysis turns out to be just the opposite—she is child labor. Her time—and her parents' too—is actually an important commodity exploited in the capitalist system. Whatever meager wages her parents receive for their manual labor, they at least get paid, but Mai-bo's time spent laboring, though also supporting the capitalist system, does not generate any monetary profit of her own. During the forty-minute stroll, Mai-bo chances upon a dead man who has jumped from the San Fran Hotel, a residential hotel for the urban poor. Having already heard enough stories about death from her mother, Mai-bo quickly walks away. Although the scene of the dead man is brief, the macabre image haunts the whole story. In a way, the dead man is emblematic of the unrewarding life of Chinatown laborers.

The story "Last Night" is about a Chinatown couple who rent their apartment from an old Italian landlady and her mute son. As in Ng's other stories, the husband is a retired merchant seaman and the wife a seamstress. He hangs around the Portsmouth Square every afternoon "playing chess and telling stories about himself as a young man" (24). Their children have grown up and moved away, while they themselves are content with living in Chinatown, virtually their whole world, as their knowledge of English is limited and they like the convenience of having the Chinese grocery and the sewing shop nearby. Their life is uneventful until one night when the landlady has an accident while her son is away working at a restaurant. The husband, despite his old age, climbs into the landlady's apartment by the fire escape, runs several blocks to fetch her son, and calls up the paramedics in his Pidgin English. The following day things return to normal. They tell their story from the night before, the husband with his usual fanfare at the Square, the wife to other seamstresses too busy sewing at the sweatshop to pay attention. Such is the life of an old Chinatown couple.

The stories "Backdaire," "Farewell," and "A Red Sweater," all excerpts from Ng's novel *Bone*, have appeared as independent pieces. Set in San Francisco's Chinatown, *Bone* captures the poignancies, vulnerabilities and occasional cheeriness of a Chinese immigrant family in its day-to-day life. The Leong family, already perceived by the Chinatown community as cursed with three daughters and no son, grieves over the death of the second daughter, Ona, who jumps from the thirteenth floor of a Chinatown housing project. As the narrator, the eldest sister Leila, tells the familial story in a reverse chronological order, the reader reads about the family's struggles—Mah and Leon's ceaseless laboring to assure the daughters a better life—and realizes that the Leongs have already been inflicted with a variety of problems before Ona's suicide. Her death remains an unsolved mystery that takes the reader back to the heart of the novel: the toils, adjustments, and survival of the Leong family.

"Backdaire," first printed in *Harper's* in 1989, makes up the last chapter of *Bone*. It tells the story of Mah's first marriage to Leila's father Lyman Foo, a "flower picker" (66), her second to Leon, the merchant seaman for his green card, Leon's fatherly affection for Leila, Leila's realization that Mah actually does love Leon, and Leila's moving out of Chinatown with her boyfriend Mason, a foreign-car mechanic. The story begins with Mah's busy preparation for Leon's return from the sea. Because Leila has asked Leon to look for her father in Melbourne, she is especially excited. However, Lyman Foo does not have any affectionate message for Leon to bring back. Leila realizes that Leon is the one who is always there for her. As she is moving away from Salmon Alley to the Mission with Mason, Leila looks back at the address "#2-4-6 Back-daire" and reassures herself, "[T]he ghosts of the old-timers hang over us, wanting us to look back, to remember" (68). By maintaining Leila's ties to her parents, the story hints at the ambivalent concept of filial obligation as well as presents Ng's homage to the memories of the old-timers.

In an interview with Renee Schoof, Ng mentions a childhood experience that inspired her to become a writer: frightened after an old-timer's funeral, she got comfort from the thought of writing about him as "a way to remember him" (01C). "Farewell" is a story revolving around such an old-timer's funeral. Grandpa Leong is the old-timer from whom Leon bought his identity as a paper son. Without any progeny but his "paper descendants," Grandpa Leong is given a hastily prepared funeral. Chinatown life is hard, at least for an old-timer like him. The funeral house "is as makeshift as his coffin" (210). At the funeral other old-timers come to pay their respects and have to leave immediately to go back to work. Having worked at gold mines and farms, Grandpa Leong ends up in a crowded cemetery, where the Leongs come to visit during the Ghost Festival. Leon tries to take pictures with a new camera he has bought in Japan. However, the children are impatient in the hot sun, and when the pictures come back, only one comes out: Ona standing alone in front of the grave. It is an ill omen; as readers familiar with the story of *Bone* know, she later commits suicide and aggravates the Leongs' misfortune.

"A Red Sweater" features a prominent symbol, the red sweater, which is written out in its counterpart in *Bone*. While *Bone*'s narrator is the eldest sister Leila, "A Red Sweater" is told from the youngest sister's perspective, and the eldest sister is named Lisa instead. Nevertheless, the import of the narrative remains as rich and poignant. "A Red Sweater" centers on the annual dinner meeting of the two sisters. The family has three sisters: the eldest has a decent job and lives with the parents; the middle one jumped off a tall building three years ago; the third, scorned by her parents for her rebellious behavior, including pregnancy and abortion out of wedlock, moved away to Honolulu as a flight attendant. The parents are Chinese immigrants; Mah works as a seamstress at a sweatshop, and Deh toils from one job to another—laundry, merchant cruise, take-out place, and Alaskan canneries. The parents work hard and live frugally so that their "marriage of toil" may insure a better life for the next generation. Although Lisa and the narrator appear financially more secure than their parents, the hard life has taken a toll on the emotional well-being of the family. In addition to quarreling between themselves, the parents impose strict expectations on the daughters, and hence the generational conflict. Geographically apart, the narrator feels an emotional void, and her annual dinner with Lisa serves to compensate her need for familial connection. This year they choose an American restaurant for its atmosphere. At dinner, the sisters reminisce about their past. Chinese food prevails in their recollection: drinking Johnny Walker with Deh at banquets, Johnny Walker in shark's fin soup, squab dinners while watching "I Love Lucy," and won-tons. They remember how they used to buy and feed pigeons, calling them "our baby dove birds," until the mother without warning cooked them as a "special, nutritious treat" (51). In addition to fond memories, they inevitably talk about squabbles between Mah and Deh, their harsh words and violent threats. Feeling that Lisa is burdened with filial obligations, the narrator wants to give her a red sweater, a gift that presumably would highlight her beauty and help her find a rich man to marry so that she may be relieved from duties to her parents.

◆ CRITICAL RECEPTION

Ng is noted for her laconic style, which seems simple but resonates with suggestion. One critic, for instance, uses "sparse words, rich images" to describe her novel *Bone* (Suh 75). Noting the combined quality of simplicity and richness in Chinese poetry, Ng herself admits that she "worked very hard at creating a very simple and honest and bare language . . . to reflect the frugality of [her characters'] lives"; the immigrants in her stories are hard-working laborers "who have very little but don't waste anything" (Stetson 3).

Ng's novel *Bone* has received numerous positive reviews and much scholarly attention. Because of the short stories' affinity to *Bone*, criticisms of *Bone* aptly apply to Ng's stories. Kem Knapp Sawyer praises *Bone* as "a brilliant attempt to define family" and notes its "homage to the power of memory" (05F). Reviewers recognize *Bone* as "an immigrant's story, without a rags-to-riches ending" (Suh 75). Wendy Ho reads *Bone* as a narrative that resists the model minority discourse (210–11). Unlike model minority marriages, Ho points out, Leon and Mah's is a "marriage of toil [which] reflects the *lack* of social-economic and political options for subordinated racial-ethnic families in U.S. society" (224).

Lisa Lowe's emphasis on the gendering of labor, the racialization of sexuality, and the class association of race serves a vital approach to *Bone* and Ng's short stories. It helps explain the unremitting but unrewarding manual labor of Ng's immigrant parents. Lowe regards the spatialization of Chinatown as emblematic of Asian American social life over the past century. She observes how the seamstresses, unable to afford the clothing they themselves sew, are immobilized geographically, culturally, linguistically, and economically. The encroachment of the workplace on the private space of home (they take the sewing work home after hours) further exposes the prioritization of "the relations of production over Chinese family relations," and hence the "racialized exploitation of Chinese workers by the dominant society" (119). Lowe looks at *Bone*'s Chinatown community as a "richly sedimented, dialectical space," where "several incompatible spaces or temporalities" coexist (121). For example, the Hoy Sun Ning Yung Benevolent Association represents a space where various seemingly incompatible activities coalesce: leisure and work, family and business. In "Farewell," the narrator (Leila) observes how the space of the funeral parlor has served different purposes through the years: grocery warehouse, bookstore, martial arts club, and the Chinese Educational Services. Drawing on Foucault's notion of heterotopia, Lowe locates in Chinatown a potential "to expose the untenability of the hierarchized divisions of space into domains of public and private, leisure and work, or legitimacy and illegitimacy" (121).

Donald C. Goellnicht's discussion of the suicide motif in *Bone* may shed light on Ng's short stories, where suicide is also a haunting image. Goellnicht regards Leon's immigration as a paper son to the United States as a symbolic suicide, from which he never recovers (305). Despite his "Going-back-to-China fund," Leon can never return due to his economic failure in the United States. After so many rejections and disappointments in business ventures, Leon finally realizes the deception of the American dream. Goellnicht reads Ona's suicide as signifying both the parents' "failure to win 'America' and of their failure to hold onto 'China' in 'America,' the symbol of the broken body of the traditional family" (320). Asian American suicide, Goellnicht suggests, becomes "a trope of the failure to negotiate hybrid subjectivities" (322).

So far all of Ng's critics have focused on the novel *Bone* except Sau-ling Cynthia Wong. In her book chapter on alimentary imagery in Asian American literature, Wong uses Ng's story "A Red Sweater," among other Asian American texts, to explore the motif of quasi-cannibalism and its sociohistorical context. Drawing on the history of Asian immigration and assimilation, Wong reads alimentary images in Asian American literature as symbolic of "Necessity—all the hardships, deprivations, restrictions, disenfranchisements, and dislocations that Asian Americans have collectively suffered as immigrants and minorities in a white-dominated country" (20). She observes generational differences between immigrant parents and their children in eating; Asian American immigrants are often omnivorous eaters who manage to extract nutrients from food sources considered implausible by their children, who tend to be fastidious eaters and "treat lovers." The parents' dietary habits are dictated by Necessity; their ability to turn unlikely sources into nourishment serves as a survival strategy; their inclusive eating reflects their capacity to endure and tolerate hardships. On the contrary, their children, enjoying somewhat better economic standing, often owing to the parents' hard work and economical lifestyle, prefer restaurant and store-bought food to homemade cooking; their liking for candies and snacks reflects their aspiration for Extravagance and assimilation to mainstream American culture.

Acting on the principle of Necessity, the mother in "A Red Sweater" sees the pigeons as a food source, while the daughters consider them pets, which in the Necessity mentality not only fail to make tangible contributions but also consume allegedly limited resources. The immigrant generation toils and conserves to give their children a more affluent life, as does the mother who gives the daughters the meaty parts while she herself nibbles the head, backs, and necks of the pigeons, claiming, "Bones are sweeter than you know" (52). Admitting that the mother's consumption of less-meaty parts, while required by Necessity, could also indicate her gourmet taste (39–40), Wong detects entrapment for the daughters in such "parental self-sacrifice," which "generates expectations of filial self-sacrifice" (32). All three daughters have invariably been sent on guilt trips. Wong points out various images of "quasi-cannibalistic sacrifice" in the story. The parents are like "emotional monsters" with their "murderous" bickering with each other and relentless demands on the daughters. Caught between "love and violence" in the family, the daughters are like "a food source, valued only for what they can give, to be slaughtered, cashed in on, when the time for repaying previous feeding comes" (Wong 32–33). Highlighting the narrator's description of the red sweater ("swollen with good cheer" and "a fierce rouge on [Lisa's] naked breasts"), Wong points to the invocation of images of "physical battery and pathology in *swollen*," the association of the color red with blood—menstrual, virginal, and sacrificial, and the comparison of Lisa's naked breasts to those "bared for slaughter" (34, emphasis in original). As the daughter most tied up with the parents, Lisa is thus seen as a sacrificial offering, devoured by parental neediness.

Although the conflicts in "A Red Sweater" are unraveled in the familial setting, they should be put in the larger sociohistorical context. After all, the frustrations within the family have much to do with "the parents' disadvantaged positions in a race- and gender-linked labor market" (Wong 42). Food consumption in "A Red Sweater" is not only ethnicized but also class coded. Dining with her sister at an American (read Western, non-Chinese) restaurant, the narrator compares Chinese and Western cooking in both cultural and socioeconomic terms. "Chinatown places," despite the good food, remind her of hard living and "bare issues," whereas American restaurants have "nice light and a view and handsome waiters" (49). Admitting that she does not particularly care for Western flavors, the narrator wonders if they should have chosen a Chinese restaurant after all, since what they crave are Chinese dishes like "[d]uck liver sausage, bean curd, jook, salted fish, and fried dace with black beans" (52). While Chinese restaurants offer flavors they "grew up with, [and] still dream about," they have opted for an American restaurant for its surroundings: "Three pronged forks. Pink tablecloths. Fresh flowers. Cute waiters" (52). In this way, the sisters' avoidance of Chinese restaurants masks their wish to detach themselves from Necessity and hard labor—associated with the immigrant generation—while the attraction of American restaurants is precisely their extravagant associations, pointing toward socioeconomic upward mobility.

The image of the red sweater at the end conjures up the ambivalent blessing/curse of parental supervision, which offers at the same time sanctuary and incarceration. Drawing attention to Ng's language in the final paragraphs,

Wong notes, "The pounding rhythm of mono- and disyllabic words hints at inexorability, at bargains clinched and fates sealed" (34). Successfully combining the poetic elements with its sociohistorical context, Wong's reading of "A Red Sweater" provides a productive model for reading other Asian American texts.

◆ BIBLIOGRAPHY

Works by Fae Myenne Ng

Short Stories and Articles

"The First Dead Man." *San Francisco Chronicle* (March 9, 1986): Sunday ed., 10+.
"A Red Sweater." *The American Voice* 4 (1986): 48–56. Rpt. in *Charlie Chan Is Dead: An Anthology of Contemporary Asian American Fiction*. With Intro. by Jessica Hagedorn, ed. New York: Penguin, 1993, 358–68. Rpt. in *Forever Sisters: Famous Writers Celebrate the Power of Sisterhood with Short Stories, Essays, and Memoirs*. Claudia O'Keefe, ed. New York: Pocket Books, 1999, 147–59, and *The Bedford Introduction to Literature: Reading, Thinking, Writing*, 5th ed. Michael Meyer, ed. Boston: Bedford, 1999, 234–42.
"Last Night." *City Lights Review* 1 (1987): 24–29.
"Backdaire." *Harper's* 278.1667 (April 1989): 64–68.
"False Gold: My Father's American Journey." *The New Republic* (July 19 and 26, 1993): 12–13.
"CHINANOW." *Travel & Leisure* 23.9 (September 1993): 62–75, 113+.
"Farewell." *Granta* 54 (Summer 1996): 209–13.
"My Dragon-Dancing Years." *Gourmet* 60.2 (February 2000): 108, 110, 125.

Novel

Bone. New York: Hyperion, 1993.

Studies of Fae Myenne Ng

Brostrom, Jennifer. Interview. *Contemporary Literary Criticism* 81 (1993): 87–88.
Chuang, Jay. "Bone in *Bone*." *Hitting Critical Mass: A Journal of Asian American Cultural Criticism* 2.1 (1994): 53–57. http://socrates.berkeley.edu/~critmass/v2n1/chuangprint.html. Accessed February 1, 2002.
Eder, Richard. "A Gritty Story of Assimilation." Rev. of *Bone*. *Los Angeles Times* (January 14, 1993): E5.
Garcia, Cristina. "Reading Chinese Fortunes." Rev. of *Bone*. *Washington Post* (January 10, 1993): 8.
Goellnicht, Donald C. "Of Bones and Suicide: Sky Lee's *Disappearing Moon Café* and Fae Myenne Ng's *Bone*." *Modern Fiction Studies* 46.2 (Summer 2000): 301–30.
Ho, Wendy. "The Heart Never Travels: Fathers in the Mother-Daughter Stories of Maxine Hong Kingston, Amy Tan, and Fae Myenne Ng." In *In Her Mother's House:*

The Politics of Asian American Mother-Daughter Writing. Walnut Creek, CA: AltaMira Press, 1999, 195–231.

Jones, B. Louis. "Dying to Be an American." Rev. of *Bone. New York Times Book Review* (February 7, 1993): 7, 9.

Kakutani, Michiko. "Building on the Pain of a Past in China." Rev. of *Bone. New York Times* (January 29, 1993): C26.

Kim, Thomas W. " 'For a Paper Son, Paper Is Blood': Subjectivation and Authenticity in Fae Myenne Ng's *Bone*." *MELUS* 24.4 (Winter 1999): 41–56.

Lee, A. Robert. "Imagined Cities of China: Timothy Mo's London, Sky Lee's Vancouver, Fae Myenne Ng's San Francisco and Gish Jen's New York." *Wasafiri* 22 (Autumn 1995): 25–30.

Lowe, Lisa. "Decolonization, Displacement, and Disidentification: Asian American 'Novels' and the Question of History." In *Cultural Institutions of the Novel.* Deidre Lynch and William B. Warner, eds. Durham, NC: Duke University Press, 1996, 96–128.

Marcus, James. "*Bone* by Fae Myenne Ng." *Village Voice Literary Supplement* 38.6 (February 9, 1993): 5.

Miller, Heather Ross. "America the Big Lie, the Quintessential." *The Southern Review* 29.2 (Spring 1993): 420–30.

Samuel, Suzanne. "Time Heals No Wounds." Rev. of *Bone. Women's Review of Books* 10.8 (May 1993): 27.

Sawyer, Kem Knapp. "A Suicide Unravels a Family." Rev. of *Bone. St. Louis Post-Dispatch* (February 14, 1993): 05F.

Schoof, Renee. "Story of Broken Dreams in San Francisco's Chinatown." *St. Louis Post-Dispatch* (January 24, 1993): 01C.

Stetson, Nancy. "Honoring Her Forebears." Rev. of *Bone. Chicago Tribune* (April 4, 1993): 3.

Suh, Mary. "Fae Myenne Ng: Sparse Words, Rich Images." *Ms.* 3.6 (May–June 1993): 75.

Sze, Julie. "Have You Heard? Gossip, Silence, and Community in *Bone*." *Hitting Critical Mass: A Journal of Asian American Cultural Criticism* 2.1 (1994): 59–69. http://socrates.berkeley.edu/~critmass/v2n1/szeprint.html. Accessed February 1, 2002.

Waller, Nicole. "Past and Repast: Food as Historiography in Fae Myenne Ng's *Bone* and Frank Chin's *Donald Duk*." *Amerikastudien/American Studies* 40.3 (1996): 485–502.

Wong, Sau-ling Cynthia. "Big Eaters, Treat Lovers, 'Food Prostitutes,' 'Food Pornographers,' and Doughnut Makers." In *Reading Asian American Literature: From Necessity to Extravagance.* Princeton, NJ: Princeton University Press, 1993, 18–76.

Yen, Xiaoping. "Fae Myenne Ng." In *Asian American Novelists: A Bio-Bibliographical Critical Sourcebook.* Emmanuel S. Nelson, ed. Westport, CT: Greenwood Press, 2000, 261–66.

HUALING NIEH

(1925–   )

Su-ching Huang

♦ **BIOGRAPHY**

Hualing Nieh was born in Hubei Province, China, in 1925, when most of the Republic of China (ROC), founded in 1911, was still divided among the warlords. Nieh's father belonged to one of those political cliques. He was eventually coopted by Chiang Kai-shek and assigned to Guizhou Province to serve as an administrative chief, but only for eight months before he was killed by Mao Zedong's army. Nieh thus began her refugee existence in her teens in war-torn China. She attended Central University, relocated to Sichuan Province during the Anti-Japanese War and back to Nanjing in 1945 when the Japanese surrendered. Post–World War II China was divided between the Nationalists and the Communists, and Nieh witnessed student movements firsthand during the political upheavals. She graduated in 1948 and was married in Beijing, when the city was being "liberated" by the Communists, who changed the nation's official name to the People's Republic of China (PRC). The defeated Nationalists, who hold onto the official name of ROC, withdrew to Taiwan in 1949.

Moving with her family to Taiwan in 1949, Nieh started to work as the literary editor at *Free China Fortnightly*. During this period, she published two collections of short stories, *Feicui Mao* (*The Emerald Cat*) and *Yiduo Xiaobaihua* (*A Little White Flower*), a novella *Geteng* (*Creeper*), and a novel *Shiqu de Jinlingze* (*The Lost Golden Bell*). Her short stories from this period were republished in different collections in both Hong Kong and mainland China. In 1960 the publisher of *Free China Fortnightly*, Lei Zhen, was imprisoned for antigovernment activities—*Free China Fortnightly* had carried editorials criticizing the Chiang Kai-shek regime, and Lei himself was campaigning to form a new political party. The magazine was seized by the Justice Department, and Nieh and her colleagues were placed under surveillance.

Nieh subsequently taught creative writing at National Taiwan University in Taipei and Donghai University in Taichung. She met Paul Engle at the American poet's reception in Taipei in 1963. As director of the Writers' Workshop at the University of Iowa, Engle invited Nieh to work as a consultant to the program in 1964. There Nieh completed her M.F.A. in 1966, and with Engle, cofounded the International Writing Program in 1967. Every year they invited 30 to 40 writers from around the world to participate in a three-month workshop at the University of Iowa and spend one month touring the United States. Many renowned international writers took part in the program, including Nobel Prize laureate Czeslaw Milosz. Nieh and Engle married in 1971. In 1976 they were nominated for a Nobel Peace Prize by writers from more than twenty countries, who commended them for contributing to international cooperation through bringing writers around the world together. In 1982 Nieh received the Award for Distinguished Service to the Arts from the Governors of Fifty States.

Nieh's first novel after immigration to the United States was *Mulberry and Peach*. Originally written in Chinese, *Mulberry and Peach* was first serialized in the literary section of Taiwan's *United Daily News* in 1970. Before the completion of the novel, however, *Mulberry and Peach* was censored by the Taiwanese government for its political satire against the Nationalist regime and for its "overt" sexual content. Hong Kong's *Mingbao* continued the serialization, and the complete novel was published in Hong Kong in 1976. The English translation was published simultaneously in Beijing and New York in 1981. In 1988 the Beacon Press in Boston reissued the novel and it went on to win the American Book Award from the Before Columbus Foundation.

In 1984 Nieh published her latest novel, *Qianshan Wai, Shui Changliu* (*Lotus, or Far Away, a River*). Aside from fiction writing, Nieh translated American and European writers into Chinese, including works by André Gide, Henry James, Stephen Crane, William Faulkner, Willa Cather, Sherwood Anderson, F. Scott Fitzgerald, and so forth. She also wrote a critical biography of the modern Chinese writer Shen Congwen. In addition, Nieh edited two volumes of Chinese literature written during the "Hundred Flowers" period (mid-1956 to mid-1957). She and Engle traveled and lectured frequently around the world and published their impressions and interviews in *Sanshi Nian Hou* (*After Thirty Years*) and *Heise, Heise, Zui Meili de Yanse* (*Black, Black, the Most Beautiful Color*).

Nieh considers herself a Chinese in exile. She writes mainly in Chinese, has contacts with Chinese on both sides of the Taiwan Straits, and has enjoyed readership among Chinese all over the world. She retired from the International Writing Program in 1988 and now lives in Iowa.

◆ MAJOR WORKS AND THEMES

Nieh's short stories are noted for their sympathetic portrayal of common people. Nieh is skilled at using simple details to reflect her characters' psychological state. Her stories focus on mainland Chinese exiles in Taiwan and their disillusionment with the Nationalist regime and on women's existence as manipulated both by personal choice and political upheavals in modern Chinese history.

Nieh's work always concerns the Chinese nation and the Chinese people, whether they are in Taiwan, mainland China, or the United States. In her 1981 interview with Peter Nazareth, Nieh talks of her "obsession" with "the tragic situation of the Chinese" and states, "the longer I am away from my own country, the more I am concerned with the heart of the situation of the country" (11). The two collections of short stories published in Taiwan before her emigration to the United States, *Feicui Mao* (*The Emerald Cat*) and *Yiduo Xiao-baihua* (*A Little White Flower*), both focus on mainland Chinese expatriates in Taiwan. The characters are all common people: old widows and widowers left alone by their adult children, low-level government employees dreaming of getting rich overnight, couples torn apart by wars, couples dealing with marital problems, lonely old maids and bachelors lamenting the passing of their youth, and so forth. Her ironic tone notwithstanding, Nieh presents a sympathetic portrayal of these "little people." For example, the stories "Yuan Laotou" ("Old Man Yuan") and "Gao Lao Taitai de Zhoumo" ("Old Lady Gao's Weekend") both focus on the loneliness of widowhood. "Yuan Laotou" begins with widower Yuan's excitement over his son's recent marriage. Eager to share his happiness, he tries to chat with his neighbors, a service woman, and his son's friend, but none of them lends a sympathetic ear. Even his son and daughter-in-law are too immersed in their conjugal merriment to pay him any attention. "Gao Lao Taitai de Zhoumo" paints a comic picture of Widow Gao, who vows never to speak with her widow friend ever again after a tiff. She calls her son and daughter back home to spend the weekend but only to find that the young have their own lives. In the end, she lets them go out partying with friends. Reminiscing about past marital bliss and realizing that the widow friend is probably the only friend she has now, she relents and shares snacks with her.

Nieh's characters have led a fugitive existence through Chinese civil wars and the Anti-Japanese War. Uprooted and settling down in Taiwan, most of them feel trapped on the island and look nostalgically toward their mainland home and the past. After a decade in Taiwan they feel restless and sometimes hopeless, but lack an outlet for such angst. Although Nieh does not explicitly allude to Taiwan's political situations in her short stories, the characters' disillusionment and discontented life hint at the macrocosmic politics. Many mainland Chinese settlers have left their families and/or spouses behind on the mainland, and are leading a miserable existence in Taiwan. For instance, the female protagonist in the story "Yi'nianhong" ("Red Blossom") came to Taiwan with her son on the premise that her husband would follow soon after, but he never could. Alone and without any means, she has no choice but to serve as a concubine to a man whose wife was also left on the mainland.

The inertia of mainland Chinese expatriates is best captured in those short stories where the characters can find solace only in memories of old times but do little about the present. "Wang Danian de Jijian Xishi" ("The Several Blessings of Wang Danian," a rewrite of "Wancan" [Dinner]) is representative of the unpromising situation of an average Chinese in Taiwan. On the surface it appears to be a story about the daily life of a schoolteacher, but it really sums up the frustrations and disillusionment of not only ordinary people but specifically Chinese expatriates in Taiwan. Danian, a schoolteacher married with two children, has recently moved from a pigeon cage-like house into a two-room apartment, crammed with worn-out furniture such as bamboo beds, rattan chairs with rickety hind legs, a desk with its paint worn off, and bookshelves made of wooden boxes. Ironically, Danian counts the congested apartment assigned by the school as a blessing. He pins a schedule on the wall of practicing English and studying Chiang Kai-shek's and Nixon's essays but never really sticks to the plan. One of his entertainments in the monotonous life of a schoolteacher is to play military review with his son, and he pretends to be a high-ranking military officer inspecting his son marching. At the outset of the story, Danian has just received a bonus and a certificate of merit from the principal. He invites old friend Fuzi home for dinner. Overjoyed, Danian even predicts that they will be able to fight back to mainland China the following year. At dinner, he reveals his scheme to get rich by raising fish and invites Fuzi to give up teaching to be a partner. However, when asked by his wife for further details about his proposal, Danian does not seem to have a well-thought-out plan. Teased by her and playing with his son, Danian laughs so hard that he inadvertently tumbles in the rattan chair. The story ends with him seeing Fuzi off in the chilly evening air and acting as if he were fearless.

Likewise, the story "Aiguo Jiangquan" ("Lottery Ticket") portrays the disillusionment of a group of Chinese expatriates sharing an apartment. These people pool their savings to buy a lottery ticket in the hope of winning the grand prize to upgrade their living conditions. They even go over the meticulous procedure of drafting and signing a contract for this partnership; however, the bubble of their get-rich dream pops off when the winning number is finally announced, only to their great disappointment.

The story "Shanshan Ni Zai Nar?" ("Where Are You, Shanshan?") features another disillusioned protagonist. Lixin, a thirtyish bachelor, is riding a bus to meet his high school crush Shanshan at her home address. On the bus he reminisces about the good old times with Shanshan in Chongqing, but his recollection keeps being interrupted by other passengers, including two plump, gossipy, middle-aged women, who make such a contrast to the pretty and innocent Shanshan that he remembers. The surprise comes at the end of the story when one of the garrulous women steps off the bus at the same stop where Lixin is supposed to get off; Lixin overhears her giving her address to her friend, which happens to be that of Shanshan's. Unable to accept the fact that the crude, flabby woman is the very Shanshan for whom he has yearned all along, Lixin collapses on the bus seat. Shanshan the innocent young woman serves as a symbol of good old times that can never be retrieved. Lixin's disenchantment at the end of the story, read politically, may hint at the wide-spread frustration of mainland Chinese settlers with the political leaders in Taiwan.

Another story about unfulfilled desires is "Junzi Haoqiu" ("Bachelor"). Dong Tian-an used to be a good-looking young man with girls in pursuit. Aware that he is not getting younger in his thirties, Dong starts to look seri-ously for a wife. After several unsuccessful quests, he chances upon his first romance, Sun Wanqing, who ten years ago was dumped by Dong because she was not his ideal feminine type. Now Sun looks even more attractive and feminine and is well dressed. After several failed attempts to find a fiancée, Dong is eager to get back with Sun. He writes her a love letter regretting what he did before but only to discover later that she is happily married to a wealthy man. Another pursuit thwarted, Dong is suddenly aware of his bald-ing forehead and decides to buy himself a bottle of hair-growing medicine. Nieh's light-hearted tone paints at once a comic and sympathetic picture of her pitiable characters.

Nostalgia for the past and discontent with the present is a recurrent theme in Nieh's stories. For instance, in "Yiduo Xiaobaihua" ("A Little White Flower"), the narrator, a mother of five, visits her high school buddy after they parted sixteen years ago in mainland China. The high school buddy, a tomboy who used to be nicknamed "A Little White Flower," is now Principal Tan of a private elementary school in southern Taiwan. She runs a tightly controlled school. Even in the scorching summer heat, the narrator feels icy in Tan's official residence. While the narrator complains about being tied up by familial responsibilities, Tan as the principal seems burdened with all sorts of personal and personnel requests. After the initial uneasiness, however, the two old friends start to reminisce about their youthful days in Chongqing, and at the end of the story both are transported back to their carefree good old days.

Gender issues are another significant theme in Nieh's short fiction. Due to gender inequities, women's existence is more susceptible to historical contin-gencies than that of men. Nieh utilizes quotidian details to capture women's psychological struggles. In addition to "Yi'nianhong" ("Red Blossom"), several other Nieh stories feature female protagonists who lead a miserable existence owing to the political upheavals of modern China. In "Zhonggen Jiuma" ("Aunt Zhonggen"), told from the perspective of a little Chinese girl, the af-fectionate Japanese aunt, who used to love Chinese people and their culture, turns into a bitter woman and refuses to associate with Chinese after her only son joins the Communist Army and leaves her alone. At the end of the story the girl narrator misses the warm and friendly Japanese aunt but seems also able to sympathize with the poor widow aunt, whose life has been shattered by wars and who has nothing left but endless sorrow and mourning.

The story "Qiao" ("Bridge") offers another take on how women negotiate cross-cultural connection/encounters. It depicts the dilemma a young woman faces in a budding interracial romance. Bill, an American anthropologist, is driving Aidan home after a dinner party. He is scheduled to leave Taiwan the following day. While they are walking across the bridge to his car, it starts to rain. As the rain falls harder and harder, their conversation becomes more and more engaging and the mutual attraction more and more palpable. During the ride home, Aidan silently savors the overwhelming but supposedly transitory encounter. When they say goodbye, she abruptly tells Bill she will not see him off at the airport. In a determined gesture, she begins to run in the direction of home.

Some of Nieh's female characters are middle-aged women lamenting their lost youth. Although Nieh does not overtly criticize society's double standard for the sexes in her stories, her portrayal of women's problems points up the predicaments facing women in a repressive patriarchal society. In "Li Huan de Pibao" ("Li Huan's Purse"), the female hero is relocated to Taiwan and separated from her family due to the Communist-Nationalist conflict. While Li Huan's real age is thirty-four, she carries an identification card that says forty-two, the eight-year difference resulting from a fraud she committed at twenty-two: she borrowed a friend's identity for government employment. Now at thirty-four, she is acutely aware of her facial wrinkles and of people, mistaking her for forty-two, whispering "old maid" behind her back. Furthermore, she feels she can no longer find true love after several missed opportunities. The narrative spans less than two hours, during which Li Huan calls up a male friend, who has made it clear he is not into serious relationships, for a date; ruminates about the inevitability of aging; reminisces about past romances triggered by the content of her purse; and eventually decides to cancel the date and walks toward the City Court to change her age back. The attempt to get the eight years back could be read as her determination to stop pitying herself and turn over a new leaf.

In "Yongbu Bimu de Wutai" ("The Stage Where the Curtain Never Falls"), the female narrator witnesses obliquely an illicit love affair between a middle-aged woman and her second cousin. Through the misplaced diary of the aunt, the narrator reads about her female sexual desire and feels for her instead of judging her as other people do. Such a sympathetic description of female desire reminds one of the pioneering Chinese feminist writer Ding Ling, whose novella *Shafei Nüshi de Riji* (*Diary of Lady Sophie*), published in the 1930s, was among the first fiction by modern Chinese women writers to deal explicitly with active female desire.

Nieh's sympathy for transgressive women becomes most evident in her longer works. The novella *Geteng* (*Creeper*) centers on an illicit affair between Bai Ling, whose husband is in jail, and the narrator, who is a writer and schoolteacher. *Geteng* is seldom mentioned by critics, perhaps due to its excessive sentimentality and deus-ex-machina ending: Bai Ling drowns herself and thus ends the entangled affair. However, like "Yongbu Bimu de Wutai" ("The Stage Where the Curtain Never Falls"), *Geteng* merits attention for its compassionate portrayal of an "immoral" woman and her active desires. Another interesting woman in the novella is the narrator's wife. He seldom mentions her, but she occupies a pivotal position in the story. At the end the narrator realizes that she knows about his extramarital affair all along but has decided not to disclose it to protect the marriage, like the wife in Edith Wharton's *Age of Innocence*. Nieh's female characters, in this novella, turn out to be non-traditional and resilient. All three of Nieh's novels portray female characters who resist the gender role traditionally prescribed for women: *Shiqu de Jinlingze* (*The Lost Golden Bell*) revolves around the sexual awakening of a young girl and her widow aunt's illicit affair; *Mulberry and Peach* features a sexually liberated woman; *Qianshan Wai, Shui Changliu* (*Lotus, or Far Away, a River*) depicts the reconciliation between a mother and her daughter, both of whom dare to traverse boundaries to pursue their dreams.

◆ CRITICAL RECEPTION

Nieh's short stories are noted for their narrative techniques and political implications. Critics of Nieh's short stories have all praised her employment of ordinary trivia to penetrate the psychological depths of her characters. W. Yeh applies the concept of epiphany to discuss how Nieh builds up a sense of enlightenment at the end of her stories through detached descriptions of seemingly trivial objects and happenings, which gradually develop into external manifestations of the characters' internal psychological undulations. Using "Yuan Laotou" ("Old Man Yuan") as an example, Yeh observes, Yuan's fervent attempts at sharing his good news and the busy activities of his inattentive listeners slowly but surely point up the contrast between the excitement outside and Yuan's loneliness inside ("Turu Yeshun" 278–79). Another example of epiphany is the story "Qiao" ("Bridge"). Yeh points out how Nieh relates the complex psychological transformation of her female hero to the capricious weather. While Nieh hardly reveals the inner struggles of her characters directly, she achieves a sense of epiphany through depicting the flow of the water under the bridge and the interweaving rainfalls, which correspond to the internal commotions of the characters. Eventually the walk across the bridge becomes an act of bridge building itself, bringing the two characters from two different cultures closer to each other (282–85).

Critics have observed how Nieh adroitly employs realistic details for symbolic meanings. Chen Shixiang praises Nieh for selecting seemingly ordinary fragments from daily life that also abound with symbolic significance. He focuses on "Wang Danian de Jijian Xishi" ("The Several Blessings of Wang Danian") and argues that a symbolist interpretation would reveal "disaster" in "blessings," hopelessness in Danian's pipe dreams, ridicule of Chiang Kai-shek's military rule in the father-son mock parade, the deterioration of education in Danian's failure to stick to his schedule on the wall, and Taiwan's dismal future in the setting of dusk at the end of the story (266). In addition to symbolism, Chen applauds Nieh for her ironic but at the same time sympathetic portrayal of her characters (267).

The most comprehensive study of Nieh's works thus far is Shiao-ling Yu's essay "The Themes of Exile and Identity Crisis in Nieh Hualing's Fiction." Yu offers a close reading of Nieh's short stories and commends Nieh's dexterity in blending the realistic with the symbolic. Also using the short story "Wang Danian de Jijian Xishi" as an example, Yu observes Nieh's realistic depiction of a schoolteacher's dwelling and shows how the details of the dilapidated furnishings, along with the protagonist's naive dream to get rich, serve as a symbolic representation of Taiwan's bleak political situation (128). Toward the end of the story the reader sees that Danian's pipe dreams, like the Nationalist government's slogan to recover the mainland, are never likely to materialize. The only relief these "little people" can get "to assuage the pain they suffer in the present" therefore is to reminisce about the past (130).

The theme of exile and cultural identity is another focus of critical attention. In "The Wandering Chinese: The Theme of Exile in Taiwan Fiction," writer/critic Hsien-yung Pai looks at émigré writers from the mainland to Taiwan and contends that these émigré writers, due to censorship by the Nationalist government, turned to the study of individual psyche rather than tackling social and political issues upfront (207). Pai remarks that Nieh's short stories are "mostly ironic studies of the frustrations of the mainlanders in Taiwan." He focuses instead on Nieh's novel *Mulberry and Peach*, which "has elaborated the theme of exile to its fullest extent" (210).

Yu uses another story, "Aiguo Jiangquan" ("Lottery Ticket"), to further explore the theme of exile and confinement in Nieh's work (130–31). The story itself is simple, but Nieh uses a variety of details to illustrate the everyday living of these people and their frustrations, and how their lives are intricately related to the political climate in Taiwan. For instance, the sense of entrapment on a small island is illustrated by a character's walking exercise in his tiny room, where he has to keep turning when running into walls; the married couple's only recreation now is procreation; and another character's life/job is so boring and meaningless that he spends hours transcribing the personnel directory from work only to cross the names out as people keep passing away.

Elaborating on the theme of exile and disillusionment in Nieh's stories, Yu observes how personal loss is not merely "the fickleness of fate" but also closely related to political turmoil such as wars and revolutions in "Shanshan Ni Zai Nar?" ("Where Are You, Shanshan?") (131). She points to Nieh's contrasting of "the youthful dreams of the past with the lackluster present" in "Yiduo Xiaobaihua" ("A Little White Flower") (132). Compared with the exilic existence in Taiwan, the war years turn golden in the female characters' reminiscences.

Nieh continues her political satire and engagement with history in her novels written in the United States. While her characters crisscross gender/racial/ national borders, she herself also crosses boundaries by combining various literary genres and conventions in her fiction writing.

◆ BIBLIOGRAPHY

Works by Hualing Nieh

Short Story Collections

Feicui Mao [*The Emerald Cat*]. Taipei: Minghua Shuju, 1959.
Yiduo Xiaobaihua [*A Little White Flower*]. Taipei: Book World, 1963.
Wang Danian de Jijian Xishi [*The Several Blessings of Wang Danian*]. Hong Kong: Haiyang Wenyishe, 1980.
Taiwan Yishi [*Taiwan Stories*]. Beijing: Beijing Chubanshe, 1980.
Shanshan Ni Zai Nar? [*Where Are You, Shanshan?*] Beijing: Xinhua Shudian, 1994.

Novels

Geteng [*Creeper: A Novella*]. Taipei: Free China Magazine, 1953.
Shiqu de Jinlingze [*The Lost Golden Bell*]. Taipei: Xuesheng Chubanshe, 1960.
Sangqing yu Taohong [*Mulberry Green and Peach Pink*]. Hong Kong: Youlian Chubanshe, 1976.
Qianshan Wai, Shui Changliu [*Lotus, or Far Away, a River*]. Sichuan: Renmin Chubanshe, 1984.

Other Prose and Essays

Meng Gu Ji [*Dream Valley*]. Hong Kong: Chengwen Chubanshe, 1965.
A Critical Biography of Shen Congwen. Boston: Twayne Publishers, 1972.
Aihehua Zhaji: Sanshi Nian Hou [*Notes from Iowa: After Thirty Years*]. Hong Kong: Joint Publishing Co., 1981.
Heise, Heise, Zui Meili De Yanse [*Black, Black, the Most Beautiful Color*]. Hong Kong: Joint Publishing Co., 1983.
Sanshi Nian Hou: Mengyou Guyuan [*After Thirty Years: Dream-Walking the Old Country*]. Taipei: Hanyiseyan Wenhua Shiye Youxian Gongsi, 1988.
Renzai Ershi Shiji [*People, 20th Century*]. Teaneck, NJ: Global Publishing Co., 1990.
Renjing yu Fengjing [*Reminiscence*]. Xi'an: Shanxi Renmin Chubanshe, 1996.
Luyuan Qingshi [*Anecdotes from Deer Garden*]. Shanghai: Shanghai Wenyi Chubanshe, 1997.

English Translations of Nieh's Works

The Purse and Three Other Stories of Chinese Life. Taipei: The Heritage Press, 1962.
"Many Things to Tell, but Hard to Tell." Trans. Jane Parish Yang. In *Nativism Overseas: Contemporary Chinese Women Writers*. Hsin-sheng C. Kao, ed. Albany: State University of New York Press, 1993, 113–26.
Mulberry and Peach: Two Women of China. 1976. Trans. Jane Parish Yang and Linda Lappin. Beijing: World Books, 1981. Rpt., Boston: Beacon Press, 1988, and New York: The Feminist Press at the City University of New York, 1998.

Translations and Compilations

Madame de Mauves by Henry James. Taipei: The Heritage Press, 1959.
Selected American Short Stories. Taipei: The Heritage Press, 1960.
Eight Stories by Chinese Women. Taipei: The Heritage Press, 1963.
Poems of Mao Tse-tung. Co-trans. with Paul Engle. New York: Simon and Schuster, 1972.
Writing from the World: Poetry, Fiction, and Criticism in Translation and in Original English by Members of the International Writing Program from the First Ten Years of Its Life. Coed. with Paul Engle. Iowa City: University of Iowa Press, 1976.
Literature of the Hundred Flowers. 2 vols. New York: Columbia University Press, 1981.
Writing from the World, II: Selections from the International Writing Program, 1977–1983. Coed. with Paul Engle, Marilyn Chin, David Hamilton, and Walter Knupfer. Iowa City: University of Iowa Press, 1985.
The World Comes to Iowa: Iowa International Anthology. Coed. with Paul Engle and Rowena Torrevillas. Ames: Iowa State University Press, 1987.

Studies of Hualing Nieh

Chen, Shixiang. "Cong 'Wang Danian de Jijian Xishi' Tanqi [Beginning with 'The Several Blessings of Wang Danian']." In *Wang Danian de Jijian Xishi*, by Hualing Nieh, 264–68.
Denton, Kirk. "A Review of *Mulberry and Peach: Two Women of China.*" *Journal of the Chinese Language Teachers' Association* 34.2 (1989): 135–38.
Lee, Leo Ou-fan. "On the Margins of the Chinese Discourse: Some Personal Thoughts on the Cultural Meaning of the Periphery." In *The Living Tree: The Changing Meaning of Being Chinese Today*. Wei-ming Tu, ed. Stanford, CA: Stanford University Press, 1994, 221–38.
Nazareth, Peter. "An Interview with Chinese Author Hua-ling Nieh." *World Literature Today* 55.1 (1981): 10–18.
———. Rev. of *Mulberry and Peach: Two Women of China*. *World Literature Today* 56.2 (1982): 403–4.
Pai, Hsien-yung. "The Wandering Chinese: The Theme of Exile in Taiwan Fiction." *The Iowa Review* 7.2–3 (1976): 205–12.
Wong, Sau-ling Cynthia. "The Stakes of Textual Border-Crossing: Hualing Nieh's *Mulberry and Peach* in Sinocentric, Asian-American, and Feminist Critical Practices." In *Orientations: Mapping Studies in the Asian Diaspora*. Kandice Chuh and Karen Shimakawa, eds. Durham: Duke University Press, 2001, 130–52.

————. "Afterword". In *Mulberry and Peach: Two Women of China*, by Hualing Nieh. Trans. Jane Parish Yang and Linda Lappin. New York: The Feminist Press at the City University of New York, 1998, 209–31.

Xiang Yang. "Xiongyongzhe de Penquan: Du Nieh Hualing Xiaoshuo *Shiqu de Jinlingzi* [Bubbling Fountain: Reading Nieh Hualing's *The Lost Golden Bell*]." In *Shiqu de Jinlingzi*, by Hualing Nieh. Taipei: Linbai Chubanshe, 1987, 265–70.

Xiao, Hailing. "Hualing Nieh." In *Asian American Novelists: A Bio-Bibliographical Critical Sourcebook*. Emmanuel S. Nelson, ed. Westport, CT: Greenwood Press, 2000, 271–76.

Yeh, Wei-lian. "*Shiqu de Jinlingzi* Zhi Taolun [Discussions on *The Lost Golden Bell*]." In *Shiqu de Jinlingzi*, by Hualing Nieh, 241–56.

————. "Turu Yishun de Tuibian li: Celun Nieh Hualing [The Epiphany in Nieh Hualing's Fiction]." In *Wang Danian de Jijian Xishi*, by Hualing Nieh, 269–85.

Yu, Shiao-ling. "The Themes of Exile and Identity Crisis in Nieh Hualing's Fiction." In *Nativism Overseas: Contemporary Chinese Women Writers*. Hsin-sheng C. Kao, ed. Albany: State University of New York Press, 1993, 127–56.

SUSAN NUNES
(1943–   )

Alice D'Amore

◆ BIOGRAPHY

Susan Nunes, short story writer and nationally recognized author of children's literature, was born in 1943 in Hilo, a small town on the eastern coast of the Big Island of Hawaii. A descendent of an interracial union of Japanese and Portuguese cultures, the source for much of her writing, Nunes resided in Hilo until 1959, when she moved with her family to Honolulu. While in Hawaii, she worked as a writer and editor at the University of Hawaii and published a series of children's books and short stories, along with a collection *A Small Obligation and Other Stories of Hilo* (1982). In 1991, she moved to Berkeley, California, with her husband and son and now writes full time. She began publishing once more and the Hawaii Book Academy awarded her children's book, *To Find the Way*, the *Ka Palapala Po'okela* Award in 1994. The following year, *The Smithsonian* selected *The Last Dragon* as one of its "Notable Books for Children." Nunes has also published several non-fiction pieces in the *San Francisco Chronicle* and is currently working on a longer project.

Most of Nunes's writing portrays the joys and pains of familial bonds. Discussing the nature of her work, she states, "I think many writers begin with stories about family because families are what we know, and because, when you think about it, families provide a dynamic out of which stories naturally grow" (e-mail). Throughout her writings, she also explores the individual's painful yet necessary search for identity in an environment of geographic and cultural displacement. Reflecting on the journey of her grandmother from Japan to Hawaii, Nunes notes, "When she stepped on board a ship back in 1914 to join her betrothed, my grandfather, she had no idea she'd one day be gazing at a great-grandchild with fair hair and green eyes. I see the journey, despite its sadness and loss (for there is always loss), its giving up of one identity for another, as a worthy one" (e-mail).

◆ MAJOR WORKS AND THEMES

"We are all wanderers looking for a place to call home" (e-mail). In this reference to her work, Nunes summarizes her exploration of the individual's search for identity in a multicultural, and often hostile, world. In *A Small Obligation and Other Stories of Hilo*, Amy, the protagonist and occasional narrator, seeks her identity in a vague mixture of Japanese and Portuguese ancestry similar to that of Nunes's. In "The Grandmother," Amy, seeing herself as a hybrid, rebels against the "purebred" orchid, something she interprets as a symbol of an ancient and unattainable cultural wholeness that evades her. However, Nunes counters Amy's sense of loss with positive characters who express a measure of hope for Amy as she seeks her identity in the midst of the chaotic cycle of change.

In "The Yardman," Nunes describes Amy's relationship with the equally displaced Mr. Naito, a silent yet observant fixture of the damp basement of the Kinoshita house, the home of Amy's maternal grandparents. Amy as an adult downplays his influence, noting that "he is not particularly symbolic, nor is his story" (". . . and Mud Lane shall be known as Piopio" 67); however, his story reveals his importance in Amy's youth. Nunes notes that he had arrived twenty years prior in the midst of change, when the bucolic "Mud Lane" became "Piopio Street" ("pio" being the local expression for "gone" or "ended"). As he works, Naito observes the stony nature of Mrs. Kinoshita, Amy's maternal grandmother, and her resistance to change that takes the form of disapproval for Amy's Portuguese father. As Amy misinterprets Mrs. Furuisato's actions in "The Grandmother," she also sees Mrs. Kinoshita's actions as a rejection of her heritage. In childish confusion, Amy approaches Mr. Naito, asking, "How come I'm only half Japanese?" (23). Unable to respond, Mr. Naito can only offer her the consolation of flowers, thimbleberries, ducks, and water. He is a return to Nature for Amy, a wizened river god who lives in the "damp" beneath the earth. An aged loner, he comes from a realm where all things are equal. Nunes surrounds him with water imagery that, in turn, reflects Amy's childhood search for identity.

For example, when Amy poses her question to him, Mr. Naito realizes that "whatever it was she had done had caused the question to rise like a fish to the surface of a pond" (23). Later, as he inwardly searches for an answer to Amy's dilemma, he gazes at his reflection in Waiakea Pond:

> The pond was still, except at the water's edge where a few ducks swam among the water lilies. Mr. Naito took some bread from a paper bag and threw it piece by piece into the water. The ducks bobbed and splashed, disturbing the placid surface of the pond. He watched the

ripples cross the water to where the abandoned cane mill stood. So quiet. Before Amy was born the mill had droned day and night.(23)

As the water ripples and grows still, Mr. Naito comes to realize that change, whether cultural or natural, is constant. The ripples alter the linear stability of the water, scattering random images, but when ripples die, the continuity of the water returns to its external constancy. Facing a sleepless night in his damp domain, he returns to the water, noting, "Between himself and the pale glow of the Kilauea Street lights all was blackness. Then the headlights of a car flashed briefly, sending out long, fan-shaped beams that cut through the dark and were momentarily transfigured on the surface of the pond. Pio. Gone" (24–25). Again, Mr. Naito realizes that change is constant *and* necessary, despite the cultural strictness of Mrs. Kinoshita and Mrs. Furuisato, and he is hopeful for Amy as he "chuckles" to himself.

◆ CRITICAL RECEPTION

Susan Nunes's work has been a dominant influence on Hawaiian writing for nearly two decades. Cathy Song, author of the collection *The Land of Bliss*, among others, and a writer whose work has received the Elliot Cades Award for Literature as well as other honors, comments on Nunes's influence on her writing: "I saw Susan Nunes' book, *A Small Obligation*, and that to me was very transforming. To see a collection of short stories that were about Hawaii by someone I kind of remotely knew . . . It made writing something you could do with what you had, because it was here, by someone you kinda knew . . . It meant a lot to me as a young writer" (qtd. in Oi 2). Nunes's work appeals to many of her Hawaiian contemporaries because of its exploration of the individual's search for identity in society.

In her reflection on Amy in "Hilo Story," Gayle K. Sato writes:

We feel the tension surrounding the marriage . . . a tension generated less by deteriorating relations between Japan and America than the antagonism of Amy's maternal grandparents. The story's exaggerated omissions reflect the parents' method of expressing disapproval—conspicuous absence from the wedding ceremony. "Hilo Story" thus offers a stark contrast to "The Ebesu Girls" on the theme of Amy's Japanese heritage. Whereas the Ebesus accept Amy wholeheartedly though by custom they are not obliged to do so, not being blood relations, Amy's mother is alienated by her own parents for choosing a non-Japanese husband. Their wedding photograph with two unsmiling faces captures the beginning of Amy's future struggles with biracial identity. (269)

As Sato notes, with the exception of the Ebesu girls and Mr. Naito, Amy's interpretation of the rejection of her bicultural lineage by those who surround her is prevalent throughout the stories: in Mrs. Kinoshita's refusal to acknowledge Sumi's attempt to defend Amy's Portuguese father in "The Yardman," in Mrs. Furuisato's ambivalent contrast between Amy's ancestry and that of the ancient and "purebred" orchid in "The Grandmother," and in Amy's self-recognition that "the face in the mirror was neither Asian nor Caucasian" in "The Confession." Like her predecessors, Jean Rhys's Antoinette Mason and William Faulkner's Joe Christmas, Amy is on a quest for racial and cultural self-knowledge; and her painful metamorphosis is vital to finding her place in society.

◆ BIBLIOGRAPHY

Works by Susan Nunes

Short Stories

"What Would You Do If I Sang Out of Tune?" In *Hapa*. Michael McPherson, ed. Maui: Xenophobia Press, 1983.
"Villa Franca." *Chaminade Literary Review* 4 (Spring 1989): 32–43.
"A Moving Day." In *The Graywolf Annual Seven: Stories from the American Mosaic*. Scott Walker, ed. Saint Paul, MN: Graywolf Press, 1990, 130–37.
"The Science of Symmetry—A Love Story." In *Sister Stew: Fiction and Poetry by Women*. Juliet S. Kono and Cathy Song, eds. Honolulu: Bamboo Ridge Press, 1991, 299–308.
"The Yellow Umbrella." *The Hawai'i Writers' Quarterly* 63, 64 (Summer and Fall 1994): 140–48.
"The Poor Pagan Children." In *Growing Up Local: An Anthology of Poetry and Prose from Hawai'i*. Eric Chock, James R. Harstad, Darrell H. Y. Lum, and Bill Teter, eds. Honolulu: Bamboo Ridge Press, 1998, 86–96.
"The Man with the Package." *San Francisco Chronicle* (October 10, 2000): B10.
"Good Signs Make Bad Neighbors." *San Francisco Chronicle* (March 16, 2001): C18.
"In Norwalk, Ohio, It's Still Vanilla." *San Francisco Chronicle* (April 5, 2001): B10.
"Flowers for Remembrance." *San Francisco Chronicle* (July 12, 2001): E12.

Short Story Collection

A Small Obligation and Other Stories of Hilo (Bamboo Ridge Series; No. 16). Honolulu: Bamboo Ridge Press, 1982.

Children's Literature

Coyote Dreams. New York: Atheneum, 1988.
Tiddalick the Frog. New York: Atheneum, 1989.

To Find the Way. Honolulu: University of Hawaii Press, 1992.
The Last Dragon. New York: Clarion Books, 1995.

Academic Publications

Language Functions. With Edith Kleinjans. Honolulu: Hawaii State Department of Education, 1983.
Pathways. With Leon Burton. Boston: Addison Wesley Publishing, 1984.

Studies of Susan Nunes

Nunes, Susan. E-mail to author, December 16, 2001.
Oi, Cynthia. "Chick Chat: A Four-Way Conversation with Hawaii's Foremost Writing Women." Rev. of *For the Love of Words*. *Honolulu Star-Bulletin* (February 5, 2001). http://www.bambooridge.com/danews.asp. Accessed October 31, 2001.
Ramirez, Tino. "Home Is a Cultural Welcome Mat." Rev. of *Home to Stay: Asian American Women's Fiction*. *Sunday Star-Bulletin & Advertiser* (July 15, 1990): G7–9.
Sato, Gayle K. "Susan Nunes." In *Reading Japanese American Literature: The Legacy of Three Generations*. Teruyo Veki and Gayle K. Sato, eds. Osaka: Sogensha, 1997, 266–71.
Usui, Masami. "The Global/Local Past Encounters the Local/Global Future: The Japanese Local Literature in Hawaii." *AALA Journal* 6 (10th Anniversary Issue, Asian American Literature Association, Kobe, Japan, 2000): 79–92.

GARY PAK
(1952–   )

Michael Oishi

◆ BIOGRAPHY

Gary Yong Ki Pak, a third-generation Korean American, or *samse*, was born on April 30, 1952, in Honolulu, Hawaii to Francis Chin Chan Pak and Etta Chung Hee Pak, second-generation Korean Americans, or *ise*. At the age of three, Pak and his parents moved from their home in the Honolulu suburb of Makiki to the town of Kane'ohe on the Windward, or northeastern, side of Oahu where Pak, his wife, and his children reside today.

Following his graduation from 'Iolani School, a prestigious private school in Honolulu, in 1970, Pak enrolled in Boston University. During this time Pak deepened his extant interest in community and global politics, provoking his engagement in various social conflicts such as the United States' involvement in Vietnam and Boston's 1974 school bussing crisis. He graduated from Boston University in 1974 with a B.A. in Social Psychology.

After graduation, Pak returned to Hawaii and renewed his engagement in local community struggles by becoming involved in, among other things, the urban development of agricultural lands in the Wai'ahole and Waikane valleys, and the eviction of low-income residents from Honolulu's Chinatown tenements—struggles which would later find expression in his works of fiction. To support himself and his political commitments, Pak held odd jobs as a roofer, construction worker, press operator, truck driver, and private investigator, among others.

But Pak's foray into creative writing would not begin in earnest until the birth of his first son in 1980. At that time, Pak became acutely aware of the abundance and importance of stories in his life and the need to set those stories to paper for the benefit of his son and others: "I just felt this huge sense of responsibility, a need to tell him and pass on certain things" (Cob Keller, "A Writer with a Sense of Place" B1). That sentiment would eventually lead to two different but parallel pursuits in Pak's life: creative writing and literary criticism. In 1990, Pak received an M.A. in English with an emphasis in creative writing, and in 1997 a Ph.D. in English, both from the University of Hawaii at Manoa. His M.A. thesis, titled "Kanewai," would serve as a testing ground for his first published collection, *The Watcher of Waipuna and Other Stories* (1992). His doctoral dissertation, " '*E ala mai kakou e na kini na mamo*' ('We, the multitudes of descendants, are waking up'): 19th Century Hawaiian Historiography and the Historical Novel of Hawai'i," a postcolonial reading of Native Hawaiian and "Local" immigrant historical texts, however, would serve to satisfy his curiosity into the social conditions and political functions of Hawaii's literatures.

During his pursuit of advanced degrees, Pak published the works for which he is currently best known: a collection of short fiction, *The Watcher of Waipuna and Other Stories* (1992), and a novel, *A Ricepaper Airplane* (1997). An eclectic mix of short stories, *The Watcher of Waipuna* won the Association for Asian American Studies' fiction award in 1993 and was later adapted and performed as a play by Kumu Kahua Theatre in May 1996. Pak's novel, *A Ricepaper Airplane*, was later adapted and performed by Kumu Kahua in March 2002.

From September 1996 through June 2002, Pak taught English at Kapi'olani Community College. In February 2002, Pak accepted a position as Assistant Professor of English at the University of Hawaii at Manoa.

◆ MAJOR WORKS AND THEMES

Of Pak's works of short fiction, the most popular and well received are those collected in *The Watcher of Waipuna and Other Stories*, published by Bamboo Ridge Press in 1992. While varied and unique, these stories share important thematic and formal similarities. As Morris Young notes in his review of the book for *Amerasia Journal*, "While each of the eight stories can be seen as a self-contained entity, they form couplets where each pair emphasizes a particular theme: land, community, childhood, and land once again" (108).

In "The Valley of the Dead Air," the story that opens *The Watcher*, the residents of Waiola Valley believe that the ghost of the old Hawaiian hermit and *kahuna* (priest), Jacob Ho'okano, has cursed the community, causing a strong, putrid odor to linger in the air. As the residents attempt unsuccessfully to discover the source of the odor and mask it, they eventually come to the realization that Jacob's curse is the result of their failure to include Jacob in the community and to acknowledge his organic and sacred relationship to the valley. Only after the residents offer tribute to Jacob and restore their communal bonds by way of a three-night, two-day party does the stench pass away. The second and title story, "The Watcher of Waipuna," similarly touches on the issue of land by way of the story's protagonist, Gilbert Sanchez.

A character reminiscent of Cervantes's Don Quixote, the good-hearted, mentally unstable, Portuguese-Hawaiian Gilbert stands as the dreamy "watcher" or guardian of Waipuna as greedy investors and Gilbert's own sisters attempt to cajole him into selling his land so that it may be converted into a beachfront resort. But supernatural things begin to happen in Waipuna, forcing the investors to abandon their plans, rendering the land safe from the destruction and desecration of urban "development."

Utilizing magical realism, Pak introduces the *'aina* or land as a major character in these two stories to comment on the ravaging of the environment as well as the dispossession and alienation of Native Hawaiians whose culture is so deeply bound to that environment. Yet in employing magical realism in his works, Pak also rehearses formal conventions of Native Hawaiian storytelling, that frequently incorporate references to the fantastic.

In the third and fourth stories of this collection, "For the Sake of a Christ" and "The Trial of Goro Fukushima," respectively, Pak examines personal dynamics and morality in the context of community. In "For the Sake of a Christ," Pak ventures into the gothic to explore how prejudice destroys a town as it gossips about Gloria DeSilva's new baby—who no one has ever seen but who many believe to be either part dog, part shark, or Christ or the devil reborn. Rumor eventually destroys the DeSilvas, causing a terrible smell to fall over the neighborhood—the palpable reminder and remainder of the community's complicity and guilt. In "The Trial of Goro Fukushima," a Japanese gardener unable to speak English is accused and lynched for murdering the plantation manager's wife. During the course of the story, the plantation community realizes that Goro is in fact innocent and that the community's own viciousness, suspicion, and prejudice directly contributed to his death.

The fifth and sixth pieces—rites of passage stories—reflect on the lessons learned from those alienated to society's margins. In "A Toast to Rosita," the *mahu* (homosexual) Hawaiian neighbor Rosita Kamali'i emerges as a hero to a group of kids despite the rest of the community's ridicule of him. Though the entire neighborhood is threatened with dissolution by the state's proposed freeway, only Rosita takes the initiative to do anything about it as he collects petition signatures and chains himself to the statue of Father Damien in front of the state capitol to protest the construction of the freeway. But the neighborhood's homophobia prevents it from joining forces with Rosita, and Rosita commits suicide, believing himself alone in his crusade for community. Ironically, it is the community's inability to accept Rosita's sexuality that will prove its own destruction. "The Gift," meanwhile, grapples with a group of boys' misperceptions of and prejudices toward a fellow classmate, Chunky Kalama. Though a bully, Chunky is in fact vulnerable and lonely—more than anyone, especially the young protagonists, had previously thought. Yet the boys only learn of this side of Chunky after his death, when rapprochement is too late.

The last pair of stories, "An Old Friend" and "The Garden of Jiro Tanaka" return to the issue of land and Locals' relationships to it. When a volcanic steam vent opens up behind his duplex, Dennis Lim, a Local Korean once active in the Hawaiian Sovereignty Movement, begins to imagine ways he might exploit and profit from the land. But Dennis's capitalistic thoughts quickly betray him as he muses over the significance and sacredness of the land, particularly as he imagines the Hawaiian fire goddess, Pele, exacting violent revenge on him for his act of avarice. In "The Garden of Jiro Tanaka," Pak again employs magical realism to fill the void of an elderly man's heart. A recently retired groundskeeper, Jiro Tanaka allows his garden—his land—to grow wild. Later he dreams that he plants a tree in his garden and wakes to find that its fruits have metamorphosed into tiny, thumb-sized children whom he warmly receives into his open arms. Here the land nurtures the one who nurtured it, underscoring the ethic of ecological and humanistic reciprocity so important in Native Hawaiian culture.

If a thread of commonality can be identified in all eight stories, it is perhaps in the creation of a recognizable reflection of Hawaii's Local community—its triumphs, its failures, its possibilities. As author and critic Nora Cobb-Keller observes in her review of the book, "Amazingly, instead of getting lost or tangled in family lineages, we find ourselves immersed in enchanted and enchanting communities we come to recognize as our own. The real magic in Pak's storytelling is his gift for imparting a sense of home—with all its surprises and burdens, ignorance and love—to those of us who have half-forgotten where we live" (" 'Waipuna' a Village World" G6). Yet in making the Local community intelligible to itself, Pak defamiliarizes it—renders it somewhat unlike itself—to enable Locals to see more clearly the ways they have naturalized and reified various social relationships. It is perhaps in this way that Pak proves himself a truly remarkable artist.

◆ CRITICAL RECEPTION

Reviews of Pak's short fiction—which have heretofore focused exclusively on *The Watcher of Waipuna*—have been overwhelmingly positive. Even in those instances when he has been criticized for lapsing into the stereotypical to represent his characters (see reviews by Robin Bott, Michael McPherson, and David Takami) or for misrepresenting and modifying Hawaiian myths (see Bott), reviewers have made a point to underscore the novelty and artistry of Pak's work. Most frequently, reviewers point to Pak's representation of a multicultural Hawaii—a Hawaii that both revels in and grates against its unique racial and ethnic diversity. As Robin Bott notes in her review of *The Watcher of Waipuna*, "Unlike some other contemporary writers in Hawaii, such as Darrell Lum, Susan Nunes, and Milton Murayama, whose works focus on a single ethnic background—Chinese, Portuguese, and Japanese, respectively—Pak writes about racially, religiously, and socially mixed communities in Hawai'i" (18). Indeed, if there can be said to be a common thread in *The Watcher of*

Waipuna beside its Hawaiian setting, it is its representation of communal ties—which, in Hawaii, means panethnic ties.

In her article "Between Nationalisms: Hawaii's Local Nation and Its Troubled Racial Paradise," Candace Fujikane builds on extant observations of Pak's emphasis on community to argue that "Local" or non-Native Hawaiian narratives reveal a psychic ambivalence over Local cultural nationalists' claims to sovereignty and self-determination—claims that often run counter to Native Hawaiian claims to sovereignty and self-determination. Using representative stories from *The Watcher of Waipuna*—namely, "The Valley of the Dead Air," "The Watcher of Waipuna," "A Toast to Rosita," and "An Old Friend"—Fujikane demonstrates how Local narratives evince an anxiety over Local dispossession of Native Hawaiians, particularly the colonization and development of the *'aina* or land to which Native Hawaiian culture is so deeply bound.

Brenda Kwon's book-length study *Beyond Ke'eaumoku: Koreans, Nationalism, and Local Culture in Hawaii* likewise analyzes Pak's representation of community, though does so to point out how dominant conceptions of "Local" frequently marginalize and elide Local Koreans in Hawaii. Noting how traditional definitions of "Local" derive from Hawaii's plantation history—a history that most Local Koreans cannot claim—Koreans are often considered outsiders to Hawaii's Local community. That Pak, a Local Korean writer, lays bare in his stories the conflicts, exclusions, and inequalities belying popular characterizations of Hawaii as a "racial paradise" for Kwon opens up a space where Koreans might finally come to be seen as legitimate members of Hawaii's Local community.

To date, there has been little published criticism of Pak's short stories, though more is sure to come as Pak's work reaches and interests wider audiences.

◆ BIBLIOGRAPHY

Works by Gary Pak

Short Stories

"My Friend Kammy." *Hawai'i Review* 12.2 (1988): 61–73.
"A House of Mirrors." *Hawai'i Review* 15.2 (1991): 129–40.
"Hae Soon's Song." In *The Best of Honolulu Fiction: Stories from the* Honolulu Magazine *Fiction Contest.* Eric Chock and Darrell Lum, eds. Honolulu: Bamboo Ridge, 1999, 194–204.

Short Story Collection

The Watcher of Waipuna and Other Stories. Honolulu: Bamboo Ridge, 1992.

Novels

A Ricepaper Airplane. Honolulu: University of Hawaii Press, 1997.
Children of a Fireland. (Forthcoming from University of Hawaii Press).

Plays

Only the Wind's Home. Kennedy Theatre, Honolulu. December 1991.
Beyond the Falls. Honolulu Theatre for Youth, Honolulu. April–May 2001.

Creative/Critical Essays

"Catching a Big Ulua." *Bamboo Ridge* 47 (1990): 17–27.
"In That Valley Beautiful Beyond." In *Bold Words: A Century of Asian American Writing*. Rajini Srikanth and Esther Y. Iwanaga, eds. New Brunswick, NJ: Rutgers University Press, 2001, 133–39.

Ph.D. Dissertation

" '*E ala mai kakou e na kini na mamo*' ('We, the multitudes of descendants, are waking up'): 19th Century Hawaiian Historiography and the Historical Novel of Hawai'i." Ph.D., diss. University of Hawaii at Manoa, 1997.

Studies of Gary Pak

Bott, Robin L. "Hawaiian-Style Mixed Stew." Rev. of *The Watcher of Waipuna and Other Stories*. *American Book Review* 16.2 (1994): 18.
Cobb-Keller, Nora. " 'Waipuna' a Village World Full of Magic, Dreams." Rev. of *The Watcher of Waipuna and Other Stories*. *Honolulu Advertiser* (September 20, 1992): G6.
———. "A Writer with a Sense of Place." *Honolulu Star Bulletin* (September 21, 1992): B1.
Fujikane, Candace. "Between Nationalisms: Hawaii's Local Nation and Its Troubled Racial Paradise." *Hitting Critical Mass: A Journal of Asian American Cultural Criticism* 1.2 (1994): 23–57.
Gima, Charlene. "Writing the Pacific: Imagining Communities of Difference in the Fiction of Jessica Hagedorn, Keri Hulme, Rodney Morales, and Gary Pak." Ph.D. diss., Cornell University, 1997.
Kwon, Brenda Lee. *Beyond Ke'eaumoku: Koreans, Nationalism, and Local Culture in Hawai'i.* New York: Garland, 1999.
———. "Gary Pak." Interview. In *Words Matter: Conversations with Asian American Writers*. King-Kok Cheung, ed. Honolulu: University of Hawaii Press, 2000, 303–19.
McPherson, Michael. Rev. of *The Watcher of Waipuna and Other Stories*, by Gary Pak. *Manoa: A Pacific Journal of International Writing* 6.1 (1994): 181–83.

Muromoto, Wayne. "Gary Pak and *The Watcher of Waipuna*: Recording an Oral Tradition." Rev. of *The Watcher of Waipuna and Other Stories*. *Hawaii Herald* [Honolulu] (May 21, 1993): A10–11.

Takami, David. "Spinning a World of Colliding Cultures, Places." Rev. of *The Watcher of Waipuna and Other Stories*. *International Examiner Literary Supplement* [Seattle] (April 7, 1993): 6.

Young, Morris. Rev. of *The Watcher of Waipuna and Other Stories*. *Amerasia Journal* 20.3 (1994): 108–10.

TY PAK
(1938–   )

Seiwoong Oh

Seiwoong Oh

◆ BIOGRAPHY

Born in Korea in 1938, Ty Pak (Tae Young Pak) grew up witnessing two of the most momentous events in Korea's modern history: the liberation of the country in 1945 from Japan and the Korean War between 1950 and 1953. The latter, in particular, has had a profound impact on his psyche and subsequently on his literary landscape, mainly because his father died during the war.

Upon graduation from Seoul National University with a degree in law in 1960, Pak worked for five years as a reporter for *The Korean Republic* and later *The Korea Times*. In 1965, he came to the United States to study at Bowling Green State University and received his Ph.D. degree in English in 1969. From 1970 to 1987, he taught at the University of Hawaii.

His debut book was *Guilt Payment*, a collection of short stories, published by Bamboo Ridge Press in 1983. Years later, he left Hawaii to try a hand at business in Los Angeles. After moving to New York, he published two more books in 1999: *Moonbay*, another short story collection, and *Cry, Korea, Cry*, his first novel about the odyssey of a mixed-blood Korean War orphan.

◆ MAJOR WORKS AND THEMES

Pak's stories help contextualize the lives of Korean Americans in Hawaii and elsewhere. In doing so, Pak also attempts to subvert the Korean American stereotypes by portraying them as surgeons, generals, professors, and pastors who are capable of reflection as they struggle to reconcile themselves with their past failures and bitter memories.

His thirteen short stories collected in *Guilt Payment* share not only similar characters but also closely related thematic threads. With mostly Korean male immigrants in Hawaii as protagonists, Pak explores the traumatic impact of their Korean past on their American lives. In the title story, for example, an English professor at the University of Hawaii recalls his moral failure in the past: when North Korean soldiers were on a killing spree in Seoul, he abandoned his wife and their infant baby during a bombardment, only to find later that his wife was dead. This sense of guilt forces him to accept his teenage daughter's unreasonable demands.

In "Possession Sickness," another single father in Hawaii with a young daughter is haunted by his past in Korea. When his wife turned a Shaman, he ran away to Honolulu with their daughter. Now that his former wife is in Honolulu on a TV show, yelling curses at him from the screen, he believes that his daughter's sickness is caused by the former wife's curse. Several other stories run in a similar vein. "Steady Hands" features a surgeon who hears about the plight of his former lover during the Vietnam War, a woman who saved his life and now rears their child alone. "Nostalgia" reveals the reason behind the suicide of a retired Korean general in Honolulu, who during the Korean War killed his epileptic wife while trying to keep her quiet in a hideout, and who killed another woman for not acceding to his sexual advances. An English professor in "A Second Chance" receives a visit from his former fiancée, only to remember his affair with her brother's fiancée while they lived in Korea. "The Water Tower" introduces another love triangle. When a friend working on a building project in Saudi Arabia commits suicide, John Bay, an architectural engineer in Honolulu, receives a phone call from his friend's wife asking him to wrap up her husband's business in Saudi Arabia. He agrees to go, but only after she asks him to do it for "our kid's sake," revealing him to be the biological father of her son.

While the stories above share a similar narrative pattern—a Korean immigrant male being haunted by his past—other stories in the collection aim to reveal the inner lives of Korean immigrants in Hawaii. In "A Fire," a Korean orphan adopted by an American couple goes back to Korea to find his roots. He is, however, conned by a woman who uses a fake pregnancy to marry him. After coming to Hawaii, she steals his belongings and runs away in his absence. "A Regeneration" describes a Korean reporter who falls in love with a married woman out of sympathy. "Exile" depicts the odyssey of an ex–political activist who escapes from Korea when his life is threatened by his own party. "The Grateful Korean" deals with the complicated past life of a fisherman in Honolulu; when his wife realizes she and her idiot son might stand in the way of his emigration to America, she kills her son and herself so as to allow him to move on.

The remaining three stories are not necessarily about residents of Hawaii, but they also explore male psychology under pressure in times of war. "The

St. Peter in Seoul" features a protagonist who is manipulated by a woman to rescue her pastor-father. Upon the pastor's death, he becomes the successor, yet feels guilty about preaching with no faith of his own. Both "Identity" and "Wartime" investigate the camaraderie among men and their struggle with their conscience during wartime.

Four of the seven stories in *Moonbay* revisit the themes in *Guilt Payment* and use similar characters; however, irony pervades the tone of each story, and the settings are now diversified to include, besides the Korean and Vietnam Wars, such historical landmarks in Korean American history as the Soviet attack on the Korean Airlines plane and the Los Angeles riots. "The Tiger Cub," for instance, introduces a Korean War orphan who has become a Stanford professor advocating the rights of adopted children from Korea. "A Debt" depicts a Korean lieutenant in Vietnam who feels guilty when he is saved by a racist white soldier. In "Contrition," an English professor experiences an extreme sense of guilt when his estranged wife, who left him after catching him cheating with a graduate teaching assistant, is killed in the Korean Airlines plane shot down by the former Soviet Union. Loosely based on a historical event during the L.A. riots, "The Court Interpreter" is about a retired university professor who is asked to work as a court interpreter for a Korean-speaking woman on trial for killing a black shoplifter. When she gets off with a light sentence, a riot breaks out, and he feels guilty and partly responsible for causing the riot by competently and eloquently interpreting for the woman.

The last three stories in *Moonbay* treat different themes. In the manner of Conrad's "Secret Sharer," Pak deals with the question of identity in the title story about a boat captain whose mistaken identity leads him to death. "The Foe" describes an encounter between enemies during the Vietnam War. The last story in the collection, "The Gardener," reveals the profound changes in human relations brought by the Korean War and immigration. After his pregnant girlfriend is forced into a marriage with the son of a rich family, a young man marries a pregnant semi-autistic woman abandoned by the biological father of her soon-to-be-born baby. The baby grows up to marry a G.I., and invites her legal father to live with her in the United States; when he finds out his biological son is orphaned, the father wants to find a way to bring him to the United States.

◆ **CRITICAL RECEPTION**

Sustained criticism on Pak has been scarce. When *Guilt Payment* was first published, the volume included introductory remarks by James Harstad, who praised Pak's "vigorous prose" and realistic rendering of the Korean War and its consequences via the personal experiences of victims. Harstad also valued the stories for providing "clues" to the identity of second-generation Korean Americans (2–3).

Presumably because Pak was considered not a "Korean American" but an "immigrant" writer in the early phase of Korean American literary studies, he had been excluded from discussions of Korean American literature. In recent years, however, after the term "Korean American" began to gain a broader definition, his *Guilt Payment* has been receiving some attention. In 1997, for example, Brenda Lee Kwon completed a doctoral dissertation on Korean American authors in Hawaii, including Ty Pak, Margaret Pai, and Gary Pak. Kwon examines these authors to illustrate the "complex relationship between 'American,' 'Local,' and 'Korean,' and 'Korean-American' identifications" and to demonstrate the "diasporic and transnational nature" of Korean American identity in Hawaii.

Also in 1997, Elaine Kim introduces Pak's first book in her chapter on "Korean American Literature" and criticizes it for being male-centered and for often describing female characters as "seductive objects of male desire." Though action-packed and vividly described, the stories, according to Kim, display "various manifestations of misogyny" (165).

In 1999, when Pak's second collection of short stories was published, *Publishers Weekly* praised the "coolly unruffled prose" that befits the ironies confronted by the Korean American characters as they wrestle with their collective and individual history and memory in a new land (59). In a 2001 article on "The Court Interpreter," King-Kok Cheung finds Pak's representation of the ethnic characters problematic. According to Cheung, Pak subscribes to the divisive stereotyped images of Asians and blacks in the story: the black girl is described as an obese teenaged mother weighing 250 pounds, and the court interpreter as a crass materialist "obsessed with the goal to get rich quick" (189).

In a book published in 2001 in Korea, Sunmo Yoo credits Pak for competently crafting stories about the identity questions in the lives of Korean Americans. He also points out how no character, regardless of success as an immigrant, is immune from the traumatizing impact of the past (127). In an engaging book—probably the most extensive treatment of Ty Pak to date—Kirsten Twelbeck argues that *Guilt Payment* is largely a number of variations on the same theme of trauma. After noting the similar framework of the stories and Pak's pervasive use of irony, Twelbeck further argues that the central figures in Pak's stories—the prostitute, the rape victim, the "racially mixed child"—are allegories of the wounded nation and that Pak uses these to criticize Korean society and Korean Americans who live in denial of their ancestral nation's misogynist past.

◆ BIBLIOGRAPHY

Works by Ty Pak

Short Story Collections

Guilt Payment. Honolulu: Bamboo Ridge Press, 1983.
Moonbay. New York: Woodhouse, 1999.

Novel

Cry, Korea, Cry. New York: Woodhouse, 1999.

Studies of Ty Pak

Cheung, King-Kok. "Fictional Re-presentation of the Los Angeles Riots: 'The Court Interpreter' by Ty Pak." *Journal of American Studies* (Seoul) 33.2 (Winter 2001): 183–200.

Harstad, James. "Introduction." In *Guilt Payment*, by Ty Pak. Honolulu: Bamboo Ridge Press, 1983, 1–3.

Kim, Elaine H. "Korean American Literature." In *An Interethnic Companion to Asian American Literature*. King-Kok Cheung, ed. Cambridge: Cambridge University Press, 1997, 156–91.

Kwon, Brenda Lee. "Beyond Keeamoku: Koreans, Nationalism, and Local Culture in Hawai'i." Ph.D. diss., University of California, Los Angeles, 1997. *DAI* A 58/06 (1997): 2210.

Rev. of *Moonbay: Short Stories*. *Publishers Weekly* 246.10 (May 17, 1999): 59.

Twelbeck, Kirsten. *No Korean Is Whole—Wherever He or She May Be: Erfindungen von Korean America seit 1965*. Berlin: Peter Lang, 2002.

Yoo, Sunmo. *Understanding US Minority Literatures: Korean American Literature* (title translation mine). Seoul, Korea: Shina-sa, 2001.

NAHID RACHLIN
(1947–   )

Robert D. Sturr

♦ **BIOGRAPHY**

Nahid Rachlin was born in Abadan, Iran. Her mother had previously given birth seven times (with five surviving children), and so she readily agreed to allow her childless sister to have her new baby. Thus, from six months to nine years old, Rachlin lived with her aunt in Teheran in the ancient and decayed neighborhood of Ghanat Abad. This enclave of traditionalism is typically the location of Rachlin's stories set in Iran.

Rachlin has described her aunt as a "staunchly religious Muslim" who was nevertheless "lenient with me" ("A Bitter Homecoming" 76). Her more secular father, a lawyer, feared that Rachlin would, according to custom, be married while still a child. Accordingly, he kidnapped her when she was nine and took her to the family's home in the southwestern city of Ahvaz. This move was deeply traumatic because Rachlin had viewed her aunt as a mother and was made to feel unwelcome by her biological mother and siblings (with the exception of one sister). The sense of disruption and alienation stemming from this period appears repeatedly in Rachlin's fiction. She particularly dramatizes the struggles of women who must contend against callous and even abusive fathers and husbands who have ultimate control over their lives.

Rachlin found inspiration in American movies during her teenage years. As she has described it, the roles for women in these films led her "to realize that there were other possibilities in life besides getting married . . . having children, and settling for passive domesticity." To escape that fate, she excelled academically and in 1964 was allowed to attend Lindenwood College in Missouri. However, its curricular emphasis on domesticity and enforcement of Christian worship was frustrating, and Rachlin has written that its many rules were as "limiting as those I chafed against in Ahvaz" ("Five Stories" 51, 52).

Upon graduating, Rachlin found some measure of freedom in New York where she settled in Greenwich Village. She worked, took graduate courses, and began to write. She married Howard Rachlin, a psychology professor, and became a naturalized U.S. citizen in 1969. Rachlin completed her first novel, *Foreigner*, in 1978 and also began to teach creative writing. Her second novel, *Married to a Stranger* (1983), was followed by *Veils* (1992), a collection of new and previously published short stories. Her most recent novel is *The Heart's Desire* (1995), and Rachlin's short stories have continued to appear in leading journals and magazines.

◆ MAJOR WORKS AND THEMES

Rachlin's three novels, which are primarily set in Iran, all focus on the struggle of a female protagonist to escape a repressive cultural system that empowers men, especially through marriage and family, while leaving women with few opportunities to live independent and fulfilling lives. Inevitably, Rachlin's protagonists must define themselves separately from the influence of male authority figures, and these transformations typically require their removal from family settings and, ultimately, Iran itself. The themes of repression, alienation, removal, and regret that appear in the novels are also evident in Rachlin's short stories. The first six pieces in *Veils* take place in Iran, and are set in the Ghanat Abad neighborhood, while the last four stories are located in the United States.

Among the earlier stories, the overt oppressiveness of political and religious institutions, as well as the terrible human cost of the Iran-Iraq war, is dramatized through the sufferings of frustrated yet ultimately submissive mothers. Fatemeh, the eponymous protagonist of one story, tries desperately to gain an exemption for her son from military service during war. While dealing with uncaring political and religious officials, she also learns the location of her lost daughter, who had been taken by her abusive ex-husband many years before. The status of her son, as well as the outcome of her fragile reunion with her daughter, is left open-ended at the story's close. Farogh, whose only son is about to be inducted into the army in "Departures," is panic-stricken as she plans his farewell luncheon. "War," to her, "was like a wild, blood-thirsty animal, merciless in its killing," and she cannot help but notice the black flags that indicate mourning hung on so many of her neighbors' doors. While her husband casually says that their son is "lucky to be given the chance to fight," Farogh is constrained from expressing her true feelings about the supposed glories of martyrdom. While this surface drama unfolds, Farogh also has a reunion with Karim, a former suitor who has become a professor in the United States. His coldness and formality only exacerbates her sense of frustration, entrapment and emptiness. Finally, in "The Son," Parvin is powerless to stop her son from becoming involved in dissident activities. The story charts her unsuccessful attempts to draw him back into proper religious thinking, and it ends as he is taken away by the police. During one exchange with her son, Parvin feels "as though a window to his mind had opened suddenly, revealing to her a storm raging" (41). All three of these earnest mothers struggle to protect their sons and to maintain the status quo even as they cannot help but understand the impossibility of holding back both the social and psychological turmoil of the times.

Other stories in the collection are not so directly focused on political events. In "A Poet's Visit," two teenage girls vie for the attention of a famous author. They both had agreed to "fight hard not to become typical wives and mothers, not to marry men selected for them by their families" (71). The visiting poet represents the academic and artistic world that is, in their eyes, a pathway to escape. However, as a consequence of their nervous attempts at flirtation, as well as the poet's ambiguous sexual suggestions, jealousy comes between them. They are united in their desire to avoid dreary domestic lives, but their fantasies of romance, love and freedom—all located in the contested figure of the poet—cannot be shared.

The stories set in the United States are also primarily psychological, with only oblique references to events in Iran. They all feature deeply conflicted Iranian immigrants who feel the need to wear cheerful masks around American spouses, friends, and coworkers while experiencing guilt and a painful lack of true communication. To some extent, they find the same limitations in the United States that they thought they had left behind in Iran. For example, Samira, the protagonist of "Dark Gravity," fears a second pregnancy even though her American husband, Steve, is thrilled. She recalls her mother's bitterness and her father's sullenness because they had too many children and fears the same situation even though she is supposedly living in a place where women are said to have more choices than in Iran. Similarly, Mohtaram, the older protagonist of "The Calling," becomes disenchanted with living in the United States when her devout sister visits from Iran. She is disconnected from her Americanized adult children and feels guilty about the compromises she has made. Capturing these internal conflicts succinctly, Rachlin writes that Mohtaram "wished she could break out of the prison of this new self, and be reborn again into the old one" (108). She eventually decides to return to Iran because, as her sister dubiously insists, it is at least a place of moral stability.

Displacement and disorientation are combined with tentative feelings of love and connection in the closing stories of *Veils*. "Forces of Attraction" is told from the perspective of an American woman who earnestly wishes to penetrate the loneliness and depression of her new Iranian boyfriend. He is pulled by emotional forces from Iran that, at least temporarily, outweigh the sweetness of a new romance. In "Dreamers," Paula is the American mother of a college-aged Iranian American son, who must contend with depression stemming from his parents' divorce and his father's return to Iran. He is flunking out of college and in their visit together one weekend, he finally speaks honestly about his feelings. Abbas decides that he will, one day, visit his father in Iran—that he will, one day, come to terms with both his Iranian and American identities. The story ends appropriately as Paula, while grading papers, begins to feel that "[t]here was a feverish, excited awareness in the air that anything was possible" (131).

◆ CRITICAL RECEPTION

Nahid Rachlin is primarily known as a novelist, and has been praised for a minimalist style that heightens the drama and psychological tension of her narratives. *Foreigner* was lauded by Anne Tyler when it first appeared for providing "a rare intimate look" at Iranian society on all levels, and V. S. Naipaul has claimed that it was the first novel written in English by an Iranian. Accordingly, it has been scrutinized and debated for its accuracy in portraying Iranian life and culture. Rachlin's later novels have received generally positive reviews, but less attention from scholars.

Veils garnered only a few brief reviews in American periodicals when it appeared and has yet to receive significant scholarly attention. The notices generally take up the question of authenticity and praise Rachlin for exposing American readers to the complex cultural dilemmas faced by her female protagonists. According to the *New York Times* review, "[b]y portraying families divided against themselves, [Rachlin] effectively illustrates a culture in conflict" (Graeber 18). Some reviewers criticize Rachlin's spare prose style, claiming that certain characters and situations are undeveloped. However, other reviews take note of Rachlin's achievement in bringing the variety and depth of Ghanat Abad and the Iranian immigrant community to life.

◆ BIBLIOGRAPHY

Works by Nahid Rachlin

Uncollected Stories

"Far Away Love." *Virginia Quarterly Review* 76.3 (Summer 2000): 403–15.
"Dangers." *Prairie Schooner* 74.3 (Fall 2000): 141–50.

Short Story Collection

Veils: Short Stories. San Francisco: City Lights, 1992.

Novels

Foreigner. New York: W. W. Norton, 1978.
Married to a Stranger. San Francisco: City Lights, 1983.
The Heart's Desire: A Novel. San Francisco: City Lights, 1995.

Essays

"Five Stories." *Natural History* (March 1998): 50–56.
"A Bitter Homecoming." *New York Times Magazine* (April 14, 2002): 76.

Studies of Nahid Rachlin

Filbin, Thomas. "The Expatriate Memory: Four Iranian Writers in America." *The Literary Review* 40.1 (Fall 1996): 172–77.

Graeber, Laurel. Rev. of *Veils. New York Times Book Review* (November 29, 1992): 18.

Helou, Paul. "Ancient Tehran Area Forms Setting for Stony Brook Author." *New York Times* (October 3, 1993): C10.

Jaleshgari, Ramin P. "The Liberation of Language." *Poets & Writers* 26.5 (September–October 1998): 56–59.

Naipaul, V. S. *Among the Believers.* New York: Alfred A. Knopf, 1982, 13–15.

Rev. of *Veils. Publishers Weekly* (April 20, 1992): 49.

Sharma, Maya M. "Nahid Rachlin." In *Asian American Novelists: A Bio-Bibliographical Critical Sourcebook.* Emmanuel S. Nelson, ed. Westport, CT: Greenwood Press, 2000, 296–301.

Solomon, Charles. Rev. of *Veils. Los Angeles Times Book Review* (May 10, 1992): 18.

Tyler, Anne. Rev. of *Foreigner. New York Times Book Review* (February 18, 1979): 35.

Wright, Carolyne. Rev. of *Veils. Harvard Review* 2.1 (Spring 1993): 1–2.

RAJA RAO

(1908–   )

Chandrima Chakraborty

◆ BIOGRAPHY

Raja Rao was born in Hassan, Karnataka, in India, into a well-known Brahmin family in 1908. He went to Montpellier University, France, for his postgraduate education. Rao began his literary career writing for the periodical *Jaya Karnataka* in Kannada, his native tongue. His first short stories were published in French and later translated into English. Stories written in various periodicals were published in *The Cow of the Barricades and Other Stories* in 1947. Select stories from this anthology along with three pieces published in periodicals were later anthologized as *The Policeman and the Rose*. His reputation rests primarily as a writer of novels.

Rao received the Sahitya Akademi Award (1964) and the prestigious *Padma Bhusan* (Order of Lotus, 1969) from the Government of India. He is the recipient of the Neustadt International Prize for Literature (1988). He settled in the United States in 1965 and retired as Professor Emeritus of Philosophy from the University of Texas in Austin in 1980. He lives in Texas.

◆ MAJOR WORKS AND THEMES

Raja Rao's works are deeply rooted in Brahmanism and Hinduism. Most of the stories in *The Cow of the Barricades* and *The Policeman and the Rose* are set in rural South India, in the 1930s, during Mahatma Gandhi's Quit India Movement. Many of them bear testimony to Rao's appreciation and deep regard for Gandhian teachings and illustrate the interminable link between the legendary and the historical-political in the life of the Indian villages.

In "Narsiga" the historical figure of Gandhi is merged with legendary/

mythical heroes of the Hindu tradition. The illiterate orphan, Narsiga, after hearing about Gandhi, feels that the "Mahatma is an incarnation of God" (*Cow* 105). In the boy's imagination the political icon becomes indistinguishable from the hero of the Indian epic, *Ramayana*. In "The Cow of the Barricades" the "holy" cow is named Gauri after the mother Goddess. Elements of mysticism, incarnation of gods, and Gandhi's Swadeshi campaign surround this traditional sacred animal of the Hindus. Significantly, the story ends with the sacred cow becoming a martyr in the cause of the modern Indian freedom struggle by dying of a bullet fired by a British officer.

Rao's short stories, described by Naik as "vignettes of Indian village life" (392), portray the sexual and economic exploitation of the marginalized—lower caste, women, and the poor. In "The Little Gram Shop" Motilal's grandfather squanders his wealth among his ten concubines and Chota, Motilal's son, has a mistress. Chota kicks his pregnant wife, Rati, in the stomach, which results in a miscarriage. Rati and her mother-in-law are both subjected to routine physical abuse by their respective husbands. Condensing the lives of over three generations of a family in one story superbly highlights the continuing oppression of the women within the familial sphere. Gendered oppression under the guise of tradition is vividly portrayed in "Javni" and "Akkayya." Javni and Akkayya are widows—the former belongs to a rich, reputable Brahmin family and the latter is a low-caste, poor Hindu. However, their oppression and discrimination transcends class. Javni is ill-treated by her in-laws and verbally abused every day by her sister-in-law. Akkayya, a child-widow, spends her entire adult life taking care of the children of her brothers only to have these same individuals dismiss the news of her death as "a nuisance."

The child narrator's insistent questioning to grasp the meaning of the term "widow" in "Akkayya" encapsulates the life of a rural Indian widow in the 1930s. He notes Akkayya's shaven head, her "same dull sari," the absence of "bangles" and "holy vermilion" (*Policeman* 44). Akkayya was married at the age of eight or nine to a man whose "son already had three children of his own" (47). Soon after her marriage the husband died. The pathos of the story lies in the child-wife/widow's indifference to this momentous event: "Akkayya did not understand anything of what happened and she perfectly enjoyed the doll-show" (*Policeman* 47).

Lack of education and economic freedom coupled with casteist and gendered upbringing make the women of "The Little Gram Shop" and "Akkayya" unable to interrogate/resist the feudal societal structures. Rati and Akkayya are both superstitious and their casteist upbringing is entrenched in them. The plague-stricken Rati prefers death because in the hospital "[t]hey . . . did a million unholy things" (*Policeman* 80), and Akkayya refuses medicines prepared by "irreligious, low-born" doctors (*Policeman* 50). For the female characters in Rao's stories, in spite of the death of a husband or a child, "everything went on in the household as usual" (*Policeman* 78). But the emerging nationalist ideologies and changing male psyche are evident in "In Khandesh," as the young men of the village voice their subversive "city ideas" about resistance and nationalism to the consternation of the elders, and in "Javni," where the narrator questions the rigid casteist customs his sister upholds, which do not allow her to eat with Javni because "eating with a woman of lower caste is irreligious" (*Policeman* 88).

Rao's preoccupation with his Brahmanic heritage along with his search for a spiritual mentor (Guru) in his later life resulted in experiments at evolving a diction, which combined native Sanskritic features with English. "The Policeman and the Rose" comprises layers of religion, ritual, metaphysics, myth, legend, folklore and history. Critics believe that the difficulty in understanding this story arises from Rao's metaphysical quest along with the private appropriation of cultural symbols from European and Indian traditions.

As a first-generation Indian English writer faced with the challenge of using "a language that is not one's own to convey the spirit that is one's own" ("Foreword," *Kanthapura* vii), Rao Indianizes the English language and establishes it as a model. He expresses an Indian rural sensibility through his similes, metaphors, and abundant use of nature imagery to describe characters and landscape. For instance, in the extreme heat in "In Khandesh" Dattopant is "[b]lazing like a frying-pan" (*Policeman* 23) and the land is "[b]lack and grey as the buffalo, and twisted like an endless line of loamy pythons" (*Policeman* 16). Rangappa refuses brides "beautiful as new-opened guavas, and others tender as April mangoes" ("The Story of Kankapala" *Policeman* 2), while the old widow Akkayya has a face "wrinkled like a dry mango" ("Akkayya," *Policeman* 42). He literally translates vernacular idioms and phrases into English. Akkayya did all the cleaning and the sweeping, "as though she was born with a vessel at her waist and a broom in her hand" (*Policeman* 48), but her stepson said mean things about her because "[w]hen people hate others they always mix milk and salt" (49). Sita scolding Javni for re-telling the story of a suicide in the village says, "Always the same *Ramayana*" ("Javni," *Policeman* 85).

The rural habit of prefixing an adjective to a proper name based on status, occupation, habit, and so on is illustrated in such names as "Eight-verandahed-house Chowdayya," "Cardamom-field Venkatesha," "Big House Subbayya" ("The Story of Kanakapala"), "red-men's government" ("The Cow of the Barricades"), and "concubine Chowdy," "barber Venka" ("Javni"). The stories replace calendrical time with incidents of significance in the life of the rural community or the individual narrator. For instance, Javni identifies the pipal tree that Ramu rode by as the one "where-the fisherman-Kodi-hanged-himself-the-other-day" (*Policeman* 85), and the narrator in "The Story of Kanakapala" says that Seetharamu's wife died "when our little Ramu was going through his initiation ceremony" (*Policeman* 7).

In some of the stories Rao infuses "[t]he tempo of Indian life" into the English language ("Foreword," *Kanthapura* vii) by replicating the folkloric form of story-telling, which simulates the inflections and rhythms of Indian oral narrative. The introduction of "The Story of Kanakapala," which describes the behavior of serpents, has one sentence that is twenty-four lines on the printed page and ends with the traditional Hindu style benediction: "May you live a thousand years!" (*Policeman* 2). The narrator is an old, gossipy grandmother with a rambling, distorted syntactical style whose repetitions, turns of phrase, and consistent digressions successfully evoke the spirit of India's traditional folk narrative, the *Puranas*. She tells the local legend to the male listener/narrator interspersed with her opinions: "Sata . . . was greedy, malicious, and clever as a jackal" (*Policeman* 7); sympathies: "poor Seetharamu!" (*Policeman* 11); material concerns: "Oh, when our grandfathers were alive, . . . We bought a khanda of rice for half a rupee" (*Policeman* 9); and philosophizings: "who can save us from karma?" (*Policeman* 6).

The religious and metaphysical symbols unmistakable in Rao's short stories and his experiments with style and diction were developed in depth in his later writings. His successful experimentation to infuse his stories with "a near native sound and structure" ("Preface," *The Policeman and the Rose* xv) illustrates his exemplary contribution to Indo-English literature.

◆ CRITICAL RECEPTION

Critical analyses of Raja Rao's novels are many, but critical work on his short stories is sparse. Narasimhaiah noted in 1978 that "his short stories have yet to receive critical attention" ("Afterword" 127), and this comment holds ground even today. Mukherji critiques Rao's stories as "merely vehicles" for the manipulation of symbols (68). Narasimhaiah finds faults with some of the stories for their "failure to resist the cliché, an easy surrender to the sentimental and the abstract" (134), and for letting into some of the new stories in *The Policeman and the Rose* "much unassimilated material" (137). While Narasimhaiah locates the "popular appeal" of the stories in *The Cow of the Barricades* in their "social preoccupations" (128), Naik finds them significant in that "there is much in this picture that is more or less true, even today" (394). Describing Rao as "a master of descriptive prose" (395), Naik regrets that Rao has written so few short stories.

Numerous critics have applauded Rao's innovative literary style and diction. Parthasarathy commends Rao as an "innovative novelist" (157) "unique in his attempt not only to nativize but also to Sanskritize the English language" (159). Gemmill views Rao's "early experiments with narrative" as an exploration of "a very communication device which insures for a culture a vision of the sacred undivorced from everyday life" ("Elements" 161).

◆ BIBLIOGRAPHY

Works by Raja Rao

Short Story Collections

The Cow of the Barricades and Other Stories. Champak Library, Madras: Oxford University Press, 1947.
The Policeman and the Rose. Delhi: Oxford University Press, 1978.

Novels

The Serpent and the Rose. London: John Murray, 1960.
Kanthapura. New York: New Directions, 1963.
The Cat and Shakespeare; a Tale of India. New York: Macmillan, 1965.
Comrade Kirillov. New Delhi: Orient, 1976.
The Chessmaster and His Moves. New Delhi: Vision Books, 1988.
On the Ganga Ghat. New Delhi: Vision Books, 1989.

Edited Books

With Iqbal Singh. *Changing India: An Anthology*. London: G. Allen & Unwin Ltd., 1939.
With Iqbal Singh. *Wither India*. Bombay: Padma, 1948.
With K. Natwar Singh, Narayana Menon, Ahmed Ali, Mulk Raj Anand, and Santha Rama Rau. *"Recollections of E. M. Forster." E. M. Forster: A Tribute with Selections from His Writings on India*. New York: Harcourt Brace & World, 1964, 15–32.

Essays

"The Writer and the Word." *The Literary-Criterion* 7.1 (1965): 76–78.
"On Translating from Sanskrit." Paper delivered at Conference on Literary Translation, New York City, May 1970, under Auspices of PEN American Center. In *The World of Translation*. Gregory Rabassa and Lewis Galantiere, eds. New York: PEN American Center, 1987, 281–89.
"The Climate of Indian Literature Today." *The Literary-Criterion* 10.2 (1972): 1–7.
"The Caste of English." In *Awakened Conscience: Studies in Commonwealth Literature*. C. D. Narasimhaiah, ed. New Delhi: Sterling, 1978, 420–22.
"Autobiography: Entering the Literary World." *The Journal of Commonwealth Literature* 13.3 (1979): 28–32.
"The Cave and the Conch." In *The Eye of the Beholder: Indian Writing in English*. Maggie Butcher, ed. London: Commonwealth Institute, 1983. 44–45.
"The Meaning of India." In *New Perspectives in Indian Literature in English: Essays in Honour of Professor M. K. Naik*. C. R. Yaravintelimath, G. S. Gupta Balarama, C. V. Venugopal, and Amritjit Singh, eds. New Delhi: Sterling, 1995, 1–5.

Studies of Raja Rao

Agnihotri, G. N. *Indian Life and Problems in the Novels of Mulk Raj Anand, Raja Rao and R. K. Narayan*. Meerut: Shalabh Prakashan, 1993, 61–82.

Bhattacharya, P. C. *Indo-Anglian Literature and the Works of Raja Rao*. Delhi: Atma Ram, 1983.

Dayal, P. *Raja Rao: A Study of His Works*. New Delhi: Atlantic Publishers, 1991.

Dey, Esha. *The Novels of Raja Rao: The Theme of Quest*. New Delhi: Prestige, 1992.

Gemmill, Janet P. "Raja Rao: Three Tales of Independence." *World Literature Written in English* 15 (1976): 135–41.

———. "Raja Rao's *The Cow of the Barricades*: Two Stories." *Journal of South Asian Literature* 13.1–4 (1977–1978): 23–30.

———. "Elements of the Folktale in Raja Rao's *Cow of the Barricades*." *World Literature Written in English* 20.1 (Spring 1981): 149–61.

Mukherji, Meenakshi. "Raja Rao's Shorter Fiction." *Indian Literature* 10.3 (1967): 66–76.

Naik, M. K. *"The Cow of the Barricades and Other Stories*: Raja Rao as a Short Story Writer." *Books Abroad* 40 (1966): 392–96.

———. *Raja Rao*. New York: Twayne, 1972.

Narasimhaiah, C. D. *Raja Rao*. New Delhi: Arnold-Heinemann, 1973.

———. "Raja Rao: The Short Stories, An Afterword." In *The Policeman and the Rose*. Delhi: Oxford University Press, 1978, 127–38.

Niranjan, Shiva. *Raja Rao: Novelist as Sadhana*. Gaziabad, India: Vimal, 1985.

Parthasarathy, R. "Tradition and Creativity: Stylistic Innovations in Raja Rao." In *Discourse across Cultures: Strategies in World Englishes*. Larry E. Smith, ed. Englewood Cliffs, NJ: Prentice-Hall, 1987. 157–65.

"Raja Rao: Our 1988 Neustadt Prize Laureate." *World Literature Today* 62.4 (Autumn 1988). [Journal dedicated to Rao.]

Rao, K. R. *The Fiction of Raja Rao*. Aurangabad, India: Parimal, 1980.

Sharma, K. K., ed. *Perspectives on Raja Rao: An Anthology of Critical Essays*. Gaziabad, India: Vimal, 1980.

Sharrad, Paul. *Raja Rao and Cultural Tradition*. New Delhi: Sterling, 1988.

Srivastava, Narsingh. *The Mind and Art of Raja Rao*. Bareilly: Prakash Book Depot, 1980.

PATSY SUMIE SAIKI
(1915–   )

Amy W. S. Lee

◆ **BIOGRAPHY**

Patsy Sumie Saiki was born on March 12, 1915, the daughter of immigrants
from Hiroshima, Japan. Her parents, Shukichi and Chise Okada Kawatachi,
who had seven children, were among the first wave of Japanese workers con-
tracted to work in Hawaiian sugar plantations. In the 1880s, due to the lack
of laborers, King Kalakaua of Hawaii signed a treaty with Emperor Meiji of
Japan to allow workers to go to Hawaii and work on the plantations starting
from 1885. After they had completed a contract, these workers were free to
choose whether or not to stay. Saiki's parents completed their three-year contracts on a plantation, saved enough money and purchased a fifty-acre home-
stead in Ahualoa, Honokaa, on the Big Island.

When Saiki was fifteen, she went to McKinley High School on Oahu. Her
mother died of cancer before she was graduated, but her legacy of words and
compassion inspired Saiki to write. She entered the University of Hawaii, and
in 1952, during her sophomore year, she won the Charles Eugene Banks
Award for short story writing. She graduated with honors from the University
of Hawaii, and then continued to pursue a doctorate at Teachers College,
Columbia University, specializing in curriculum design. Saiki has taught at
the local university and served as an administrator in Hawaii's public school
system for many years.

Saiki's work has won her two Wall Street Journal fellowship prizes, and
the 1996 Japanese Imperial Order of the Precious Crown, a recognition of her
contribution to enhance cultural understanding between Japan and America.
To pass on the catalysis she received when she won the Charles Eugene Banks
Award, Saiki made an endowment to the Creative Writing Program of the

University of Hawaii, to offer a prize for the best short story written by a student in that university every year. The best short story should carry on the mission of reflecting Hawaii's history, culture, or traditions.

◆ MAJOR WORKS AND THEMES

Patsy Sumie Saiki has devoted her work to recording the experiences of first- and second-generation immigrants to Hawaii, among whom were her parents. Through the documentation and re-telling of these individual stories of the immigrants, Saiki provides a vivid picture of the dreams and fears, joy, and hardship this group shared; the vast range of characters appearing in the stories, each with his or her own life and thoughts, makes the story collections insightful explorations of humanity. Of particular interest in her stories is how the land of Hawaii becomes a focal point for the acting out of cultural forces from Japan, America, and Hawaii.

Sachie, A Daughter of Hawaii is her first collection of short narratives. It is followed by *Ganbare! An Example of Japanese Spirit* and, later, *Japanese Women in Hawaii: The First 100 Years*, and *Early Japanese Immigrants in Hawaii*. Although there are no particular unifying themes in each collection, the focus has always been the individual experiences of these early immigrants and how this spirit of the pioneers has affected later generations who were born in this culturally mixed land. Through the depiction of cultural differences between generations, the stories become a private documentation of cultural interaction.

Cultural mixing and changes from one's orientation has been a consistent theme found in Saiki's stories, as can be glimpsed from the title chosen for each collection. This has much to do with her own cultural background. In *Japanese Women in Hawaii: The First 100 Years*, Saiki refers to her own mixed background. "I'm grateful I was able to live in a marvelously rich community and era. We were money-poor but culture-rich. We had a heritage of three cultures—American, Japanese and Hawaiian, plus a sprinkling of others—to serve as a background from which to grow" (158).

True to the title, *Japanese Women in Hawaii* is a collection of stories about named and unnamed women who helped to make Hawaii what it is today. Tracing the history of Japanese women who set foot in Hawaii, the collection is structured to show the various and changing roles Japanese women have played in the 100-year history drawn by the narratives. As stated in the introduction to the collection, the harsh lives borne by these pioneer Japanese women did not stop them from staying in Hawaii after their contracts ended because they had a vision of "what could be" (1) their life. The first women to arrive in Hawaii brought with them the dream and the preparation to lead a better life and create a better future for their children.

The chapter headings give a taste of the interesting variety of women included in the narratives: the drifters, those working for the Christian church and Buddhist temples, the fighters, teachers, artists, up to the contemporary generation who have become administrators and important countrymen. Personalities recorded range from notables such as Kosone, the geisha "with skin like fine porcelain and hands that moved like a gentle breeze among white birch or bamboo forest in spring" (7), who could have been one of the first groups of Japanese workers reaching Hawaii, to thousands of unnamed women who came to Hawaii with their husbands to work on the plantations. Named or unnamed, these early Japanese settlers have founded a tradition with their lives.

Early Japanese immigrants in Hawaii share this celebration of human courage with colorful character drawing. As reflected in the titles, these stories reach different layers of that community and reveal poignant human experiences. In the twelve stories, a combination of fictional and biographical details form highly individual characters: the loving parents who quietly worked for the future of their children in a new culture; the cultural misfit who had problems adjusting to the demands of a mixed culture; those whose hopes were thwarted by the strict and unfair rules; tough fighters who went through numerous struggles to bring about a better life for the others; and foreigners of different kinds. Sometimes main characters in one story appear as peripheral characters in another. These recurrent characters give the collection an extra touch of realism and intimacy, for the stories read more like biographical reminiscence than creative fiction.

◆ CRITICAL RECEPTION

Despite recent attention to Asian American writing, advocated by writers such as Shirley Lim and King-Kok Cheung, Patsy Sumie Saiki's works have not caught massive attention like other Japanese American writers who write about the traumatic World War II internment. While Saiki has been recognized as one of the most devoted writers of Japanese American literature in the Pacific Islands, the intermediate position of the island in relation to America and Japan might have contributed to a relatively quiet response to this culturally rich body of writing.

In an essay about Japanese Hawaiian literature and how the location has become history, Stephen Sumida clearly points out that the "local" history of Hawaii has either been misconceived or ignored for years, so that general knowledge only extends to the last 250 years since Captain Cook landed. Given this historical condition, it is not difficult to understand the seeming lack of popular attention to Saiki's work.

That aside, Saiki's work has been firmly recognized as devoted to the documentation and glorification of the courageous human spirit in the face of hardship. Although many of her short stories are descriptive of the specific historical and cultural situations of a few generations of Japanese immigrants in Hawaii, the stories have not been outlived by the change of time. The fact that Saiki's stories, whether presented in written form or live readings, still draw attention and interest is a tribute to the eternally valid human courage they have documented.

◆ BIBLIOGRAPHY

Works by Patsy Sumie Saiki

Short Story Collections

Sachie, A Daughter of Hawaii. Honolulu: Kisaku, Inc., 1977.
Ganbare! An Example of Japanese Spirit. Honolulu: Kisaku, Inc., 1981.
Japanese Women in Hawaii: The First 100 Years. Honolulu: Kisaku, Inc., 1985.
Early Japanese Immigrants in Hawaii. Honolulu: Japanese Cultural Center of Hawaii, 1993.

Studies of Patsy Sumie Saiki

Asian American Literature: A Selective Bibliography. http://www.library.csustan.edu/pcrawford/asianlit/. Accessed February 18, 2002.
Enomoto, Catherine Kekoa. "Author Continues Circle of Compassion, Creativity." *Honolulu Star Bulletin* (October 2, 1997). http://starbulletin.com/97/10/02/features/books.html. Accessed February 20, 2002.
GetLit: New Media for New Fiction. http://www.getlit.net/. Videotape of Saiki reading the short story "Communion." Accessed February 18, 2002. http://www.hawaii.edu/ur/News_Release/NR_Feb/saiki.html. Accessed February 18, 2002.
Sumida, Stephen H. "Sense of Place, History, and the Concept of the 'Local' in Hawaii's Asian/Pacific Literatures." In *Reading the Literatures of Asian America*. Shirley Geok-lin Lim and Amy Ling, eds. Philadelphia: Temple University Press, 1992, 215–37.

BIENVENIDO N. SANTOS
(1911–1996)

Nikolas Huot

◆ BIOGRAPHY

Bienvenido Santos was born on March 22, 1911, in the Manila slums. Despite losing his mother to cancer at the age of thirteen and his father to tuberculosis two years later, Santos managed to earn a baccalaureate in education at the University of the Philippines in 1931. For the next ten years, Santos taught and wrote profusely. From the publication of his first story in 1930 to his first trip to the United States in 1941, ninety-two of his stories appeared in the pages of various magazines. In 1941, Santos received a government scholarship to study in the United States. Stopping first at the University of Illinois, Santos went on to study creative writing at Columbia and then English at Harvard. His studies were interrupted, however, by World War II, when he was summoned to Washington, D.C., to work in what would become the Philippine embassy. Later during the war, the United States Office of Education asked him to tour the country and lecture about the value of the Filipinos, America's new allies against Japan.

In 1946, Santos returned to his wife and three daughters in the Philippines, where he wrote *You Lovely People* (1955) in memory of the Pinoys he met and whose lives he shared while traveling in the United States. In 1958, Santos received a Rockefeller creative writing fellowship and, along with his wife, left for the Writers Workshop at the University of Iowa. In Iowa, Santos completed his first two novels, *Villa Magdalena* (1965) and *The Volcano* (1965), while on a Guggenheim Fellowship. Upon his return to the Philippines in 1961, Santos took the position of dean and then of vice president of the University of Nueva Caceres and, in 1965, was awarded the Republic Cultural Heritage Award in Literature. A year after receiving the most prestigious literary award in the Philippines, Santos returned once more to Iowa, this time as an Exchange Fulbright Professor.

In the summer of 1972, as he was about to return to his homeland once again, the Marcos government declared martial law, which effectively compelled Santos into exile. During his forced expatriation, Santos accepted the position of Distinguished Writer in Residence at Wichita State University, a position he held until 1982. He became an American citizen in 1976, and, in 1979, won an American Book Award for *Scent of Apples: A Collection of Short Stories*. (Out of the sixteen stories in the collection, there is one new story, eleven previously published in *You Lovely People*, and four that first appeared in *The Day the Dancers Came*.) Frequently traveling between the United States and the Philippines in his later years, Santos finally retired to his family home at the foot of Mount Mayon, where he died on January 7, 1996, at the age of eighty-four.

During his prolific career, Bienvenido Santos was awarded the National Achievement Award for Literature in Fiction, the U.S. National Endowment for the Arts Award in Creative Writing, and the Southeast Asia Writer's Award. He also received honorary degrees from the University of the Philippines, Bicol University in Legazpi City, Wichita State University, and De La Salle University, which also established the Bienvenido N. Santos Distinguished Professorial Chair in Creative Writing.

◆ MAJOR WORKS AND THEMES

Whether writing about Filipinos in their native villages or in exile in the United States, Bienvenido Santos is mostly concerned with the feelings of belonging and of community as internalized by his characters. In his early stories, collected in *Dwell in the Wilderness* (1985), Santos writes of the predecessors of the Pinoy expatriates found in his later fiction. Set in the Philippines, Santos's stories present the poor farmers, the young married couples, and the students who must deal with sickness, passion, aging, and death. In these stories, as well as in his later ones, Santos records the many facets of the "pain that lies at the heart of the human condition" (Aureus-Briscoe ix). Although the setting for his stories often changes, this centralized issue remains constant.

In *You Lovely People* (1955), the pain in the hearts of the Filipinos have to do with their displacement, forced or not, and their preoccupation to belong. The Filipinos who now live in the United States, especially those who do not believe they will ever return to their homeland, try to deal with the loneliness and the distance by creating a sense of community around them. As such, the old-timers (the first wave of Filipinos to migrate to the United States) and "the hurt men" pretend to be brothers to give themselves strength and so as not "to appear the homeless waifs that [they] were" ("The Door," *You Lovely People* 124). This sense of community is extremely important in the lives of old-timers as it creates a sense of belonging and of identity. Adding to the feelings of dislocation and isolation is the difficulty for all exiles of "reconciling the Filipino dream of solidarity with the American dream of individualism" (Casper, "Introduction," *Scent of Apples* xi). As Leonard Casper points out in his introduction to *Scent of Apples*, this theme of belonging and of holding on to one's Filipino identity is central to Bienvenido Santos's fiction:

> [H]ow hard it always is, yet how important, to be "Filipino" at heart, with all that implies about human decency, good humor, and honor, consideration beyond courtesy, and putting both hands to a common burden; while at the same time trying to make a life out of being overseas Filipinos, Philippine-Americans, temporary "permanent residents" obligated to be buried "at home," or those assimilated beyond recovery of any heritage whatsoever. (xvi)

Through the alienation and isolation suffered by Filipino exiles, however, comes the strength of character in the midst of this dislocation.

In Santos's stories, the strength of the Filipinos in exiles comes from their acceptance of the reality of their situation and, at the same time, from their dreams of the Philippines. Realizing that "as the years pass, in the home of [their] young manhood, [they] become nothing but a name mentioned now and then, casually, and always, without love" and looking at their empty lives in the United States, the old-timers create and passionately hold on to a romanticized view of their home country ("Lonely in the Autumn Evening," *You Lovely People* 104). Although seemingly paradoxical, the idealized images of their homeland allow the old-timers and the exiles to accept their plight and their isolation in the United States. As Santos explores in numerous stories, every Filipino in the United States "must have held on to certain ideals, certain beliefs, even illusions peculiar to the exile" as mementos of his homeland ("Scent of Apples" 181). As old-timers meet other Filipinos, the former need confirmation that there is "no cause to regret one's sentimental investment," that the Philippines is just like their idealized homeland (182). Even though modern Filipinas have changed ("Brown Coterie"), the face in the picture has become blurred ("Scent of Apples"), and the visiting Filipinos laugh at the old-timers ("The Day the Dancers Came"), the exiles hold on to their visions of the Philippines, as they are the only things worth holding on to and the only things tying them to their homeland.

In Santos's second collection of short stories, the reader finds some of the same characters from *You Lovely People* returning home. Homecoming is the theme that links the stories of *Brother, My Brother* (1960). In Santos's stories, many of those returning home (re)discover their affinities and closeness with their fellow Filipinos. However, homecoming in *Brother, My Brother* may also be "to the physical body's final destination, the grave [or] to one's awakening to [one's] responsibilities" (Carpio 60). Regardless of the kind of homecoming,

Santos stresses that all men, regardless of racial or ethnic background, are part of the brotherhood of men. Whether the story deals with war, school, life, or death, there is always something (a house, a church, a grave, a flood, a city, a family member) that ties all the characters together. Santos partly achieves this emphasis through the use of his narrators. Often using a first-person narrator (something he frequently does in all of his collections) to divulge inner perspectives, Santos brings the reader along with the narrator on his journeys to his heritage and to the revelation that he, too, belongs to the brotherhood of men.

In his third collection of short stories, Santos returns to the plight of the old timers exiled in the United States. In *The Day the Dancers Came* (1967), the old timers are still yearning for a sense of community and are still reaching out to the new exiles and to the Filipinos in transit. Desperately out of touch with the younger generation of exiles and seen as assimilated old fools by visiting Filipinos, the old timers are more than ever alone in their adopted country. To reconcile their isolation and their yearning to belong, the exiles are "forever listening to news from the warfront" in the Philippines (Cruz). Although the same predominant themes of displacement, alienation, and the exiled Filipino's identity are found in this third collection of short stories, *The Day the Dancers Came* differs from *You Lovely People* by the underlying violence present in the majority of the stories. As they hear of the violence that ravages their homeland, the exiles are also busy fighting wars and battles. In the United States, however, the battles are mostly internalized and fought with oneself about one's identity and one's place. Here again, the difficulties of remaining Filipino at heart in the United States are presented in many ways and in many lives.

◆ CRITICAL RECEPTION

Epifanio San Juan, Jr., is certainly the harshest critic of Bienvenido Santos. In his oft-published essay, "Filipino Writing in the United States: Reclaiming Whose America?" San Juan considers Santos's fiction to be "integrationist" and writes: "Santos's imagination is attuned to an easy purchase on the hurts, alienation, and defeatism of *pensionados*, expatriated *ilustrados*, petit bourgeois males marooned during World War II in the East Coast and Midwest, and other third wave derelicts. His pervasive theme is the reconciliation of the Filipino psyche with the status quo" (451). Most critics, however, are not as acerbic or as trenchant as San Juan. In fact, the great majority of readers find Santos's writing to be exceptional in its depiction of the strength Filipinos mustered in the face of alienation and dislocation. Reviewing *Scent of Apples*, Maxine Hong Kingston even speaks of the representativeness of Santos's collection of stories: "Filipino-Americans now have a book" (28).

Often considered to be the most successful of Santos's writings, *You Lovely People* has been praised by critics like Gonzalez for its coherent unity and its profound humanity in the person of Ambo, one of the main narrators. That same humanity, believes Francisco Arcellana, is even more apparent in Santos's second collection of short stories, *Brother, My Brother*. According to Arcellana, the masterpieces found in *Brother, My Brother* make it "an even more valuable collection than *You Lovely People*, which is already in its own way priceless" (718). Although not as enthusiastic, Rustica Carpio points out that some of the stories in Santos's second collection are weak, but, she concludes, the "majority of them are very convincing and entertaining" (58). The praise for Santos continues as Isagani Cruz writes of his third collection of short stories: "*The Day the Dancers Came* is a masterpiece of subtlety, a grand adventure into innocence, an epic initiation rite" (n.p.). The acclaim Santos has received in the Philippines has been echoed in the United States with the publication of *Scent of Apples*, his only book published in the United States. Such distinguished critics and authors as Maxine Hong Kingston, Hisaye Yamamoto, Elaine Kim, and N.V.M. Gonzalez have reviewed and applauded Bienvenido Santos's depiction of Filipino old-timers.

In addition to his apt discussion of the pain and isolation of his characters, Santos is also praised for his "simple yet entertaining" writing style, which "is amply enhanced by a vivid imagery in the description of places and people" (Carpio 64). Using "restraint and narrative control" in his stories, Santos "[holds] sentiment in check [and sharpens] the reality of pain and loss" (Rico 99). "Above all, Santos has depth," writes Rustica Carpio. "He can penetrate into the minds and emotions of characters without being unconvincing" (64). This persuasiveness, notes Kingston, comes from Santos's expertise at using colloquial language: "Mr. Santos is a master at giving the reader a sense of people speaking in many languages and dialects" (28).

As more and more of his stories are anthologized, Kingston's wish that Santos's writing "[makes] its way into the mainstream of American literature" is slowly coming true (28). "Scent of Apples," "Immigration Blues," and "The Day the Dancers Came" will certainly highlight Bienvenido Santos as one of the best chroniclers of the Filipino experience in the United States.

◆ BIBLIOGRAPHY

Works by Bienvenido Santos

Short Story Collections

Scent of Apples: A Collection of Stories. Seattle: University of Washington Press, 1979.
Dwell in the Wilderness: Selected Short Stories (1931–1941). Quezon City: New Day, 1985.
You Lovely People. 1955. Makati City, Philippines: Bookmark, 1991.
Brother, My Brother: A Collection of Short Stories. 1960. Makati City, Philippines: Bookmark, 1991.
The Day the Dancers Came. 1967. Makati City, Philippines: Bookmark, 1991.

Poetry

The Wounded Stag: A Collection of Poetry. Manila: Capitol Publishing House, 1956.
Distances in Time: Selected Poems. Quezon City: Ateneo de Manila University Press, 1983.

Novels

The Praying Man. Quezon City: New Day, 1982.
The Man Who (Thought He) Looked Like Robert Taylor. Quezon City: New Day, 1983.
The Volcano. 1965. Quezon City: New Day, 1986.
What the Hell for You Left Your Heart in San Francisco? Quezon City: New Day, 1987.
Villa Magdalena: A Novel. 1965. Quezon City: New Day, 1999.

Autobiography

Memory's Fictions: A Personal History. Quezon City: New Day, 1993.
Postscript to a Saintly Life. Pasig City, Philippines: Anvil, 1994.
Letters (Book One). Pasig City, Philippines: Anvil, 1995.
Letters (Book Two). Pasig City, Philippines: Anvil, 1996.

Essays

"The Filipino Novel in English." In *Brown Heritage: Essays on Philippine Cultural Tradition and Literature.* Antonio G. Manuud, ed. Quezon City: Ateneo de Manila University Press, 1967, 634–47.
"Filipino Old Timers: Fact and Fiction." *Amerasia* 9.2 (1982): 89–98.
"The Personal Saga of a 'Straggler' in Philippine Literature." *WLWE: World Literature Written in English* 15.2 (November 1976): 398–405.

Studies of Bienvenido Santos

Arcellana, Francisco. "Bienvenido N. Santos." In *Brown Heritage*. Manuud, ed., 714–21.
Aureus-Briscoe, Leonor. "Foreword." In *Dwell in the Wilderness*. v–ix.
Bresnahan, Roger J. "The Midwestern Fiction of Bienvenido N. Santos." *Society for the Study of Midwestern Literature Newsletter* 13.2 (Summer 1983): 28–37.
Campomanes, Oscar V. "Filipinos in the United States and Their Literature of Exile." In *Reading the Literatures of Asian America.* Shirley Geok-lin Lim and Amy Ling, eds. Philadelphia: Temple University Press, 1992, 49–78.
Carpio, Rustica C. "Bienvenido Santos and *Brother, My Brother.*" *Solidarity* 5.12 (1970): 58–64.
Casper, Leonard. "Introduction." In *Scent of Apples*, ix–xvi.
———. "Introduction." In *Brother, My Brother*, n.p.
Cruz, Isagani R. "Introduction." In *The Day the Dancers Came*, n.p.
Cruz, Isagani R., and David Jonathan Bayot. *Reading Bienvenido Santos.* Manila: De La Salle University Press, 1994.
Fernandez, Doreen G. "Introduction." In *Dwell in the Wilderness*, xi–xv.

Gonzalez, N.V.M. "Introduction." In *You Lovely People*, vii–x.

Gonzalez, N.V.M., and Oscar Campomanes. "Filipino American Literature." In *Interethnic Companion to Asian American Literature*. King-Kok Cheung, ed. Cambridge: Cambridge University Press, 1996, 62–124.

Kim, Elaine H. "Multiple Mirrors and Many Images: New Directions in Asian American Literature." In *Asian American Literature: An Introduction to the Writings and Their Social Context*. Philadelphia: Temple University Press, 1982, 265–72.

Kingston, Maxine Hong. "Precarious Lives." Rev. of *Scent of Apples*. *New York Times Book Review* (May 4, 1980): 15+.

Mannur, Anita. "Bienvenido N. Santos." In *Asian American Novelists: A Bio-Bibliographical Critical Sourcebook*. Emmanuel S. Nelson, ed. Westport, CT: Greenwood Press, 2000, 317–22.

McDowell, Edwin. "About Books and Authors." *New York Times Book Review* (March 28, 1982): 34.

Rico, Victoria S. "*You Lovely People*: The Texture of Alienation." *Philippine Studies* 42.1 (1994): 91–104.

San Juan, Epifanio Jr. *The Philippine Temptation: Dialectics of Philippines-U.S. Literary Relations*. Philadelphia: Temple University Press, 1996.

———. "Filipino Writing in the United States: Reclaiming Whose America?" In *The Likhaan Book of Philippine Criticism (1992–1997)*. J. Neil C. Garcia, ed. Quezon City: University of the Philippines Press, 2000, 441–64.

Valdez, Maria Stella. "The Myth and the Matrix in Bienvenido N. Santos' 'Scent of Apples': Searching for Harmony among Incongruities." *DLSU Dialogue* 25.1 (1991): 73–86.

Yamamoto, Hisaye. Rev. of *Scent of Apples*. *MELUS* 7.2 (Summer 1980): 92–93.

KATHLEEN TYAU
(1947–   )

♦ Gayle K. Sato

♦ **BIOGRAPHY**

Kathleen Tyau, of Chinese and Hawaiian descent, was born in California and grew up in Waikiki and Pearl City, Oahu. She left Hawaii in 1965 to attend Lewis and Clark College in Oregon, and has lived there ever since. After college, Tyau married and found work as a hand weaver, the first of several and varied occupations that have included legal secretary, freelance journalist, and creative writing instructor at Pacific University. She and husband Paul Drews live on a fifty-two-acre tree farm outside Portland.

Tyau has published two book-length works of fiction, *A Little Too Much Is Enough* (1995) and *Makai* (1999), which were both well received. *A Little Too Much Is Enough* (henceforth called *ALTMIE*) was chosen as the 1996 Best Book of the Year by the Pacific Northwest Booksellers Association and was also a finalist that year for the Oregon Book Award in fiction as well as the Barnes and Noble Best New Writers Award. *Makai* was a finalist for the 2000 Oregon Book Award.

Certain aspects of Tyau's personal history shape her fiction in understated yet significant ways. Tyau's knowledge of hand weaving, her passion for blue-grass music, and experience at St. Andrew's Priory, a private Catholic girls' school in Honolulu, furnish important details for setting and character in *Makai*. Tyau's near drowning at age five is reworked into the episode "Ocean Is for Drowning" from *ALTMIE* as well as the narrator's fear of water in *Makai*, a decisive factor in both works' complex representation of Hawaii. Tyau's part-Hawaiian father, born on Niihau, has probably influenced the creation of a Chinese-Hawaiian father in *ALTMIE* who figures in two of the book's most striking representations of indigenous culture—chapters dealing with hula, surfing, and shark *aumakua* (in Hawaiian cosmology, divinities that serve as a family's guardian spirits).

◆ MAJOR WORKS AND THEMES

Tyau's two books reflect on Hawaii's postwar development through the perspectives of working-class Hawaiian-Chinese women, one about to leave for a mainland college and the other dealing with the return of her adult, mainland-educated daughter. Mahealani Suzanne Wong, the restless daughter and central narrator of *ALTMIE*, remembers her childhood from the perspective of a local girl who found independence from her family by moving to the mainland, while Alice Lum, the aging mother and narrator of *Makai*, is remembering a life that evolved around her need to stay home and never go "far." Both Mahi and Alice, however, understand leaving and staying as an interconnected difference and create lifestyles for themselves that enable inhabitation of different locations at once—Oregon and Hawaii, present and past, departure and return.

Though marketed as a novel, there are good reasons for reading *ALTMIE* as a collection of short stories. Structurally, the book consists of forty chapters, most of them quite short and several of which were previously published as independent stories. Chapters are written as sharply focused episodes that together build a picture of the relationships within an extended Chinese-Hawaiian family, narrated mainly by the daughter Mahi at different points in her growing up but occasionally by her mother, father, and elder brother. Roughly half of the chapters concern the preparation or consumption of meals, a motif that has structural as well as thematic significance. As Tyau puts it, "I wanted to convey the local spirit—the exuberance, the craziness, and the often overwhelming generosity. So I wrote about food and eating—what else? I also shaped the book so that the chapters are like dishes at a potluck supper—some small, like pupus; some big, like main dishes. These chapters may be read independently, but together they tell the story of a girl growing up local in a big family with big appetites and big hearts" (Tyau 376).

Tyau's potluck analogy is a poetic version of the "unified miscellany" identified by Kirk Curnutt as the hallmark of a "short-story cycle" (803). Citing the work of Louise Erdrich, Gloria Naylor, Ruth Sasaki, and Sandra Cisneros, whose *The House on Mango Street* influenced the construction of *ALTMIE*, Curnutt notes the short story cycle's "special value for women writers" dealing with "the relationships and rituals that weave a particular community together" (804). Tyau's *ALTMIE* is clearly affiliated with this tradition. Through a narrative of female development extending from Mahi Wong's birth to her departure from family and homeland, Tyau depicts a lifestyle situated within and shaped by the geography and history of a particular place: here, multicultural, multiracial Hawaii during the postwar phase of its problematic development into an economy controlled by the interests of the U.S. military and corporate tourism.

The representation of place is a central theme in Tyau's fiction, but her focus on the social meaning of location endows *ALTMIE* (and *Makai*) with a subtle critique of the Hawaii-is-Paradise genre. "Ocean Is for Drowning," a chapter from *ALTMIE*, is less about the ocean's physical nature than about Mahi's relationship to older brother Buzzy, whom she adores and fears for whenever he swims, and about Buzzy's own troubled relationship to family. This emphasis on cultural geography over physical geography fosters respect for the particularity of physical environments, enabling readers to see why, for example, Sandy Beach, Oahu, and Sarasota, Florida, are not interchangeable beaches, or why a New England clam bake is not the same kind of family picnic as the Wong clan's beach luau in honor of Buzzy's graduation from high school. When Tyau creates the scene of Buzzy's luau, the beach is not identified but it is nonetheless intimately familiar to readers who have attended such parties on Oahu's shores. The story concludes through a dramatic moment that asserts the continuation of an ancestral past in the present, as Buzzy performs an impromptu hula affirming his ties to family, friends, and Hawaii, accompanied only by the music of crashing waves, silent moon, and his father's "singular, haunting voice" (157–58). These indigenous and local lifestyles and subjectivities of Mahi and her community embody aspects of island living that remain unassimilated into the dominant economic and cultural paradigms of U.S. society.

◆ CRITICAL RECEPTION

The response to Tyau's work from scholars of Asian American literature or other academic disciplines is not yet visible, but reviews of both *ALTMIE* and *Makai* were excellent. Although a few found Tyau's characters somewhat superficial (Ross, Lu, Pennybacker), even they, like all other reviewers, admired the style, structuring, and handling of themes in both works. There is much praise for Tyau's language (Cline, D'Erasmo, Gray, Joyce), portrayal of women's relationships (Cline, Heller, See), and refocusing of transnational historical events, such as Pearl Harbor and Vietnam, from a personal perspective (Stead, Ross). Articles by Wanda Adams, Jeff Baker, and Suzannne Tswei provide useful biographical information and speak of the importance and effectiveness of Tyau's memory work. Of *ALTMIE*, Adams writes: "The book is, in part, for the people who've approached her at readings in Oregon and California during her book tour, homesick Hawaiians like herself. And for her nieces and nephews and others of their generation, who can't remember the islands that she knew" (F-5).

Reviews of *Makai* by Mindy Pennybacker and *ALTMIE* by Stacey D'Erasmo provide insightful commentary on the cultural politics of Tyau's work without losing sight of her artistry. Pennybacker places Tyau's work in the context of

Hawaii's "sovereignty movement," which aims to restore political and land-based sovereignty to Native Hawaiians. Some of the debate surrounding this movement is centered on (re)definitions of "local" identity. Whereas until recently "local" was assumed to signify a cultural and political coalition among non-white residents of Hawaii, it is now understood by some as a false claim to Hawaii as homeland, a right that by definition belongs solely to Native Hawaiians (see Trask, *From a Native Daughter*; Fujikane and Okamura, *Amerasia Journal*). In Pennybacker's view, Tyau's narrative represents a critical understanding of "local" as a heterogeneous, unevenly empowered identity, evolving within a larger history of economic, cultural, and military colonization. D'Erasmo's review offers the best literary analysis of *ALTMIE*, pinpointing the source of the book's political critique in its poetry and plotting: "[O]ne of the great pleasures of reading *A Little Too Much* is watching Tyau coax eruptions from words one might have thought dormant: *poi, luau, hula, muumuu*" (86). In place of a "terribly accessible" Hawaii promoted by tourism, the kind reduced in the end to "a browning lei, a trinket carved from coconut shell," Tyau's Hawaii is "a string of islands of language and family," made from chapters "jumbled and various, like a drawer full of emotional snapshots," which trace "the arc of a personal history" (86).

Rob Wilson's *Reimagining the American Pacific*, which analyzes a long history of literature from and about Hawaii for its relationships to the current debate on Hawaiian sovereignty, offers a very brief reading of "Family Shark" from *ALTMIE* that illuminates the critical depths of Tyau's writing, a reading quite different from that of the reviewer in Westerville, Ohio, who found *ALTMIE* "an eye-opening but not terribly involving glimpse into an unusual culture" (Ross 168). "Family Shark" is a comic depiction of Mahi's father's mixed-up encounters while surfing with a Chinese *gui* (ancestral ghost), Hawaiian *aumakua*, and future father-in-law (very much alive, who eventually teaches Mahi's father the surfing skills he himself learned from the legendary Duke Kahanamoku). Wilson reads "Family Shark" as "a *local story*, a little story with its own abiding claims to make on Pacific identity and these Hawaiian harbors," thus "counter[ing] the reigning master narrative of capitalist teleology and nature as real estate" (211–12). It seems likely that Tyau's stories of nostalgic and critical remembering will be appreciated by a growing body of readers seeking local-based ways of living to counteract globalism.

◆ BIBLIOGRAPHY

Works by Kathleen Tyau

Short Story Collections

A Little Too Much Is Enough. New York: Farrar, Straus and Giroux, 1995.
Makai. New York: Farrar, Straus and Giroux, 1999.

Studies of Kathleen Tyau

Adams, Wanda A. "For Author Kathleen Tyau, 'Little Too Much Is Enough.' " Rev. of *A Little Too Much Is Enough. Honolulu Sunday Advertiser* (July 16, 1995): F-5.

Baker, Jeff. "The Tides of Her Craft." Rev. of *Makai. The Oregonian* (May 5, 2001): C-1+.

Cline, David. "A Wartime Friendship Hits the Rocks on the Maui Coast." Rev. of *Makai. San Francisco Chronicle* (June 27, 1999): 8.

Curnutt, Kirk. "Short-Story Cycles." In *The Oxford Companion to Women's Writing in the United States.* Cathy N. Davidson and Linda Wagner-Martin, eds. New York: Oxford University Press, 1995, 803–5.

D'Erasmo, Stacey. "Wild Palms." Rev. of *A Little Too Much Is Enough. Village Voice* (July 25, 1995): 86.

Fujikane, Candace, and Jonathan Okamura, eds. "Asian Settler Colonialism in Hawai'i." *Amerasia Journal* 26.2 (2000).

Gray, Julie. Rev. of *Makai. New York Times Book Review* (August 29, 1999): 21.

Heller, Amanda. "Short Takes." Rev. of *Makai. Boston Globe*, City ed. (July 11, 1999): C-2.

Joyce, Alice. Rev. of *A Little Too Much Is Enough. Booklist* 91 (July 1995): 1861–62.

Lu, Lynn. Rev. of *Makai. Ms.* 9.4 (June–July 1999): 88.

Pennybacker, Mindy. "Decolonizing the Mind." Rev. of *Makai. The Nation* 269.10 (October 1999): 31–35.

Ross, Patricia. Rev. of *A Little Too Much Is Enough. Library Journal* 120 (June 1995): 168.

See, Carolyn. "Heaven in Small Bites." Rev. of *A Little Too Much Is Enough. Washington Post*, Final ed. (July 28, 1995): B-2.

Stead, Deborah. "Books in Brief: Fiction." Rev. of *A Little Too Much Is Enough. New York Times Book Review* (October 15, 1995): 20.

Trask, Haunani-Kay. *From a Native Daughter: Colonialism and Sovereignty in Hawai'i.* Rev. ed. Honolulu: University of Hawaii Press, 1999.

Tswei, Suzanne. "All Roads Lead to *Makai*." Rev. of *Makai. Honolulu Star-Bulletin* (July 9, 1999): B-1.

Tyau, Kathleen. "Author's Notes." In *Growing Up Local: An Anthology of Poetry and Prose from Hawai'i.* Eric Chock, James R. Harstad, Darrell H. Y. Lum, and Bill Teeter, eds. Honolulu: Bamboo Ridge Press, 1998, 376.

Wilson, Rob. "Shark God on Trial." In *Reimagining the American Pacific: From South Pacific to Bamboo Ridge and Beyond.* Durham, NC: Duke University Press, 2000, 191–213.

JOSÉ GARCIA VILLA
(1908–1997)

Nikolas Huot

◆ **BIOGRAPHY**

José Garcia Villa was born in Manila on August 5, 1908 (many other years of birth have been suggested, but in an interview with Nick Carbó, Villa gives 1908 as the year of his birth [*Anchored Angel* 223]). After graduating from high school, he enrolled at the University of the Philippines in medicine, conforming to the wish of his father who used to be a doctor in the revolutionary army of Emilio Aguinaldo. More interested in painting and writing than in his studies, Villa, along with friends, founded the UP Writers Club. In 1929, he published a series of erotic poems, "Man Songs," for which he was suspended from the university and fined for obscenity by the Manila Court of First Instance. The same year, his "Mir-i-Nisa" was judged best short story in a contest sponsored by the *Philippines Free Press*. With the money he won, he relocated to the United States and enrolled at the University of New Mexico.

In 1933, Villa published a collection of twenty-one short stories entitled *Footnote to Youth: Tales of the Philippines and Others* and moved to New York. Following the publication of his first book, Villa decided to dedicate himself entirely to poetry. After publishing two collections of poems in the Philippines, his first volume of poetry to appear in the United States, *Have Come, Am Here* (1942), won the American Academy of Arts and Letters Award and was shortlisted for the Pulitzer Prize. His fourth collection of poetry, *Volume Two* (1949), was not received with as much praise as his "comma poems" (a comma with no surrounding spaces linked every word in the poems) and was regarded by many as typographical games. Employed as associate editor at New Directions Books between 1949 and 1951 and as instructor at City College of New York between 1952 and 1960, Villa published another selection of poems, *Selected Poems and New*, in 1958, for which he was awarded the Shelley Memorial Award of the Poetry Society of America.

In 1959, Villa was conferred the degree of Doctor of Literature, *honoris causa*, by Far Eastern University, an honor duplicated by the University of the Philippines in 1973. Villa was also the recipient of the Philippines Pro Patria Award for literature (1961), the Philippines Cultural Heritage Award for literature (1962), as well as Guggenheim and Rockefeller Fellowships (1942, 1963). In 1968, he was appointed Presidential Advisor in Cultural Affairs by President Ferdinand Marcos and, in 1973, was elected Philippines National Artist. After he abandoned lecturing at the New School for Social Research in 1973, he continued to hold private poetry workshops in his apartment. Though he would publish another collection of poems, *Appassionata: Poems in Praise of Love* (1979), Villa completely stopped writing poetry for fear of repeating himself. Two days after being found unconscious in his apartment, José Garcia Villa died at a New York hospital on February 7, 1997.

◆ MAJOR WORKS AND THEMES

Other than "Mir-i-Nisa," a story about the "patriarchal feudal order," all the original short stories Villa ever wrote can be found in *Footnote to Youth* (San Juan, "Articulating" 191). Of these twenty-one stories, five were republished in *Selected Stories* (1962), four (the same as in *Selected Stories*) were included in *The Essential Villa* (1965), and three ("Footnote to Youth," "Untitled Story," and "The Fence") were selected for *The Anchored Angel* (1999). Although there is no continuity between the stories in *Footnote to Youth*, all of the stories, as Roger Bresnahan notes, can be grouped in five categories: love stories, Christ stories, José Rizal stories, loss of youth stories, and experimental stories.

"The Fence" is the first love story found in *Footnote to Youth*. In this story, a fence has been erected out of spite to separate two women's houses. Every night, a sickly young boy waits for the girl on the other side of the fence to play part of a song on a guitar. After three years of never hearing the entire piece, the young man speaks to the young girl for the first time and asks her to play it for him. At 2:00 A.M., after desperately waiting, the young man dies; unknowingly, the girl plays the whole piece at 3:00 A.M., which angers the dead man's mother blinded to the love by her hatred. As in "The Fence," Villa's love stories never end happily, since love is permeated with pain and cruelty. In "Given Woman," Villa explores another common theme in his love stories: denial of the self. Ponso asks Flora to live with him. She agrees, and he builds a house for her. After their son dies in infancy and even though they seem to love each other, Ponso decides to leave Flora and to provide her with a better man. The decision to leave is unexplained and enigmatic, but it is clear that Ponso believes he is doing the right thing by Flora. Villa's love stories involve little or no communication between the lovers, and they usually revolve around the man; although women generally suffer greatly from the cruelty of love, Villa depicts the man as the one who hurts the most. Other love stories in the collection include "Valse Triste," "Malakas," and "Kamya."

The Christ stories invariably involve a revelation of some kind. However, more often than not, the characters fail to understand the presence of a greater force intervening in their lives. The simple-mindedness or lack of insight lends a comic twist to such stories as "The Woman Who Looked Like Christ," "Resurrection," and "Like My Boy." The exception comes in "Yet Do They Strife," where a young boy feels at peace when he helps a weary stranger. Revelations of another kind arise in "Footnote to Youth," "Death into Manhood," and "Young Writer in a New Country." In these three stories about the loss of youth and the loss of innocence, the main characters come to terms with their relationships with their parents.

In "Footnote to Youth," the seventeen-year-old Dodong demands that his father accept his marriage; the father complies with reluctance. Eighteen years later, Dodong's young son stands up to his father and announces that he will marry; Dodong realizes that his son is too young to marry and is doomed to repeat the same mistakes he committed, but he still gives his blessing to the union. In the loss of youth stories, as well as many other stories in the collection, the main cause of the conflicts originates from the father-son relationship. In Villa's stories, the father is an incredibly powerful force that is not to be confronted or denied, unless, in an oedipal fashion, the young boy is ready to become a man.

In *Footnote to Youth*, the stories centering on the national hero of the Philippines, José Rizal, are "Son of Rizal," "The Daughter of Rizal," "The Man Who Looked Like Rizal," and "Story for My Country." In these four stories, Villa examines the power of the national hero on individuals who are told they look like him or who believe they have some kinship to him, albeit improbable. Simply being associated with José Rizal affects the personality of the characters. Whether they are embodying the noble characteristics of the national hero or are attempting to bask in the glory of Rizal, the characters are empowered by this connection. In "The Man Who Looked Like Rizal," for example, the title character, a lowly and ugly man, achieves some kind of self-esteem and dignity as he is told of his resemblance to Rizal; after being cuckolded, he even refuses to fight with his wife's lover because the "father of Philippine independence" would not lower himself to the level of petty violence. In these stories, however, the transformations are mostly comical and tend to reflect the pathetic nature of those who believe that being remotely associated with a great man will automatically elevate them to the same level of admiration.

The last five stories found in Villa's collection are composed of numbered paragraphs and deal with the poet's coming to America. "Song I Did Not Hear," "Little Tales," "Untitled Story," "White Interlude," and "Walk at Night: A Farewell" (the last three comprise "Wings and Blue Flame: A Trilogy") are autobiographical in nature and deal with the poet's refuge into language and fantasy. Here again, the conflict with the father manifests itself, as is the resulting creation of the self who transcends the father figure. In these stories, "more concerned with the pyrotechnics of language," the young man not only becomes a man but also a poet (Bresnahan 66).

◆ CRITICAL RECEPTION

Little has been written in the United States about the short fiction of José Garcia Villa. Mostly considered a poet, his short stories have been forgotten for years or dismissed as lesser works. A few of his short stories (especially "The Fence," "Untitled Story," and "Footnote to Youth") have appeared in anthologies published in the United States, but, in general, little recognition has been awarded to Villa's fiction. Although "Untitled Story" was included in *The Best Short Stories of 1932* and "The Fence" appeared in *The Best Short Stories of 1933*, these retrospective volumes are poor in quality and mostly show the lack of lasting talent in the genre of the short story in those years rather than indicate the true merit of Villa's fiction.

The few who have analyzed his short stories, however, do not seem to agree on the value of Villa's fiction writing. Edward J. O'Brien, who edited *Best Short Stories* in 1932 and 1933 and who wrote the introduction to *Footnote to Youth*, believed that Villa was "among the half dozen short story writers in America who [counted]" and thought that his talent for fiction would redefine the American scene (4). In Villa's stories, O'Brien found "passionate feeling" and "a native sensuousness of perception and expression" (4). Though not as enthusiastic as O'Brien, Roger Bresnahan sees the potential for Villa to have "become a considerable force in American fiction," only, however, had he "continued to write short stories in the manner of Sherwood Anderson" (66). Overall sympathetic in his assessment of *Footnote to Youth*, Bresnahan points out the lack of unity and the scarcity of "local color" in the collection of short stories (59–60). He also mentions Villa's alienated attitude toward his characters and how it causes the reader to feel detached and apathetic to their situations. Despite these flaws, which might have been corrected had Villa continued to write fiction, he supposes, Bresnahan considers some of the stories found in *Footnote to Youth* to be "very powerful" (66).

E. San Juan, Jr., perhaps the most devoted critic to the works of Villa, perceives *Footnote to Youth* as Villa's response to the fragmented world of the Philippines in the late 1920s. The perfect example of his modernism, the collection of short stories demonstrates how Villa, the writer, was in a "no-man's land" between the "vulgar Americanizers," the vernacular writers, and the propagandists ("Articulating" 188). Completely alienated from peasants' armed insurrections, militant union organizers, or from the independence struggle, Villa buried himself in the study of the English language, "trying to find his unique individual voice" and pursuing his personal exploration (188).

Through his fiction, San Juan asserts, "Villa exemplifies the colonized subject who revolts against the philistine milieu of a society divided by caste and class" (186). His short stories, especially those set in the United States, are cathartic exercises to get rid of his colonial deracinated self alienated from his surroundings and of his father's overpowering presence (192–93). As such, and even though his stories do not conform to the requirements of the short story as established by Villa himself in his essay "The Contemporary Short Story" (found in *The Anchored Angel*), San Juan believes that the short fiction of Villa is successful in establishing the modernity of the writer.

Far from the previous critics' assessments, Leonard Casper believes that Villa's fiction is most interesting when examined as an experimental precursor to his poetry. Through his fiction, Casper believes, Villa "found his rhythmic repetitions, his sense of the cyclic, his delight in color symbol and allegory, his inability to sustain narrative momentum, his passion for the ineffable or the aphoristic, as well as the sometimes bizarre wrenching of his words" (105). As for the stories themselves, Casper affirms, they are overall monotonous, repetitive, and sentimental; *Footnote to Youth* never achieves a narrative quality nor presents different perspectives of the everyday world in which the characters live. His only collection of short stories, Casper concludes, "has become a footnote to Villa" (105).

◆ BIBLIOGRAPHY

Works by José Garcia Villa

Short Story Collections

Footnote to Youth: Tales of the Philippines and Others. New York: Scribner's, 1933.
Selected Stories of José Garcia Villa. Manila: Alberto S. Florentino, 1962.
Mir-i-Nisa: A Tale of the South Seas. Manila: Alberto S. Florentino, 1966.

Poetry

Many Voices. Manila: Philippine Book Guild, 1939.
Poems by Doveglion. Manila: Philippine Writers' League, 1941.
Have Come, Am Here. New York: Viking, 1942.
Volume Two. New York: New Directions, 1949.
Selected Poems and New. New York: McDowell, Obolensky, 1958.
Appassionata: Poems in Praise of Love. New York: King and Cowen, 1979.

Collections

Poems in Praise of Love: The Best Love Poems of José Garcia Villa. Manila: Alberto S. Florentino, 1962.

Poems 55: The Best Poems of José Garcia Villa as Chosen by Himself. Manila: Alberto S. Florentino, 1962.

The Portable Villa. Manila: Alberto S. Florentino, 1962.

The Essential Villa. Manila: Alberto S. Florentino, 1965.

The Anchored Angel: Selected Writings by José Garcia Villa. Eileen Tabios, ed. New York: Kaya, 1999.

Edited Volumes

Philippine Short Stories: Best 25 Stories of 1928. Manila: Philippines Free Press, 1929.

A Celebration for Edith Sitwell. New York: New Directions, 1948.

A Doveglion Book of Philippine Poetry. Manila: L. Arguilla Sallas, 1962.

Studies of José Garcia Villa

Arcellana, Francisco. "Period of Emergence: The Short Story." In *Brown Heritage: Essays on Philippine Cultural Tradition and Literature.* Antonio G. Manuud, ed. Quezon City: Ateneo de Manila University Press, 1967, 603–17.

Bautista, Cirilo F. "Conversations with José Garcia Villa." *Archipelago* (August 1979): 29–31.

Bresnahan, Roger J. "José Garcia Villa and Sherwood Anderson: A Study in Influence." In *Exploring the Midwestern Literary Imagination.* Marcia Noe, ed. Troy, NY: Whitston, 1993, 57–67.

Casper, Leonard. "A People of Many Pasts and Complex Parts: José Garcia Villa." In *New Writing from the Philippines: A Critique and Anthology.* Syracuse, NY: Syracuse University Press, 1966, 103–10.

Davis, Rocío G. "José Garcia Villa." In *Asian American Poets: A Bio-Bibliographical Critical Sourcebook.* Guiyou Huang, ed. Westport, CT: Greenwood Press, 2002, 305–10.

Espiritu, Augusto Fauni. " 'Expatriate Affirmations': The Performance of Nationalism and Patronage in Filipino-American Intellectual Life." Ph.D. diss., UCLA, 2000.

Gonzalez, N.V.M., and Oscar Campomanes. "Filipino American Literature." In *Interethnic Companion to Asian American Literature.* King-Kok Cheung, ed. Cambridge: Cambridge University Press, 1996, 62–124.

Grow, L. M. "José Garcia Villa: The Poetry of Calibration." *World Literature Written in English* 27.2 (Autumn 1987): 326–44.

Hagedorn, Jessica. "The Time of Mirrors." Foreword. In *The Anchored Angel*, Tabios, ed., xi–xv.

O'Brien, Edward J. "Introduction." *Footnote to Youth*, 3–5.

Olson, Ray. "Adult Books: Nonfiction." Rev. of *The Anchored Angel*. *Booklist* 96.7 (December 1, 1999): 680–81.

San Juan, Epifanio, Jr. "Articulating a Third World Modernism: The Case of José Garcia Villa." In *The Philippine Temptation: Dialectics of Philippines–U.S. Literary Relations.* Philadelphia, Temple University Press, 1996, 171–214.

———. "Filipino Writing in the United States: Reclaiming Whose America?" In *The Likhaan Book of Philippine Criticism (1992–1997).* J. Neil C. Garcia, ed. Quezon City: University of the Philippines Press, 2000, 441–64.

Sitwell, Edith. "Preface." *Selected Poems and New*, ix–xiv.

Tinio, Rolando S. "Villa's Values; Or, the Poet You Cannot Always Make Out, or Succeed in Liking Once You Are Able To." In *Brown Heritage*, Manuud, ed., 722–38.

University of the Philippines Library. *José Garcia Villa: A Bio-Bibliography*. Quezon City: University of the Philippines Library, 1973.

Yabes, Leopoldo Y. "Pioneering in the Filipino Short Story in English (1925–1940)." In *Philippine Short Stories, 1925–1940*. Leopoldo Y. Yabes, ed. Quezon City: University of the Philippines Press, 1974, xix–xxxvii.

SYLVIA A. WATANABE
(1953–   )

Gayle K. Sato

◆ BIOGRAPHY

Born in Wailuku, Maui, and raised in Kailua, Oahu, Sylvia Watanabe is a third-generation Japanese American. She majored in art history at the University of Hawaii (B.A. 1980), earned an M.A. in English and creative writing at SUNY-Binghamton in 1985, and spent the next ten years on the road with husband William Osborn in search of tenured positions. They now commute between Michigan, where Osborn teaches, and Ohio, where Watanabe has taught in the Creative Writing Program at Oberlin College since 1995. Hawaii, however, remains the primary setting and inspiration for Watanabe's work, including her major achievement in the short story genre, *Talking to the Dead*.

Watanabe's reflections on her journey from Maui to the Midwest can be found in "Knowing Your Place," an award-winning essay first published in *Michigan Quarterly Review*. Focusing on a particularly difficult uprooting from Hayward, California, to Grand Rapids, Michigan, in the summer of 1988, Watanabe interprets relocation through two conflicting histories of ancestral home-seeking and home-founding, represented by John Coggeshall, a distant ancestor on Osborn's side of the family, and Yakichi Watanabe, the author's paternal grandfather. Whereas Coggeshall, as Watanabe observes, became "the first governor of Rhode Island after testifying in the trial of Anne Hutchinson" (321), her grandfather, a missionary-educated Presbyterian minister from Japan, was interned at a military prison in New Mexico during World War II after thirty-five years of Christian service to his Maui community (317, 322). Watanabe herself, in the eyes of many, would appear to have traveled vast distances from her grandfather, but she wraps up her reflections on relocation by noting that if white neighbors—however earnest and well-intentioned their neighborly gestures—persist in seeing her as the unassimilable foreigner in their midst, she and Grandfather still occupy the same place.

Watanabe says that the stories comprising *Talking to the Dead*, her first and to date only collection of short fiction, grew out of her parents' memories of Maui, especially her father's stories of growing up in the small towns of Wai-kapu and Maliko (Ronck C-1). During one trip to Maui with her husband, Watanabe's father drew a layered map of the island for them, showing not only present landmarks but what used to stand in their place: "the places to catch certain fish, where the sugar cane and pineapple once grew, where the houses of friends and family once stood" (Cobb-Keller D-3). An entomologist for the State Board of Health, his work and sensibilities have had a major impact on Watanabe's own vision and craft as a writer. One of her recent essays, "A Book of Names," describes the hours she spent with him as a child learning to identify, observe, collect, and appreciate his passion for insects. At age eight she received a notebook like his, clothbound with waterproof pages, on the cover of which he had written "A Book of Names," instructing her that knowing the names of things meant knowing their nature and histories. In contrast, Watanabe has said very little about the influence of her mother, who was a schoolteacher, but the fact that *Talking to the Dead* is narrated through women's experience and its sense of humor attributed to Watanabe's mother (Muromoto A-10) suggests a pervasive, if less tangible, maternal influence.

Besides her parents, Watanabe has acknowledged Professor Dorothy Vella as a key figure in her development as a writer. Vella's popular non-fiction workshop at the University of Hawaii is described in an essay called "Looking," which accompanies a story about the death of Watanabe's mother in *Passing the Word: Writers on Their Mentors*.

Watanabe's contributions to Asian American literature include scholarly and editorial work. In July 1997, she chaired a public forum titled "Regional Constructions of Cultural Identity in Media, Literature, and Community Organizing," the first of several events celebrating the twentieth anniversary of *Bamboo Ridge*, a pioneering literary journal based in Hawaii. Her interviews with Hisaye Yamamoto and Wakako Yamauchi, conducted with William Osborn, are important contributions to criticism and biographical studies of the first generation of Asian American writing in English. It might also be added that Watanabe's work bears a strong resemblance to that of Yamauchi and Yamamoto in its nuanced, critical use of humor and nostalgia to represent first- and second-generation Japanese American women. Watanabe is also the coeditor of two influential anthologies, *Home to Stay: Asian American Women's Fiction* and *Into the Fire: Asian American Prose*, which have introduced Asian American/women's writing to a broad spectrum of readers while promoting the development of young writers. In fact, Watanabe's own piece in *Home to Stay*, selected for inclusion from her master's thesis, caught the attention of an editor at Doubleday and led to a contract for *Talking to the Dead* (Muromoto A-10).

Talking to the Dead was published in 1992 to excellent reviews. Included in *People Magazine*'s Ten Best Books of 1992, it also won the 1993 Josephine Miles Award from the Oakland chapter of PEN and was a finalist for the 1992–1993 PEN/Faulkner Award for Fiction. Recognition for individual stories or essays includes a 1991 O. Henry Award for "The Prayer Lady," a 1985 Japanese American Citizens League National Literary Award for "Colors" (the original version of the lead story in *Talking to the Dead*), and Pushcart Prizes for "Knowing Your Place" (1998) and "Colors" (1989–1990). "Where People Know Me" was selected as a Distinguished Story for *Best American Stories*, 1995, and "The Prayer Lady" was chosen as a PEN Syndicated Fiction Project for 1992–1993. Watanabe has received grants from the Ohio Arts Council (1998) and the National Endowment for the Arts (1989–1990). At present, she is completing a novel, *Things That Fall from the Sky*, and a volume of personal essays, *How Long Are You Staying?* "Trees," a chapter from the novel, has been published in *American Literary Review*.

◆ MAJOR WORKS AND THEMES

Talking to the Dead (1992) is a short story cycle set in Maui during the period between the end of World War II and Hawaii's transformation from an agricultural to a tourist-based economy during the 1970s. The book paints a picture of the Japanese community in Luhi, a fictional coastal town reflecting Hawaii's unique physical environment and intermingling of indigenous and immigrant cultures.

Marriage and memory are also major themes running subtly yet insistently through the entire collection, weaving individual stories into a larger narrative of a local community in constant negotiation between development and preservation. Each story is built around a dilemma faced by a female character at a critical point in her life cycle, and with the exception of one sketch about two school-age girls who dress up for an afternoon of innocent fun in their mothers' evening gowns, each protagonist faces some obstacle to pursuing a long-held ambition or confronts a threat to her emotional well-being. Some are embarking upon or concluding careers as artists, others are grooming reluctant, naive daughters for lifestyles they dreamed of and failed to achieve. Several are nursing physically or mentally disabled family members, and all must contend with the ghosts of dead, dying, or missing loved ones and the choices they or their mothers have made regarding marriage.

Three stories anchoring *Talking to the Dead* exemplify Watanabe's deft intermingling and framing of themes and stories. "The Prayer Lady" and "Talking to the Dead," which conclude the collection, and the opening story,

"Anchorage," are all built around portraits of female healers who manage death and illness through a mixture of Hawaiian and Japanese remedies.

The title story stages a conflict between tradition and modernization through a "half-Hawaiian kahuna lady" (104) known as Aunty Talking to the Dead. She must find an apprentice to replace her son, who has graduated from mortician's school on the G.I. Bill and started a modern funeral home that spells the end of his mother's influence as a practitioner of the old ways. Aunty adopts as her successor another marginalized member of the community, a young woman at loose ends because she is unable to attract a prospective husband. This new apprentice faints at the sight of dead bodies and seems destined to become nothing more than the town's laughingstock, until the death of Aunty herself finally enables the successor to come into her own powers.

In "The Prayer Lady," the wife of an aging Buddhist minister disobeys her husband by soliciting a renowned healer's help after three medical specialists and her own store of folk remedies prove unable to cure him of a mysterious paralysis in both legs. Within minutes of the Prayer Lady's coming and going, the minister stalks out of his house, cured by a few well-placed taunts that loosen the knot of anger, grief, pride, and stubborn resistance to change underlying his self-induced paralysis. He had become depressed over dwindling attendance at his church and plans for modernization, but the Prayer Lady reminds him that everyone must accept the flow of time and cultural transformation.

"Anchorage," rounding out the collection's trio of stories about female healers and alternative healing practices, focuses on an ordinary woman's restorative powers. Watanabe's Little Grandma, reminiscent of the matriarch featured in Toshio Mori's "The Woman Who Makes Swell Doughnuts," ministers to a grown son suffering from Alzheimer's and his daughter, who has inherited her father's passion for painting and whose long-awaited chance to leave the islands for a job as an art teacher in Anchorage is now marred by guilt over leaving her grandmother alone with an ailing father. In the end, it is shown that Little Grandma's method of home care enables both of her progeny to preserve their vital connection to art. Hana is given permission to leave when she realizes that her grandmother's house, affording all-day access to views of ocean, sky, and neighborhood, provides what a care home could not: an opportunity for her father to let go of the world at his own pace, and creative activity, in the form of a commemorative patchwork quilt being pieced together secretly in the attic, to help him cope with the fading of memory.

The quilting project began accidentally when Hana's father stole laundry off a neighbor's clothesline and Little Grandma could neither return nor discard it. She decided instead to construct a quilt around the stolen laundry, a tableau featuring relatives and neighbors each represented by one special item of clothing to be stolen in the same fashion as the first piece. Little Grandma thus accepts and manages her son's condition by transforming the evidence of "forgetting sickness" (5) into a work of remembering. But as the other nine stories in the collection unfold, featuring in turn each of Little Grandma's quilted figures, it becomes apparent that economic development of Hawaii puts everyone, not just Hana's father, in danger of forgetting what is beautiful and important to living well. Articulated through patterns with names like "Ocean Waves" and "Mongoose in the Pigeon Coop" (14) that honor Luhi's local cultural and physical geographies, the quilt's remembrance of a personally meaningful past implies a critique of the erasure of individual lives and local histories through globalization and dominant "narratives of development" (see Candace Fujikane and Rob Wilson on the definition, representation and politics of "local" culture and "development" as played out in Hawaii).

◆ CRITICAL RECEPTION

Talking to the Dead is admired for its subtly complex structure and language. Reviewers consistently praise Watanabe's gentle humor and unpretentious style as the source of her stories' poignancy, freshness, and insight (Harris, Johnson, Lawrence, Rochman, Seaman), and the book's flawless integration of separate stories into a larger whole (Muromoto, Pearlman). One reviewer compares the interconnectedness of the stories to the intricate yet natural beauty of a spider's web (Bauermeister) and others to the likewise humble but powerfully articulate beauty of Little Grandma's quilt (Cobb-Keller, Harris). In Zhou Xiaojing's article on Watanabe, the most detailed discussion of her work by a literary scholar, *Talking to the Dead* is ranked alongside the short story cycles of Maxine Hong Kingston, Amy Tan, and Lois-Ann Yamanaka. Zhou notes the skill with which Watanabe interweaves themes and characters to create the impression of "a live multiethnic community" (557), and her masterful exploitation of all elements within a story to enhance its thematic unity and dramatic effect.

Watanabe's readers are equally impressed by her balanced and subtle, yet passionate handling of subject matter, particularly in regard to themes of progress versus preservation and Hawaii's local and indigenous cultures. Watanabe's treatment of conflict between old and young is identified as a central strength of the collection (Johnson), along with the stories' insightful depiction of the older generation (Harris) and women's struggles to balance "the demands of traditional culture against 20th-Century American mores" (Solomon 11). Amy Ling identifies Watanabe as one of the best Asian American fiction writers from Hawaii, noting that her representation of Hawaii, "far from being a profit-making tourists' paradise, is alive with a host of quirky but sensitively portrayed characters" (38). Donna Choo's review for *Manoa: A Pacific Journal of International Writing*, the most extensive discussion of the book's portrayal of tradition and change in Hawaii, criticizes Watanabe for "inconsistent use of local terms" but praises her portrayal of "ambivalence towards change without campaigning for one or the other as sole cause for salvation or devastation" (248).

Watanabe's writing has not received the critical attention it deserves, but this situation should not continue for long. New essays and fiction published in the last few years, including a chapter from her forthcoming novel, and a steady rise in the number of women's, regional, and multicultural anthologies representing her work, suggest that Watanabe's writing is entering a new phase of heightened productivity and appreciation.

◆ BIBLIOGRAPHY

Works by Sylvia A. Watanabe

Short Stories

"Colors." In *Love, Struggle & Change: Stories by Women*. Irene Zahava, ed. Freedom, CA: Crossing Press, 1988, 21–37.
"Trees." *American Literary Review* 12.2 (Fall 2001): 25–28.
"Where People Know Me." In *Passing the Word: Writers on Their Mentors*. Jeffrey Skinner and Lee Martin, eds. Louisville, KY: Sarabande Press, 2001, 157–70.

Short Story Collection

Talking to the Dead: Stories. New York: Doubleday, 1992.

Prose

Watanabe, Sylvia, and William Osborn. "A Conversation with Hisaye Yamamoto." *Chicago Review* 39.3–4 (1993): 34–38.
"Knowing Your Place." *Michigan Quarterly Review* 35.2 (Spring 1996): 316–28.
"Introductory Remarks." Regional Constructions of Cultural Identity Forum, July 6, 1997. *Bamboo Ridge: A Hawai'i Writers' Journal* 73 (Spring 1998): 17–18.
"Asian-American Literature." In *The Facts on File Companion to the American Short Story*. Abby H. P. Werlock, ed. New York: Checkmark Books, 2000, 24–25.
"A Book of Names." In *Father*. Claudia O'Keefe, ed. New York: Pocket Books, 2000, 185–95.
"Looking." In *Passing the Word*. Skinner and Martin, eds., 153–56.
"A *MELUS* Interview: Wakako Yamauchi." *MELUS* 23.2 (1998): 101–10.

Edited Collections

Watanabe, Sylvia, and Carol Bruchac, eds. *Home to Stay: Asian American Women's Fiction*. Greenfield Center, NY: Greenfield Review Press, 1990.
Into the Fire: Asian American Prose. Greenfield Center, NY: Greenfield Review Press, 1996.

Studies of Sylvia A. Watanabe

Bauermeister, Erica. "Talking to the Dead." In *500 Great Books by Women*. Erica Bauer-meister, ed. New York: Penguin, 1994, 262.

Choo, Donnna J. Rev. of *Talking to the Dead*. *Manoa: A Pacific Journal of International Writing* 5.1 (Summer 1993): 248–50.

Cobb-Keller, Nora. "Maui-Born Writer Stitches a Quilt of the Islands." Rev. of *Talking to the Dead*. *Honolulu Star-Bulletin* (November 17, 1992): D-1+.

Fujikane, Candace. "Reimagining Development and the Local in Lois-Ann Yamanaka's *Saturday Night at the Pahala Theatre*." In *Women in Hawai'i: Sites, Identities, Voices*. Joyce N. Chinen, Kathleen O. Kane, and Ida M. Yoshinaga, eds. Special issue of *Social Process in Hawai'i* 38 (1997): 40–61.

Harris, Michael. "In Brief: Fiction." Rev. of *Talking to the Dead*. *Los Angeles Times* (August 9, 1992): 6.

Johnson, Greg. Rev. of *Talking to the Dead*. *New York Times Book Review* (September 27, 1992): 18.

Lawrence, Keith. "Watanabe, Sylvia (1953–)." In *The Facts on File*, Werlock, ed., 437.

Ling, Amy. "The Asian American Short Story." In *Columbia Companion to the Twentieth-Century American Short Story*. Blanche H. Gelfant and Lawrence Graver, eds. New York: Columbia University Press, 2001, 34–41.

Muromoto, Wayne. "Sylvia Watanabe: 'Talking to the Dead' Finds a Live Audience." Rev. of *Talking to the Dead*. *Hawaii Herald* (December 4, 1992): A-10.

Pearlman, Mickey. "From Asian Shores." In *What to Read: The Essential Guide for Reading Group Members and Other Book Lovers*. New York: HarperCollins, 1994, 122–26.

Rochman, Hazel. "The Asian American Experience: Fiction." Rev. of *Talking to the Dead*. *Booklist* 89 (December 1992): 660–61.

Ronck, Ronn. Rev. of *Talking to the Dead*. *Honolulu Advertiser* (November 17, 1992): C-1.

Seaman, Donna. Rev. of *Talking to the Dead*. *Booklist* 88 (August 1992): 1996.

Solomon, Charles. "Paperbacks." Rev. of *Talking to the Dead*. *Los Angeles Times* (August 8, 1993): 11.

Wilson, Rob. *Reimagining the American Pacific: From South Pacific to Bamboo Ridge and Beyond*. Durham, NC: Duke University Press, 2000.

Zhou Xiaojing. "Sylvia A. Watanabe (1953–)." In *Columbia Companion to the Twentieth-Century American Short Story*, Gelfant and Graver, eds., 556–60.

HISAYE YAMAMOTO (DeSOTO)

(1921–   )

Seiwoong Oh

◆ BIOGRAPHY

Since Hisaye Yamamoto has written memoirs and given interviews during which she has made specific and helpful comments about her life and work, there is a substantial amount of information regarding the author. A second-generation Japanese American, Yamamoto was born in Redondo Beach, California, in 1921 to parents who immigrated from Kumamoto, Japan, and who "eked out a living on the land in southern California," mainly growing strawberries ("The Situation" 241). She spoke no English until she began kindergarten; as soon as she could read in English, she became a voracious reader. Using a pseudonym, Napoleon, she started writing as a teenager, receiving her first rejection slip at the age of fourteen. Throughout her youth—for twelve years—she attended Japanese language schools. After graduating from Excelsior Union High School, she went on to Compton Junior College to study foreign languages.

Following Japan's bombing of Pearl Harbor in December 1941, twenty-one-year-old Yamamoto, along with 110,000 other Japanese Americans, was taken to the Poston Relocation Center in Arizona, as mandated by the Japanese Relocation Act of 1942. Her experiences at this camp profoundly influenced her life, resulting in such touching stories as "The Legend of Miss Sassagawara." The character of Miss Sassagawara is based on a real person, a writer-poet who later died at the age of fifty-eight at a nursing home in Los Angeles.

During her stay at the camp, Yamamoto developed a lasting friendship with Wakako Yamauchi—an author often compared with Yamamoto—and was able to publish her first fictional works, including a serialized mystery entitled "Death Rides the Rails to Poston" and a piece called "Surely I Must

Be Dreaming," both in the *Poston Chronicle*, the camp newspaper. While briefly staying in Springfield, Massachusetts, in 1944, she worked as a cook, from which experience came "The Pleasure of Plain Rice."

Released from the camp in 1945, Yamamoto went to California to work as a reporter and columnist for the *Los Angeles Tribune*, an African American newspaper, from 1945 to 1948. Her experiences working for the newspaper formed the basis of her memoir, "A Fire in Fontana." When she left the newspaper to write full-time after her first story, "The High-Heeled Shoes," was published in *Partisan Review*, she adopted her son Paul, a five-month-old baby born in a family where no one could take care of him. For a while, she was assisted financially by her brother Jemo and later by an insurance bequest from her other brother Johnny, who was killed as an American soldier in Italy at the age of nineteen. In 1950, she received a John Hay Whitney Foundation Fellowship that allowed her to write full-time for a year. Despite the demanding job of motherhood, Yamamoto was able to produce such stories as "Seventeen Syllables," "Yoneko's Earthquake," "The Legend of Miss Sassagawara," and "Wilshire Bus."

Yamamoto's father worked in a cannery in Utah after the war. He then went to Los Angeles and then to Las Vegas, where he washed dishes in a Chinese restaurant. Parts of his life found their way into her story, "Las Vegas Charley" (Crow, "A *MELUS* Interview" 353). In 1953, Yamamoto was invited to study at Stanford University with Ivor Winters; however, inspired by Dorothy Day, founder of the Catholic Worker, Yamamoto traveled instead with her son to New York, to work as a volunteer at Peter Maurin Farm on Staten Island, a Catholic Worker rehabilitation camp. She married Anthony DeSoto there in 1955 and returned to California and had four more children. Her experiences at the farm are reflected in a short story entitled "Epithalamium."

A number of Yamamoto's short stories have been published in major literary periodicals such as *Partisan Review*, *Kenyon Review*, *Carleton Miscellany*, and *Harper's Bazaar*. She has also written stories and essays for audience-specific periodicals such as *Rafu Shimpo*, *Hokkubei Mainichi*, and *Pacific Citizen*. "Yoneko's Earthquake" made its way into the *Best American Short Stories of 1952*. Her other pieces—especially "Seventeen Syllables," "The Legend of Miss Sassagawara," "Las Vegas Charley," and "The Brown House"—have not only made Martha Foley's annual lists of "Distinctive Short Stories" but also have been included in numerous anthologies. In 1985, her first collection of short stories, entitled *Seventeen Syllables: 5 Stories of Japanese American Life*, was published in Japan. For her work and her nurturing of other writers, Yamamoto received in 1986 the American Book Award for Lifetime Achievement from the Before Columbus Foundation. In 1988, another collection of her short stories, *Seventeen Syllables and Other Stories*, was published in the United States.

◆ MAJOR WORKS AND THEMES

From gender issues to interethnic relations, Yamamoto's themes are wide-ranging. Her first work of fiction published in a literary magazine, "The High-Heeled Shoes: A Memoir," investigates sexual perversion. Narrated by a young woman who receives an obscene phone call, the story reflects on previous instances of sexual perversion she is aware of: a would-be rapist who asks his victim to choose between a kiss and a rape; and a young man who sits in his car naked, with his legs in black high-heeled shoes sticking out of the car door. She wonders, Hamlet-style, what to make of these perverts, given her understanding that the bizarre acts are desperate measures of extremely lonely persons.

In her best-known and most anthologized story, "Seventeen Syllables," the author depicts Japanese American life on the farm before World War II. Narrated from the limited perspective of Rosie, a teen-aged nisei who is on the threshold of a romantic relationship with a farmhand, the story gradually reveals the conflict between her issei parents. When the mother occupies herself with writing haiku, the father, preoccupied with farmwork and upset by his wife's violation of her traditional gender role, burns a painting that she has received as a prize for winning a haiku-writing competition. The story reveals the general state of issei women at the time who were isolated and found neither comfort nor understanding from either their husbands or children.

"Yoneko's Earthquake," also set on a little tenant farm before the war, examines similar themes: unhappy marriage, generation gap, and traditional gender roles. Like "Seventeen Syllables," this story is also narrated from the perspective of a young girl who does not necessarily understand what goes on in her household. Through bits of information she spills here and there, attentive readers can piece together a serious conflict between her parents. Young Yoneko grows up on an orange farm with her parents, her five-year-old brother, and Marpo, a Filipino farmhand who is good at many things. After an earthquake, Yoneko's father becomes an invalid and gets upset when his authority is undermined by his wife and Marpo. Through narrative clues, readers gradually become aware of the mother's adulterous affair with Marpo and of her abortion of a pregnancy as a consequence of the affair.

Another story, "Life Among the Oil Fields, A Memoir," is also set on a farm, this time on the oil fields in Redondo Beach, California—the author's hometown—during the depression. Life goes on for a little girl in second grade as the family works on the farm until a white couple in their roadster almost run over her little brother but deny any wrongdoing. The girl, now grown, says her memories are dim but her anger against the racism of the couple, and the larger society, remains.

"A Day in Little Tokyo" takes a Japanese American family out of a strawberry farm to Little Tokyo in Los Angeles. It is narrated from a thirteen-year-old girl's viewpoint. When her father and brother go to see a wrestling match, the girl remains in Little Tokyo. She is approached by two white men, who appear to have been World War II veterans, one of them with a missing leg. They give her coins with which she buys a newspaper, but she later regrets accepting money from them when she should be the one giving it.

Yamamoto's analysis and portrayal of racism are even more realistic and ironic in other stories. In "Underground Lady," for instance, a nisei woman is approached in front of a grocery store by a homeless white woman who talks about how her house is burned down by her Japanese American neighbors. After the nisei woman is picked up by her husband, readers learn that the bigoted homeless woman has been approaching others, regardless of their race, to maintain her contact with humanity and presumably to talk about her life. As the nisei woman wonders about the homeless woman's existence, readers are left second-guessing her thoughts, whether they be of sympathy, envy, or anger.

"Wilshire Bus," set during World War II, again portrays a racist society in which minorities are forced to compete against each other to dodge racist hatred. Esther, on her bus ride to visit her hospitalized husband, witnesses a white drunkard harassing a Chinese couple in the same bus. Esther feels detached because she is Japanese and not Chinese. She then remembers some Koreans wearing "I'm Korean" badges to avoid anti-Japanese violence. As the old Chinese couple get off the bus, presumably to visit their child injured in the war as an American soldier, the protagonist feels guilty and helpless about a country where people of Asian descent must, but do not, establish an alliance against the racist majority.

While the stories discussed above expose the negative side of American race relations, "The Eskimo Connection" shows a possibility of interethnic connections. Emiko, an old widow and babysitter for her grandchildren, gets a letter from an Eskimo in a prison who has read one of her poems published years ago. They communicate, and she even tries to visit him only to be denied, presumably because he has committed a serious crime. As he becomes a devout Christian and later is released from prison, he no longer writes to her and she returns to her life's routines. The characters' fundamental human understanding of each other makes it possible for them to cross ethnic boundaries.

"Reading and Writing" also portrays the possibility of cross-ethnic understanding and acceptance. As the narrator, a Japanese American woman, gets to know the wife of her husband's friend, she learns that the wife, a hillbilly, is illiterate. She also learns, however, that the woman, despite her troubled marriages and hardships, remains undefeated until the moment of her peaceful death. The narrator's admiring tone suggests a way in which cross-ethnic acceptance may be possible: understanding the human behind the stereotyped image.

Yamamoto's study of various characters, some of whom are drawn from her own life, demonstrates her interest in human psychology and family relationships. "The Legend of Miss Sassagawara," in particular, portrays an artist trapped in a sterile environment. Set in a relocation camp in Arizona, the story is narrated by Kiku, a young girl who is intrigued when Miss Sassagawara, a former ballet dancer, moves into the neighborhood with her Buddhist-priest father. According to the biased reports of the narrator, Miss Sasawagara is aloof, arrogant, and unfriendly. The priest father is too absorbed in his spiritual salvation to notice his daughter's mental anguish; and the daughter turns insane as she tries to resist the devastating life in the detention camp.

"Epithalamium" also explores the psychology of women as the author depicts the irrational nature of love. Yuki, a thirty-year-old spinster from California, goes to a Catholic rehabilitation center in New York. She falls in love with an Italian American sailor who is an alcoholic, against the advice of her supervisor. The supervisor tries to send her back to California, but Yuki marries the sailor the day before her planned departure—accepting his demand but wondering why.

Fatherhood and domestic relationships is another subject that holds Yamamoto's interest and is evident in several of her stories. In "My Father Can Beat Muhammad Ali," the author depicts, with humor and sympathy, an issei father's futile efforts to establish his manhood in front of his sons whose idea of manhood involves athletic abilities and body sizes. After drinking more beer than usual, the father boasts that he can beat Muhammad Ali and throw a javelin as well as anyone else. When his demonstration of javelin throwing with a stick utterly fails, he is laughed at by his sons.

More failed fathers are featured in "The Brown House" and "Las Vegas Charley." In the former, Hattori begins to gamble in a Chinese-run gambling house while his family is waiting for him outside. His wife leaves him, but upon seeing him stop gambling she returns only to find him resume the habit. Completely defeated and hopeless, she again waits outside the gambling house while he is gambling inside. The wife's return and decision to stay with her gambler-husband against her better judgment suggest marriage as a trap for women who have children from their marriage.

In "Las Vegas Charley," based on the life of the author's father, an issei man marries a picture bride only to see her die after giving him two sons. He sends the sons to his parents back in Japan and starts to gamble because he has no other joy in life. After he brings his sons back to America, one of them dies in the war, and the other gets married and lives in California. Charley, now working as a dishwasher in a Chinese restaurant in Las Vegas, again has only gambling to look forward to every day.

In "Morning Rain," Yamamoto presents a lyrical view of the father-daughter relationship. In addition to her everyday housework for her children and husband, the narrator takes care of her recently widowed father. As she realizes that her father is losing his hearing, her pathos and filial affection are mixed in the narrative tone.

◆ CRITICAL RECEPTION

Most of Yamamoto's well-known works were written between 1948 and 1961. However, her works had not received the attention they deserved until the 1970s, when Asian Americans became part of the civil rights movement to demand fair representation. When Jeffery Chan, Frank Chin, Lawson Inada, and Shawn Wong started to rediscover and rebuild an Asian American literary history in 1976, they found Yamamoto's works and praised her artistry as a short story writer. By 1980, Yamamoto had become a favorite author for many scholars of Asian American literature.

In their 1980 essay, "Relocation and Dislocation: The Writings of Hisaye Yamamoto and Wakako Yamauchi," Dorothy Ritsuko McDonald and Katharine Newman compare the works of the two nisei writers who became close friends after spending months together in the relocation camp in Poston, Arizona. Whereas Yamauchi writes "totally within the Japanese American community," argue McDonald and Newman, Yamamoto's stories, "with a blend of irony, forbearance, and connectedness," present a world interacting with the world outside Japanese America (132). McDonald and Newman also note Yamamoto's stylistic features as shown in "High-Heeled Shoes": her allusions to European authors to allow a wider perspective; references to real events, places, and people; listing of foods, flowers, and oddments to render a sensory appeal and realistic quality; soliloquies and imaginary dialogues. McDonald and Newman are impressed by Yamamoto's "analytic, meditative, honest, compassionate, and ironic" disposition (133).

Another general assessment of Yamamoto as a short story writer appeared in 1982. Robert T. Rolf, looking at seven stories written between 1948 and 1961, examines Yamamoto's style and themes. Rolf points out the "inductive" exposition of her narrative exposition, how she opens with a specific event in the lives of the characters and moves on to explore its broader implications (91). An exception to this pattern is found in "Las Vegas Charley," "the least successful" of the seven stories, according to Rolf. Yamamoto's language is "quintessentially American, marked by precision, playfulness, and irony," and as for her handling of the theme of sex, Rolf argues that sex is portrayed or imagined to be distasteful and perverted, with attendant images of "adultery, abortion and remorse" (93, 100). Miss Sassagawara's alleged voyeurism, the still-born child of Rosie's mother, and Mrs. Hosoume's abortion, all point to a repressed attitude about sex. Other themes discussed by Rolf include Japanese American family life and clashes between Japanese and American cultural values, which gives rise to the confusion in the young characters.

In *Asian American Literature: An Introduction to the Writings and Their Social Context* (1982) Elaine H. Kim credits Yamamoto for chronicling Japanese

American social history with insight and subtle humor, and for accurately depicting the psychology of women, both adolescent and mature. For Kim, Yamamoto's stories are "consummately women's stories," in which mothers attempt to convey their wisdom to their daughters (160). She also notes how all characters, male and female, try to find ways to transcend difficulties posed to them by society.

Charles Crow, in a 1984 essay about how Los Angeles is represented in literature, writes that Yamamoto's narrative strategy in "Yoneko's Earthquake" is one of the few successful works in capturing the devastation of earthquakes. Yamamoto makes the earthquake "correlative to the emotional climax of the characters," and she uses the illegal abortion, the central event of the story, as a symbol of the destruction brought by the earthquake (Crow 200). Especially for Yoneko, her faith and family life have been ruined by the earthquake and its aftershock: her father's debilitation, the death of her brother, and, without her knowledge, her mother's affair with Marpo and its subsequent abortion. Only by singing and playing word games can she overcome her overwhelming sense of loss.

In 1986, a year before his informative interview with Yamamoto, Crow again writes about Yamamoto, with an emphasis on her portrayal of the issei father. In five of the best known stories, Crows finds two prominent themes related to generational conflict: the failure of issei fathers and the struggle of issei mothers for self-expression. According to Crow, the issei fathers in Yamamoto, "withdrawn and indifferent, sometimes violent," are associated with the images of "sterility, death, and disintegration" ("The Issei Father" 119). In "Seventeen Syllables" and "Yoneko's Earthquake," the father figures are inept and violent; in "The Legend of Miss Sassagawara," the father, absorbed in his own spiritual salvation, lets his daughter suffer from mental problems; and in "The Brown House," the father is weak-willed, undisciplined, and finally unfit to be a father. Not until we get to "Las Vegas Charley," says Crow, does Yamamoto for the first time treat the father figure with sympathy and understanding. Charley is an alcoholic, a compulsive gambler, and a burden to his children. Yet the narrator reminds us of his love for his dead wife, his affectionate memories of his homeland and his parents, and the hardships he had to endure because of external circumstances such as the depression, the war, and the relocation.

After a new collection, *Seventeen Syllables and Other Stories*, was published with an introduction by King-Kok Cheung, scholarship on Yamamoto became much more prolific. In his 1989 essay, "Legacies Revealed: Uncovering Buried Plots in the Stories of Hisaye Yamamoto," for instance, Stan Yogi examines "Seventeen Syllables" and "Yoneko's Earthquake" to reveal Yamamoto's use of hidden plots and subtexts in her portrayal of Japanese American women's plights. By using young narrators with limited perspectives, asserts Yogi, Yamamoto develops what he calls "buried plots": "veiled means of conveying stories that link her work with feminist critical theory as well as with Japanese

American communication patterns" (365). "Seventeen Syllables," for example, opens with a focus on the plot involving Rosie's relationship with Jesus Carrasco, but the author shifts the focus to another plot intertwined with the first one, this time involving Rosie's mother and father. Likewise, "Yoneko's Earthquake" unfolds with an idyllic plot around Yoneko's education and life on the farm leading up to the earthquake, but Yamamoto subtly reveals another plot involving Yoneko's mother, father, and Marpo. While the two plots are connected by the earthquake, Yoneko serves as "an innocent foil which mirrors the more serious relationship the mother develops with Marpo" (367). Yamamoto does not explicitly describe much of the second plot but only drops a series of hints, so as to force the reader to put things together to construct a coherent narrative. By "layering her stories and developing buried plots," Yogi writes, "Yamamoto fully explores the tremendous psychological and emotional costs to Issei women who attempt to pursue their desires in a context hostile to their wishes" (369).

In 1990, Zenobia Baxter Mistri argues in her "Seventeen Syllables: A Symbolic Haiku" that haiku serves as a metaphor for the themes of "Seventeen Syllables." After explaining haiku's spiritual significance, Mistri maintains that haiku is a metaphor of Tome's separation from Mr. Hayashi, who insists upon her traditional role as a wife, as well as from her daughter Rosie, whose language barrier and immaturity prevent her from understanding her mother. Explaining the main conflict in the story as one between Eastern and Western values, Mistri adds that the picture Tome receives as a prize is also associated with the spiritual nature of haiku: a state of mind that remains identical with things around it without losing its individuality.

Yogi's article "Rebels and Heroines: Subversive Narratives in the Stories of Wakako Yamauchi and Hisaye Yamamoto" asserts that the two authors' depiction of rebellious issei women is subversive of issei culture. Narrated from the nisei daughters' point of view, the stories are sympathetic to the mothers' rebellion—even when they are drinking or committing adultery. The stories further suggest the transformation of the very cultural codes against which the mothers rebel. In "Yoneko's Earthquake," for example, while Mrs. Hosoume's adultery challenges the patriarchal order of the family, Yoneko's "unknowing compliance and silence about the ring's origin suggest generational rebellion against the patriarchy" (140).

Based on feminist theory about female writers' narrative strategies, Cheung in her essay, "Double-Telling: Intertextual Silence in Hisaye Yamamoto's Fiction," demonstrates the "multiple levels of silence embedded" in Yamamoto's stories. In both "Seventeen Syllables" and "Yoneko's Earthquake," argues Cheung, the conspicuous action is presented via the perspective of young and naive girls, but the more serious drama is concealed in the narrative. Although such a strategy is consistent with modernist experimentation with the limited point of view, Yamamoto "tailors the method to the Japanese American context": namely, her stories "capitalize not only on the infrequent verbal communication between issei spouses . . . but also on the peculiar interaction" between issei parents and nisei children (278). Yamamoto's "double-telling" is, according to Cheung, "especially suited to evoking suppressed feelings, revealing the anxieties and hurts that lie beneath the surface of language" (291).

Under a broad thesis about the interdependence between New Criticism and cultural criticism, Cheung's 1992 essay "Thrice Muted Tale: Interplay of Art and Politics in Hisaye Yamamoto's 'The Legend of Miss Sassagawara' " performs a close reading of the story to demonstrate the domestic and communal layers of the text's meaning and then moves on to offer a cultural-historical reading to illuminate the political layer of the text's message. On the domestic level, according to Cheung, the story explores the theme of father-daughter relationship, one between a "rejecting father" and an "admiring daughter" (111). On the communal level, the story demonstrates how the community reacts to the pair differently: the father's attitude is "respected" but hers "suspected" (111). To discuss the political dimension of the text's meaning, Cheung brings in historical documents to support her claim that the story, if read against the reality of Japanese Americans in the relocation camps, is an allegory about Japanese American history: the insensitive father parallels the U.S. government's "callousness to its own citizens," and the anguished daughter represents Japanese Americans in the camp (119). The story, then, is "thrice muted" because there is "neither direct confrontation with the father, nor explicit criticism of the Japanese American community, nor open protest against the government" (120). According to Cheung, Yamamoto camouflaged the political allusions because she, a Japanese American woman writing shortly after the war when internment was a very sensitive issue, probably "felt the pressure of personal, communal, and societal censorship" (121).

Cheung wrote several other pieces on Yamamoto, including one on teaching strategies, "Reading Between the Syllables: Hisaye Yamamoto's *Seventeen Syllables and Other Stories*"; an introduction to Hisaye Yamamoto's *Seventeen Syllables and Other Stories*; another introduction to *Seventeen Syllables: Hisaye Yamamoto*, a volume in the Women Writers: Texts and Contexts series from Rutgers University Press; and an essay on "A Fire in Fontana." In the introduction to the "casebook" volume from Rutgers University Press, Cheung argues that Yamamoto's best stories measure up to the masterpieces of other canonical authors such as Katherine Mansfield, Toshio Mori, Flannery O'Connor, Grace Paley, and Ann Petry. In her essay, "The Dream in Flames: Hisaye Yamamoto, Multiculturalism, and the Los Angeles Uprising," Cheung analyzes the double structure of the narrative of "A Fire in Fontana." While the external plot involving the killing of a black family is at the forefront of the memoir, the internal plot tracing the "narrator's evolving racial consciousness and her deepening black allegiance" sets an example of what multiculturalism ought to be like, especially in the face of what we have learned from the Los Angeles riots. In short, Cheung contends that Yamamoto was ahead of her time in recognizing the need for cross-ethnic understanding and for interethnic alliances. Moreover, Yamamoto's act of writing, and thus "reporting the crime," is to be seen as an act of revenge against the racist society (385).

In 1991, PBS broadcast *Hot Summer Winds*, a film adaptation of "Seventeen Syllables" and "Yoneko's Earthquake"—two stories merged into one, written and directed by Emiko Omori. Robert M. Payne's essay, "Adapting (to) the Margins: *Hot Summer Winds* and the Stories of Hisaye Yamamoto," examines the narrative differences between the film and the adapted stories. While the production is a landmark in film history for having Japanese Americans take center stage, the changes made to Yamamoto's stories—especially removing the narrative gaps and offering an optimistic ending in which the father abruptly transforms himself into a sweet man—cause the film to remain "content" within the master narrative of the dominant culture and thus fail to create new ways to think about race and ethnicity (213).

To counter the critics' reading of the issei father as a cruel and violent tyrant and the mother as a victim, Ming L. Cheng writes that, if read against the cultural and social context of the time, the issei father in Yamamoto should be understood as driven to act violently to "regain a necessary measure of control, economic and social, within the limitations inherent in the struggle of first-generation immigrant life" (374–75). Given the economic hardship of the issei generation, Cheng argues, the father figure acts according to the pragmatic concerns and necessities of farm life.

Donald C. Goellnicht provides an analysis of the significance of haiku in "Seventeen Syllables." Since haiku is traditionally regarded as a high art, a sphere for the ruling class, the tension between Mr. and Mrs. Hayashi, according to Goellnicht, is to be understood as a class conflict. Having failed to achieve upward social mobility after the rejection from her higher-class former lover's family, Mrs. Hayashi makes another "attempt to adopt a veneer of sophisticated, urbane speech in order to prove herself good enough" for her former lover (184).

In "Issei Mothers' Silence, Nisei Daughters' Stories: The Short Fiction of Yamamoto," Naoko Sugiyama investigates Yamamoto's use of silence not only as a sign of repression for the women in the stories but also as a means for them to convey their stories. In both "Seventeen Syllables" and "Yoneko's Earthquake," writes Sugiyama, issei mothers are "forced into silence" by difficult living conditions as first-generation immigrants and by Japanese traditional patriarchal norms (387). However, Sugiyama contends that the narrative silence in crucial moments helps convey the stories powerfully without appropriating the mothers' voices.

Two more essays appeared in recent years. Maire Mullins maintains that the silence of Esther in "Wilshire Bus" is representative of "ordinary, everyday lives of women" who are spoken to but silenced. Grace Kyungwon Hong examines how "A Fire in Fontana" suggests a "possible basis for cross-racial solidarity" (293). After reviewing the various ways in which both African and Japanese Americans have been denied full access to property rights—through segregation and internment, for example—Hong argues that the very act of writing the memoir is an attempt to form a cross-racial alliance through revealing the connection between each other's common experience of oppression.

◆ BIBLIOGRAPHY

Works by Hisaye Yamamoto (DeSoto)

Short Story Collections

Seventeen Syllables: 5 Stories of Japanese American Life. Robert Rolf and Norimitsu Ayuzawa, eds. Tokyo: Kirihara Shoten, 1985.

Seventeen Syllables and Other Stories. Latham, NY: Kitchen Table: Women of Color Press, 1988.

Seventeen Syllables: Hisaye Yamamoto. King-Kok Cheung, ed. Women Writers: Texts and Contexts Series. New Brunswick, NJ: Rutgers University Press, 1994.

Memoir and Interview by Questionnaire

"Pleasure of Plain Rice." *Rafu Shimpo* (December 20, 1960): 9–10, 14. Rpt. in *Southwest: A Contemporary Anthology*. Karl Kopp and Jane Kopp, eds. Albuquerque, NM: Red Earth Press, 1977, 295–301.

"A Fire in Fontana." *Rafu Shimpo* (December 21, 1985): 8–9, 16–17, 19. Rpt. in *Rereading America: Cultural Contexts for Critical Thinking and Writing*, 2nd ed. Gary Columbo, Robert Cullen, and Bonnie Lisle, eds. Boston: Bedford Books, 1992, 366–73.

"The Situation of American Writing 1999." *American Literary History* 11.2 (Summer 1999): 215–353.

Studies of Hisaye Yamamoto (DeSoto)

Cheng, Ming L. "The Unrepentant Fire: Tragic Limitations in Hisaye Yamamoto's 'Seventeen Syllables.'" *Short Story Criticism*, vol. 34. Anna Sheets Nesbitt, ed. Detroit, MI: Gale Research, 2000. 374–81. Rpt. from *MELUS* 19.4 (Winter 1994): 91–107.

Cheung, King-Kok. "Introduction." In *Seventeen Syllables and Other Stories*, Cheung, ed., xi–xxv.

———. "Double-Telling: Intertextual Silence in Hisaye Yamamoto's Fiction." *American Literary History* 3.2 (Summer 1991): 277–93. Rpt. in *Seventeen Syllables: Hisaye Yamamoto*, Cheung, ed., 161–80.

———. "Thrice Muted Tale: Interplay of Art and Politics in Hisaye Yamamoto's 'The Legend of Miss Sasagawara.'" *MELUS* 17.3 (Fall 1991–1992): 109–25.

———. *Articulate Silences: Hisaye Yamamoto, Maxine Hong Kingston, Joy Kogawa*. Ithaca, NY: Cornell University Press, 1993.

———. "Interview with Hisaye Yamamoto." In *Seventeen Syllables: Hisaye Yamamoto*, Cheung, ed., 71–86.

———. "Introduction." In *Seventeen Syllables: Hisaye Yamamoto*, Cheung, ed., 3–16.

———. "The Dream in Flames: Hisaye Yamamoto, Multiculturalism, and the Lost Angeles Uprising." In *Short Story Criticism*, vol. 34, 381–86. Rpt. from *Bucknell Review* 39.1 (1995): 118–30.

———. "Reading Between the Syllables: Hisaye Yamamoto's *Seventeen Syllables and Other Stories*." In *Teaching American Ethnic Literatures: Nineteen Essays*. John R. Maitino and David R. Peck, eds. Albuquerque: University of New Mexico Press, 1996, 313–25.

Crow, Charles L. "A *MELUS* Interview: Hisaye Yamamoto." In *Short Story Criticism*, vol. 34, 352–57. Rpt. from *MELUS* 14.1 (1987): 73–84.

———. "The Issei Father in the Fiction of Hisaye Yamamoto." In *Seventeen Syllables: Hisaye Yamamoto*, Cheung, ed., 119–28. Rpt. from *Opening Up Literary Criticism: Essays on American Prose and Poetry*. Leo Truchlar, ed. Salzburg, Austria: Verlag Wolfgang Neugebauer, 1986, 34–40.

———. "Home and Transcendence in Los Angeles Fiction." In *Los Angeles in Fiction: A Collection of Original Essays*. David Fine, ed. Albuquerque, NM: University of New Mexico Press, 1984, 189–205.

Goellnicht, Donald C. "Transplanted Discourse in Yamamoto's 'Seventeen Syllables.' " In *Seventeen Syllables: Hisaye Yamamoto*, Cheung, ed., 181–94.

Hong, Grace K. " 'Something Forgotten Which Should Have Been Remembered': Private Property and Cross-Racial Solidarity in the Work of Hisaye Yamamoto." *American Literature* 71.2 (June 1999): 291–310.

Kim, Elaine H. *Asian American Literature: An Introduction to the Writings and Their Social Context*. Philadelphia: Temple University Press, 1982.

Koppelman, Susan, ed. *Between Mothers and Daughters: Stories Across a Generation*. Old Westbury, NY: The Feminist Press, 1985.

McDonald, Dorothy R., and Katharine Newman. "Relocation and Dislocation: The Writings of Hisaye Yamamoto and Wakako Yamauchi." In *Seventeen Syllables: Hisaye Yamamoto*, Cheung, ed., 129–42. Rpt. from *MELUS* 7.3 (1980): 21–38.

Mistri, Zenobia B. " 'Seventeen Syllables': A Symbolic Haiku." In *Seventeen Syllables: Hisaye Yamamoto*, Cheung, ed., 195–202. Rpt. from *Studies in Short Fiction* 27.2 (Spring 1990): 197–202.

Mullins, Maire. "Esther's Smile: Silence and Action in Hisaye Yamamoto's 'Wilshire Bus.' " *Studies in Short Fiction* 35.1 (Winter 1998): 77–84.

Osborne, William P., and Sylvia A. Watanabe. "A Conversation with Hisaye Yamamoto." *Chicago Review* 39.3–4 (1993): 34–43.

Payne, Robert M. "Adapting (to) the Margins: *Hot Summer Winds* and the Stories of Hisaye Yamamoto." In *Seventeen Syllables: Hisaye Yamamoto*, Cheung, ed., 203–218. Rpt. from *East West Film Journal* 7.2 (Jul 1993): 39–53.

Rolf, Robert T. "The Short Stories of Hisaye Yamamoto, Japanese American Writer." In *Seventeen Syllables: Hisaye Yamamoto*, Cheung, ed., 89–108. Rpt. from *Bulletin of Fukuoka University of Education* 31.1 (1982): 71–86.

Sugiyama, Naoko. "Issei Mothers' Silence, Nisei Daughters' Stories: The Short Fiction of Hisaye Yamamoto." *Short Story Criticism*, vol. 34, 386–92. Rpt. from *Comparative Literature Studies* 33.1 (1996): 1–14.

Usui, Masami. "Prison, Psyche, and Poetry in Hisaye Yamamoto's Three Short Stories: 'Seventeen Syllables,' 'The Legend of Miss Sasagawara,' and 'The Eskimo Connection.' " *Studies in Culture and the Humanities* 6 (1997): 1–29.

Yogi, Stan. "Legacies Revealed: Uncovering Buried Plots in the Stories of Hisaye Yamamoto." *Short Story Criticism*, vol. 34, 364–71. Rpt. from *Studies in American Fiction* 17.2 (1989): 169–81. Rpt. in *Seventeen Syllables: Hisaye Yamamoto*, Cheung, ed., 143–60.

———. "Rebels and Heroines: Subversive Narratives in the Stories of Wakako Yamauchi and Hisaye Yamamoto." In *Reading the Literatures of Asian America*. Shirley Geok-lin Lim and Amy Ling, eds. Philadelphia: Temple University Press, 1992, 131–50.

LOIS-ANN YAMANAKA
(1961–   )

Kyoko Amano

Lois-Ann Yamanaka was born on September 7, 1961 in Ho'olchua, Molokai, Hawaii. She is the daughter of a taxidermist from Kaua'i, Harry, and a school teacher from Kona, Jean. Yamanaka is best known for her novel published in 1997, *Blu's Hanging*, which Mika Tanner describes as "a brutally frank portrayal of three Japanese American children on the island of Molokai as they struggle with their mother's death." As soon as the book appeared in bookstores, readers and critics pointed out the book's racist descriptions of Filipino Americans. It was nominated for the Association for Asian American Studies' (AAAS) National Fiction Award in the summer of 1998, and Yamanaka's students of Filipino origin received the award as the author's representatives. However, because of the novel's depiction of a Filipino American as sexually deviant, the award was rescinded the day after the award ceremony, and nearly all of the board members resigned from their positions. Regarding the characterization of Uncle Paulo, Yamanaka tells Caroline Wright in an interview that she drew that particular character from her most frightening girlhood experience in a small town on the Big Island when her classmates were being raped: "They were being picked up, one by one, on their way home from school, on their way home from the movies. . . . And it so happened to be . . . he was a Filipino young man, he had just graduated from high school." The AAAS's decision caused controversy among Asian American writers, such as Amy Tan, Maxine Hong Kingston, Lawson Fusao Inada, Frank Chin, and Shawn Wong, who argued that the AAAS's decision was unconstitutional: it went against freedom of speech and artistic creativity. Critics who support Yamanaka, like Stephanie Green, point out the fact that

Uncle Paulo is not the only character that is portrayed unfavorably. Green writes, "No ethnicity is singled out and all are part of the problem" in *Blu's Hanging*.

Yamanaka's family lived above her father's taxidermy store, which is also the setting for her novel, *Heads by Harry*. Yamanaka was raised Southern Baptist, but her mother was quite open to other denominations—if there wasn't a Southern Baptist church, the family went to a Methodist church. During the third grade, Yamanaka went to a Catholic Church for experience. The family moved to the Big Island during the 1960s. In her interview with Wright, Yamanaka says that in her girlhood, she read Ruth Tabrah's *Hawaiian Heart* and *The Red Shark* because Tabrah wrote books set on the Big Island. Yamanaka's favorite book was *To Kill a Mockingbird*. In college, however, Yamanaka admits that she depended upon Cliff's Notes because she was "a very slow reader." She says to Wright, "I have been discovering, for the first time in my life, William Faulkner." Yamanaka received her bachelor's degree in education in 1983 from the University of Hawaii at Manoa and a master's degree in education in 1987 from the same institution.

Despite her educational background, Yamanaka did not start writing fiction until she was twenty-seven years old. She grew up speaking Pidgin English, Hawaiian Creole English of the rural working class. She was led to believe that pidgin was a substandard language and that she would never get ahead speaking pidgin. Like many others, she tried to get rid of the dialect until one of her professors at the University of Hawaii at Manoa said to her that pidgin was her "voice." She realized that her stories must be told in pidgin.

Encouraged by a National Endowment for the Humanities grant in 1990, she wrote fiction in pidgin and her first collection of verse novellas, *Saturday Night at the Pahala Theatre*, was published in 1993 by Bamboo Ridge Press, a publishing house that grew out of the 1978 conference for new-wave Hawaiian voices. In her interview with Mary Kaye Ritz, Yamanaka recalls that the publication of *Saturday Night at the Pahala Theatre* changed her life completely because her son, John ("JohnJohn"), was diagnosed with autism that year. Yamanaka says, "When he was diagnosed, my life was forced to change, but it was forced to change anyway. . . . I had to stay home. My life as a teacher was going to be over." That year, *Saturday Night at the Pahala Theatre* won Pushcart Prize 18; in 1994, it brought her an Asian American Studies National Book Award and a National Endowment for the Arts creative-writing fellowship. In 1994, her short work "Yarn Wig" won Pushcart Prize 19. She was a recipient of the Elliot Cades Award for Literature in 1993 and the Carnegie Foundation in 1994. Her first novel, *Wild Meat and the Bully Burgers*, was published in 1996. A year later, her second and controversial novel, *Blu's Hanging*, was published. She received the Rona Jaffe Award for Women Writers in 1996, the Lannan Literary Award and Asian American Literary Award in 1998. In 1999, she published a highly autobiographical novel, *Heads by Harry*. *Heads by Harry*, along with *Wild Meat and the Bully Burgers* and *Blu's Hanging*, is a part of the Hilo trilogy, novels set in Hilo on the Big Island. She published *Name Me Nobody*, an adolescent novel, in 1999 and *Father of Four Passages* in 2001. In *Father of Four Passages*, Yamanaka does not use pidgin, and she fears, as she says to Ritz, "people will say, 'Oh, she sold out.' 'This is a desire to be mainstream,' 'This is a desire to have a wider audience.' " She lists Nora Okja Keller as her favorite Island writer and friend. She is working on a historical novel set in turn-of-the-twentieth-century Hawaii.

While continuously working on poetic fiction, Yamanaka raises her autistic son, John, with her husband John Inferrera, a high school health and physical education teacher. She teaches English to children of diverse socioeconomic backgrounds, takes medication for clinical depression, and keeps a depression diary. She lives in Honolulu, and visits her grandmother in Molokai once a year.

◆ MAJOR WORKS AND THEMES

Many of Yamanaka's works focus on young, working-class Japanese Americans in Hawaii, who face puberty while searching for their identity as the descendants of Japanese immigrant laborers on Hawaiian plantations. Her short story "What Love Is" perhaps best represents the recurrent themes of her works: adolescence and sexuality. The teenage narrator, Lovey, examines her relationship with a gay friend, Jerry, and attempts to define what love is and what her friendship with Jerry is. Sensitive and self-conscious of her awkwardness, Lovey wants to always be Jerry's best friend, but she catches herself teasing Jerry for his sexuality and sometimes hurting his feelings just like other, inconsiderate people who use derogatory terms like queer, queen, fag, lez, and hag. In describing ambiguous feelings between Lovey and Jerry, Yamanaka captures bittersweet moments of adolescence. Regarding her use of teenage narrators in her stories, Yamanaka says to Ritz that she needs "a 15-year emotional distance from a time, from a place." She adds, "That 15 years offers perspective."

Lovey is also the narrator in "My Nanny and Billy the Kid," which, like "What Love Is," is a short story from *Wild Meat and the Bully Burgers*. In this story, Yamanaka strings together several scenes from Lovey's home videos that chronicle Lovey and her sister Calhoon's baby goat named Nanny and baby ram named Billy the Kid. As Lovey watches the videos that depict her relationship with Nanny and Billy the Kid comically, she records her feelings behind the scenes in the videos, such as her fear when Billy the Kid attacked them, her uncertain feeling when her father killed Billy the Kid, her sorrow when she parted from Nanny, who was taken to a zoo.

Her characters speak pidgin, the language Yamanaka and other Bamboo Ridge-school writers are trying to preserve. Her prose poem, "Yarn Wig," exemplifies her use of pidgin. It starts with seemingly ungrammatical opening lines. The speaker uses pidgin not only to narrate the story and to express her feelings but also to record store clerks' comments on the long, black, wig that the mother made out of yarn from Ben Franklin. Upon seeing the speaker of the poem and her sisters, the soda fountain lady calls for a clerk from the fabric section, repeating, "try come." Harriet, the fabric lady, praises the speaker's mother. The speaker's extensive use of pidgin thus creates the sense of community rather than alienation of the speaker and her family.

The genre of her short works is sometimes difficult to determine. For example, "Empty Heart" has the appearance of both prose and verse. While the first-person narrator describes how WillyJoe touches her, she makes frequent line breaks to reflect WillyJoe's touch and to slow down the narration: "Crawl slow/slow there too/then stop/ in his finger tracks" (545). Besides Yamanaka's vivid description of a young girl's relationship with an older dropout, whom her teacher calls "child molester," "Trespasser," "Scram," and "big good-for-nothing," Yamanaka uses images drawn from the movie *The Wizard of Oz* to depict the narrator and WillyJoe (546). The narrator calls herself "Empty heart" (545, 550), "Judy Gar-land" (548), and "Dor-ty" (548, 550); WillyJoe has "so-sho and emo-sho [social and emotional] handicap" and calls himself "the Big Scarecrow" (548). Apparently, mingled within the narrator are Dorothy and the Tinman, while WillyJoe represents the Cowardly Lion and the Big Scarecrow. Thus, Yamanaka cleverly uses the images drawn from popular culture on the mainland.

The world Yamanaka portrays in her fiction is not the tropical paradise that readers might expect from the Hawaiian author and setting. Her Hawaii is violent and cruel. For example, in Yamanaka's verse poem, "Saturday Night at the Pahala Theater: Kala, Jimmy Boy and His Brother Mugs See 'Cheerleaders Growing Up,'" the inquisitive narrator, Kala, with Jimmy Boy and Mugs, goes to watch an X-rated movie in which a Caucasian cheerleader is raped by the principal and a teacher. During the movie, Jimmy Boy and Mugs take advantage of Kala. In "Sunnyside Up," the narrator's father, Harry, is brutal and merciless to animals. He strikes the rooster that had spurred first into his eyelid and next in the ankle. In revenge, Harry hangs the rooster upside down until it dies. When he finds that a huge rat is stealing the papaya rind, seeds, and chicken bones meant for the chickens, he poisons the rind and bones. He finds two dogs attacking the chickens, and he sets up a cage to catch them and practices slingshot and pitchfork throwing. Eventually, he kills the dogs owned by a Portuguese neighbor. Although Yamanaka's short stories have disturbing elements, they are also full of comical anecdotes that string her work to reveal the brutal reality of Hawaii with conflicts arising from race and class discrimination. Such is the case with "Sunnyside Up": the narrator vividly describes these scenes of slaughter, while interweaving them with rather comical scenes of her father's preparations for the killings.

◆ CRITICAL RECEPTION

Yamanaka's critical reception cannot be illustrated without touching upon the controversy surrounding her third book and second novel, *Blu's Hanging*, and the literature award from the Association for Asian American Studies in the summer of 1998. The novel is written from the point of view of Ivah Ogata, a thirteen-year-old girl who copes with the death of her mother with her younger brother Blu and sister Maisie while her father works two jobs in the poverty-stricken neighborhood. Jamie James calls the novel "a Hawaiian *Catcher in the Rye*, the story of a confused thirteen-year-old girl" (92). In her father's absence, Ivah raises her younger siblings, learning how to cook, babysitting neighbor's children, and washing dogs. While she goes through puberty without a mother, Blu is molested by Uncle Paulo, a Filipino neighbor who has sexual intercourse with his young nieces during their mother's absence.

It is the depiction of Uncle Paulo as a sexual predator and his nieces' cruelty toward animals that irritated the ethnic community, scholars, and critics of Hawaii when *Blu's Hanging* received the literature award from the Association for Asian American Studies. According to Edward Moran's *Current Biography*, Jonathan Okamura, a sociologist at the University of Hawaii, was "deeply offended and outraged" by the depiction of Filipino Americans as villains, and Candace Fujikane, a professor of English, also at the University of Hawaii, criticized "Yamanaka's failure to invest *Blu's Hanging* with a therapeutic purpose to help provide uplift for disempowered groups" (623). The AAAS granted the award, which was received by three of Yamanaka's Filipino students, while a number of association members wore black armbands and sat with their backs turned to the stage in protest. Following the resignation of the officers and executive director, the association decided to revoke the award. On the other hand, eighty-two Asian American writers stood in Yamanaka's defense by writing letters. Fourteen Filipino American authors, including Jessica Hagedorn, also defended Yamanaka against AAAS. According to Edward Moran, they argued that "the vote to rescind the award was a threat to free speech and literary creativity" (623).

According to Jamie James, Yamanaka's first novel, *Wild Meat and the Bully Burgers*, was also nominated for the AAAS literature award in 1996. However, the committee decided not to issue a prize that year because some of the committee members complained that Yamanaka's previous work, *Saturday Night at the Pahala Theatre*, and her new novel, *Blu's Hanging*, had some offensive passages. While there are not very many reviews and articles on Yamanaka's individual short stories, there are some on her *Wild Meat and the Bully Burgers*, a novel that includes many of Yamanaka's previously published short stories. Jamie James comments that *Wild Meat and the Bully Burgers* is "an exuberant, crazily comic series of anecdotes, virtually plotless, about a girl on the threshold of adolescence" (91). The stories mainly focuses on a teenage protagonist, Lovey Nariyoshi, who narrates her story of growing up in Hawaii as a poor Japanese American. Betsy Levins and Shirley E. Havens consider the protagonist and her best friend Jerry's adventures "hilarious and heart-breaking" and point out, "Yamanaka's voice is fresh, honest, raw, and funny" (136). Kiana Davenport, also a Hawaiian, praises Yamanaka's novel: "most of the stories [are] funny, poignant, scathingly authentic and often stabbingly beautiful." Davenport continues, "The book is full of the authentic sights and smells of childhood in Hawai'i." Alice Joyce remarks that Yamanaka's novel is "an exceptional and expressive cultural document" (611). While David A. Beronä praises the novel, writing, "this engrossing novel is strongly woven together, with chapters that swing from heartfelt, childhood memories of Lovey's father, Hubert, to the fiendish behavior of her neighbors," some re-viewers disagree with Beronä's opinion (101). Because each chapter of the novel is very short and focuses on a single episode, the novel as a whole gives an impression that it is highly episodic and anecdotal. For example, Merle Rubin points out in "New Voices Spin Tales of Fiction, Mostly Fiction," that Yamanaka's novel is "little more than a string of anecdotes serving up the usual teen angst with a slightly crude tang of resentment" (14). Davenport also acknowledges the structural weakness of the novel in her review: "*Wild Meat and the Bully Burgers* is less a novel than a series of linked vignettes chronicling the coming of age of Lovey Nariyoshi." Yet, Davenport concludes the review, noting its "lyrical, irreverent language" of Pidgin English used in narrating the moving anecdotes.

While Yamanaka's use of Pidgin English is the target of criticism, it is also the strength of her voice, just as it is for her narrator-protagonist in *Wild Meat and the Bully Burgers*. "Words Short List" expresses positive comments that Yamanaka's use of Pidgin in *Wild Meat and the Bully Burgers* is "a new voice, with narrator Lovey at the wheel, slaloming between the culture gap and her tough/tender dad." Noting that many stories set in Hawaii have been pre-viously written by writers from mainland, not by native Hawaiian, Jamie James calls Yamanaka "a bard of sorts" (90). On the contrary, while admitting Yamanaka's "darkly comical [language], with an underlying poetic lilt," the review of *Wild Meat and the Bully Burgers* in the October 1995 issue of *Publishers Weekly* comments that "Lovey's pidgin English is sprinkled with so much unfamiliar island vernacular that a glossary would be helpful" and that Lovey's language is "crude and ungrammatical" (51).

While Yamanaka continued to use pidgin in *Wild Meat and the Bully Burger*, *Blu's Hanging*, and *Heads by Harry*, she used standard English in her novel *Father of Four Passages*. The *Asian Reporter* comments that "Ms. Yamanaka's nearly exclusive use of Standard English in her . . . *Father of Four Passages* . . . now stirs nearly as much ire from her indigenous allies, who suggest that she 'sold out' to her top-drawer mainland publisher's market." Yamanaka explains in her interview with the *Asian Reporter*, "Though some people want me to stick to Pidgin, that language is not my whole experience" (12).

◆ BIBLIOGRAPHY

Works by Lois-Ann Yamanaka

Short Stories

"Saturday Night at the Pahala Theatre: Kala, Jimmy Boy and His Brother Mugs See 'Cheerleaders Growing Up.' " *Parnassus: Poetry in Review* 17.1 (1991): 79–81.

"Empty Heart." In *Charlie Chan Is Dead*. Jessica Hagedorn, ed. New York: Penguin, 1993, 544–50.

"Yarn Wig." *Michigan Quarterly Review* 32.1 (Winter 1993): 36–38.

"Dominate and Recessid Jeans." *Bamboo Ridge: A Hawai'i Writers' Quarterly* 57 (Winter 1993): 128–31.

"Sunnyside Up." *Chicago Review* 39.3–4 (1993): 175–78.

Excerpt from *American Eyes: New Asian American Short Stories for Young Adults*. Lori M. Carlson, ed. New York: Holt, 1994, 6–10.

"Alexander Fu Sheng Kicks Bruce Lee's Ass, Sonny Chiba and Toshiro Mifune Too." *Bamboo Ridge: A Hawai'i Writers' Quarterly* 60 (Winter 1994): 71–75.

"Blah Blah Blah." *Bamboo Ridge: A Hawai'i Writers' Quarterly* 60 (Winter 1994): 62–66.

"Oompah Loompah." *Bamboo Ridge: A Hawai'i Writers' Quarterly* 60 (Winter 1994): 67–70.

"Pin the Fan on the Hand." *Bamboo Ridge: A Hawai'i Writers' Quarterly* 60 (Winter 1994): 76–80.

"My Nanny and Billy the Kid." *The American Poetry Review* 25.1 (1996): 31–32.

Novels

Saturday Night at the Pahala Theatre. Honolulu: Bamboo Ridge Press, 1993.
Wild Meat and the Bully Burgers. New York: Farrar, 1996.
Blu's Hanging. New York: Farrar, 1997.
Heads by Harry. New York: Farrar, 1999.
Name Me Nobody. New York: Hyperion, 1999.
Father of the Four Passages. New York: Farrar, 2001.

Children's Book

Sand Angel, Snow Angel (Work in progress)

Studies of Lois-Ann Yamanaka

Beronä, David A. "Wild Meat and the Bully Burgers." *Library Journal* (15 Nov. 1995): 101. *Academic Search Elite*. Hanley Library, University of Pittsburgh at Bradford, PA. http://ehostvgw20.epnet.com/. Accessed February 19, 2002.

Davenport, Kiana. "Cultural Crossroad." Rev. of *Wild Meat and the Bully Burgers* by Lois-Ann Yamanaka and *A Little Too Much Is Enough* by Kathleen Tyau. *Women's Review of Books* 13.10–11 (July 1996): 37.

Foote, Donna. "Trouble in Paradise: A Hawaiian Novelist Sparks a P.C. Protest." *Newsweek* (August 17, 1998): 63. *Academic Search Elite*. Hanley Library, University of Pittsburgh at Bradford, PA. http://ehostvgw20.epnet.com/. Accessed February 19, 2002.

Green, Stephanie. "Book Is Raw, But Not Racist." *Asian Week*. http://www.asianweek.com/080698/a_e.html. Accessed February 19, 2002.

James, Jamie. "This Hawaii Is Not for Tourist—Heads by Harry." *Atlantic Monthly* 283.2 (1999): 90–94.

Joyce, Alice. "Wild Meat and the Bully Burgers." *Booklist* 92.7 (December 1, 1995): 611. *Academic Search Elite*. Hanley Library, University of Pittsburgh at Bradford, PA. http://ehostvgw20.epnet.com/. Accessed February 19, 2002.

Levins, Betsy, and Shirley E. Havens. "Words of Mouth." *Library Journal* 121.4 (March 1, 1996): 136. *Academic Search Elite*. Hanley Library, University of Pittsburgh at Bradford, PA. http://ehostvgw20.epnet.com/. Accessed February 19, 2002.

"Lois-Ann Yamanaka." Literature Resource Center 3.1 *Contemporary Authors*. http://galenet.galegroup.com/. Accessed February 19, 2002.

Moran, Edward. "Lois-Ann Yamanaka." *Current Biography Yearbook* 60.6 (June 1999): 57–59.

Morgan, Peter. "Lois-Ann Yamanaka." In *Asian American Poets: A Bio-Bibliographical Critical Sourcebook*. Guiyou Huang, ed. Westport, CT: Greenwood Press, 2002, 337–41.

Nguyen, Lan N. "Hawaiian Eye-Opener: Talking with . . . Lois-Ann Yamanaka." *People Weekly* (May 26, 1997): 42. *Expanded Academic ASAP*. Infotrac. Hanley Library, University of Pittsburgh at Bradford, PA. http://infotrac.galegroup.com/itweb/upitt_main. Accessed February 19, 2002.

Publishers Weekly 242.40 (October 2, 1995): 51. *Academic Search Elite*. Hanley Library, University of Pittsburgh at Bradford, PA. http://ehostvgw20.epnet.com/. Accessed February 19, 2002.

Ritz, Mary Kaye. "Lois-Ann Yamanaka Tells of Special Meaning Behind Her New Book." *HonoluluAdvertiser.com Island Life*. http://the.honoluluadvertiser.com/2001/Feb/04/24islandlife1.html. Accessed February 19, 2002.

Rubin, Merle. "New Voices Spin Tales of Fiction, Mostly Fiction." *Christian Science Monitor* 88.31 (January 10, 1996): 14. *Academic Search Elite*. Hanley Library, University of Pittsburgh at Bradford, PA. http://ehostvgw18.epnet.com/. Accessed February 19, 2002.

Steinberg, Sybil S. "Forecasts: Fiction." Rev. of *Heads by Harry. Publishers Weekly* 244.8 (February 24, 1997): 62. *Academic Search Elite*. Hanley Library, University of Pittsburgh at Bradford, PA. http://ehostvgw20.epnet.com/. Accessed February 19, 2002.

Tanner, Mika. "The Real-Life Sequel to 'Blu's Hanging': Reaction to Her Book Was a Story in Itself—Here's What She Has to Say." *Asian Week*. http://www.asianweek.com/080698/a_e.html. Accessed February 19, 2002.

"Words Short List." Rev. of *Wild Meat and the Bully Burgers. Village Voice* 41.11 (March

12, 1996): 13. *Academic Search Elite*. Hanley Library, University of Pittsburgh at Bradford, PA. http://ehostvgw18.epnet.com/. Accessed February 19, 2002.

Wright, Caroline. "Lois-Ann the Warrior: An Interview with Lois-Ann Yamanaka." *Wright for You Copy Development & Services*. http://www.wrightforyou.com/loisannyamanaka.html. Accessed February 19, 2002.

"Writer Profile: Lois-Ann Yamanaka." *The Asian Reporter* 11.8 (February 20–26, 2001): 12. http://www.asianreporter.com/stories/profiles/08yanareka%20profile.htm. Accessed February 19, 2002.

KAREN TEI YAMASHITA
(1951–   )

Robin E. Field

♦ BIOGRAPHY

Karen Tei Yamashita, a third-generation Japanese American, or sansei, was born on January 8, 1951, in Oakland, California. She spent most of her childhood in Los Angeles and then attended Carleton College in Minnesota, studying English and Japanese literature. Yamashita spent her junior year abroad at Waseda University in Japan. During this year and a half, she pondered questions of global migration and ethnic and national identities, issues which figure prominently in her later fiction. To her acquaintances in Japan she was considered "pure Japanese," able to trace her family history back fourteen generations. But Yamashita was uncomfortable with a label that prioritized race without acknowledging nation and culture; and in an essay in her recent collection *Circle K Cycles*, she instead claims the term nikkei, of Japanese ancestry, whether a Japanese emigrant or Japanese American (10). Her story "The Bath" (1975) illustrates the cultural differences between three generations of a Japanese and nikkei family.

In 1975 Yamashita's interests in identity, migration, and assimilation led her to research Japanese immigration to Brazil, which is home to the largest population of nikkei in the world. Funded by a Thomas J. Watson Fellowship, she researched the lives and accomplishments of these Japanese emigrants and their descendants. The story "Tucano" (1975) tells of one such emigrant seeking his fortune by farming reclaimed rainforest land. Yamashita spent a total of nine years in Brazil, where she married a Brazilian architect and artist, Ronaldo Lopes de Oliveira, and had two children. She and her family moved to Los Angeles in 1984, which meant, according to Yamashita, "immigrating back to my own country" (*Circle K Cycles* 13). Yamashita's research and experiences in Brazil are reflected in her first two novels, *Through the Arc of the Rainforest* (1990) and *Brazil-Maru* (1992).

Upon returning to the United States, Yamashita worked with a variety of genres and artistic media, which include a screenplay, plays, short stories, novels, performance art, essays, and an electronic journal and short story collection. She was hired by the University of California at Santa Cruz in 1996 to teach creative writing and Asian American literature. In 1997 Yamashita spent six months in Seto, Japan, funded by a Japan Foundation Fellowship to study Brazilians living in Japan. Her time there is chronicled both in her electronic journal and short story collection published electronically at the Cafe Creole website and in *Circle K Cycles* (2001). This book contains journal entries, short stories, and scrapbook-like pages with advertisements, photos, and graphics that illustrate her experience of being both nikkei and gaijin (foreigner).

Yamashita's writing garnered critical acclaim from the very first. Her story "The Bath" won first place in the *Amerasia Journal* Short Story Contest in 1975 and was reprinted in *The Third Woman: Minority Women Writers of the United States* in 1980. *Rafu Shimpo*, a Japanese American newspaper, published "Tucano" in 1975 (which won first prize in the newspaper's short story contest) and "Asaka-No-Miya" in 1979 (which won the American-Japanese National Literary Award). Yamashita received a Rockefeller Playwright-in-Residence Fellowship at East West Players in Los Angeles in 1977–1978, where her play *Omen: An American Kabuki* was produced. *Through the Arc of the Rainforest* won an American Book Award in 1991 and the Janet Heidinger Kafka Award in 1992. The *Village Voice* named *Brazil-Maru* one of the twenty-five best books of 1992. Yamashita's third novel, *Tropic of Orange* (1997), set in Los Angeles, was a finalist for the Paterson Fiction Prize. The genre-defying *Circle K Cycles* has been praised by critics for its exploration of ethnic and national identities, geographic boundaries, and globalization.

◆ MAJOR WORKS AND THEMES

Yamashita's interests in migration, identity, globalization, and technology appear prominently throughout her short stories. The piercing social commentary seen in her novels is present in her short stories as well, as Yamashita takes on environmental activism, generational conflicts, and community relations. The range of her narrative voice, from the frankly personal in "Madama B" (1993) to the dry irony of "The Last Secretary" (1996), demonstrates the stylistic virtuosity of Yamashita's pen. Despite the relative obscurity of their publication, many of Yamashita's early stories laid the groundwork for the use of postmodernity, magical realism, and science fiction in her later fiction.

Environmental issues are at the heart of "Tucano," set in the rainforests of Brazil. The protagonist, a Japanese emigrant, intends to clear the land to plant coffee. Yamashita demonstrates how the life of the rainforest is at stake by placing him in dialogue with a mysterious woman who speaks in the voice of the rainforest itself. While the woman tells the secrets of the rainforest and its creatures, the man hears only how he can profit from the destruction of its natural cycles. The magical realism of "Tucano" is echoed in "The Orange" (1993), which forecasts the plot of *Tropic of Orange*. In this story the Tropic of Cancer becomes entangled in an orange and is pulled along as the orange exchanges hands. As the orange travels north from Mexico to Los Angeles with a migrant worker, Latin American countries slide northward as well. Changes in lifestyles ensue: Chinese Americans speak Spanish; tortillas are sold in Little Tokyo; and homeless people suddenly carry briefcases and wear suits. This use of magical realism demonstrates the permeability of borders, both geographic and cultural. "The Dentist and the Dental Hygienist" (1987) tells of the uncanny knowledge that Candy, a sansei hygienist, has about her patients' personal lives. Although she drives away many of the dentist's most loyal patients with her searing observations, Candy ultimately confirms to Dr. Hashikin the dissatisfaction he subconsciously feels about his prescribed middle-class existence. This confirmation inspires him to leave both his dental practice and his staid lifestyle in a California suburb. Although Yamashita uses magical realism to portray Candy's knowledge, she also delves into issues of Japanese American identity after the internment camps.

"The Bath" and "Asaka-No-Miya" explore shifting identities between the generations of families. In "The Bath" twin Japanese American protagonists first observe the cultural differences between their immigrant parents and Japanese grandmother through their varying bathing rituals. Later, while traveling in Japan, one of the young women struggles to blend in as a Japanese student, but is conscious that she sees the country from a foreign perspective. "Asaka-No-Miya" tells of a Brazilian nisei (second-generation Japanese emigrant) who impersonates a Japanese prince in order to con the issei (first-generation emigrants) out of their life savings. Yamashita contrasts this son, who chooses Brazilian opportunism over Japanese fealty, with his father, who wishes to take his life in front of the "prince" because he could not give his life for Japan during World War II.

Yamashita's "Madama B" and "The Last Secretary" demonstrate the range of her stories' subject matter. "Madama B" is the most autobiographical of her stories, telling of her quest to record a chicken's cackles for her performance art. Also autobiographical, "The Last Secretary" tells of a sansei secretary who has seen the shift from carbon paper to fax machines, suffered from Carpal Tunnel Syndrome, and watched her colleagues be replaced by temp workers. Published in an anthology of stories about the turn of the millennium, Yamashita's story probes the intersection of technology and humanity.

Although Yamashita began her writing career with short stories, she did not publish a collection of stories until *Circle K Cycles* in 2001. Yet to call this book simply a short story collection downplays the joyful polyphony that erupts from its pages. *Circle K Cycles* places graphics illustrating population trends on the same page as fiction, photographs of the local convenience store alongside essays on assimilation, and comics next to recipes for gyoza and pastel. The story of a nikkei conwoman appears first in Portuguese and then again in English. The rules for an apartment complex first are written in Japanese characters and on the next pages in English. In addition to challenging notions of genre, Yamashita collapses the boundaries between cultural and national identities to demonstrate how geography no longer dictates community.

Many of the stories in *Circle K Cycles* deal with dekasegi, the descendants of Japanese emigrants to Brazil who have come to Japan to work. In "What if Miss Nikkei Were God(dess)?" one such dekasegi is eighteen-year-old beauty pageant winner Miss Hamamatsu, who copies videotapes of Brazilian television shows to rent to other dekasegi. Her narrow social circle and focus on all things Brazilian demonstrate the social difficulties dekasegi face in placing themselves in the largely unfamiliar Japanese culture. "Three Marias" illustrates the grueling conditions that many dekasegi face as they work in factories, performing unskilled labor to support families still in Brazil. The conwoman Maria Madalena of "Zero Zero One-derful" demonstrates the fluidity of identity of dekasegi who create hybrid identities. In this story Maria Madalena maintains three telephone conversations at once: she comforts a lonely factory worker as a phone sex operator, sells advertising for a nonexistent telephone book, and chats with a friend about her former life in Brazil. The difficulties of immigration on families are demonstrated in "Hantai," as Japanese-speaking children take language courses in order to understand their dekasegi parents' Portuguese tongue. "The Tunnel" emphasizes the psychological damage of dekasegi when two lovers are murdered and the thoughts of their friends and family are revealed. The final story, "Samba Matsuri," demonstrates how racial categories matter to dekasegi as well as Japanese when a riot erupts over whether Miss Nikkei has any Japanese blood. *Circle K Cycles* demonstrates the versatility of ethnic identity in a place where a "pure blood" Japanese can be considered nikkei, dekasegi, and gaijin.

◆ CRITICAL RECEPTION

Many of Yamashita's short stories, published as they were in newspapers, regional journals, or minor anthologies, have not received the same attention from critics and readers as have her novels. Yet the publication of *Circle K Cycles* will mostly likely lead to greater notice of her short fiction. *Circle K Cycles* has been praised for its fusion of complex issues of the transnational and postmodern with compassionate portrayals of those whom Roy Osamu Kamada calls "the voiceless." Yamashita's short stories undoubtedly will receive the attention they deserve from readers and critics in the future.

◆ BIBLIOGRAPHY

Works by Karen Tei Yamashita

Short Stories

"The Bath." *Amerasia Journal* 3.1 (1975): 137–52. Rpt. in *The Third Woman: Minority Women Writers of the United States*. Dexter Fisher, ed. New York: Houghton Mifflin, 1980, 505–19.

"Tucano." *Rafu Shimpo* (December 20, 1975): 11, 35.

"Asaka-No-Miya." *Rafu Shimpo* (December 20, 1979): 8–10, 16–17, 20.

"The Dentist and the Dental Hygienist." *AsiAm* 2 (1987): 66–70.

"The Orange." *Chicago Review* 39 (1993): 12–16.

"Madama B." *International Examiner* (May 5–18, 1993): 17–19.

"The Last Secretary." In *2000andWhat?* Karl Roeseler and David Gilbert, eds. San Francisco: Trip Street Press, 1996, 191–201.

Short Story Collection

Circle K Cycles. Minneapolis, MN: Coffee House Press, 2001.

Novels

Through the Arc of the Rain Forest. Minneapolis, MN: Coffee House Press, 1990.

Brazil-Maru. Minneapolis, MN: Coffee House Press, 1992.

Tropic of Orange. Minneapolis, MN: Coffee House Press, 1997.

Poetry

"Maceio." In *Ayumi: A Japanese-American Anthology*. San Francisco: Japanese American Anthology Committee, 1979, 253–54.

"Obasan." In *Calafia: The California Poetry*. Ishmael Reed, ed. Berkeley, CA: Yardbird Books, 1979, 375–77.

Dramatic Works and Screenplay

Omen: An American Kabuki. Produced in Los Angeles, 1978.

Hiroshima Tropical. Produced in Los Angeles, 1984.

Kusei: An Endangered Species. (With Karen Mayeda.) Visual Communications, 1986.

Hannah Kusoh: An American Butoh. Produced in Los Angeles, 1989. Published in *Premonitions*. New York: Kaya Productions, 1995.

Tokyo Carmen vs. L.A. Carmen. Produced in Los Angeles, 1990. Published in part in *Multicultural Theatre: Scenes and Monologs from New Hispanic, Asian, and African-American Plays*. Colorado Springs, CO: Meriwether Publishing, 1996.

GiLAwrecks. Produced in Seattle, 1992.
Noh Bozos. Produced in Los Angeles, 1993.

Electronic Journal Publications

"Circle K." Monthly journal series for *Cafe Creole*. Ryuta Imafuku, ed. 1998. http://www.ojw.or.jp/cafecreole. Accessed September 21, 2001.

Studies of Karen Tei Yamashita

Cheung, King-Kok, ed. *An Interethnic Companion to Asian American Literature*. New York: Cambridge University Press, 1997.

Gier, Jean Vengua, and Carla Alicia Tejeda. "An Interview with Karen Tei Yamashita." *Jouvert* 2.2 (1998). http://152.1.96.5/jouvert/v2i2/yamashi.htm. Accessed September 21, 2001.

Imafuku, Ryuta, and Karen Tei Yamashita. *The Latitude of the Fiction Writer: A Dialogue*. Cafe Creole. http://www.cafecreole.net/archipelago/Karen_Dialogue.html. Accessed September 21, 2001.

Kamada, Roy Osamu. Rev. of *Circle K Cycles*. *AsianWeek.com* (May 18–24, 2001). http://www.asianweek.com/2001_05_18/ae3_circlek.html. Accessed January 17, 2002.

Murashige, Kenneth. "Karen Tei Yamashita: An Interview." *Amerasia Journal* 20.3 (1994): 49–59.

WAKAKO YAMAUCHI
(1924–   )

Bill Clem

♦ **BIOGRAPHY**

Nisei writer Wakako Yamauchi was born Wakako Nakamura in Westmore-land, California, in 1924 to Yasaku Nakamura and Hamako Machida, both issei farmers. Living in the Imperial Valley of California, the Nakamura family moved often in search of work, due mostly to the Alien Land Law, which prohibited Japanese from owning land. In 1942, when Franklin Roosevelt signed Executive Order 9066, the Nakamuras were forced to relocate to internment (or concentration) camps; Yamauchi was seventeen and in her last year of high school when she was evacuated to Poston, Arizona.

While at Poston, she rekindled her friendship with another great, future nisei writer, Hisaye Yamamoto DeSoto. The two worked at the *Poston Chronicle*, the camp's newspaper, where Yamauchi worked as a cartoonist and Yamamoto as a writer. Toward the end of World War II, Yamauchi, released from camp, worked in Chicago, but returned to camp in the final weeks of the war because of her father's death. Once the camps closed, Yamauchi and her mother moved to San Diego where the artist took painting classes. In 1948, she married Chester Yamauchi, and in 1955, they had a daughter, Joy.

Propitiously in 1959, Yamauchi was approached by Henry Mori, editor of *Rafu Shimpo*, to draw pictures for the holiday supplement. Yamauchi agreed if Mori would publish her stories. He assented, and Yamauchi wrote stories almost consistently for the paper from 1960 to 1974. Encouraged by Yamamoto to send one of her stories to Frank Chin for *Aiiieeee!*, Yamauchi sent "And the Soul Shall Dance," which was quickly accepted and brought her writing to the attention of a director who asked her to adapt it for the stage. Divorced in 1975 and devoting more time to writing, Yamauchi accepted and embarked upon a career as both playwright and short story writer, which she continues to this day. Many of her plays, some that began as short stories, have been produced by many important companies including the East West Players, Asian American Repertory Theatre, and Yale Repertory Theatre. "And the Soul Shall Dance" was produced by Hollywood Television Theatre for PBS, 1978–1979, and A&E, 1987.

Yamauchi's only collection, *Songs My Mother Taught Me: Stories, Plays, and Memoir*, edited by Garrett Hongo and published by the Feminist Press in 1994, received the National Book Award for Literature by the Association of Asian American Studies in 1995 and was included in *The Hungry Mind Review*'s list of the 100 Best Twentieth-Century American Books in 1999. Yamauchi has garnered other awards and prizes, including a Rockefeller Foundation Grant for Playwrights; Lila Wallace–Reader's Digest Literary Award, 1995–1998; the 1996 John H. McGinnis Award in Fiction from *Southwest Review*; and Phenomenal Women 2000 from California State University at Northridge Women's Studies Center.

◆ MAJOR WORKS AND THEMES

Yamauchi's short stories, eschewing sentimentality in exactly sparse prose, detail the lives of two generations of Japanese Americans before and after internment. Relocation coupled with dislocation, mother-daughter relationships, and thwarted love and repressed/wasted sexuality comprise the themes found in her work. Her best-known story, "And the Soul Shall Dance," (1966), breaks the silence of an issei woman's troubled life through the first-person narration of a nisei girl, Masako. Masako, interested but frightened by her neighbor, Mrs. Oka, an alcoholic who flaunts her husband's abuse, relates the problems of a woman who has been forced to live in the United States, married to a man she cannot love. The story also centers on Masako's understanding of the sex-gender system as she wonders about the situations of both her own mother's happiness and the eventual whereabouts of Mrs. Oka's stepdaughter, Kiyoko-san. The story ends tragically as Mrs. Oka dies and her family moves away; Masako guesses that "Mr. Oka found some sort of work, perhaps as a janitor or a dishwasher, and Kiyoko-san grew up and found someone to marry" (24).

"Songs My Mother Taught Me" (1976) is similar to "Soul" in that Sachiko, a nisei, tells the story of her mother's thwarted love for a kibei, Yamada-san, and for all that he represents: the cultural life of the homeland, Japan. Yamada-san and Hatsue, Sachiko's mother, have an affair, and she becomes pregnant; because Hatsue's husband forces Yamada-san to leave, Hatsue is both lovelorn and depressed, so much so that she accidentally allows the new baby to drown. The story concludes in ambivalent affirmation as the family unites emotionally after the tragedy. Other pieces exemplify similar themes: "The Handkerchief" (1961) presents the predicament an issei woman's children find themselves in when she leaves them to lead her own life, and "That Was All" (1980) is the story of a young woman's unrequited love for an itinerant issei. Two stories, "A Veteran of Foreign Wars" (1981) and "So What; Who Cares?" (1994) come from the perspective of an older nisei woman as she retells her stories of misspent sexuality and memories of the past.

◆ CRITICAL RECEPTION

Because Yamauchi is best known for her dramatic works, her short fiction has not received the attention it deserves. Some work, however, exists. McDonald and Newman write that in her stories, Yamauchi "push[es] beyond traditional Japanese beliefs in the sanctity of the family . . . [and] embrace[s] the freedom of the American woman of the last part of the twentieth century" (41). Stan Yogi, concerned with mother-daughter relationships, believes that "these narratives thus not only quietly subvert the rigid constructs of the Issei family . . . [but] they also subtly suggest, through the reactions of Nisei daughters to their mothers, the transformation of the very standards the mothers violate" (132). In his introduction to *Songs*, Garrett Hongo writes that Yamauchi "develops a somewhat sparse prose, nonetheless musical, graced with an affection for rendering physical details with precision" (7). Valerie Matsumoto believes that "Yamauchi's stories of love, desperation, fear, and determination show us unforgettable faces and the myriad colors of emotion" (9), and M. Dick Osumi reads "And the Soul Shall Dance" through a Jungian and Mythological lens and writes that "Yamauchi's story deals with the inner struggle of the ego to 'realize' and 'integrate' with its shadow archetype thus making a necessary step to psychic wholeness or selfhood" (93).

◆ ACKNOWLEDGMENT

My thanks to Adam Burke, librarian at Waubonsee, for research assistance.

◆ BIBLIOGRAPHY

Works by Wakako Yamauchi

Short Stories

"The Handkerchief." *Rafu Shimpo* (December 20, 1961): 13–14. Rpt. in *Songs My Mother Told Me: Stories, Plays, and Memoir*. Garett Hongo, ed. New York: The Feminist Press, 1994.
"And the Soul Shall Dance." *Rafu Shimpo* (December 19, 1966): 9+. Rpt. in *Songs*. Hongo, ed.
"Songs My Mother Taught Me." *Amerasia Journal* 5.2 (1976): 63–73. Rpt. in *Songs*. Hongo, ed.

"That Was All." *Amerasia Journal* 7.1 (1980): 115–20. Rpt. in *Songs*. Hongo, ed.
"A Veteran of Foreign Wars." *Rafu Shimpo* (December 19, 1981): 7+. Rpt. in *Songs*.
     Hongo, ed.
"So What; Who Cares?" In *Songs*, Hongo, ed.
"Rosebud." *Southwest Review* 81.1 (1996): 28–43.

Drama

And the Soul Shall Dance. West Coast Plays 11–12 (1982): 117–64. Rpt. in *Songs*. Hongo,
     ed.
The Chairman's Wife. In *Politics of Life: Four Plays by Asian American Women Playwrights*.
     Velina Houston, ed. Philadelphia: Temple University Press, 1993.
12-1-A. In *Politics of Life*, Houston, ed.
The Music Lessons. In *Unbroken Threads: An Anthology of Plays by Asian American Women*.
     Roberta Uno, ed. Amherst: University of Massachusetts Press, 1993. Rpt. in
     Songs, Hongo, ed.

Studies of Wakako Yamauchi

Berg, Christine G. "Wakako Yamauchi." In *Voices from the Gap: Women Writers of Color*.
     http://www.cla.umn.edu/authors/WakakoYamauchi.html. Accessed Decem-
     ber 10, 2001.
Hongo, Garrett. "Introduction." In *Songs*, Hongo, ed.
"HMR's 100 Best Twentieth-Century American Books." *Hungry Mind Review: An In-
     dependent Book Review* (August 17, 1999). http://www.bookwire.com/hmr/
     top100.html.
Matsumoto, Valerie. "Migrant Worker." *The Women's Review of Books* 12.3 (1994): 8–9.
McDonald, Dorothy Risuko, and Katharine Newman. "Relocation and Dislocation: The
     Writings of Hisaye Yamamoto and Wakako Yamauchi." *MELUS* 7.3 (1980):
     21–38. Rpt. in *Asian American Women Writers*. Harold Bloom, ed. Philadelphia:
     Chelsea House Publishers, 1999, 29–46.
Osumi, M. Dick. "Jungian and Mythological Patterns in Wakako Yamauchi's 'And The
     Soul Shall Dance.'" *Amerasia Journal* 27.1 (2001): 87–98.
Yogi, Stan. "Rebels and Heroines: Subversive Narratives in the Stories of Wakako Ya-
     mauchi and Hisaye Yamamoto." In *Reading the Literatures of Asian America*.
     Shirley Geok-lin Lim and Amy Ling, eds. Philadelphia: Temple University
     Press, 1992, 131–50.

JOHN YAU
(1950–   )

Sue-Im Lee

◆ BIOGRAPHY

John Yau was born on June 5, 1950 in Lynn, Massachusetts, to a father of Chinese English parentage and a mother of Chinese background, and this interracial heritage forms a constant source of thematic inquiry in his literary works. Yau received his B.A. from Bard College and his M.F.A. from Brooklyn College, and many of his short stories echo the details of his development as a young man and an artist in the New York art scene. As an art critic, Yau has written for numerous publications and catalogs, and written monographs on contemporary painters. His awareness of the current debates and concerns in visual poetics strongly influences his literary practices as well. As a creative writer, he has published more than a dozen literary works, and he has taught at various institutions, including Bard College, Brooklyn College, Emerson College, Brown University, University of California (Berkeley) and Hofstra University. He has received fellowships and grants from the National Endowment for the Arts, the Ingram-Merrill Foundation, and the New York Foundation for the Arts; and he has received a General Electric Foundation Award, a Lavan Award (from the Academy of American Poets), and the Jerome Shestack Prize (from *American Poetry Review*), among many others.

◆ MAJOR WORKS AND THEMES

In discussing Yau's short stories, one must first address the fluid interplay between the short story genre and the prose poetry genre in his works. Many of the entries in the short story collections—*Hawaiian Cowboys* (1995) and *My Symptoms* (1998)—resemble, in their brevity (some consisting of a few sentences), the prose poetry that appears in his previous collections of poetry. The difficulty of distinguishing between the two genres in Yau's oeuvre prompts an interviewer to ask how Yau, himself, distinguishes between the two. Yau points to an emphasis on "narrative" as the distinguishing marker of short story; in contrast, he asserts, prose poetry is "more concerned with surface" (Evenson, par. 5).

Yau's first collection of short stories, *Hawaiian Cowboys*, shows a stronger presence of "narrative" than his second collection, *My Symptoms*. Since many of Yau's short stories parallel the situations and places of his personal history, the notion of memory is crucial as a formal and thematic lens. Yau's use of autobiographical details in his short story production takes on a complicated significance, as Yau himself speaks ambivalently about an ethnic minority writer's use of personal history: "[O]ften it's a way to exploit something about yourself, to make yourself into a 'victim' or 'hero,' and this is an issue that I think every Asian-American writer must face. How not to exoticize yourself in ways that are expected"(Evenson, par. 7). As the exploration of a racialized ethnic identity is a central theme in Yau's short fiction, the turbulent politics of self-representation always remains at the foreground of Yau's short fiction.

Many of the entries in *Hawaiian Cowboys* explore the theme of multiracial identity, a treatment that is best known in "Toy Trucks and Fried Rice" (a short story which appears in the previous poetry collection of *The Sleepless Night of Eugene Delacroix*). As the story begins, a young boy, attending a Chinese Benevolent Association's annual Christmas party with his parents, ruminates upon the conflicting racial, cultural, and class politics and contradictions that inform his parentage. He had always been told that he was Chinese, but as he had never learned Chinese nor lived around Chinese people, his Chinese identity is a continuing source of mystery to him. His mother, a Shanghai Chinese, points scornfully at the Cantonese Chinese Americans around them; the difference, she argues, is like those between Bostonians and people from Louisiana. She also argues the physiological superiority of Shanghai Chinese (who are "taller" than average); the boy in turn notices that she is indistinguishable in height from the supposedly inferior Cantonese Chinese. The mother's pretensions (in her racial and cultural superiority) appear as a source of conflict in many of Yau's short stories (like "Family Album" and "How to Become Chinese" in *Hawaiian Cowboys* and "Anniversary" and "Incident" in *My Symptoms*), and in addition to lending an autobiographical dimension to his fiction, they highlight the formidable role that mothers—and women—play in Yau's fiction. The conflicting racial politics of the boy's life expands as he recalls that his father, a man of Chinese English parentage, aligns himself with American Indians: "His father also told him Indians were the only true Americans, and everyone else was a fake" (34). At a Chinese American Christmas gathering where Santa Claus was "never Chinese" (33), the competing discourses of race represent the young boy's confusion over his racial identity.

Many of the short stories in *Hawaiian Cowboys* explore the experience of growing up as a racialized male in America. "A New Set of Rules Every Other Day" consists of short observations evolving around a young Asian American boy's experience in high school. Under headings like "Social Studies," "Geography," "Mythology," the unidentified speaker voices the adolescent concerns and the racial stereotypes that afflict Asian youths in America—such as the model minority myth, the dominant culture's assessment that all Asians "look alike," and the exoticized Asian male sexuality. "A Little Memento from the Boys" continues the theme of multiracial identity and the effeminized Asian male sexuality in America. Set in New York's Greenwich Village, a recurring setting for many of Yau's stories of development, the story follows the friendship of three multiracial male characters. Like the narrator-protagonist, who is of Chinese English parentage, the two other characters are Eurasian in racial heritage, and the three men's bond is their mutual frustration, anger, and defiance at the neat racial categorizations and epithets ("scrawny samurai," "gimp coolie" 38) that would always stereotype them. As they express their alienation both from the Caucasian majority culture and Asian minority culture, their agonized expressions are reminiscent of the earliest Asian American literary expressions of multiracial identity—Sui Sin Far's "Leaves from a Mental Portfolio."

The three friends begin a haphazard business as interior painters, working on the apartments of wealthy New Yorkers. One of their clients is a young, successful Caucasian woman, among whose belongings they find a diary filled with tales of sexual exploits. The diary, and the woman's sexual toys, become the men's greatest attraction. Hence, in absentia, the client's race, gender, class, and sexuality become the target for their anger against white female sexual aggression that stands in contrast to the effeminization of Asian male sexuality in the dominant culture. As their penultimate expression of defiance, they ejaculate into a can of paint that eventually covers the woman's walls, and they leave behind a photo of themselves masturbating.

The interplay of racial and gender politics is explored through the relationship of interracial marriage in "How to Become Chinese." The story begins with a scene of a Chinese American male narrator-protagonist being remonstrated by a taxi driver for his inability to speak Chinese. As the story continues, the narrator's Caucasian wife announces with great fanfare that in last night's dream, her reflection in the mirror showed a "Chinese" image. The dream, she concludes, is an "indication of how close [they've] become . . . of how [she's] become Chinese" (117). The narrator is at first nonplussed, then irritated and offended, by her triumphant declaration of racial conversion. In a story where the narrator recounts numerous incidences of racial and ethnic mis-recognition (a Pakistani who is mistaken for an Arab, the narrator who is mistaken for a Japanese) and Sinophiles (a Midwestern couple who collects all things Chinese yet objects to Chinese Americans moving into their neighborhood), the wife's essentialist categorization of his identity stands as an example of the most superficial celebration of "difference" in America. Within the structure of the "he said, she said" format, in numerous other stories, the racialized husband's response to the wife's simplistic view of race functions as a critique of the Orientalist view and the reified construction of Asian identity (also occurring in "Heaven and Earth," "Sand," and "Hawaiian Cowboys").

In contrast to the strongly biographical stories of *Hawaiian Cowboys* and the attendant thematic focus on (multi)racial identity, the most dominant trait of the stories in *My Symptoms* is the recurring figure of the sexually liberated and aggressive Caucasian woman. "Guidebook to Lying" is a representative example. A woman leaves out, for her current lover to discover, sexually explicit pictures of herself and her ex-lover. When her lover confronts her, she moves between recrimination at his nosiness and gleeful admission that she has carefully orchestrated this confrontation. The female protagonist-narrator justifies her actions—her manipulation of her lover's jealousy—as her response to the ways she has been on the receiving end of hypersexuality and male sexual domination. "No matter what they do or who they are, all men are arrogant in the end. I prefer dealing with the ones whose arrogance can be turned against them. That's when you can watch them wither in the face of their own heat" (41). The recurring figure of the sexually confident woman and her explicit first-person expressions of her sexual desires are also found in "What She Told Him," "Butcher, Baker," "Come On," "Second Date," "Tree Planting Ceremony," and more.

Another aesthetic distinction of *My Symptoms* is its formally experimental and opaque nature. Much more so than those of *Hawaiian Cowboys*, the entries in *My Symptoms* blur the line between short story and prose poetry. The first sentence of "Correlation" is exemplary of this linguistic density and obscurity: "My cauda is on the blinkety-blink and my primary molecules are in need of some serious reshuffling, while the dreaded carnassial whirlpool has managed somehow to envelop the keys to the control panel" (85). The figurative use of language dominates entries like "No More Monkey Business," "Objects for a Shrine," "Pitch," "Correlation," and "Hardy Atmosphere," and the strong spirit of wordplay and non-sense making actively fight the presence of "narrative" formation. Under Yau's own terms of distinguishing prose poetry from short story, the two-to-three-sentences or single paragraph entries that constitute "Lives of the Artists," "Snow," and "Lives of the Poets" are best understood as prose poetry. As Yau explains: "The dividing line between fiction and prose poetry is one that I often try to dissolve. In 'Lives of the Artists,' I was thinking of a series of postcards or small scenes which add up to something" (Evenson, par. 5).

◆ CRITICAL RECEPTION

Existing critical writing on Yau's literary production is exclusively devoted to his poetry. "A Symposium on John Yau," appearing in *Talisman: A Journal of Contemporary Poetry & Poetics*, volume 5 (1990), offers the most diverse—albeit brief and mostly descriptive—introductions to Yau's poetry from various critics. Elaine Kim, in "Asian American Literature," discusses Yau as an example of contemporary Asian American writers who refuse to "be confined by 'Asian American' themes or by narrow definitions of 'Asian American' identity. Their writings are all the more 'Asian American' because they contribute to the broadening of what that term means" (821). Majorie Perloff, in her review of Yau's *Forbidden Entries* (1996), suggests that there was "no indication [in the earlier works] of Yau's career . . . that the poet is in fact Chinese-American" (40). These two opposing assessments express the different critical criteria at work in reading Yau as an Asian American poet, and in his interview with Evenson, Yau strongly rejects the terms of Perloff's assessment as being overly simplistic and reified in its search for "racial" markers.

Priscilla Wald in " 'Chaos Goes Uncourted': John Yau's Dis(-)Orienting Poetics" locates within Yau's formal experimentation a deliberate disorientation that rejects a singular subjective speaking voice of "I." This rejection, Wald argues, may be read as the literary expression of a material subject who inhabits a multiracial, multinational, multicultural identity. Most recently, Timothy Yu in "Form and Identity in Language Poetry and Asian American Poetry" offers the most sustained discussion of Yau's innovative form and ethnic minority representation in America. Reading Yau within the tradition of Language Poetry, Yu persuasively traces how Yau's rejection of the lyric "I" distinguishes him from the other, better known and anthologized Asian American poets, like Li-Young Lee, David Mura, and Garrett Hongo; consequently, Yu shows, Yau has been difficult to locate within the existing Asian American poetic tradition.

◆ BIBLIOGRAPHY

Works by John Yau

Short Story Collections

Hawaiian Cowboys. Santa Rosa, CA: Black Sparrow Press, 1995.
My Symptoms. Santa Rosa, CA: Black Sparrow Press, 1998.

Poetry

Crossing Canal Street. New York: Gill's Book Loft, 1976.
The Reading of an Ever-Changing Tale. Clinton, NY: Nobodaddy Press, 1977.
Sometimes. Gardiner, ME: Tilbury House Publishers, 1979.
The Sleepless Night of Eugene Delacroix. Brooklyn, NY: Release Press, 1980.
Broken Off by the Music. St. Paul, MN: Bookslinger, 1981.

Corpse and Mirror. New York: Henry Holt, 1983.
Radiant Silhouette: New & Selected Work 1974–1988. Santa Rosa, CA: Black Sparrow Press, 1989.
Edificio Sayonara. Santa Rosa, CA: Black Sparrow Press, 1992.
Berlin Diptychon (with Bill Barrette). New York: Timken Publishers, 1995.
Forbidden Entries. Santa Rosa, CA: Black Sparrow Press, 1996.

Edited Works

The Collected Poems of Fairfield Porter (with David Kermani). New York: Tibor de Nagy, 1985.
Fetish. New York: Four Walls Eight Windows, 1998.

Studies of John Yau

Campbell, Bruce. " 'Pieces of a Piece.' " *Talisman: A Journal of Contemporary Poetry & Poetics* 5 (1990): 126–34.
Chaloner, David. "On John Yau." *Talisman* 5 (1990): 113–14.
Chang, Juliana Chu. "Word and Flesh: Materiality, Violence and Asian-American Poetics." Ph.D. diss., University of California, Berkeley, 1996. Ann Arbor: UMI, 1996.
Corbett, William. "On John Yau." *Talisman* 5 (1990): 114–15.
Donahue, Joseph. "Harmonic Interferences: A Note on John Yau." *Talisman* 5 (1990): 118–19.
Evenson, Brian. "A Conversation with John Yau." *Rain Taxi: Review of Books*. http://www.raintaxi.com/yau.htm.
Foster, Edward Halsey. "An Interview with John Yau." *Talisman* 5 (1990): 31–50.
———. "John Yau: A Selected Bibliography." *Talisman* 5 (1990): 147–51.
———. "John Yau and the Seductions of Everything That Used to Be." *Multicultural Review* 3 (1994): 36–39.
Hemensley, Kris. "On John Yau." *Talisman* 5 (1990): 116–18.
Kim, Elaine. "Asian American Literature." In *Columbia Literary History of the United States*. Emory Elliott, ed. New York: Columbia University Press, 1987, 811–21.
Mobilio, Albert. "The Dream Science of John Yau's 'Dragon's Blood.' " *Talisman* 5 (1990): 119–20.
Morris, Daniel. "Strangers and Oneself: John Yau's Writings on Contemporary Art." *Talisman* (2001): 21–22, 45–57.
Perloff, Majorie. Rev. of *Forbidden Entries*. *Boston Review* 22 (1997): 39–41.
Peterson, Eric. "A Bughouse Interaction." *Bughouse* 2 (1994): 47–59.
Wald, Priscilla. "Guilt by Dissociation: John Yau's Poetics of Possibility." *Talisman* 5 (1990): 121–25.
———. " 'Chaos Goes Uncourted': John Yau's Dis(-)Orienting Poetics." In *Cohesion and Dissent in America*. Carol Colatrella and Joseph Alkana, eds. Albany: State University of New York Press, 1994, 133–58.
Wang, Dorothy Joan. "Necessary Figures: Metaphor, Irony and Parody in the Poetry of Li-Young Lee, Marilyn Chin, and John Yau." Ph.D. diss., University of California, Berkeley, 1999. Ann Arbor: UMI, 1999.

Yu, Timothy. "Form and Identity in Language Poetry and Asian American Poetry." *Contemporary Literature* 41 (2000): 422–61.
Zhou Xiaojing. "John Yau." In *Asian American Poets: A Bio-Bibliographical Critical Sourcebook*. Guiyou Huang, ed. Westport, CT: Greenwood Press, 2002, 343–56.

SELECTED BIBLIOGRAPHY

Anthologies

Aziz, Nurjehan, ed. *Her Mother's Ashes, and Other Stories by South Asian Women in Canada and the United States*. Toronto: TSAR, 1994.

Carlson, Lori M., ed. *American Eyes: New Asian American Short Stories for Young Adults*. New York: Holt, 1994.

Chan, Jeffery Paul, Frank Chin, Lawson Fusao Inada, and Shawn Wong, eds. *The Big Aiiieeeee! Anthology of Chinese American and Japanese American Literature*. New York: Meridian Books, 1991.

Chin, Frank, Jeffery Paul Chan, Lawson Fusao Inada, and Shawn Hsu Wong, eds. *Aiiieeeee! An Anthology of Asian American Writers*. New York: Meridian Books, 1997.

Chock, Eric, and Darrell H. Y. Lum, eds. *The Best of Bamboo Ridge: The Hawai'i Writers' Quarterly*. Honolulu: Bamboo Ridge Press, 1986.

———, eds. *Pake: Writings by Chinese in Hawaii*. Honolulu: Bamboo Ridge Press, 1989.

———, eds. *The Best of Honolulu Fiction: Stories from the Honolulu Magazine Fiction Contest*. Honolulu: Bamboo Ridge Press, 1999.

Chock, Eric, Darrell H. Y. Lum, Dave Robb, Frank Stewart, Gail Miyasaki, and Kathy Uchida, eds. *Talk Story: An Anthology of Hawaii's Local Writers*. Honolulu: Petronium and Talk Story, 1978.

Chock, Eric, James R. Harstad, Darrell H. Y. Lum, and Bill Teter, eds. *Growing Up Local: An Anthology of Poetry and Prose from Hawai'i*. Honolulu: Bamboo Ridge Press, 1998.

Fenkl, Heinz Insu, and Walter K. Lew, eds. *Kori: The Beacon Anthology of Korean American Fiction*. Boston: Beacon Press, 2001.

Gillan, Maria Mazziotti, and Jennifer Gillan, eds. *Growing Up Ethnic in America: Contemporary Fiction about Learning to Be American*. New York: Penguin Books, 1999.

Hagedorn, Jessica, ed. *Charlie Chan Is Dead: An Anthology of Contemporary Asian American Fiction*. New York: Penguin Books, 1993.

Hsu, Kai-yu, and Helen Palubinskas, eds. *Asian-American Authors*. Boston: Houghton Mifflin Company, 1972.

Hutcheon, Linda, and Marion Richmond, eds. *Other Solitudes: Canadian Multicultural Fictions*. Toronto: Oxford University Press, 1990.

Kang, Hyun Yi, ed. *Writing Away Here: A Korean-American Anthology*. Oakland, CA: Korean American Arts Festival Committee, 1994.

Karlin, Wayne, Le Minh Khue, and Truong Vu, eds. *The Other Side of Heaven: Postwar Fiction by Vietnamese and American Writers*. Willimantic, CT: Curbstone, 1995.

Kudaka, Geraldine, ed. *On a Bed of Rice: An Asian American Erotic Feast*. New York: Anchor Books, 1995.

Lim, Shirley Geok-lin, ed. *Asian American Literature: An Anthology*. Chicago: NTC/Contemporary Press, 1999.

———, ed. *Tilting the Continent: An Anthology of Southeast Asian American Writing*. St. Paul, MN: New Rivers Press, 2000.

Lim, Shirley Geok-lin, Mayumi Tsutakawa, and Margarita Donnelly, eds. *The Forbidden Stitch: An Asian American Women's Anthology*. Corvallis, OR: Calyx Books, 1989.

Lum, Darrell H. Y., Joseph Stanton, and Estelle Enoki, eds. *The Quietest Singing*. Honolulu: Bamboo Ridge Press, 2000.

Watanabe, Sylvia, ed. *Into the Fire: Asian American Prose*. Greenfield Center, NY: Greenfield Review Press, 1996.

Watanabe, Sylvia, and Carol Bruchac, eds. *Home to Stay: Asian American Women's Fiction*. Greenfield Center, NY: Greenfield Review Press, 1990.

Wong, Shawn, ed. *Asian American Literature: A Brief Introduction and Anthology*. New York: HarperCollins, 1996.

Secondary Sources

Brown, Julie, ed. *Ethnicity and the American Short Story*. New York: Garland Press, 1997.

Cheung, King-Kok. *Articulate Silences: Hisaye Yamamoto, Maxine Hong Kingston, Joy Kogawa*. Ithaca: Cornell University Press, 1993.

———, ed. *An Interethnic Companion to Asian American Literature*. New York: Cambridge University Press, 1997.

———, ed. *Words Matter: Conversations with Asian American Writers*. Honolulu: University of Hawaii Press, 2000.

Davis, Rocío G. *Transcultural Reinventions: Asian American and Asian Canadian Short Story Cycles*. Toronto: TSAR, 2001.

Gelfant, Blanche H., and Lawrence Graver, eds. *Columbia Companion to the Twentieth-Century American Short Story*. New York: Columbia University Press, 2001.

Huang, Guiyou, ed. *Asian American Autobiographers: A Bio-Bibliographical Critical Sourcebook*. Westport, CT: Greenwood Press, 2001.

———, ed. *Asian American Poets: A Bio-Bibliographical Critical Sourcebook*. Westport, CT: Greenwood Press, 2002.

Kaylor, Noel Harold, Jr., ed. *Creative and Critical Approaches to the Short Story*. Lewiston, NY: The Edwin Mellen Press, 1997.

Kim, Elaine H. *Asian American Literature: An Introduction to the Writings and Their Social Context*. Philadelphia: Temple University Press, 1982.

Lee, Rachel C. *The Americas of Asian American Literature: Gendered Fictions of Nation and Transnation*. Princeton, NJ: Princeton University Press, 1999.

———. "Asian American Short Fiction: An Introduction and Critical Survey." In *A Resource Guide to Asian American Literature*. Sau-ling Cynthia Wong and Stephen H. Sumida, eds., New York: MLA, 2001, 252–84.

Leonard, George J., ed. *The Asian Pacific American Heritage: A Companion to Literature and Arts*. New York: Garland Press, 1999.

Li, David Leiwei. *Imagining the Nation: Asian American Literature and Cultural Consent*. Stanford, CA: Stanford University Press, 1998.

Ling, Amy. "The Asian American Short Story." In *Columbia Companion to the Twentieth-Century American Short Story*. Blanche H. Gelfant and Lawrence Graver, eds., NY: Columbia University Press, 2001, 34–41.

———. *Between Worlds: Women Writers of Chinese Ancestry*. New York: Pergamon Press, 1990.

Liu, Miles X, ed. *Asian American Playwrights: A Bio-Bibliographical Critical Sourcebook*. Westport, CT: Greenwood Press, 2002.

Ma, Sheng-mei. *Immigrant Subjectivities in Asian American and Asian Diaspora Literatures*. Albany, NY: State University of New York Press, 1998.

Maitino, John R., and David R. Peck, eds. *Teaching American Ethnic Literatures: Nineteen Essays*. Albuquerque: University of New Mexico Press, 1996.

Nelson, Emmanuel S., ed. *Asian American Novelists: A Bio-Bibliographical Critical Sourcebook*. Westport, CT: Greenwood Press, 2000.

Trinh, Minh-ha. *Woman, Native, Other*. Bloomington: Indiana University Press, 1989.

Trudeau, Lawrence J., ed. *Asian American Literature: Reviews and Criticism of Works by American Writers of Asian Descent*. Detroit: Gale Research, 1999.

Wong, Sau-ling Cynthia. *Reading Asian American Literature: From Necessity to Extravagance*. Princeton, NJ: Princeton University Press, 1993.

Wong, Sau-ling Cynthia, and Stephen H. Sumida, eds. *A Resource Guide to Asian American Literature*. New York: MLA, 2000.

Journals/Periodicals

Amerasia Journal
Asian Pacific American Journal
Bamboo Ridge: A Hawai'i Writers Journal
Hitting Critical Mass: A Journal of Asian American Cultural Criticism
Journal of Asian American Studies
Manoa: A Pacific Journal of International Writing
MELUS: Multiethnic Literature of the United States
Multicultural Review
Studies in Short Fiction

INDEX

Page numbers in **bold** indicate the location of the main entry.

ABOUT THE EDITOR AND CONTRIBUTORS

KYOKO AMANO was Cultural Diversity/Minority Fellow at the University of Pittsburgh at Bradford in 2001–2002; currently she is Assistant Professor of English at the University of Alabama at Birmingham.

SARAH CATLIN BARNHART is a doctoral candidate in English at the University of Missouri, where she teaches literature, folklore, and film. Her dissertation deals with kitchens as gendered space in literature of the southern United States.

CHANDRIMA CHAKRABORTY was born in Hooghly, West Bengal, India. She came to Canada in 1999 to pursue a Ph.D. in English at York University, Toronto. Her area of interest is discourses of nationalism in postcolonial literatures.

FU-JEN CHEN is Assistant Professor in the Department of Foreign Languages and Literatures at National Sun Yat-sen University, Taiwan, where he teaches American ethnic literature. He has published numerous essays on Asian American literature.

JANET HYUNJU CLARKE is a librarian at SUNY-Stony Brook.

BILL CLEM is a doctoral student in Multicultural American Literatures and Women's Studies at Northern Illinois University. He has recently published bio-bibliographic and encyclopedic entries on Fatima Lim-Wilson and Ann Petry. He received the Sarah E. Wright Best Graduate Paper Award at the

2001 American Women Writers of Color Conference. He is instructor in English at Waubonsee Community College.

JEAN LEE COLE is an Assistant Professor in the Department of English at Loyola College in Baltimore, Maryland. She is the author of *The Literary Voices of Winnifred Eaton: Redefining Ethnicity and Authenticity* (2002), and the co-editor, with Maureen Honey, of a reprint edition of John Luther Long's *Madame Butterfly* and Winnifred Eaton's *A Japanese Nightingale* (2002).

ALICE D'AMORE has an M.A. in English from Kutztown University of Pennsylvania.

ROCÍO G. DAVIS is Associate Professor of American and Postcolonial Literature at the University of Navarre, Spain. She has recently published *Transcultural Reinventions: Asian American and Asian Canadian Short-Story Cycles* (2001) and coedited, with Sämi Ludwig, *Asian American Literature in the International Context: Readings on Fiction, Poetry, and Performance* (2002).

VANESSA HOLFORD DIANA is Assistant Professor of English at Westfield State College in Westfield, Massachusetts. She specializes in multicultural American women writers and has published essays on such writers as Sui Sin Far, Louise Erdrich, Zitkala Sa, Gloria Naylor, and Paula Gunn Allen.

ROBIN E. FIELD is a Ph.D. candidate at the University of Virginia. She is writing a dissertation on sexual trauma in contemporary ethnic fiction.

GUIYOU HUANG is Chair of the English Department as well as Director of University Honors Program at Kutztown University of Pennsylvania. He is author and editor of numerous books and articles.

SHUCHEN SUSAN HUANG is a Ph.D. candidate in Comparative Literature and Women's Studies at the University of Massachusetts at Amherst. Her areas of specialty include feminist theories, cultural studies, ethnic studies, and postcolonial diaspora.

SU-CHING HUANG received her Ph.D. in English from the University of Rochester and is Assistant Professor of English at Edinboro University of Pennsylvania, where she teaches writing and modern American literature. Her major teaching and research interests are ethnic American literature, Chinese diasporic literature, and cultural studies.

NIKOLAS HUOT is a doctoral candidate in English at Georgia State University. His research interests include Asian American and African American literatures.

LEELA KAPAI has a Ph.D. in English literature with a concentration in Victorian fiction. She is a Professor of English at Prince George's Community College in Largo, Maryland, and has published several articles on multicultural literature.

AMY W. S. LEE is an Assistant Professor in the Department of English Language and Literature, Hong Kong Baptist University. She is currently teaching for the Humanities Program. Her research interests include marginal and minority female writings, feminism, gender studies, twentieth-century novels in English, detective fiction, and popular children's fiction.

SUE-IM LEE is currently an Assistant Professor of Contemporary American Fiction at Temple University. Her publications include "Suspicious Characters: Realist Narrativity, Asian American Identity, and Theresa Hak Kyung Cha's Dictee" in *The Journal of Narrative Theory* (forthcoming).

WENXIN LI is an Assistant Professor of English at SUNY Old Westbury and teaches courses in Multi-Ethnic Literature, Asian American Literature, and composition. He holds a Ph.D. in Twentieth-Century British and American Literature from Purdue University and has published on Ezra Pound, David Lodge, Ha Jin, and Maxine Hong Kingston. Other authors he is currently working on include Ernest Hemingway, John Okada, and Sui Sin Far.

KIM-AN LIEBERMAN is a Ph.D. candidate in the University of California-Berkeley English Department, where she is currently completing a dissertation on Vietnamese American literature. She is also a writer whose poetry appears in several journals, including *Prairie Schooner, Quarterly West, Threepenny Review, ZYZZYVA*, and the *Asian Pacific American Journal*.

SEIWOONG OH, Associate Professor of English at Rider University, has written articles on various Asian American authors as well as on Shakespeare and Milton. His articles appeared in *MELUS, CCTE Studies, The Explicator*, and *English Studies in Texas*.

MICHAEL OISHI is a doctoral candidate in English at the University of Washington. His research and teaching interests include the literatures of Hawaii, Asian American literatures, theories of canon formation and literary history, and nationalist and postcolonial discourses. His current engagement with these fields takes the shape of a dissertation that examines the relationship of Hawaii's popular and canonical literatures to ethnic and racial hierarchies in the islands.

ALICIA OTANO has degrees from Manhattan Marymount College (New York) and the University of Navarre (Spain), where she teaches English. Her research interests include Asian American literature, narrative perspective, and life writing.

JOHN H. PARK is a doctoral candidate in English at the University of Illinois, Chicago. Apart from his scholarly interests in Asian American and postcolonial literature and theory, he is actively involved in the development of an Asian American Studies Program and Cultural Center at UIC.

JOONSEONG PARK is a Ph.D. candidate in Creative Writing at Florida State University. His short stories have appeared in several U.S., Canadian, and Australian literary magazines.

GAYLE K. SATO is Professor of English at Meiji University in Tokyo. She has been living and teaching in Japan since 1987. Her articles have appeared in journals and anthologies, including *MELUS, Amerasia Journal, Japanese Journal of American Studies, Reading the Literatures of Asian America, The Oxford Companion to Women's Writing in the United States,* and *Asian American Poets: A Bio-Bibliographical Critical Sourcebook.*

KENNETH J. SPEIRS is Assistant Professor of English at Kingsborough Community College, CUNY in Brooklyn. Currently he is coediting a collection of essays on multiraciality entitled *Mixing It Up: Racing and E-race-ing,* to be published by the University of Texas Press in 2003.

ROBERT D. STURR is an Assistant Professor of English at Kent State University on the Stark campus and has published articles on the Chinese American writer Ha Jin.

DOUG SUGANO teaches early British, multicultural and Asian American literatures at Whitworth College, Spokane, Washington. He has also contributed to the Greenwood Press sourcebooks on *Asian American Novelists* and *Asian American Playwrights.*

JIE TIAN is a reference librarian at California State University, Fullerton. Her education includes an M.A. in English from Sichuan University, China, an M.A. in American Studies from California State University, Fullerton, and an M.L.S. in Library and Information Science from the University of Illinois at Urbana-Champaign. Her interests encompass nature, art, literature, music, cultural studies, ethnic studies, and gender studies. She also writes stories, poems, and essays.

AIPING ZHANG received his Ph.D. in English from Harvard University. He is Associate Professor of English and Adviser of the Graduate Program of the

English Department at California State University, Chico. He is the author of *Enchanted Places: The Use of Settings in F. Scott Fitzgerald's Fiction* (Greenwood Press, 1997) and has published articles on James Fenimore Cooper, Mark Twain, F. Scott Fitzgerald, James Joyce, Timothy Mo, Jessica Hagedorn, and others.